BEYOND THE SUNSET

A STUDY IN BIBLICAL ESCHATOLOGY

Perry B. Cotham

Perry B. Cotham
1814 Santa Cruz
Grand Praire, Texas 75051

Unless otherwise noted, Bible quotations are taken from the American Standard Version.

3rd Printing, June 2009

Printed in the United States of America

Publisher's Cataloging-In-Publication Data

Cotham, Perry B., 1912—
Beyond the Sunset. / Perry B. Cotham
404 pp.
Twenty-eight chapters. Includes study questions.
1. Man's origin. 2. Immortality—Resurrection—
Heaven—Hell. 3. Death—Purgatory. 4. Judgment.
ISBN 978-0-615-24390-0
236

Edited and designed by

Publishing Designs, Inc.
P.O. Box 3241
Huntsville, Alabama 35810

To all those who have lost precious loved ones

And mourn their departure from this life

and

To Ben and Nannie Cotham, my parents,

Who worked so hard and made so many sacrifices,

That I, and my two brothers, Harry and Preston, might have a

Christian education and be enabled to better

Preach the glorious gospel of Jesus Christ,

This volume is lovingly dedicated, by

The Author

We think of an object with many facets—a diamond. Turn it. See more. Turn it again. See more still. Such is an apt metaphor for this study of Beyond the Sunset, *a delightful title on the subject of eschatology. There is no paucity of Scripture cited, no scarcity of turns on the subject, no lack of insightful and relevant poems collected through the years. With this book in your hands, you have the rare opportunity to hold, in one volume, a collection of material from a gentle, 96-year-old preacher of 79 years, writing on a subject that, it is evident, has deep meaning to him. Perry has provided a resource of study for independent thinkers. Having reviewed the book, I already have marked areas that I intend to use.*

—George F. Beals, Co-Director, Michigan Bible School
Senior Technical Writer

Perry B. Cotham was reared by Christian parents. He began preaching at age 17. Perry and I are natives of western Kentucky. We were college classmates at Freed-Hardeman and Murray State University. We have preached at many of the same places. Our parents worshiped together at the old Antioch church in Graves County.

What a great depth of knowledge brother Cotham has of the Scriptures; what enthusiasm when he preaches the gospel of Christ; and what willingness to go and preach in hard places! Perry has preached in all fifty states and in all the inhabited continents of the world. He has become one of the most outstanding gospel preachers in the brotherhood and is recognized as one of the most loyal to the church. Perry has distributed Bibles in all parts of the world. Also, his tracts are widely distributed.

—Adron Doran, President Emeritus
Morehead State University, Morehead, Kentucky

After a brief review of Beyond the Sunset, *I anxiously await its publication so I may read it carefully. I can commend it because I have known Perry B. Cotham for 65 years. I have worked with churches in local ministry where he once lived and worked. They love him! Perry loves the Lord. He loves the souls of men and women. He loves and preaches the gospel both at home and abroad. In my opinion, no living person is more capable of writing about what lies* Beyond the Sunset *than Perry B. Cotham. I rejoice that he took time to write it.*

—Mack Lyon, Television Host
In Search of the Lord's Way

Perry B. Cotham has blessed our brotherhood and the world through the many excellent tracts and books he has written during his long and fruitful ministry. His book, Beyond the Sunset, *on eschatology is his crowning work! It is the product of a long lifetime of study and thought. I know of no work on the subject that is its equal. I predict it will become a classic in Restoration literature and will bless students of God's Word for generations to come. I am happy to commend it to every serious student of God's Word.*

—Rod Rutherford, Evangelist

CONTENTS

PREFACE

No teaching is more remarkable in the whole of Biblical truth than the doctrine of man—his origin, nature, duty, and destiny. People want to know about the end of the world and man's condition beyond death. Man shall pass out of this world in a brief time; death waits for all the living. As long as death stalks the land, men will ask, "If a man die, shall he live again?" Hence, the theme discussed in this book is one of intense interest to every rational person in all the world.

Revelation, the Bible, comes to man's aid and proclaims that man is immortal, that the body shall be raised changed, that death shall be conquered, that the grave does not end all, and that there shall be life after death—a life which stretches beyond the grave. Man shall live on, personally, consciously, and forever. There is no need for the righteous to fear death. To the Christian death is but the gateway to a brighter, better world. The inspired Scriptures should always be recognized as authoritative and final. The purpose, therefore, of this study is to ascertain and explain what the Bible teaches on the life in the hereafter. However, the Bible does not answer all of one's questions on this subject; but the Lord has given to man all that he needs to know about death and the existence that follows it.

This book has been written for the masses, during a busy ministry of preaching, teaching, counseling, and conducting evangelistic meetings. It is the result of much study and teaching on the subject and is in answer to many requests for the material to be placed in book form.

All quotations of the Scriptures, unless otherwise noted, are from the American Standard (1901) Version of the Bible. This version is widely used in the English-speaking world. However, special attention is called at times to the reading of other versions of the Scriptures, especially the King James Version (1611) and the New King James Version.

It would be impossible to give credit to all printed works consulted over a period of years in gathering the material for this book. No originality, therefore, is claimed, except perhaps in the arrangement of the material. With sincere appreciation the author wishes to thank his many friends for their invaluable assistance in the preparation of the manuscript for publication. Especially I wish to mention the help given by Dale T. Lemons, L. O. Sanderson, Gary Colley, Glenn Reynolds, Grace Carriger, Rod Rutherford, Randall Morris,

George Beals, Naomi Ford, Sarah Clem Smith; and thanks to Sidna Jo Andrews and Eadie Falkner for typing much of the material for the printer.

The book is divided into chapters, with review questions at the end of each chapter, so that it may be used also for class study, as well as for preaching.

May the reading of this book cheer and encourage the Christian, console and comfort the bereaved, awaken and warn the thoughtless, and convict and help bring sinners back to God. To this end it is now commended to the grace of God and to the favor of His people.

—Perry B. Cotham
March 2008

WORTH TREASURING

We search the world for truth; we cull
The good, the pure, the beautiful,
From graven stone and written scroll,
From all old flower fields of the soul;
And weary seekers of the best,
We come back laden from our quest,
To find that all the sages said
Is in the Book our mothers read.
—Whittier

– 1 –

Is There a God?

". . . there is a God in heaven"
Daniel 2:28

People want to know about death and the hereafter—what is to take place. They ask, "Is there life beyond the grave, or does death end all?" As long as death stalks the land, men will ask, as did Job: "If a man die, shall he live again?" (Job 14:14).

God has spoken on the subject. His revealed Word gives to man the meaning of death and the states that follow it. "The doctrine of last things" is used by scholars to define Biblical teaching concerning the end of this life, the interim between death and the resurrection, the second coming of Christ, final judgment, and eternal destiny.

An integral part of any study of the destiny of man after physical death demands an investigation first of the existence of God, the creation of man and his nature, and then the states that follow. Here the study begins.

God is. Daniel affirmed in the long ago, "There is a God in heaven" (Daniel 2:28). David wrote: "The heavens declare the glory of God; and the firmament showeth his handiwork" (Psalm 19:1). The universe is here. How did it begin? Man is here. How did he come into existence? The book of Genesis gives us the only detailed and true account of how man and this world and all things in it came into existence. Matter is not eternal; it had a beginning. God is eternal. Man and this world and everything in it had a beginning. Moses did not see with his eye nor experience the creation of the world, but he was inspired by the Holy Spirit to write after the creation.

For the study of any religious subject it is necessary for two important questions to be settled: "Is there an eternal God and is the Bible the inspired, inerrant Word of God?" These are the most crucial questions that confront the world today.

The Bible is here. It claims to be of God, who created the universe and man. It further claims to be "given by inspiration of God" (2 Timothy 3:16 KJV, cf. 2 Peter 1:21).

Moses, who wrote the book of Genesis, begins by assuming the existence of God, and says: "In the beginning God created the heavens and the earth" (Genesis 1:1). But man wants to know, "From where did I come?" "Why am I here?" "Who am I?" and, "Where am I going?" Only the Bible can answer these questions.

God is eternal. God is the One who has always been, is now, and will forever be. It is self-evident that something cannot come from nothing. Therefore, the study begins with the belief in the eternal existence of God. Atheism is the doctrine that there is no God.

"There Is a God"

Dr. A. W. Dicus was the head of the Department of Physics at Tennessee Tech University for many years. By his diligent study and teaching, he gained the reputation of being one of the most influential physics professors of his time. During World War II, when American scientists were developing the atomic bomb in the Oak Ridge Laboratories, it was said that Dr. Dicus sent more young physicists into the laboratory than any other physics teacher in America.

Dr. Dicus died in 1980 at the age of 90. His legacy is not so much his science, though. It was his faith in God. Dr. Dicus was a believer in God as the creator. In 1966, A. W. Dicus wrote the song, "Our God, He Is Alive," both the words and the music. It soon became one of the most popular hymns sung by Christians in all parts of the world.

> There is, beyond the azure blue,
>   A God, concealed from human sight.
> He tinted skies with heav'nly hue,
>   And framed the worlds with His great might.

True science is not in conflict with faith in God. It never has been and never will be. Though God cannot be seen or analyzed scientifically, the honest observant scientist sees the evidence of God in all the universe. Indeed, "The fool hath said in his heart, There is no God" (Psalm 14:1).

God, the creator, is eternal. This great truth concerning God is set forth in the Scriptures by Moses in these words: "Lord, thou has been our dwelling-place in all generations. Before the mountains were brought forth, or ever thou hadst formed the earth and the world, even from everlasting to everlasting, thou art God" (Psalm 90:1–2). Hence, the Creator, being self-existent and underived, has life in Himself and is the source of life to others (cf. John 5:26). Therefore, all human life came from God. No life came by accident or blind chance.

> The day in which the belief in an after-life vanishes from the earth will witness a terrific moral and spiritual decadence. There is no lever capable of raising an entire people if once they have lost their faith in the immortality of the soul.
>
> —Renan

> Were the belief in God and immortality to die out in the human heart, the flood-gates of vice would open wide, plunge the world into the grave of despair, and consign humanity to the dungeons of the damned.
>
> —Madison C. Peters

The Foolishness of Atheism

The atheist denies divine creation and pictures man as an accident. He would have all believe that all life came from dead matter. This theory is contrary to the Scriptures. Likewise, the theory of theistic evolution (which admits God and creation of life by Him) denies the Biblical account of man's origin. This theory has God working through countless ages, evolving from some infinitesimal form of life, a myriad species of animal organisms, until man became. The Bible says God created man, not that which later evolved into man. In Genesis 1, the word *create* is used five times: verse 1, in reference to the origin of matter, the universe; verse 21, in reference to the origin of animal life; and three times in verse 27, between non-spirit and spirit, or brute and man. The heavens and the earth were created. Animal life and vegetable life were created. Man, endowed with life and spirit, was created.

Those who deny God as creator are obligated to show how life began and to illustrate how life can come from non-life. What is the origin of life? Life can come only from pre-existent life. Only God is the giver of life; only God could create. Scientists know that life does not come from non-life, but only from previous life. Rejection of God requires that one accept the amazing or incredible theory that life came from non-life by spontaneous generation. This is absurd. If evolution of all life from one cell were true, the atheist cannot explain how or where that one-cell life began. Besides this fact is the question that if the blind forces of nature ever created life, why cannot they do it again? What stopped the process? Matter did not originate life. Matter did not create the mind of man, for nothing can give to another what it does not itself possess. It is unreasonable, then, to think that the world is eternal or that it came from nothing and that the world by blind chance created life.

In addition, the theory of the origin of the species by evolution is, and always shall be, incapable of proof. At creation, God said that the living creatures should bring forth "after their kind [species] . . . and it was so" (Genesis 1:24). It was so then, and it is so now. There is no evidence that one kind ever changed into another. Man cannot cross the kinds or originate a new kind. Why is this true? Too, what caused the abrupt termination of evolution of life into other species when man was produced? Why are not lower animals now evolving into human beings? The evolutionist cannot answer.

Hence, the theories of evolution—both atheistic and theistic—are unscientific and contrary to the Scriptures. Evolution is only a dogma, an unproved assertion, which is believed in spite of the facts, and not because of them. Atheism offers nothing to man beyond this life but an eternal sleep. In the last moments of one's life on earth, there is a great difference between the man who can say, "The Lord is my shepherd" and the man who says, "There is no God."

The Universe—From Whence Did It Come?

God's revelation to man declares that the universe and all that is in it (the entire cosmos) came into existence by the creative power of the eternal God. "By the word of Jehovah were the heavens made, and all the host of them by the breath of his mouth . . . For he spake, and it was done; He commanded, and it stood fast" (Psalm 33:6–9). "For he commanded, and they were created" (Psalm 148:5). "By faith we understand that the worlds have been framed by the word of God, so that what is seen hath not been made out of things which appear" (Hebrews 11:3). The universe had a beginning which was caused. It cannot be self-existent. God is the uncaused cause of all things! Where nothing exists, only God can originate it by creation.

It is reasonable, therefore, for modern man to believe in God. Yet some ask: Can man believe in God? One thing is certain: either God or matter is eternal, as there are but two things in existence—namely, mind (the attribute of God) and matter. The question is, which one of the two is eternal? The universe exists. Man, endowed with intelligence and free will, exists. There must be a cause for everything. That is, there must be a sufficient cause for every effect. Things do not happen without cause. An effect implies a cause. The world is an effect. Man is an effect. The universe and man have not always existed. The Bible teaches that the heavens and the earth and all life were called into existence by the command of Jehovah God. (The word *create,* as used in Genesis 1:1, means to bring into existence something where nothing previously was.) Since the world and man are effects, as all admit, there must have been an original cause sufficient to produce them.

Note this argument:

1. If something is and something cannot come from nothing, then something must be eternal.
2. Something is.
3. Something cannot come from nothing.
4. Therefore, something must be eternal.

Furthermore, that which first existed must have had in it the potency or the power to cause all that now exists. Thinking, intelligent beings exist and they come only from thinking, intelligent beings. Hence, the first cause must have been a thinking, intelligent being.

Too, the first cause must have been an uncaused cause. Surely there could have been no uncaused beginning of the universe and man. Behind all beginnings there must have been something unbegun. Man, in his reasoning, must start somewhere with something. If there ever was a time when absolutely nothing existed, then nothing could have existed at any time. For out of nothing, nothing comes. All the works of man are nothing but products of causation. Everything made has a maker. A house has a builder. No house came into existence by mere accident and chance. "For every house is builded by some one; but he that built all things is God" (Hebrews 3:4).

These are undeniable axioms. Hence, something has existed from all eternity, for what was before creation is eternal. What is that eternal something? Consistent with this thinking, the Bible says, "He that built all things is God" (Hebrews 3:4). So the Christian declares it is God who is eternal and who, "In the beginning" (whenever that was, no one knows), created all things. Back of that no man can venture. God has always been. He is. We will ever be. Only God is without beginning or end. He alone is eternal—the sufficient first cause, the uncaused cause. Thus, the Creator, being self-sufficient and underived, has life in Himself and is the source of life. Christ declared: "For as the Father hath life in himself, even so gave he to the Son also to have life in himself" (John 5:26).

Man Incapable of Producing Life

Man has never been able to create life. Man has never created anything. Man could never have created the world. Since everything conceivable was caused by something else before it, if this chain of cause and effect could be traced back to its beginning, there must have been a first uncaused cause. Now, what was it? The answer is God. God, without pre-existent material, created the heavens and the earth. Only God can be the creator of the universe and man. Jehovah, therefore, spoke by revelation concerning man's origin and said: "For I have created him for my glory, I have formed him; yea, I have made him" (Isaiah 43:7 KJV).

True, man cannot fully comprehend God, but this should not prevent his believing that God is. The finite cannot fully comprehend the infinite. Zophar asked, "Canst thou by searching find out God? Canst thou find out the Almighty unto perfection?" (Job 11:7). And Paul spoke of that "which is known of God" (Romans 1:19), implying that there are some things that we cannot know about God in this physical life. Then he continued by saying: "For the invisible things of him since the creation of the world are clearly seen" (Romans 1:20). We know, therefore, that God is, that "there is a God in heaven" (Daniel 2:28). We know, also, that the Bible is the inspired, inerrant, authoritative Word of God, and that the Bible is the only inspired, inerrant revelation from God (2 Timothy 3:16–17; 2 Peter 1:21).

We can be certain that God exists and that man was created by Jehovah. Nevertheless, all over the world young people especially are being taught from textbooks in public schools and universities that evolution is an established scientific fact. But this definitely is not true! The universe functions on the basis of law, order, and design. So there must have been a lawgiver and a designer. The universe bears every mark of divine causation. The visible world declares a Creator, and it bears witness to His intelligence. There are unmistakable evidences of a well-designed plan and not chance. The harmonious workings of nature all reveal intricate planning. Since nature gives evidence of intelligent causation, there must have been an intelligent cause. A watch, for instance, declares there must have been an intelligent designer and maker. So, "The heavens declare the glory of God; and the firmament showeth his handiwork. Day unto day uttereth speech, and night unto night showeth knowledge" (Psalm 19:1–2).

Since the atheist denies God who made all things, he is asked to name that "something" that always was, which is responsible for man and all things that exist. How did the world come to be? What caused the beginning? The atheist cannot answer, but the Christian can. To the atheist, the "eternal something" must be non-living matter in some form. But matter gives no evidence of self-existence. Matter is not eternal. Matter was created. Hence, atheism can never be proved. To know that God is not would require a person to know all there is to know. But man has not been everywhere and does not know everything. This shows man's inadequacy to prove there is no God. It is reasonable to begin with a self-existent Being (God) as the first cause. It is not reasonable to begin with self-existent, non-living matter as the first cause. The fundamental reason, therefore, for the existence of all things is God, and the universe may be viewed as a big neon sign merely proclaiming its own Creator in large letters: G-O-D!

The universe is not God. The creation must never be identified as the Creator. Although God is invisible to the human eye, He is clearly manifested in His handiwork. A workman is known by his works. The Holy Scriptures clearly affirm: "For the invisible things of him since the creation of the world are clearly seen, being perceived through the things that are made, even his everlasting power and divinity" (Romans 1:20). The visible world bears witness to the invisible Creator (Acts 14:17). Truly, the words of David are appropriate: "The fool hath said in his heart, There is no God" (Psalm 14:1). To which may be added the converse: "The wise man hath said in his heart, God is a wonderful reality." The heavens were made by the fingers of God. The beautiful stars are, in the words of Joseph Addison,

> Forever singing as they shine,
> "The hand that made us is divine."

That the scholarship of the world substantiates the claims of evolutionists is absolutely false. Further, many great scientists accept the Biblical account of creation and the divine origin of man. True, some who call themselves scientists reject the inspired record of the creation of the universe and of man's origin and his nature. They say the Bible is unscientific. But there is no conflict between the Bible and true science. The word *science* means "to know," and what man really knows—has proof for—does not contradict any statement in the Bible. However, some of the theories of would-be scientists often contradict the Holy Scriptures, but a true understanding of scientific data and a true understanding of Biblical teaching are always harmonious.

Actually, the Bible is pre-scientific, instead of un-scientific—that is, it was written long before the day of modern scientific investigation. For example, in the nineteenth century Herbert Spencer declared that there are only five things in existence: time, force, action, space, and matter. This was not a great discovery, for the Bible states this truth in the very first verse. "In the beginning"—time; "God"—force; "created"—action; "the heavens"—space; "and the earth"—matter. In 1735, Linnaeus discovered there were only three kingdoms or realms in the world—mineral, vegetable, and animal. The Bible lists these in the first chapter of Genesis.

For centuries men argued about the shape of the earth. Some said it was flat. Others said it was round. Later, Columbus, Magellan, and others proved that it was round. Centuries earlier the Bible had stated that it was in the form of a circle. "It is he that sitteth above the circle of the earth" (Isaiah 40:22). Men also debated what held the earth up or what supported it. Scientists finally determined that nothing tangible supports it. This truth was stated by Job in the long ago, centuries before the birth of Christ: "He stretcheth out the north over empty space, and hangeth the earth upon nothing" (Job 26:7). Until recently astronomers did not know there is an empty space in the North. Yet Job also declared that fact. The Bible is in harmony with scientific discoveries.

These truths were then unknown by humans. So Job wrote by inspiration of God—God told him what to write (2 Peter 1:21). These examples are only an indication of the scientific truths that are found in the Bible. Believers in divine creation are not opposed to science. They do oppose the theories that cannot be reconciled with God's Word. Paul referred to this in admonishing the young preacher Timothy to avoid "oppositions of science falsely so called" (1 Timothy 6:20 KJV).

Science and the Bible in Complete Accord

Where there is an apparent conflict between religion and science, someone has attributed to the Bible a position that it does not teach (for example, that the earth is flat), or else scientists are teaching as facts principles which are in reality only assertions (for example, Darwinian evolution).

Creationists deny that evolution is science or that it is scientific. It is neither. Someone has asked, "If it took 'mind' to design the modern computer, why is it not perfectly reasonable to conclude that it took mind to design the human computer that is many times more complex?" It is often the case that when some people determine that they will not believe in God—in spite of the evidence—they become wholly unreasonable.

To speak of creation without a creator is as unreasonable as to speak of a plan without a planner or a house without a builder. The idea of life beginning on earth spontaneously is untenable. The theory of evolution as to man's origin is not true science. Science can no more prove evolution than it can disprove creation, for both are outside the realm of science's ability to determine. Hence, the question of the ultimate origin of human beings is beyond the purview of natural scientists.

Let this one fact be well established: there is no conflict between the Bible and the facts of science. There may be many conflicts between the Bible and the assertions of so-called scientists. There may be conflicts between the facts of science and the assertions of so-called Bible scholars. A true understanding of the teaching of the Bible and a correct understanding of the facts of science are always harmonious.

Can Accept Both

In view of all these facts, man can accept both the Bible and science, for not a single ascertained fact of science conflicts with any statement of the Holy Scriptures. The student of the Bible has nothing to fear from true science. There never has been and never shall be a single scientific fact that contradicts God's Word, because the Author of the Bible is also the Author of nature. Since truth is consistent, facts cannot be in conflict with each other, and science is far from being the enemy of faith.

Thus, "In the beginning God," that is, the Godhead—three co-eternal and co-equal beings, the same in essence (God the Father, God the Son, and God the Holy Spirit)—cooperated in the creation of the universe and man (cf. Acts 17:29; Romans 1:20; Colossians 1:17–19). With God the Father was Christ the Son, as the agent who assisted in creation. "In the beginning was the Word, and the Word was with God, and the Word was God . . . All things were made through him; and without him was not anything made that hath been made"

(John 1:1–3). "For in him [Christ] were all things created, in the heavens and upon the earth, things visible and things invisible . . . all things have been created through him, and unto him; and he is before all things, and in him all things consist" (Colossians 1:16–17). Scripture teaches that Christ was (and is) eternal, for He that had an existence before anything was created must be eternal. The Holy Spirit also had a part in creation: "The Spirit of God moved upon the face of the waters" (Genesis 1:2; cf. Isaiah 45:18). The Spirit put forth His creative power in the word uttered: "Thou sendest forth thy Spirit, they are created" (Psalm 104:30; cf. Job 26:13; 33:4). The Spirit was the organizer of the material universe and the giver of laws. All things began with a miracle. They continue through laws which the Holy Spirit has given.

All the Bible Inspired

The inspired Bible is reliable, trustworthy, and indestructible. It is the Word of God. Jehovah, in His Word, has told us how the universe and man began. Strangely enough, most people who attack the Bible are ignorant of what it contains. When asked to produce a real contradiction or inconsistency in it, they are unable to do so, though some try. The person who denies the existence of God is an atheist. The position of an atheist is one of complete folly, because he affirms a negative proposition which is incapable of proof. How wonderful it is for a person to say, "I believe in God." Men will believe in and be ruled by God, or they may be ruled finally by tyrants.

When Paul and Barnabas came to Lystra on their first missionary journey, they found many people worshiping idols and knowing nothing of the true and living God. In teaching them, Paul stated that they "should turn from these vain things unto a living God, who made the heaven and the earth and the sea, and all that in them is" (Acts 14:15). This was new teaching to them. Ignorance of God only leads to idolatry. Man will worship something.

When Paul was on his second missionary journey, he came to the intellectual city of Athens, Greece. Here he found many idols being worshiped. Finally, he was invited to speak on Mars' Hill. In this address, he told them that he had observed their altar, TO AN UNKNOWN GOD. Then he told them of "the God that made the world and all things therein" and that "he made of one every nation of men to dwell on all the face of the earth" (Acts 17:24–26). They were educated from one standpoint but very ignorant from another standpoint. They knew nothing of the one true and living God, the Creator of the universe and man. Only God can create something out of nothing. The word *create* means to bring something out of nothing: "In the beginning God created the heavens and the earth" (Genesis 1:1). The word *made* does not mean "create."

Why Hate the Bible?

Through the ages some people have hated the Bible (cf. Jeremiah 36:1–23). This is true today. The Bible is hated because of its condemnation of sin and because it demands humble submission to God's will. There is, indeed, a direct connection between human conduct and one's concept of his origin and purpose in life. If a person is convinced that he is only an animal and that the Bible is not the inspired Word of God, he will have little motivation to behave other than as an animal. Without moral guidelines, he may live a wanton life. There are others, however, who love the Bible and believe with all their hearts that it is the inspired word of God and the one and only authoritative and all-sufficient guide in righteous living. Believing they are people made in God's image, they strive to live godly lives (Titus 2:12). There is, therefore, a great need for the home and the church to stand firm and strong against the godless influences that have been unleashed upon the world in the last few years. The fruit of atheism is generally vice, wickedness, immorality, and irreligion. The inevitable sin that follows the false doctrine of atheism is evidence of its damnable nature. Surely all honest people are forced to the conclusion that a great Mind or Power is responsible for the origin of the universe and man; that all must accept by faith the sublime statement that in the beginning God created the heavens and the earth and man (Genesis 1:1, 27).

By reading Romans 1:18–32 one can note what happened to the ancient pagan world when they gave up God and put Him out of their mind. The fruits of atheism are always bad in every nation. A good reason for belief in God and morality is that atheism and immorality do not work to lift man to a higher plane of living. The same God who created man and gave him his desires and appetites gave him the Bible for a code of conduct. Jehovah knew what would bring to man his greatest happiness here on earth and in eternity. The reason that people are atheists is that they do not want to believe in God and obey the teaching of the Bible, the inspired Word of God. He who is without knowledge of the Holy Scriptures is destitute of information on two vital matters. First, he is ignorant of the one true God, and second, he is ignorant of himself. He does not know where he came from, why he is here, or where he is going when he passes from the scenes of this earthly existence. However, the Bible is a revelation of man's origin, mission in life, and ultimate destiny. The Bible presents to man the only plausible and sensible account of his beginning. It unfolds a system of ethics superior to that offered by the earth's wisest philosophers, and it specifies his eternal destiny, either heaven or hell.

Surely all honest people are forced to the conclusion that a great Mind or Power is responsible for the origin of the universe and man. If this conclusion is accepted, then all must accept by faith the sublime and inspired statement that in the beginning God created the heavens and the earth (Genesis 1:1), that

God created man (Genesis 1:27). "In six days Jehovah made heaven and earth, the sea, and all that in them is" (Exodus 20:11). There is no gap of millions or billions of years between Genesis 1:1 and 1:2. And the universe is five days older than man. Moses was inspired to write the truth of the origin of the universe and man. God is! This is fundamental, "for he that cometh to God must believe that he is, and that he is a rewarder of them that seek after him" (Hebrews 11:6).

Questions for Discussion

1. What is the purpose of this course of study? How does the Bible begin?
2. Did the world come into existence by chance or by creation?
3. Did matter exist before mind?
4. What are some reasons for believing in the existence of God as an eternal Being? Is God the uncaused cause?
5. In Genesis 1 what does the word *create* mean?
6. Can man produce life? Does life come from previous life?
7. What is meant by transmutation?
8. It has often been said that one reason some do not believe in a divine Creator is not due to a lack of evidence but due to their unwillingness to live by the teaching of the Word of God. Do you agree?
9. What is the only reliable source of information regarding the origin, duty, nature, and destiny of man?
10. Who is the eternal, self-existent One?
11. Is it a self-evident fact that "something cannot come from nothing"?
12. Define the term *Biblical Eschatology*.
13. Is it reasonable to believe in God? Give your reasons for believing in God.
14. What are some of the reasons often offered for not believing in an eternal God?
15. Define "All Scripture is given by inspiration of God" from 2 Timothy 3:16–17 (KJV).
16. In what way do the universe and man show marks of intelligent causation?
17. What are some of the fruits of the teaching of atheism? Discuss Romans 1:18–32.
18. Why do some live as evolved animals?
19. What is theistic evolution? Why is it contrary to the teaching of the Bible regarding man's origin?
20. Is the idea that man cannot fully know God a valid reason for denying the existence of God?

21. Is the Bible unscientific? What are some of the pre-scientific statements found in the Scriptures? How could these have been written when this information was not in the realm of human learning at the time they were written? Explain 2 Peter 1:21.
22. Has evolution regarding the origin of man ever been proved? Can it be?
23. Do the Bible and true science contradict each other? If so, where?
24. Is the Bible a textbook on science or a textbook on religion (the science of living)? Does the Bible present basic standards of living and morality?
25. What is meant by the Godhead? Did the three Persons cooperate in the creation of the universe and man?
26. What role does logic play regarding the existence of God, the origin of the universe, and the origin of man?
27. Which one of these three explanations is correct for the origin of the universe and man?
    a. Materialism: Matter is eternal and mind is a result of certain combinations and properties of matter.
    b. Dualism: Both mind and matter are eternal.
    c. Theism: Mind is eternal, and matter is a creation of mind.
28. Some skeptics ask, "Where did the dinosaurs come from?" Did God promise that all animals He created would exist as long as time continues?
29. Pantheism is the belief that God is the force and law of the universe. Why is pantheism wrong?
30. Does the Bible give the age of the earth, or the age of man on the earth?
31. What is meant by the missing link?
32. Does the theory of evolution explain the origin of matter? Of the first single cell? Of man? Or why the process of evolution has ceased?
33. Henry Fairfield Osburn gave this definition of science: "Science consists of the body of well-ascertained and verified facts and laws of nature. It is clearly to be distinguished from the mass of theories, hypotheses, and opinions which are of value in the progress of science."
    a. What do you think of this definition?
    b. Is there not often a contradiction between true science and the opinions of men who are studying in the field of science?
    c. If the Word of God had agreed with science two hundred years ago would it agree with science today?
    d. If there can be false ideas of scientists, can there not be false ideas as to what the Bible really teaches?
34. Can the doctrine of evolution as to man's origin be a real substitution for the facts of scientific discovery? Why?

35. Why should evolution not be taught as fact in public schools?
36. How does the "Big Bang Theory" contradict the Bible's teaching that the entire universe, including the sun, the moon, the stars, and the earth came into being during the six literal days of the creation week?
37. Did not the human family come into existence the same week of the universe and has it not been in existence from the beginning of the creation?
38. Define and discuss the gap theory. (Note: In the discussion, consider billions of years between Genesis 1:1 and Genesis 1:2.)
39. What alone is eternal?

THE EVOLUTIONIST'S ANSWER

As the evolutionist sat with his son upon his knee,
"Tell me of the beginning," was the little fellow's plea.
So the scholar with his learning and diploma on the wall
Quoted from his textbooks all he could recall.

"In the beginning there was nothing but a little bit of gas;
But finally it got together and made a lot of mass.
Now where the gas had come from and how it came about,
Is not discussed by scholars, it's taken without doubt.

"When the elements cooled off and the gasses ceased their strife,
All of a sudden life sprang up, from whence there was no life.
At first, of course, there was but a fish by the ocean tossed and thrown,
Then some decided they would walk, so legs and feet were grown.

"Others decided they'd like to fly up in the heaven's blue;
They wished so hard that soon, it seems, that wings had sprouted through.
Finally apes began to think, with brains they'd decided to grow;
The smartest one became a man—natural selection, you know."

As he ended his wise discourse and glanced at the lad upon his knee,
'Twas hard for the simple-minded lad to understand, he could see.
Then, as if in defense of his cause, the scholar said with a nod,
"If you don't believe this just happened by chance,
Then you'll have to believe there's a God."

—Author Unknown

–2–

What Is Man's Origin?

"God created man in his own image"
Genesis 1:27

From the beginning of time, trembling lips have asked the question of the origin, nature, and constitution of man. For truly, "Man, that is born of a woman, is of few days, and full of trouble. He cometh forth like a flower, and is cut down: he fleeth also as a shadow, and continueth not . . . Yea, man giveth up the ghost, and where is he?" (Job 14:1–10).

People ask: "Is man destined to live after this earthly life is over?" "Is there any life beyond the grave, or does death end all?" "If there is life after death, what are some of the characteristics of that life?" Man's questions are always, "Is there a future life and, if so, what is that life like?" Or, "Is it really possible for man to survive death?" Man has incessantly searched for the answer to these questions. What is man, and whence did he come?

As an example of man's quest for an answer, note this story from history related by William E. Burton, in *My Faith in Immortality:*

> When Christian missionaries made their way to England in 597, and journeyed as far inland as Northumberland, they came to the domain of King Ethelbert. It was a serious question with the king whether these men should be allowed to teach a religion different from that which had been taught in the realm. It involved many religious, social, and political uncertainties. He called a council of his nobles and chiefs. There was diversity of opinion. Then an aged chief arose and said: "The king will remember that now and then as the king sits at night with his men, a little bird will fly in at a window, and across the room, and out again through an opposite window into the night. From the darkness it comes, and into the darkness it goes, and it is for a brief space only in the light between. Such is the spirit of man. If these men can tell us concerning it, whence it comes and whither it goes, let us hear them."
>
> They were heard. Britain heard their message. America heard it. Successive generations have heard it and there is need that they shall still hear. For the spirit of man continues to make its swift flight through the narrow interval of life between the two great areas of darkness and silence. If there be any

> voices that can tell us whence this life comes and whither it goes, let us listen to them.[1]

Colonel Robert Ingersoll, a well-known agnostic of the nineteenth century, after a life of effort to destroy the very hope of immortality, standing by the casket of his deceased brother, said:

> Every cradle asks us, Whence? Every coffin asks us, Whither? The poor barbarian weeping over his dead can answer the question as intelligently and as satisfactorily as the robed priest of the most authentic creed. The tearful ignorance of the one is just as consoling as the learned and unmeaning words of the other.
>
> Life is a narrow vale between the cold and barren peaks of two eternities. We strive in vain to look beyond the heights. We cry aloud and the only answer is the echo of our wailing cry. From the voiceless lips of the unreplying dead, there comes no word; but in the night of death hope sees a star and listening love can hear the rustle of a wing.[2]

This is eloquent language, but it contains no definite answer to the question concerning life beyond the grave. Although man has sought spiritual information from many sources, knowledge of life after death can only be derived from the Holy Scriptures. Man's only authoritative source for this information is a "thus saith the Lord." The Bible speaks about the end of this life, the interim between death and the resurrection, the second coming of Christ, final judgment, and eternal destiny. This teaching about life beyond is called *eschatology* or, in simpler language, the doctrine of last things. It shall be demonstrated in this Biblical study that there is a life beyond and that death is not the end of man's existence.

"What Is Man?"

Of all the questions that engage attention in the spiritual realm concerning man, four rise above all others in importance: (1) Whence came man? (2) What is man? (3) What is man's duty? (4) What will be man's destiny? Whence? What? Why? Whither? These questions involve a study of the Bible concerning the origin, nature, duty, and destiny of man. Until the correct answers to the first two questions come, man will never know the answers to the other two. The psalmist asked, "What is man, that thou art mindful of him?" (Psalm 8:4). Man still asks: "Is man wholly mortal?" "Does man possess an immortal soul?" "Is he a spirit-being dwelling in a mortal body?" "Is he created for eternity?"

---

1 William E. Barton, *My Faith in Immortality* (Cornwall: The Cornwall Press, Inc., (1926), pp. 34–35.

2 Robert G. Ingersoll, as quoted by W. L. Oliphant in the Oliphant-Smith Debate, p. 176, held in Shawnee, Oklahoma, August 15–16, 1929; F. L. Rowe, publisher, Christian Leader Publishing Co., Cincinnati, Ohio, 1929.

The answers to these questions are vital. For an integral part of any study of the destiny of man after death demands an investigation into the origin, nature, and constitution of man himself. Here the study must begin.

Man Was Created By Jehovah

There are but two possible answers as to what man is and from whence he came: (1) Man is a mere animal who erupted from the unknown ages past through a process of evolution, or (2) man is a spirit-being who was created by an act of God. If man evolved from lower life and is wholly mortal, as some claim, then all questions concerning the dead can be quickly answered. The dead have ceased to be; they are extinct, and all who die will likewise become extinct. The theory of evolution as applied to the origin of man is unproved—and unprovable.

The Bible definitely affirms that man was created by God and made in His own image: "And God said, Let us make man in our image, after our likeness . . . And God created man in his own image, in the image of God created he him; male and female created he them" (Genesis 1:26–27). John 4:24 tells us that God is a Spirit. And Luke 24:39 says that "a spirit hath not flesh and bones." Further, Zechariah says, "Jehovah . . . formeth the spirit of man within him" (Zechariah 12:1). Genesis 2:7 says, "And Jehovah God formed man of the dust of the ground; and breathed into his nostrils the breath of life; and man became a living soul." These Biblical statements show that man was divinely created a compound being—a material body and an inbreathed part by Jehovah. There is a great difference between man and animals. Man was created in the image of God, but animals were not. Adam, the first man, was "the son of God" (Luke 3:38). Hence, all praise belongs to the Lord, "for thou didst create all things, and because of thy will they were, and were created" (Revelation 4:11). Definitely, man was created by Jehovah God. Jesus also said, "He who made them from the beginning made them male and female" (Matthew 19:4). "But from the beginning of the creation, male and female made he them" (Mark 10:6).

As we continue our study to ascertain the correct teaching of the Holy Scriptures on life in the hereafter, we are now ready to inquire into the very nature of man himself. The account of man's creation not only shows that man is divine in origin but also that he was created a compound being. God first formed man of the dust of the ground; that is, He made his body, the material part. The human body was inanimate and lifeless and not yet a complete man. The second step in the process of creation was the animation of this body of dust by the special inbreathing of the Lord. God "breathed into his nostrils the breath of life; and man became a living soul" (Genesis 2:7). "Breath of life" here literally means "breath of lives"; it also occurs in Genesis 6:17; 7:15; and

7:22, where it applies to beasts of the field. Yet God created man "a little lower than God [the angels, KJV] and crownest him with glory and honor" (Psalm 8:5). So this inbreathing by the Creator was not the imparting of mere human (physical) life; it also was the infusion of a spiritual (intelligent) nature into the material body. Adam was first a body, but he became a living soul; that is, he became a living creature bearing the image of God. Let us now notice some other Biblical statements which show that man was divinely created a compound being—a material body made from the dust of the earth and an immortal spirit inbreathed by Jehovah Himself.

Body, Soul, and Spirit

God's Word teaches that man's whole nature is spirit, soul, and body. The apostle Paul wrote: "And the God of peace himself sanctify you wholly; and may your spirit and soul and body be preserved entire, without blame at the coming of our Lord Jesus Christ" (1 Thessalonians 5:23). Man, in this respect then, is a triune being. (1) The body is the fleshly or material part of man's constitution. But there is more about man than the body; Paul also said soul and spirit. (2) The word *soul* in the Bible sometimes refers to the physical life, as for example: "He made a path for his anger; he spared not their soul from death, but gave their life over to the pestilence" (Psalm 78:50). (3) Soul is occasionally used in a synecdochical sense (in which a part stands for the whole). For example: "All the souls that came with Jacob into Egypt, that came out of his loins . . . all the souls . . . were threescore and ten" (Genesis 46:26–27). So the Word often refers to the whole man: "Eight souls were saved through water" (1 Peter 3:20). (4) And soul is sometimes used interchangeably with the spirit—as in this study—as for example: "Father, into thy hands I commend my spirit," said Christ as He was dying on the cross (Luke 23:46). But Peter on the day of Pentecost, in referring to Christ's resurrection, quoted from David's psalm: "Because thou wilt not leave my soul unto Hades" (Acts 2:27; cf. Psalm 16:10). (5) The spirit is the immortal nature of man. Paul wrote, "For who among men knoweth the things of a man, save the spirit of the man, which is in him?" (1 Corinthians 2:11). The part that knows is the mind, and Scripture makes the mind and heart synonymous: "on their heart" (Hebrews 8:10; 10:16); "your mind" (Romans 12:2); "my heart" (Psalm 119:11). The Bible affirms that "God is a Spirit" (John 4:24), and that God is "immortal" and "eternal" (1 Timothy 1:17). Man, then, having been created in the image or likeness of God (Genesis 1:26–27), is like God, and his spirit is immortal and eternal. (Further study will be given to the soul and spirit in chapters that follow.)

Scripture often refers to man as body and soul, or body and spirit, rather than the three-fold division of body, soul, and spirit, meaning that soul and spirit are one and the same entity. For example, note: In Romans 8:10, Paul spoke of body and spirit; in 1 Corinthians 7:34, he mentioned "body and spirit"; in 1 Corinthians 5:5 he said "flesh" and "spirit"; in Luke 8:55, reference is made to the return of the spirit of the maiden into her body when Christ brought her back to life; in Acts 2:31, Peter spoke of the resurrection of Christ that his soul was not "left unto Hades, nor did his flesh did see corruption"; in Genesis 35:18, mention is made of the death of Rachel, "as her soul was departing," and yet when Stephen died, he said, "Lord Jesus, receive my spirit" (Acts 7:59). Thus, man's whole nature is body, soul, and spirit, or more commonly referred to as body and soul, or body and spirit. The spirit dwells within the body, and sometimes the word *soul* means the same as *spirit*.

Error of Materialism

There are those who teach that matter is everything and, therefore, man is wholly mortal. They deny that man is a spirit, dwelling in a physical body. They affirm that man is nothing but matter in motion, and that when a man dies, he ceases to exist. These are often referred to as materialists. (There is reference to their teaching throughout this study.) Indeed, man's human body is mortal ("your mortal body," Romans 6:12), but his spirit or soul is immortal.

The purpose of this study is to show the teaching of the Scriptures on the origin, nature, and destiny of man. However, as we proceed, this study will also show the error in the teaching of the materialists. Although materialists are very energetic in the propagation of their doctrine, it can be easily answered by God's Word. When they come to your door do not be rude. Invite them in, or make an appointment with them for future study. Be interested in their soul. Try to turn the contact into an effort to teach them the truth. Tell them that you appreciate their interest in your soul, and that you are just as interested in their soul. Tell them that you believe that they are teaching error but that you are willing to study with them if they will be honest with you in this study. Agree to listen to them on the basis that they will listen to you an equal length of time. (They usually want you to sit and listen to them do all the talking without disagreeing or offering counter arguments. Do not agree to this. If they will agree to study, then do not interrupt them while they talk, and do not permit them to interrupt you while you talk.) Most generally their arguments follow five themes: (1) man does not have an immortal soul; (2) physical death means ceasing to exist; (3) there is no eternal punishment (hell); (4) future life will be here on this earth and not in heaven; and (5) Jesus Christ is not divine but a created being. All of these points of false doctrine are answered in this study.

Other passages of Scripture also teach the divine origin and nature of man. Let us note some of these.

Man, Offspring of God

Paul in his speech at Athens declared that God had "made the world and all things therein" and had "made of one every nation of men," that "in him we live, and move, and have our being" (Acts 17:24–28). He also quoted a statement consistent with this from Greek poetry to prove to those educated philosophers that man descended from God; for certain of their own poets had said: "For we are also his offspring."

Then Paul added: "Being then the offspring of God, we ought not to think that the Godhead is like unto gold, or silver, or stone, graven by art and device of man (v. 29). Furthermore, the apostle stated that God "giveth to all life, and breath, and all things" (v. 25). He said that all nations are "of one" (of one blood, KJV) (v. 26). This emphasizes that we are all related, for all humans are descendants of the first man and woman.

Scientists have also shown through the study of mitochondrial DNA that all people trace their ancestry to a single mother. It should be of no surprise that the Bible speaks of just such a woman, Eve, whose name means "mother of all living" (Genesis 3:20). Thus, astonishingly, all the groups of people living today are closely related. The Bible and science are in remarkable harmony. Biologically, there is only one race of human beings, regardless of minor variations.

Therefore, in this address Paul declared several things which are vital to this study:

- There is one God who is the Creator and Sustainer of all mankind.
- There has been one common origin of all men.
- The whole human family, having been created in God's image, is of one and the same species of blood.
- Adam is not spoken of as the progenitor of any certain race of mankind, but he is the common ancestor of all races of men.
- All nations on this earth are equally cared for by Jehovah God, the Creator.
- Only man is the offspring of God.
- There is no reason for man to continue groping for God because He is not far from any one.
- It is the spirit of man that is the offspring of God and in God's likeness.

God, Father of Spirits

One of the most enlightening passages on this topic comes from the author of Hebrews: "Furthermore, we had the fathers of our flesh to chasten us, and we gave them reverence: shall we not much rather be in subjection unto the Father of spirits, and live?" (Hebrews 12:9). In this verse it is said that God is the Father of spirits. In the footnote of the American Standard Version the phrase is rendered "our spirits." (See also translations by Goodspeed, Moffett, and Weymouth.) In this passage, then, the fathers of the flesh and the Father of people's spirits are contrasted, and the writer emphasizes that man should obey God. The Lord is both the Maker of man's body and the Father of man's spirit. This harmonizes with Paul's statement in Acts 17:29.

The Body a House

Daniel declared that man is possessed of a body and spirit: "As for me, Daniel, my spirit was grieved in the midst of my body" (Daniel 7:15). Daniel affirmed man was a spirit enshrined in a body, the spirit being the true self. The real "I" of man is this invisible spirit within the body.

Zechariah insisted that "Jehovah . . . stretcheth forth the heavens, and layeth the foundation of the earth, and formeth the spirit of man within him" (Zechariah 12:1). This spirit within the body of a man is just like a tenant within a house; they are distinct, yet real. The spirit dwells within the body.

Man in House of Clay

Eliphaz made reference to people as those that dwell in houses of clay (Job 4:19). Here again the soul is as clearly distinguished from the body, as the occupant of the house is distinguished from the house. To confound the spirit with the body would be to say that the house and he who dwells in it are one and the same. The body is only the house in which the real man dwells.

Paul is also conclusive on this point: "Wherefore we faint not; but though our outward man is decaying, yet our inward man is renewed day by day" (2 Corinthians 4:16). Here the Holy Scriptures affirm that man is a compound being, having both an inward and outward reality. The outward man is the body, and the inward man is the spirit which dwells within the body. A good question to pose is: Where does the Bible speak of any brute beast possessing an inner and an outer being, as it does of man's compound being? Comparing Paul's statement with that of Genesis 2:7, one would say that God formed man out of the dust of the ground (the outer man), and then breathed into this body the breath of life (the inner man), and man became a living soul (an animate being, endowed with an intellectual spirit).

The thought is further developed in Ecclesiastes 12:7. Here the different destinations of body and spirit at death are distinctly stated, with allusion to different origin and alliance: "The dust returneth to the earth as it was, and the spirit returneth unto God who gave it." Man's body came from the ground; his spirit came from God. At death the dust, or body, returns to the earth as it was, and the spirit returns unto God who gave it. Each returns to its place—matter to matter, spirit to Spirit.

Body and Spirit Are Different

Flesh and spirit are not the same. God is declared to be "the God of the spirits of all flesh" (Numbers 16:22). Job asserted that the flesh and the soul are distinct: "But his flesh upon him hath pain, and his soul within him mourneth" (Job 14:22). Note that the flesh is upon him, that is, it envelops the soul. The soul is within him, that is, it is in the body. These two parts—the flesh without and the spirit within—form man as he is here upon the earth. The inward man is not identical with the earthly form, the body, but is distinct from it and master over it. The spirit is invisible; the bodily form is visible, "for a spirit hath not flesh and bones" (Luke 24:39).

Elihu expressed the truth when he said: "But there is a spirit in man, and the breath of the Almighty giveth them understanding" (Job 32:8). Here the spirit in man is plainly distinguishable from the physical man, in whose body it dwells. The understanding, instead of being the result of mere animal organization, is attributed to the inbreathing of the Almighty. Again he said: "The Spirit of God hath made me, and the breath of the Almighty giveth me life" (Job 33:4). In the same book it is stated that the real man is the self-conscious person, the indweller, the "I" of the body, for God asked, "Who hath put wisdom in the inward parts? Or who hath given understanding to the mind?" (Job 38:36).

Isaiah taught that man is more than a body: "With my spirit within me will I seek thee earnestly" (Isaiah 26:9). He spoke of both soul and body (10:18), of God giving "breath unto the people" on earth and "spirit to them that walk therein" (42:5). These statements are in harmony with Daniel 7:15; Zechariah 12:1; and other portions of Scripture which have already been noted.

Man: Son of God

Luke, in his genealogy of Christ, teaches the divine origin of man and the continuance of the image of God: "The son of Enos, the son of Seth, the son of Adam, the son of God" (Luke 3:38). The inspired writer said man came from God, that the first man (Adam) was the son of God—meaning that man was created by the Lord.

Man's Life Is Sacred

Jehovah's ancient law against murder shows that man's life is sacred because man is made in God's image. "Whoso sheddeth man's blood, by man shall his blood be shed: for in the image of God made he man" (Genesis 9:6). The sacredness of human life was again emphasized when the law of Moses was given: "Thou shalt not kill" (Exodus 20:13). This same law was later repeated by Christ in His Sermon on the Mount with added emphasis on anger in the heart (Matthew 5:21–24). Murder has always been a terrible sin against

Jehovah. It is a crime against man as well as a crime against God in whose image man is created. To launch an immortal soul into eternity is a fearful thing. Murder is sacrilege. Wherever there is a human being, regardless of how wicked he may be, there is an image of God. It dishonors the Lord for man to murder a being that is in that image. The Scriptures urge all men to respect their fellow men as individuals created in God's image. The body and its integral union with the spirit ought to impress all people with the true worth and dignity of all mankind. Human life is made in the image of the divine.

Furthermore, since the body is the spirit's dwelling place in this life, it is to be rightly cared for as the temple of God. The body should be kept pure, nurtured with suitable food, and all forms of dissipation avoided. It is also a sin to harm the body. To Christians Paul asked: "Or know ye not that your body is a temple of the Holy Spirit which is in you, which ye have from God?" (1 Corinthians 6:19). To the Christian, his body is a sacred thing; he does not want to destroy it (cf. Daniel 1:8; Proverbs 20:1; 23:29–35; 1 Corinthians 6:18).

The Image of God

Man's creation in the image and likeness of God does not refer to man's physical body but to his spiritual nature. "In the image of God" means that man was created with a spirit, as invisible and undying as the divine Spirit. Only man's body was formed from the dust of the ground; his spirit was created (Genesis 1:27; John 4:24).

The image of God in man consists of those God-like attributes of man's intellectual and moral nature. God has intelligence, will, and emotions. Man also has intelligence, will, and emotions. Man thinks, perceives, remembers, reasons, and wills. Like God, he has the ability of communication. Since man is an intelligent, reasoning being, there must be more to him than matter. Man must and does possess a spirit. Man possesses characteristics not present in any other creature. Although man has a corporeal frame with physical life, he also has additional qualities that manifest spirit which is not found in animals. Man has a mind in a sense in which animals have none. Man alone possesses self-consciousness and is capable of fellowship with his Maker. Nothing in all the animal creation measures up to the mental, moral, and spiritual nature of man. He is different from and superior to animals. An animal does not possess the image of God. In creation, therefore, both man's physical and intellectual lives began with the union of the spiritual nature with a material body. Hence, man should not think of himself as a mere biological organism. Jesus taught that a human soul is worth more than the whole world (Matthew 16:26 KJV).

How, then, is man different in comparison to the other creation of God? He was created in the image of God! He is unlike the animal. Man is unique. *Image* and *likeness* carry the idea of man's being in a spiritual resemblance to

God. Spiritually, man is made in God's image as a rational, moral, and responsible being. God breathed into the lifeless body of dust the breath of life, and then man became a living soul. It was here that the soul of man was given from God to man, and that which was given to man in this action will one day return to God who gave it.

Man did not evolve from swamp slime. He is a created being in the likeness and image of God. He is a morally responsible being who must give an answer for his actions. He must respect the moral laws of God. The fact that man's soul came, not from the dust, but from the eternal God, justifies belief in the immortality of the soul and its survival at the body's dissolution. There is a great difference between men and animals.

Anthropomorphism Used

Sometimes the Bible speaks of God as if He possesses a physical body, as "the arm of the Lord," "the eyes of God," and such like. This is a figure of speech called *anthropomorphism,* which means representation of God with human attributes or characteristics. God does not dwell in a human (fleshly) body. The arm of the Lord would suggest His strength or power; the eyes of God stand for His all-seeing (knowing) attribute, as He sees all people at all times.

A Word to Young People

We would say to young people everywhere that this truth of God as Creator is no outworn fragment of the Bible which has been scientifically disproved. It is a truth just as timely and necessary for this generation in the twenty-first century as for the Greeks in the days of Paul when he gave his great address to the educated philosophers in Athens on Mars' Hill in the first century (Acts 17:22–31). We challenge infidels to do their utmost to prove untrue those statements by Paul and other Bible writers.

The real God, unknown to the Athenians, was made known to them by Paul. With all of their altars and temples they had failed to find the true God. They did not know the characteristics of the true and living God as revealed in the Scriptures. Paul identified this God as the Creator, the one that made the heavens and the earth and created man in His own image. The world is not eternal and it is not accidental. God is not a part of nature, but above it and beyond it and before it. God is a spirit being, and man, being God's offspring and in God's likeness, must be a spirit being (John 4:24).

We are not merely bodies. These are ours, not we. That "I, myself, I" (which exists in each of us), is something different from the body; something spiritual and intangible. If such we are, then such also must be the Creator; and, therefore, the very thought of likening God to a gold or silver or marble image is absurd. God does not dwell in temples made with man's hands. He made all people: Greeks and barbarians, Jews and Gentiles. And God, in His providence, is the ruler and upholder of the world.

Finally, young people, as well as older ones, need to realize, as Paul told the people of Athens, that there will be a final judgment of the world. God will judge all men by Christ, the God-ordained man, in that judgment. In view of the judgment, God commands "all men every where to repent" (Acts 17:30 KJV). The demand for repentance implies sin. The idea of judgment implies the doctrine of retribution. Death is not the end of us. There is a judgment day and an eternity before every one of us, either of happiness in heaven or of misery in hell.

The Athenians had no belief in a life beyond the grave or in a universal Judge. They had no faith in the immortality of the soul, or the rising of the dead body from the grave. They thought that when death comes that is the end of us (1 Corinthians 15:32). They knew not that man's Savior had come, lived, and died and had been buried and raised from the dead. They knew not the one personal God who is our Creator. But these truths are the great fundamentals of Christianity, and young people today need to know them. Man possesses an immortal nature; animals do not.

Questions for Discussion

1. How was man created?
2. What does "breath of life" mean in Genesis 2:7?
3. Memorize Genesis 1:1, 26–27; and 2:7.
4. Define body, soul, and spirit as used by Paul in 1 Thessalonians 5:23.
5. From the Bible, how many parts does man have in his entirety on earth?
6. Define the doctrine of materialism.
7. What did Paul say about man's origin in Acts 17:29? How are all men like each other?
8. Who is the Father of our spirits? Who forms the spirit of man in him?
9. In what sense is man's body like a house? From what source did the body come? To what source will the body return? When?
10. In what sense was Adam "the son of God"?
11. Why is murder such a terrible sin in God's sight? Memorize Genesis 9:6.
12. In the sight of men a tiger kills a man and the tiger does not do wrong (sin). But when a man murders a child, he commits a heinous act. Why the difference?
13. In what sense is man in the image of God? Are all people in God's image?
14. What is the "inward man" and the "outward man" of Paul's language in 2 Corinthians 4:16?
15. Were animals created in God's image?
16. Define the term *anthropomorphism*.
17. Does the body of an animal differ in essence from the body (material) of a man?
18. Where did the people (or "races") come from?
19. What do you think of "racist" attitudes?
20. From this study thus far complete this sentence: "Man and woman came into being as a result of . . ." (There are only two basic views: (1) the creative act of God, or (2) the process of evolution from non-living matter. It cannot be that neither one of these is true. It must be that one of them is true and the other is false. It cannot be that both are true.)
21. Is there any scientific truth that anyone must deny in order to hold to the Biblical view of the origin of man?
22. Does not the evolutionist assume the very thing to be proved? Is the theory of evolution of the origin of man now a matter of established scientific fact?
23. Notice has been made in this chapter that the unbeliever in God must be able to answer these three important questions: If man is nothing but

matter in motion, why does he feel a sense of right and wrong? Is man a moral being? Is he free to choose?

24. Why do some hate the Genesis account of creation and the Biblical teaching of morality?
25. Would you say that the Bible is right, and that it is man's only correct guide from earth to heaven? Do you think that if one compromises on the matter of origins from Genesis 1, he will likely, sooner or later, compromise on other Biblical teaching? The statements throughout the Bible (Genesis 1:1; Exodus 20:11; Nehemiah 9:6, et. al.) plainly teach fiat creation, and not any kind of evolutionary process. Does that settle it with you?
26. How long were the days of Genesis 1? (Theistic evolution is wrong because the Bible says that the heavens, the earth, the sea, and all that is in them were created in six days. The evolution theory is that evolution took place over multiplied millions or billions of years. The Bible states that God created a fully grown and fully developed man in one day.) Is the idea of spontaneous origin of life from non-living antecedents true? Did God ever say He used evolution to create man? What is wrong with the way God said He did it? Is the universe eternal?
27. What is meant by the Bible being inspired of God?
28. Why is the position of the atheist one of complete folly?
29. What happened to the ancient pagan world when it gave up God and put Him out of its culture? Does this same result follow today in any nation of people who likewise adopt the philosophy of atheism?
30. Give evidence of the fruits of godless humanistic philosophy that is increasingly penetrating the minds of men, especially among the young people.
31. Assign some member of the class to read and report on Charles Darwin's book, *The Origin of Species,* published in 1859. Point out that Darwin did not show that the species originated by natural selection but that this might have occurred on the basis of certain assumptions. Show that he used language of assumption, speculation, and imagination more than 180 times. Pages 118 and 119, for instance, contain these phrases: "If assumed," "are supposed," "if we suppose," "may still be," "will generally tend," "I have assumed," "it is probable," and many others. There is nothing of scientific value in personal convictions or simple possibilities presented as evidence. Darwin's theories should not be taught anywhere at anytime as fact. Every science and philosophy teacher should point out that evolution is a speculation that has been elevated in the minds of some to a position equal to scientific law. *Tennessee v. John Scopes,*

sometimes known as *The Scopes "Monkey" Trial,* was held in 1925 in Dayton, Tennessee.

32. What is meant by the "Big Bang Theory" of the origin of the universe? What was there to bang?

– 3 –

When Does Human Life Begin?

"Thou didst cover me in my mother's womb"
Psalm 139:13

A question of great interest to religious people is: "When does human life begin?" "Is the embryo non-human?" David, in Psalm 139, speaking by the Spirit of God (cf. Acts 1:16; 4:25; 2 Samuel 23:2), characterized himself as a person when he was developing in his mother's body. Note the personal pronouns, "I," "me," "my," even when his substance was yet unformed.

> For thou didst form my inward parts: thou didst cover me in my mother's womb. I will give thanks unto thee; for I am fearfully and wonderfully made; wonderful are thy works; and that my soul knoweth right well. My frame was not hidden from thee, when I was made in secret, and curiously wrought in the lowest parts of the earth. Thine eyes did see mine unformed substance; and in thy book they were all written, even the days that were ordained for me, when as yet there was none of them (Psalm 139:13–16).

The angel Gabriel, in announcing the birth of Christ to Mary, informed the virgin that Elisabeth, her cousin, had conceived a son: "And behold, Elisabeth thy kinsman, she also hath conceived a son in her old age" (Luke 1:36). From these statements, one may logically conclude that the tiny living being, which has been so from the moment of conception, has also possessed a spirit from that time, and is, therefore, a human being, a person.

Murder Is Wrong

The destruction of innocent human life is evil. God has spoken on this subject.

> There are six things which Jehovah hateth; yea, seven which are an abomination unto him: haughty eyes, a lying tongue, and hands that shed innocent blood: a heart that deviseth wicked purposes, feet that are swift in running to mischief, a false witness that uttereth lies, and he that soweth discord among brethren (Proverbs 6:16–19).

It will be a day of sorrow and agony, and maybe a surprise to some, when those who performed abortions and those who had abortions stand before God in the day of judgment, and the innocent ones they murdered, to answer for their actions. However, those involved in such actions can, by the grace of God, be forgiven if they will truly turn to the Lord in sincere repentance and obedience to the gospel of Christ (1 Corinthians 6:9–11; Acts 18:8). But unforgiven murderers shall not enter into heaven. The Bible says:

> But for the fearful, and unbelieving, and abominable, and murderers, and fornicators, and sorcerers, and idolaters, and all liars, their part shall be in the lake that burneth with fire and brimstone; which is the second death (Revelation 21:8; cf. 22:15).

Human Life at Conception

Since God is the author of human life, as has already been learned from this study (Acts 17:25), then surely He is the one who has the right to declare when human personhood begins. The Scriptures teach that human life commences at conception. However, the *Roe v. Wade* decision, made in America on January 22, 1973, to legalize abortion, has resulted in many thousands of babies being killed. Less than a decade into the twenty-first century, more than 50 million American babies had been slaughtered. Annually, more than 1.2 million babies continue to be killed. Too, there are those also who are advocating the execution of adults (full-grown individuals) through euthanasia, that is, the elderly and those with infirmities. God warned Israel: "Keep thee far from a false matter; and the innocent and righteous slay thou not: for I will not justify the wicked" (Exodus 23:7). Does a mother have a right, a choice to kill her baby? Is it the mother's body that is being killed in abortion or is it the body of another person inside the mother's womb? What right does she have to kill her own child?

In the long ago, God said to the prophet Isaiah regarding the sins of His people: "Cry aloud, spare not, lift up thy voice like a trumpet, and declare unto my people their transgression, and to the house of Jacob their sins" (Isaiah 58:1). Should this not be done today? Have the religious people of our world been negligent in recent years in teaching God's Word on the sacredness of human life?

The assisted suicide approval seems to be the next step after the approval of the killing of unborn children. Suffering may be providential in some people's lives (cf. Hebrews 12:5–6). Although Job pleaded with God to put him to death (Job 6:8–9), it never entered his mind that suicide or mercy killing (assisted suicide) was an acceptable option. Job had done nothing to deserve his boils, but, unknown to him, God had a providential purpose in allowing Satan to afflict him with ulcers from the sole of his foot unto his crown (Job 2:7). Neither suicide nor being put to death by others seems to have entered Job's mind. The apostle Paul had a thorn in the flesh. He asked the Lord three times to remove it, but the Lord said to him, "My grace is sufficient for thee: for my power is made perfect in weakness." Then Paul replied: "Most gladly therefore will I rather glory in my weaknesses, that the power of Christ may rest upon me . . . for when I am weak, then am I strong" (2 Corinthians 12:7–10). So suffering can, if taken in the right way, prove helpful to a person (cf. Romans 5:3–4). Thus, in prison in Rome, near the end of his life, Paul could write: "Rejoice in the Lord always: again I will say, Rejoice" (Philippians 4:4). It is a true saying that one's attitude determines his altitude!

Jeremiah recorded in the introduction to his book what the Lord said to him when He called him to be a prophet. God knew that he was a human being prior to his birth: "Before I formed thee in the belly I knew thee, and before thou camest forth out of the womb I sanctified thee; I have appointed thee a prophet unto the nations" (Jeremiah 1:5). But some think that a baby does not have a soul and is not a person until it is born and takes its first breath. This surely is not true. A person is created and given human life as an eternal being at conception. However, while some people do not agree with abortion, that is no reason to attack or kill doctors who perform them. Rather, people need to be taught that human life is sacred.

Children Born Innocent

The Bible teaches that a child is born pure and innocent. Children do not inherit the sins of their parents. "The son shall not bear the iniquity of the father, neither shall the father bear the iniquity of the son" (Ezekiel 18:20). Jesus said concerning little children: "For to such belongeth the kingdom of heaven" (Matthew 19:14). The New International Version of Psalm 51:5 is in error: "Surely I was sinful at birth, sinful from the time my mother conceived me." But David was not conceived and born in sin. No one is. We die physically because of Adam's sin. We die spiritually because of our own sins (Ezekiel 18:20; Isaiah 59:2). If one's spirit is evil from birth, how did it get that way? It is God who is the Father of our spirits, not our parents (Hebrews 12:9). So the idea of inherited sin is a false doctrine.

Man Valuable

Jesus taught that a human soul is worth more than the whole world: "For what shall a man be profited, if he shall gain the whole world, and forfeit his life [soul KJV]?" (Matthew 16:26). Again: "How much then is a man of more value than a sheep!" (Matthew 12:12). There is a great difference between man and animals. Man was created in the image of God, but animals were not. Man has an immortal soul (spirit), but animals do not. This higher life that was given to man by an inbreathing of the spirit distinguishes man (homo) from all other species. Always keep this in mind: Man, as created by Jehovah, is (has) an immortal spirit which lives beyond death. In respect to his visible or material organism, man is mortal; but with reference to his deathless, intelligent spirit (soul) within, derived from God, he is immortal. Man shall live forever!

So human life begins at conception. That is a biological fact. Where there is union of body and spirit there is life. Unborn, John the Baptist leaped in his mother's womb when the expecting Mary, mother of our Lord, greeted Elisabeth: "And it came to pass, when Elisabeth heard the salutation of Mary, the babe leaped in her womb" (Luke 1:41). The word *babe* used in this passage literally means an embryo or fetus. But little John was very much alive, even though in his mother's womb. Hence, the prophet Zechariah said: "Jehovah . . . formeth the spirit of man within him" (Zechariah 12:1). And Paul declared to the Athenians on Mars' Hill that life is a gift from God: "He giveth to all life, and breath, and all things" (Acts 17:25 KJV).

An eighteen-week-old fetus, measuring about six inches, can suck its thumb. The person is active at this stage of development and very energetic. There is muscle-flexing, punching with the fists, and kicking with the feet. The prenatal baby has an entire organ system by the eighth week, and has a full sense of pain. That person is alive! Once precious life begins, man has not the moral right to take it away. Since life begins before the baby is born, abortion is wrong. Man, as already observed, has always been forbidden to murder his fellow human being because he is made in God's image (Genesis 9:6). Abortion on demand is the killing of one human for the convenience of another. God does not give a person this right.

The Beginning of Love

It is at the instant of conception that the new entity received the genetic code which is peculiar to a human being. If, therefore, science is able to assure us that fetuses have a human genetic code, and if prenatal medicine accepts such fetuses as patients, it seems incredible that mothers and physicians can be permitted to treat these fetuses as less than human. Sacrificing one human life to save another (i.e., abortion to save a woman's life) is one thing; sacrificing a human life at will (i.e., abortion to spare parental inconvenience) is quite something else.

Does the Bible speak concerning abortion? Moses legislated to the ancient children of Israel in these words:

> If men strive together, and hurt a woman with child, so that her fruit depart, and yet no harm follow; he shall be surely fined, according as the woman's husband shall lay upon him; and he shall pay as the judges determine. But if any harm follow, then thou shalt give life for life (Exodus 21:22–23).

One simple question clarifies the issue concerning the right or wrong of abortions: Is a living fetus in utero a natural part of a woman's body, like her hands and feet? The answer is no! She is not born with a fetus. It is not carried for a lifetime along with other parts of the body. Therefore, it must be considered a separate life with its own soul from the moment of conception until death. It is an individual human life. If not, just at what moment does it not have a right to live but the next moment it does?

Is it not wrong to take the lives of little innocent babes? The taking of human life for any reason is not a private matter. For another example, does the fact that old people can be a burden give their families a license to kill? Surely we think not. When any person looks on the handicapped as a total liability, his attitude toward life is warped.

The Abortion Issue

Because human life is sacred, God in the beginning of time commanded that the murderer be put to death for his crime (Genesis 9:6; cf. Genesis 1:27). Abortion has been legal in all fifty states of America since January 22, 1973. Since that day, over fifty million innocent babies have died in American abortion clinics. It is often said, "You cannot call someone who isn't breaking the law a murderer." The Nazis were not breaking German law when they murdered six millions of Jews. We cannot accept the notion that whatever a nation does that is legally right is also morally and ethically right. There is a higher law than man's law. Amazingly, America is now doing legally what Hitler's henchmen did back in the 1940s. Many Christians are opposed to this holocaust. They are for the protection of the lives of the unborn, the handicapped, and the elderly. This is not just a political issue; it is also a religious and moral issue. Abortion kills another living human. Even if a woman does have a right to her own body, the unborn child is not her body. The child has its own body. Why call it pro-choice when the one affected the most by the decision is given no choice? Why does the mother with an unwanted pregnancy say it is not a baby but a fetus?

When the hearts and minds of people are changed by the teaching of God's Word, the issue of abortion will be no more. More children will be adopted and receive care. The termination of innocent human life will stop. Abortion is not, as many think, the removing of some tissue from the woman's womb. Also, good, morally righteous people need to let doctors know that they cannot with a good conscience support a doctor who helps to kill innocent babies. The abortion industry is a multi-million dollar business. But there will come a day in which those guilty will stand before God in judgment to give account (2 Corinthians 5:10; Revelation 21:8; 22:15). Truly, "For the wrath of God is revealed from heaven against all ungodliness and unrighteousness of men."

(Romans 1:18). "Cursed be he that taketh a bribe to slay an innocent person" (Deuteronomy 27:25).

The Suicide Issue

One of today's major social problems is suicide. Suicide is self-murder. Each year in America alone, over 25,000 people commit suicide. That is about 55 per day. Authorities also admit that 50,000 other deaths might be attributed to suicide but cannot be proven.

Suicide is the tenth leading cause of death in the American nation. It is the fourth leading killer of teenagers and the number two cause of death among college students. Well over a thousand persons take their own life each day around the world. This equals more than three million every year. All kinds of people—rich and poor, educated and uneducated, high and low in society—commit suicide. Only about one in ten of those who attempt suicide are actually successful, and eighty percent of those who threaten suicide will actually do it.

The jailer in Philippi awakened to find the prison doors opened, drew his sword, and would have killed himself, supposing that the prisoners had fled, but Paul stopped him (Acts 16:25–28). He came close to taking his own life. There are six recorded cases of suicide in the Bible: (1) Samson (Judges 16:30); (2) King Saul, (1 Samuel 31:4); (3) King Saul's armour-bearer (1 Samuel 31:5); (4) Ahithophel (2 Samuel 17:23); (5) Zimri (1 Kings 16:18–19); and (6) Judas (Matthew 27:3–5; Acts 1:18).

Many reasons are often given for one's taking his own life. Some choose death after being found guilty of wrongdoing, rather than take the shame and humiliation. Some do so to punish another for some cause, hoping to make him feel guilty. Some do this to their parents. Partners in an unhappy marriage have been guilty of this crime. Others feel unable to cope with their problems, and come to the conclusion that life is not worth living. Still others are just lonely and dread what the future may hold. Stress often leads to extremes. But there is never a right time to do a wrong thing.

When one kills himself, he has committed a sin of which he cannot repent. Suicide is self-murder, and murder is wrong (Exodus 20:13; Romans 13:9). In many ways, the act of suicide is injustice to both family and friends. No matter how heavy the burden, how dark the night, or how intense the pain, a person should never entertain the idea of suicide. The writer of Hebrews said of God: "I will in no wise fail thee, neither will I in any wise forsake thee" (Hebrews 13:5). Many people become depressed from time to time, yet they do not attempt suicide. Suicide is always the wrong way out. Under no circumstances should one ever consider taking his own life. Wrong is wrong even if one does it thinking it is for a good cause, for sin is lawlessness (1 John 3:4). However, a person who is mentally sick or on drugs might end his or her life. God will judge these matters.

Similar to this is mercy killing—euthanasia. God does not endorse active euthanasia, whether it involves a knife or some modern means of ending one's life, often to cut spending. The Bible teaches the sacredness of human life. To deliberately shorten a life that belongs to God is wrong. "For we know him that said, Vengeance belongeth unto me, I will recompense. And again, The Lord shall judge his people. It is a fearful thing to fall into the hands of the living God" (Hebrews 10:30–31). "Be not overcome of evil, but overcome evil with good" (Romans 12:21).

Man Alone in God's Image

Man alone, of all creatures of this earth, has a spirit and bears the image of his Creator. This image of God certainly implies something higher than the physical nature which man possesses in common with the animal creation. An animal does not possess the image of God. The Bible nowhere says that animals were created in God's likeness as it says of man. The life which man possesses in common with the beasts is no part of God's image. Man has something within that differentiates him from the mere animal. God did not breathe into any animal the breath of life, as it is said about the creation of man (Genesis 2:7).

Certainly, in a material sense there is no difference between the body of a man and the body of a beast, but there is a vast difference between man and animal. Two distinct substances are united in man; namely, an earthly body and a divine spirit. It is, then, this divine nature—the spirit, derived from God—which distinguishes man from the animal creation and makes him a man. On the physical side, man is allied to the animal creation, but the thing that differentiates him from the rest of the creation is that he is a moral being created in God's image. That man is above the animals is proved by man's possessing characteristics not present in any other creature. Although man has a corporeal frame with physical life, he also has additional qualities that manifest spirit, which are not found in animals. Man has a mind in a sense in which an animal has none. How can this be accounted for? Nothing in all the animal creation measures up to the mental, moral, and spiritual nature of man. He is different from and superior to an animal in his spiritual nature. In creation, therefore, both man's physical and intellectual lives began with the union of the spiritual nature with a material body. Thus, in this way Scripture sets forth the distinction between man and the animals, as well as man's relationship to God.

God's Law in Natural Birth

Many other questions now begin to emerge. Are all men today in God's image? How does a person receive a personal spirit? At what time? These are important questions in this study. Today a person receives his spirit and body in harmony with God's divine law of natural birth, and not by a miracle as at the beginning. The spirit (soul) is now brought into existence directly from (by) Jehovah (as pure as the source from which it springs), and not from human parents. God is the Father of our spirits (Hebrews 12:9). All men today, even those marred by sin, are in God's image in these respects: (1) intelligence, (2) comprehension, (3) feeling, (4) free will, and (5) eternal existence (as shall be shown more fully later). The Bible teaches the non-ending existence of the soul. These are the features of the divine likeness which all men possess. It is in this sense that men are made after the likeness of God, as expressed by James (James 3:9). Each man, in all nations of the world, contains in his essence the image of the eternal God who created him. Therefore, the Bible teaches that all human beings today are given a peculiar place in the universe. Although by his body man is allied to this earth, yet by his spirit, derived from Jehovah, he is in the likeness of God. Man is an embodied spirit.

This truth is important to this study, for people do not believe in immortality unless they believe in God and in the divine origin of man, who was created in the image of God. The human race was originated in the first pair. The first father and the first mother had to be created; all other human beings are born. Adam was the first man (1 Corinthians 15:45). "Jehovah God formed man [his body] of the dust of the ground, and breathed into his nostrils the breath of life; and man became a living soul" (Genesis 2:7). Thus all animals and man, too, are breathers; they possess physical (animal) life. Hence, Paul in 1 Thessalonians 5:23 speaks of man's whole being as to what constitutes him. The word *soul* is used then in the sense that man has a physical body. He breathes and he has physical life, as does the animal.

But *soul* is often used for the immortal part of man that never dies, that is, his spirit. This part belongs to man alone, and is unaffected by death. It is the spirit or soul of man in this sense that distinguishes man from the brute beast. This is the part of man that is created in the image of God (Genesis 2:7). This is how the word *spirit* is used in 1 Thessalonians 5:23.

In speaking of the death of Rachel at the time of the birth of her son, Benjamin, Moses wrote: "And it came to pass, as her soul was departing, (for she died), that she called his name Benoni: but his father called him Benjamin" (Genesis 35:18). Hence, her soul, or spirit, departed from the body when she died. After Elijah, the prophet of God, had stayed some time in the house of the widow in the city of Zarephath, her son died. Elijah carried the body of the child into his bedroom and "stretched himself upon the child three times, and cried unto Jehovah, and said, O Jehovah my God, I pray thee, let this child's soul come into him again. And Jehovah harkened unto the voice of Elijah; and the soul of the child came into him again, and he revived" (1 Kings 17:21–22).

Jesus, in His public ministry, gave this warning: "And be not afraid of them that kill the body, but are not able to kill the soul: but rather fear him who is able to destroy both soul and body in hell" (Matthew 10:28; cf. Luke 12:4–5). When the apostle John was on the island of Patmos, where he received the revelation of God (Revelation 1:9), he was allowed to see "the souls of them that had been slain for the Word of God, and for the testimony which they held" (Revelation 6:9). When Jesus died on the cross, Luke records, "And Jesus, crying with a loud voice, said, Father, into thy hands I commend my spirit: and having said this, he gave up the ghost" (Luke 23:46). Yet, Peter, preaching on the day of Pentecost, quoted David's prophecy of the resurrection of Christ, and said:

> Because thou wilt not leave my soul unto Hades, neither wilt thou give thy Holy One to see corruption . . . He foreseeing this spake of the resurrection of the Christ, that neither was he left unto Hades, nor did his flesh see corruption (Acts 2:27–31).

Each of these passages is instructive of the fact that there is within man a soul that survives the death of the body.

The question therefore of this chapter in our study becomes this: Can the word *soul* be used correctly in referring to animals? The first definition definitely cannot apply to animals since animals are not persons. Yet the second definition would apply to animals if it is used to denote the physical life, just as humans have physical life. In Psalm 78:50 there is an example of the usage of soul or life when the writer said in speaking of the people of Egypt (who tried in vain to prevent the Hebrews from leaving their land) that God "spared not their soul from death, but gave their life over to the pestilence." But can the third definition be applied to animals? Do animals possess immortal souls that one day will inhabit heaven or hell? The answer is certainly no. Such an idea is completely at odds with the teaching found in God's Word.

Man and animals do not share kinship. All men are separated from the animal world by an impassable gulf. In fact, man was commanded by Jehovah God to subdue the earth "and have dominion over the fish of the sea, and over the birds of the heavens, and over every living thing that moveth upon the earth" (Genesis 1:28). God gave man permission to kill and eat animals for food (Genesis 9:3–4). However, within the same context God specifically forbade manslaughter, saying, "Whoso sheddeth man's blood, by man shall his blood be shed: for in the image of God made he man" (Genesis 9:6). If man shares kinship with the animals, or if animals possess immortal souls, why would God permit men to kill them? That would be like killing his own kin-relatives whose souls are no different from his own. The answer, of course, lies in the fact that animals are not created in the image of God.

Therefore, it is true that the word *soul* may be used to refer to the immortal souls of humans, but it is never used to refer to "immortal souls of animals." When animals die, their physical life comes to an end, but when man dies, then only the body dies. "The dust returneth to the earth as it was, and the spirit returneth unto God who gave it" (Ecclesiastes 12:7). Thus, man is an immortal being and animals are not. Only humans have been created in the image of God and possess a soul (an immortal spirit) that will never die.

What about Depravity?

People ask, "What about the theory of total depravity?" An eminent Bible scholar commented in a fine way on the false doctrine of original sin:

> Our bodies we receive from our earthly parents; our spirits are infused into us, and fathered for us, by God himself (Heb. 12:9). Were it possible, in view of this fact, (which it is not), to prove that there is some moral taint hereditarily transmitted from parent to child (which theologians style Original Sin, the Adamic Nature, etc.), the doctrine of Total Depravity would still not be established, because our spirits come to us directly from God, and not from our parents. Inasmuch as like begets like (Genesis 1:9–25, everything brings forth after its own kind), and since God begets our spirits, they are, at birth, as pure as the source from which they spring, and become sinful only through personal transgression.[1]

The Bible says that Adam "begat a son in his own likeness, after his image" (Genesis 5:3). This image of God continued through Seth's descendants, even down through Noah's sons after the flood (Genesis 9:6). Man does not inherit a sinful nature—the spirit (soul) comes from God.

What about Reincarnation?

Again, others ask, "May not the soul have lived in another body of some kind before it became embodied in this present body?" Scripture does not teach the theory of the reincarnation of the soul, a doctrine taught by Buddhists and Hindus in the East and the New Age Movement (new-pagan movement) in the West. The doctrine is that the soul must pass through numerous transmigrations before it reaches its final state. Since the doctrine of "metempsychosis" (the idea that at death the soul passes into another body, whether of an animal or a person) is not taught in the Bible, it cannot be an object of faith. Faith comes by hearing God's Word (Romans 10:17).

---

1 Guy N. Woods, *Commentary on the Epistle of James* (Nashville: Gospel Advocate Co., 1964), p. 152.

The Bible Man's Guide

The Bible is addressed to the rational qualities of man, and man is capable of understanding the revelation of God through his processes of reason. It is this rational ability of man to which God appeals through the Bible to tell him how to order his life. All men are answerable to Jehovah, and one day shall stand before Him in universal judgment. "It is appointed unto men once to die, and after this cometh judgment" (Hebrews 9:27); ". . . for we shall all stand before the judgment-seat of God" (Romans 14:10); "So then each one of us shall give account of himself to God" (Romans 14:12); "Thou wilt guide me with thy counsel, and afterward receive me to glory" (Psalm 73:24).

God has made known His will to mankind in the Sacred Scriptures. The Bible is God's revelation to man, given through men inspired by the Holy Spirit (2 Timothy 3:16–17; 2 Peter 1:21). Man says, "I know that I will go from this life before long, but what then?" The Bible has the only answer. It is the telescope that reveals the world beyond the grave and tells man about the life in the hereafter. With faith in the existence of a Divine Creator and the Holy Bible as the inspired Word of God, man can look forward to a life beyond the grave that shall never end. But when a person rejects the idea of God, who has existed from all eternity and is the Creator of everything, he becomes lost in the intricate maze of human speculation. Man gropes in his own darkness and searches for the slightest inkling of his origin or destiny when he rules out God. How pathetic is the person who, at the close of life's little day, can look forward only to a dark grave and oblivion!

Psalm 8

When the psalmist asked, "What is man, that thou art mindful of him?" he raised the question of the ages. To this point in the study, it has been established that all human beings are created in the image of God and that man is given a peculiar place in the universe, having been made but little lower than God [the angels KJV] and crowned with glory and honor (Psalm 8:5).

Man, then, is of a very honorable rank of beings; he is God's masterpiece of creation, the highest being that dwells on the earth. Although by his body he is allied to this earth, yet by his spirit he is in the likeness of Jehovah. He is above all the creatures of this world.

The Creator endues man with noble faculties and capacities, and qualifies him for dominion over all the inferior creatures. Man is their ruler.

> Thou makest him to have dominion over the works of thy hands; thou hast put all things under his feet: all sheep and oxen, yea, and the beasts of the field, the birds of the heavens, and the fish of the sea, whatsoever passeth through the paths of the seas. O Jehovah, our Lord, how excellent is thy name in all the earth! (Psalm 8:6–9).

Man on this earth is to live to the glory of God. Isaiah said man was made to exist for God's glory: "every one . . . whom I have created for my glory, whom I have formed, yea, whom I have made" (Isaiah 43:7). The animals were furnished for the use of man on earth. Man has greatness, and if he chooses to live the right way, great will be the consequences of his being.

What, then, is man, and whence came man? Man is more than body; he is more than a body with a soul; he is rather a soul dwelling in a body. Man is a being who came from God, created in God's image, rather than the product of mere physical, evolutionary processes. What a wonderful and sublime being is man! Each person can say: "Great thou art, O God!—and great is man created in thy image!" Peter also speaks of the "hidden man of the heart," that is not corruptible (1 Peter 3:4). This means that it is immortal, not subject to decay. But it is dwelling in an earthly tabernacle (2 Corinthians 5:1).

Error of Materialism

These statements of Scripture so far studied cannot be reconciled with the teaching of materialists who say that man has no spirit distinct from his material body. Herein lies the problem of the doctrine of materialism. The Bible reveals the truth of the origin and nature of man. The more one searches elsewhere, the more he presents his conflicting and changing theories to the contrary, the more clearly the simple statements of God's Word stand out: Man is the creature of God, in the image of God.

In this lofty doctrine of man's nature, which tells of the peculiar origin and alliance of his soul, originated by the very inbreathing of the eternal God, there exists the firm basis for the belief that man's soul came, not from the dust, but from the eternal God. Thus man, as created by Jehovah, is (has) an immortal spirit which lives after death.

Questions sometime asked about animals are "Do animals possess souls?" "If they do, are their souls the same as the human soul?" "Will they eventually inherit either heaven or hell?" Although little children love their pets, the answer is no. Animals do not have immortal souls or spirits.

Questions for Discussion

1. How did Jesus speak of the value of man?
2. When does one's life begin? At what time does one receive his spirit (soul)?
3. Do you think that abortion is wrong? If so, why?
4. Some do not believe the Bible. They do not believe that God created our world or that Jesus Christ is our only Redeemer. They do not believe that man will be raised from the dead, that God will judge the world in righteousness, or that He will reward the just with eternal life in heaven and punish the wicked with everlasting torment in hell. Others, confused by the errors of denominationalism, are being attracted to oriental mystic religions. Why is this a good time for true believers to be more evangelistic in presenting the teaching concerning man's origin, duty, and destiny?
5. When did Jeremiah's life begin?
6. Explain Psalm 51:5 from the translation of the American Standard Version and the King James Version and the teaching of Christ. Is there not a difference in inheriting the sins of our parents and inheriting the consequences of their sins? Study Exodus 20:4–6.
7. What is the doctrine of "original sin" or "total depravity"? Is this idea in harmony with the teaching of Scripture?
8. What is the doctrine of reincarnation? Which religions hold to this view?
9. What should guide man in his life on earth? Does each person possess tremendous possibilities for good or for evil?
10. How did David in the Eighth Psalm speak of man's dominion?
11. From this study what do you think is the basis of man's belief in the immortality of the soul and its survival at the body's dissolution?
12. Why is the doctrine of materialism wrong?
13. What is man's only correct source of authority in religion? (Study 2 Timothy 3:16–17.)
14. What is sin? Does a baby inherit sin? (See 1 John 3:4.)
15. Does the Bible teach that babies are innocent until they reach the age of accountability and then transgress God's law?
16. What did Jesus teach in Matthew 18:3 concerning little children?
17. The New International Version (1983) says, "Surely I was sinful at birth, sinful from the time my mother conceived me" (Psalm 51:5). Explain why the erroneous translation regarding total depravity is not true.
18. Sin brought physical death into the world, and sin separates from God. We die physically because of Adam's sin; we die spiritually because of our own sins (Ezekiel 18:20; Isaiah 59:1–2). Explain how this is true.
19. Explain the errors of suicide, abortion, and euthanasia.

TO AN UNBELIEVER

I'm concerned that you deny
That God created earth,
And it pains my heart when you decry
Our Savior's virgin birth!

You say that Jesus Christ our Lord
Was just another man,
While I believe with all my soul
God sent Him to our land!

You view the starry skies above
And see an accident,
I say the moon was hung by God
And the stars are heaven sent.

You say that man's immortal soul
Your imagination bends,
And that when death shall touch your heart
Your whole existence ends!

But I'm aware by God's own breath
When this body's 'neath the sod,
My soul shall fly away to stand
At the judgment bar of God!

My friend, if you are right and I am wrong
When death's cold wind shall blow,
We'll sleep forever in the ground
And neither one will ever know!

But if—as God's Word says—I'm right and you are wrong
When death shall chance to be,
Then both of us will be aware
Throughout all eternity!

—Marion Ed Lobaugh

– 4 –

WHAT IS DEATH?

". . . it is appointed unto men once to die"
Hebrews 9:27

In this world nothing is more common than death. Death is universally the king of terrors (Job 18:14). Death severs the ties of human life and removes one from the scene of this present world into the unknown, and the unknown causes man to fear death. God has planted love for life in every creature of the universe. Man does not want to die, but everyone knows that he soon must die. Since the murder of Abel, death has held men in fear of its power, but the teaching of the New Testament on this subject can do much to help take away this dread and fear.

There are four simple facts about death.

- Death is real. Each day approximately 95,000 people die—66 per minute. The legions of the dead are more than those of the living.
- Death is certain. Unless the Lord returns soon, none now living can evade it, for this is the lot of all mankind. Death will be a personal experience.
- The time of death is uncertain. True, death often serves notice in advance, but most often it comes when least expected.
- Man should make preparation for death before it comes. Isaiah said to King Hezekiah, "Set thy house in order; for thou shalt die, and not live" (2 Kings 20:1). Man needs to realize that now—in this life—is the time to prepare for life after death.

Four important days in a man's experiences are the day of his birth, the day of his marriage, the day of his obedience to Christ's commands for salvation, and the day of his death. The good and bad, the rich and poor, the high and low, the young and old must each feel the cold hand of death. Death ends physical life. It is the common fate of all men.

The following passages of Scripture affirm the reality and inevitability of death: "For, all flesh is as grass, and all the glory thereof as the flower of grass.

The grass withereth, and the flower falleth" (1 Peter 1:24). "For the living know that they shall die" (Ecclesiastes 9:5). "It is appointed unto men once to die, and after this cometh judgment" (Hebrews 9:27). "Boast not thyself of tomorrow; for thou knowest not what a day may bring forth" (Proverbs 27:1). Death will come and the event must be faced by everyone. The death rate is a hundred percent—one death for each birth, unless you are alive when Christ returns. Death comes every day to someone, and someday to everyone. But death need not be feared. The psalmist said, "Precious in the sight of Jehovah is the death of his saints" (Psalm 116:15).

Man does not want to die. He thinks of others who will die, yet somehow he tries to avoid thinking of it himself. In 1513, Ponce de Leon searched for a fountain of perpetual youth. He found no magic fountain, merely Florida. That fountain has never been found—nor will it ever be—but the search has not been called off.

The wise man wrote: "It is better to go to the house of mourning than to go to the house of feasting: for that is the end of all men; and the living will lay it to his heart" (Ecclesiastes 7:2). Why is it better to go to a funeral than to a wedding? Because all men may not choose to marry but all men must die. Death is the end of all men. It is good, then, to frequent the place of mourning, for in so doing one may meditate upon the brevity and uncertainty of this life. People are living such busy and fretful lives that there is a real danger of forgetting that death will come to them, and that it may come when they are unprepared for it. Man may say that he has no fear of death, but he may fail to consider that also he may have no hope in death. Inscribed on the great central arch leading to the main aisle of the cathedral of Milan, are these words: "That only is important which is eternal." If all could only be conscious of this great truth, they would not permit themselves to be fascinated by the carnival of material things, and they would live for the things of the hereafter.

This world is a place of probation and preparation for the next. In the monastery at Cluny, France, is written this sentence concerning the hour of death: "Of all these hours, fear only one." If one has fulfilled the purposes God had for him on this earth, then truly the day of death is better than the day of one's birth (Ecclesiastes 7:1).

Natural death is the appointment of God because of the transgression and fall of man. "Therefore, as through one man [Adam] sin entered into the world, and death through sin; and so death passed unto all men, for that all sinned" (Romans 5:12). If sin had never entered into this world, death would not have come. Therefore, physically, all individuals are subject to death because of Adam's sin. He became separated from the tree of life and could not eat of it (Genesis 3:22–24). Adam began to die physically that day. As a result of Adam's sin, all men are born separated from the tree of life and sooner or later die.

Although men do not inherit the guilt of Adam's sin, Adam's posterity suffers this consequence of his sin. Man does not inherit sin from any person—Adam or anyone else. Sin is a transgression of God's law (1 John 3:4). The prophet of God declared: "The soul that sinneth, it shall die: the son shall not bear the iniquity of the father, neither shall the father bear the iniquity of the son" (Ezekiel 18:20). (The statement in Exodus 20:5, which speaks of God visiting the iniquity of the fathers upon the children, refers to the consequences of sin on one's posterity.) Again, the apostle Paul said: "For since by man [Adam] came death, by man [Christ] came also the resurrection of the dead. For as in Adam all die, so also in Christ shall all be made alive [at the resurrection]" (1 Corinthians 15:21–22). So these passages do not teach that babies are born in sin or born sinners, or that they inherit Adam's sin or come into the world totally depraved; they teach that natural death entered into the world because of Adam's sin. The Bible also teaches that what man lost unconditionally in Adam he will gain unconditionally in Christ. So each person must die—excepting those who will be alive and remain until the coming of Christ in judgment (1 Corinthians 15:51; 1 Thessalonians 4:15). Only two of God's faithful servants evaded death here on earth: Enoch and Elijah (Genesis 5:24; 2 Kings 2:11). Each one, then, can say with Job: "For when a few years are come, I shall go the way whence I shall not return" (Job 16:22); and as David said of himself, so may each one say of himself: "There is but a step between me and death" (1 Samuel 20:3).

Now let us go to the Scriptures to learn the meaning of death, for the Bible has the only authoritative information on the subject of death and the hereafter. Having learned that man is a being composed of animated matter and spirit, it shall now be demonstrated that the Scriptures teach that natural death is the separation of these two parts—that at death the spirit leaves the body.

Separation of Spirit from Body Occurs in Death

That physical death is the separation of the spirit from the body is evident from the teaching of James: "For as the body apart from the spirit is dead, even so faith apart from works is dead" (James 2:26). This passage clearly shows that the body is dead without the spirit. The separation causes the body to be without the spirit. The Bible does not say that the spirit is dead without the body; it says the body is dead without the spirit, just as faith is dead without works. The spirit does not die. Death occurs when the occupant (the spirit) leaves the house (the body). Death is a change in which the organic life terminates by cessation of bodily functions, and the spirit is separated from the body and called away from this world. So long as that mysterious union between the body and the spirit exists, the individual lives; but when that union is dissolved, the body dies; it is separated from the spirit and cannot continue to live. Hence, physical death results when the spirit leaves the body. The unity of his compound nature is broken up. When a person dies, the body returns to dust, while the spirit returns to God who gave it. This is the nature of death.

In the description of death given by Solomon, there is a distinction between the body which goes to the dust and the spirit which returns to God who gave it: "The dust returneth to the earth as it was, and the spirit returneth unto God who gave it" (Ecclesiastes 12:7). When man sinned in the Garden of Eden and was driven out, God said to Adam: "In the sweat of thy face shalt thou eat bread, till thou return unto the ground; for out of it wast thou taken: for dust thou art, and unto dust shalt thou return" (Genesis 3:19). The body only—that which is dust—is to return to the ground, while the spirit returns to God who gave it. "Man [i.e., the body] shall turn again unto dust" (Job 34:15). In these passages Jehovah taught that only the body, which was dust and taken from the ground, was to return to dust again. But man is not all dust—only his body is (cf. Genesis 1:27; 2:7; Zechariah 12:1; Hebrews 12:9). So, according to the Scriptures, the destiny of the body is to return to the source of its origin, the dust. The mortal shall perish and return to its native element. The body dies, but not all of man dies because the spirit, the real man, returns to its origin, God. It is not dust; hence, the spirit is not doomed to return to the dust with the body at physical death. Well did the poet express this truth:

> Life is real, life is earnest;
> And the grave is not its goal;
> "Dust thou art—to dust returneth,"
> Was not spoken of the soul.
>
> —Henry W. Longfellow

Thayer gives this definition of death (*thanatos*): "The death of the body, i.e., that separation (whether natural or violent) of the soul from the body by which the life on earth is ended."[1] Physical death is that condition which occurs when the spirit, the conscious entity of man derived directly from Jehovah, leaves the body. Separated, the body returns to the dust out of which it was made, and the spirit wings its way into the unseen world.

The Soul Departs

The spirit departs from the body at death. The death of Rachel, the mother of Benjamin, is recorded in these words: "And it came to pass, as her soul was

---

1 Joseph Henry Thayer, *A Greek-English Lexicon of the New Testament* (New York: American Book Co., 1886), p. 282.

departing (for she died) . . ." (Genesis 35:18). When Rachel died, her soul departed; or, in that sad hour, soul and body became separated from each other.

Other descriptions of death convey the idea of the separation of spirit and body. For instance, death is described as the giving up of the ghost or spirit: "Abraham gave up the ghost, and died" (Genesis 25:8); "Isaac gave up the ghost, and died" (Genesis 35:29); Jacob "yielded up the ghost, and was gathered unto his people" (Genesis 49:33); "And Jesus, crying with a loud voice, said, Father, into thy hands I commend my spirit: and having said this, he gave up the ghost" (Luke 23:46). Two early members of the church in Jerusalem were killed because of sin. After trying to deceive the Lord about his money, Ananias "gave up the ghost," and later his wife, Sapphira, fell down "and gave up the ghost" (cf. Acts 5:5–10). Concerning the first Christian martyr, the Scriptures relate that he died with a prayer on his lips: "And they stoned Stephen, calling upon the Lord, and saying, Lord Jesus, receive my spirit . . . And when he had said this, he fell asleep" (Acts 7:59–60).

We Fly Away

The Bible compares the departure of the soul at death to the escape of a bird from the hands of the fowler or from a cage. "The days of our years are threescore years and ten, or even by reason of strength fourscore years; yet is their pride but labor and sorrow; for it is soon gone, and we fly away" (Psalm 90:10). This language could not be used if a man has no distinct spiritual nature. What is it that flies away? Bodies do not fly away; the bodies remain after death. The "we" who "fly away" are the spirits, not the bodies. Only by metonymy (container for the contained) or as a synecdoche (part for the whole) is the body ever called the man. It is the spirit that departs from the body at death. So death is spoken of as the soul's departure or exodus from this world.

The Body a Tabernacle

The inspired writers represent the human body as a tabernacle, a frail dwelling-place such as a tent, in which the real man lives. Death is referred to as the putting off of this tabernacle. Note these passages:

> For we know that if the earthly house of our tabernacle be dissolved, we have a building from God, a house not made with hands, eternal, in the heavens. For verily in this we groan, longing to be clothed upon with our habitation which is from heaven: if so be that being clothed we shall not be found naked. For indeed we that are in this tabernacle do groan, being burdened; not for that we would be unclothed, but that we would be clothed upon, that what is mortal may be swallowed up of life . . . Being therefore always of good courage, and knowing that, whilst we are at home in the body, we are absent from the Lord . . . and are willing rather to be absent from the body, and to be at home with the Lord (2 Corinthians 5:1–8).

The fact that the spirit is in the body—the house of clay—is proved in this language of Paul. Else, what does the writer mean here by "at home in the body" and "absent from the body" if death is not a separation of the one from the other? Does he not show that at death the soul leaves the body to be present with the Lord? The "we" of this passage surely refers to the spirits in the bodies. The body is the "earthly house of our tabernacle"; therefore, it is only the house in which the real man (the spirit) dwells. The dweller and his house are distinct (cf. 2 Corinthians 4:16). Hence, the body is merely a tent, and death is merely the spirit leaving the body.

Now, is man all mortal? What is "at home in the body," if man is all body? What is there about man which can be "absent from the body" and "at home with the Lord"? It cannot be the body, for after death it decays. Therefore, man is more than a body, and death means something other than ceasing to be. "At home" or "absent" means whether the person is in the body or out of it, whether alive or dead. The tabernacle to be dissolved and the dweller in the tabernacle are as distinct as the house and its occupant.

The apostle Peter employed the same metaphor concerning the house and its occupant in his writings.

> I think it right, as long as I am in this tabernacle, to stir you up by putting you in remembrance; knowing that the putting off of my tabernacle cometh swiftly, even as our Lord Jesus Christ signified unto me. Yea, I will give diligence that at every time ye may be able after my decease to call these things to remembrance (2 Peter 1:13–15).

The word *decease* here means departure or exodus. Peter probably recalled that Moses and Elijah conversed with Christ on the Mount of Transfiguration concerning "his decease which he was about to accomplish at Jerusalem" (Luke 9:31). It is no wonder that Peter later spoke of his own death as an exodus from this world, since he was present at this momentous occasion and greatly impressed by what occurred. To Peter, death meant leaving the tabernacle or tent of clay—because it has served its purpose—and he is moving on to the next stage of being. So here again, according to Biblical teaching, the body is only a temporary covering which clothes the real man, and death is a departure out of the covering.

Simeon also viewed death as a departure which could not be true in any sense if the soul died with the body and was not separated from it. After seeing the child Jesus in the temple at Jerusalem, he said: "Now lettest thou thy servant depart, Lord, according to thy word, in peace" (Luke 2:29). This question is in order: in what sense does one leave this tabernacle and make his exit from this world, if death is not the process which separates the soul and body?

Again, Paul spoke of his own death as a departure from this life: "But I am in a strait betwixt the two, having the desire to depart and be with Christ; for it is very far better: yet to abide in the flesh is more needful for your sake" (Philippians 1:23–24). What does the writer mean here by "abide in the flesh" if it be not living in the body? And what is meant by "depart," if it be not dying?

The Scriptures teach without doubt that physical death severs the mystical tie that binds the spirit to its material body; then these two essentially different natures part company, and man passes from one condition of existence to another. However, this separation of body and spirit is not final but temporary. The separation is only till the resurrection; at that time the body will be raised changed, and the spirit will be reunited with the body (1 Corinthians 15:35–57). Instead of being lost forever at death, those who have died in Christ, as shall be clearly shown later in this study, shall be raised with new bodies incapable of weariness, and all the redeemed shall live together in heaven (1 Thessalonians 4:13–18). There the righteous shall meet in the land where the tears and sorrows of this life are no more. These separations from loved ones and friends, caused by death, are not permanent. The resurrection of Christ and the whole of Biblical teaching have taken the fear out of death for the believer (Hebrews 2:14–15; John 5:28–29).

A beautiful figure of a Christian's passing from this life is the one used by Paul when he wrote to Timothy from his prison cell in Rome: "The time of my departure is come" (2 Timothy 4:6). The Greek word translated depart means "to loose, to unloose, or to loose anchor." It is the picture of unloosing of the anchor or ropes which held a ship to the shore, so that it may move out into the deep. Paul realized that his unmooring was at hand. Hence, as the vessel glides out to sea and slowly fades from the sight of the watching throng at the port, so it is with those who cast off life's moorings and sail away on the billowing waves of death. Though they pass for a moment from our eyes, others wait on distant shores and watch with joy their coming. If on this side death is a departure, then on the other side it is an arrival. If here a separation, there a reunion. It is a voyage to a better life.

This metaphor of dying is beautifully expressed by Tennyson in his well-loved poem, "Crossing the Bar":

> Sunset and evening star,
> And one clear call for me!
> And may there be no moaning of the bar
> When I put out to sea.
>
> But such a tide as moving seems asleep,
> Too full for sound or foam,
> When that which drew from out the boundless deep
> Turns again home.

Twilight and evening bell,
And after that the dark!
And may there be no sadness of farewell,
When I embark!

For tho', from out our borne of time and place
The flood may bear me far,
I hope to see my Pilot face to face,
When I have crossed the bar.
—Tennyson

Or, again in these words:

Like a ship that's left its mooring
And sails bravely out to sea,
So Someone Dear has sailed away
In calm serenity:
But there's promise of greater joy
Than earth could have in store,
For God has planned a richer life
Beyond the Unseen Shore.
—Author unknown

Each tick of the clock brings each one of us nearer death and eternity. Therefore, in the words of another great poet:

So live, that when thy summons comes to join
The innumerable caravan that moves
To that mysterious realm, where each shall take
His chamber in the silent halls of death,
Thou go not, like the quarry slave at night,
Scourged to his dungeon, but, sustained and soothed
By an unfaltering trust, approach thy grave
Like one who wraps the drapery of his couch
About him, and lies down to pleasant dreams.
—William Cullen Bryant

When Dorcas Died

There once lived at Joppa a great Christian woman by the name of Tabitha, or Dorcas: "This woman was full of good works and alms deeds which she did." But she became sick, and died. Friends washed the body and laid her in an upper room. The apostle Peter was in Lydda, near to Joppa, so the disciples sent for Peter to come, and Peter came. Luke records:

> When he was come, they brought him into the upper chamber: and all the widows stood by him weeping, and showing the coats and garments which Dorcas made, while she was with them. But Peter put them all forth, and kneeled down, and prayed; and turning to the body, he said, Tabitha, arise. And she opened her eyes; and when she saw Peter, she sat up. And he gave her his hand, and raised her up; and calling the saints and widows, he presented her alive (Acts 9:39–41).

When Dorcas died her body was still there, but she was not then with them. She had gone out of her body. The widows, weeping, showed Peter the coats and garments Dorcas had made for them out of a heart of love for the poor, while she was with them, still living in the body. The widows realized that Dorcas was now gone. They understood the meaning of death. After Peter had brought her back to life by miraculous power as an inspired apostle, he then presented her to them again alive, for her spirit had returned to her body. Thus she was alive physically again. Such is the meaning of physical death.

Peter had been present three times when Jesus had raised the dead: Jairus' daughter (Mark 5:40–42); the son of the widow of Nain (Luke 7:11–15); and Lazarus (John 11:36–44). As those early disciples truly rejoiced to have Dorcas back to life again, how indescribable will be the scene when all the dead shall rise and the righteous will greet each other on the shores of eternity!

The psalmist declared in Psalm 116:15: "Precious in the sight of Jehovah is the death of his saints." To the faithful child of God, death is precious. To depart from this life and to be with Christ on the other side is very far better than living in this world (Philippians 1:23).

The summary of this chapter is that life is that state when body and spirit are together, and that physical death is that condition which obtains when the spirit, the conscious entity of man derived directly from God, is no longer in the body. The spirit leaves the body and returns to God. The body returns to dust. All should live each day as if it were the last. It may well be. To the faithful child of God, death is only the portal through which his soul enters into a brighter world of bliss and happiness. But this will be studied more fully in later chapters, for when a faithful Christian goes the way of all the earth and his body sleeps in the dust, his spirit puts out to sea and arrives safely on the other shore to be welcomed by the Lord. The "I," referring to the immortal soul, continues to exist, and "you" will always be. May we live in view of eternity (Psalm 90:12).

Questions for Discussion

1. Why is it natural for man to dread death?
2. What is the Biblical meaning of death? Give Thayer's definition.
3. What is the doctrine of materialism concerning the meaning of physical death?
4. What brought physical death into the world?
5. How many parts constitute man?
6. What happens to the body at death? What happens to the spirit?
7. Using Paul's illustration of the body being the house in which man lives, what happens to the tenant at death?
8. If one should remove a bird from its cage would that necessarily kill the bird?
9. What happened when Rachel died? Abraham? Isaac? Jacob? Christ? When Jacob died, he was taken from Egypt and buried in the cave of Machpelah (Genesis 50:13); Joseph's bones were carried back to Canaan and buried in Shechem (Joshua 24:32); and loving hands buried the body of Jesus (John 19:38–42).
10. If one says that man ceases to exist entirely at death, is that a necessary conclusion?
11. What is meant by "gave up the ghost"? What is another and better word for ghost?
12. When the Old Testament speaks of the departed saints being gathered to their people at death, are the references made to their gathering together in the tombs or to the concourse of departed spirits?
13. What did Paul mean when he said the time of his departure was at hand?
14. Will the soul (spirit), dislodged from the body at death, ever have another body? If so, when and what kind of body?
15. How should one live each day?
16. How did Peter view death? Paul?
17. How is death illustrated by the account of the death and resurrection to life again in the story of the death of Dorcas?
18. Four times in the book of Genesis, death is described as being gathered to one's people (25:28; 25:17; 35:29; 49:33). But does this phrase refer to the destination of the body or of the soul? Abraham was buried in the cave of Machpelah when Sarah was the only one of his "people" buried there (Genesis 25:9–10).
19. If one could view life the way Paul did, "For me to live is Christ," then could he not view death as Paul did: "and to die is gain . . . to depart and be with Christ; for it is far better"? (cf. Philippians 1:21–23).

20. Where was the body of Jesus between His death and His resurrection? (cf. Acts 2:27, 31).

Note: Some say that since Jesus died, arose, and went to heaven, He moved Paradise and took all the righteous spirits who were there to heaven. So now saved spirits go immediately into heaven at their physical deaths. We cannot agree with this view. We shall show later that the Scriptures teach that the souls (spirits) of the dead remain in Hades (Paradise) until the resurrection of the body. The theory that Paradise was moved to heaven by Jesus at His resurrection is a basic part of the erroneous premillennial doctrine. We go to be with the Lord, if righteous at death, but the place is Paradise in Hades, not yet in heaven (cf. Matthew 25:31–46; 1 Thessalonians 4:13–18). Peter, on the day of Pentecost, some fifty days after Christ ascended to heaven, said, "For David is not ascended into the heavens" (Acts 2:34 KJV).

– 5 –

Does the Spirit Survive the Grave?

"Now he is not the God of the dead, but of the living: for all live unto him"
Luke 20:38

When death approaches, many people ask soberly: "Is this all? Are all my interests being crowded within the narrow compass of the brief span of this life? Shall I fall into nothingness so soon after I am born?" Others ask: "After death comes and severs the spirit from the body, what happens to the spirit? Is it interred with the body in the grave? Does it cease to exist after its departure from the body? If the spirit continues to exist after leaving the body, is the departed spirit conscious? Does personal identity continue after death? If the spirit survives the shock of death, where then does it go?"

These and many other questions come to every thoughtful mind in the study of man's existence after death. Science and philosophy can give no light on the subject. Only the Holy Scriptures can answer these questions and provide accurate information on life in the hereafter. What, then, does the Bible teach regarding these questions? God has not left man in complete ignorance about death, for some things concerning the life beyond the grave He has revealed.

Job exclaimed: "Yea, man giveth up the ghost, and where is he?" (Job 14:10). We shall see.

The spirit does not go to the grave, for it has been shown that at death the spirit returns to God who gave it (Ecclesiastes 12:7). The body, taken from the ground, returns to dust to await the resurrection. The destination of the body after death is out of sight, usually in the grave. Abraham, the patriarch of old, said concerning his beloved wife, Sarah, after the spirit departed from her body: "Give me . . . a burying place . . . that I may bury my dead out of my sight" (Genesis 23:4). "But what about the spirit?" people ask. "Does it survive after death?" Always, materialists ask: "When a man dies, does his soul or spirit survive?" and, "Is it possible for spirit-beings to exist out of material bodies?" The Bible clearly teaches that the soul or spirit of man does not become extinct with the death of the body. True, from all outward appearance, to those ignorant of God's Word, death looks like the end of man. They know of no hereafter. But the Scriptures teach that death is merely the spirit's departure from this earthly life; it is like a doorway to another world through which everyone must pass. Death is but the gateway to life in another state or form.

Some people claim they believe the teaching of the Scriptures, yet they reject the idea of the soul's survival after death. They claim that at death a person goes out of existence, into blank nothingness, and must so remain until the resurrection. (Some even deny a resurrection.) Materialists say to die means "to cease to exist." They argue that the dead are "wholly unconscious, being entirely out of existence except in God's memory."[1]

They teach that if the soul is a part of man, it dies too; otherwise, the man does not die. They affirm that man has no spirit that can have a separate existence out of the body, that a man dies like other animals, that everything about man dies, and that nothing survives the death of the body. Materialists affirm there is no "I"—no thinking, remembering spiritual being apart from the body; therefore, they say that when the body dies, the "I" ceases to be. Some materialists say they believe that the dead will live again and the body will be raised, but they deny that the soul survives death. This is indeed a strange doctrine and, as shall be further shown, foreign to God's Word.

The spirit does not perish with the death of the body. Life does not end at the grave. It has already been brought out in this study that the Holy Scriptures teach that death means simply the separation of the spirit from the body. The soul or spirit of the person does not become extinct with the death of the body.

---

1 For an example of such teaching see J. F. Rutherford's book, *Where Are the Dead?* (Brooklyn: Watchtower Bible and Tract Society, 1932), pp. 29, 31.

In the writings of Jehovah's Witnesses statements are found which teach that men are wholly mortal, they, like animals, cease to exist at death, that all consciousness ends when one dies. For instance, "So we see that the claim of religionists that man has an immortal soul and therefore differs from the beast is not Scriptural" *(Let God be True,* 68). "What is the soul? It is a living, breathing creature. Every man is a soul, but no man possesses a soul . . . By what authority is the claim made that death is merely the separation of the body and soul and that the soul lives on? That claim is based wholly on the Devil's lie" (*Enemies,* p. 174). "The Scriptures, without contradiction, show that the dead are unconscious, out of existence" *(Religion,* p. 100). "At death the sinner soul dies and ceases to be" (*The Truth Shall Make You Free,* p. 77).

Spirit-Beings Exist

Spirit-beings do exist apart from material bodies. There is an invisible world of beings. This fact is abundantly illustrated by the Sacred Writings. Consider the following passages: Jesus said, "God is a Spirit" (John 4:24). Goodspeed, Weymouth, and Moffatt's translations read, "God is Spirit." This verse does not say that God has a Spirit, as if His spiritual nature were united with a physical body. The passage says that God is Spirit. He is wholly a Spirit-Being—non-material and unconnected with bodily form or organs. Christ is now a glorified Spirit-Being. The Holy Spirit is also a Divine Person or a Spirit-Being, invisible, not dwelling in a physical body. He is a Person of the Godhead, in essence as one with the Father and the Son. Statements said of Him could only be said of a personality (cf. John 14:16; 16:7–14; Acts 17:29; Romans 8:26–27; Ephesians 4:30; 1 Timothy 4:1). Now, if God, Christ, and the Holy Spirit are exclusively Spirits, and can exist outside of physical bodies, the same existence is altogether possible in regard to the human soul. It has been established that man, as a spirit, is of the same nature with God, being created in the image of God. Just because the Persons of the Godhead are invisible to man on earth does not prove that God (i.e., Deity) does not exist. (There are some things on earth which are invisible to man, but exist: e.g., electricity and the atom. Even man's own spirit is invisible.) Likewise, the holy angels are spirit-beings. Speaking of angels, the Bible asks, "Are they not all ministering spirits, sent forth to do service for the sake of them that shall inherit salvation?" (Hebrews 1:14). As God is a Spirit, unembodied, so also His angels are spirits (cf. Psalm 104:4). Fallen angels are evil spirits. They were once obedient and holy, but they kept not their own principality; they sinned and were cast down to hell (Jude 6; 2 Peter 2:4). Satan, or the devil, is also a spirit or personality. The Bible never attributes a corporeal nature to angels, good or bad (cf. Mark 5:13).

After all, the Bible speaks of only two kinds of beings that are in existence, namely: (1) God (Deity), who is the eternal, self-existent One, and (2) the beings that He has created and which exist by His will; some of these exist in material bodies and some in spirit form. There are three classes of purely spirit-beings, namely: (1) God (Deity or the Godhead), (2) the holy angels, and (3) fallen angels or evil spirits. They are all spirits and as such do not possess material, physical bodies. Hence, there can be a purely spiritual existence.

There is nothing any more mysterious about the existence of spirits out of the flesh than about their existence in the flesh. Mary, the mother of Jesus, had a spirit dwelling in her material body, for she said: "My soul doth magnify the Lord, and my spirit hath rejoiced in God my Saviour (Luke 1:46–47). Likewise, Daniel, for he said: "As for me, Daniel, my spirit was grieved in the midst of my body" (Daniel 7:15). The Bible also speaks of the "spirits of just men made perfect" in referring to spirits out of their physical bodies, i.e., with the spirits of all the redeemed (Hebrews 12:23).

Therefore, a spirit—a non-material and incorporeal essence—may or may not be associated with a physical body. The spirit of man can live and act without a physical body. Scripture teaches that the spirit is not dependent upon a body for its existence. While in the body the spirit is in the earthly house; after death the spirit is outside this house (2 Corinthians 5:1).

Man Lives after Death

Now note some passages of Scripture which show that man's spirit does continue to exist after death, and that death does not imply the extinction of the soul. This is affirmed many times in the Bible.

The patriarchs died by natural death and were described as having been gathered to their people. "Abraham gave up the ghost [spirit], and died in a good old age, an old man, and full of years, and was gathered to his people. And Isaac and Ishmael his sons buried him in the cave of Machpelah" (Genesis 25:8–9). "Gathered to his people" does not mean that he was buried where they were buried. The gathering to his people is definitely distinguished from the act of burial. Abraham's father was buried in Haran, some four hundred miles from the cave of Machpelah in Hebron (cf. Genesis 11:32; Genesis 25:8–9); his more distant ancestors lived in Ur of Chaldees, some six hundred miles from Hebron (Genesis 11:28); yet, Abraham at his death was gathered to his people. The reunion was not a mere reunion of corpses but of spirits.

Of Ishmael it is said: "He gave up the ghost [spirit] and died; and was gathered unto his people" (Genesis 25:17). "And Isaac gave up the ghost [spirit], and died, and was gathered unto his people, old and full of days: and Esau and Jacob his sons buried him" (Genesis 35:29). The same is said concerning the deaths of Aaron (Numbers 20:26), Moses (Deuteronomy 32:50), and all the people contemporary with Joshua (Judges 2:10). "And when Jacob made an end of charging his sons, he gathered up his feet into the bed, and yielded up the ghost [spirit], and was gathered unto his people" (Genesis 49:33). Jacob was gathered unto his people at the moment of death. Although the patriarch died in Egypt, he was not buried until many days later in the cave of Machpelah in the land of Canaan near Hebron. How was it, then, that he was gathered unto his people at the time of his death, if it was not by the departure of his soul to the abode of his father Isaac and his grandfather Abraham? The statement affirms a reunion in a continuation of life after death, for it is certain that at death, Jacob's body was not gathered unto his ancestor's physical bodies.

These old patriarchs did not think that the mere abandonment of the body meant the cessation of life because they believed in a common gathering place of the departed spirits beyond this life. It is clear that in this sense these ancient people understood that their loved ones went to join their people when they departed this life.

The expression, "gathered unto his people," therefore, does not mean simply to die or to be buried in a family tomb. This is true for three reasons:

- Death and burial are both mentioned in the same connection as happenings distinct from being gathered unto his people.
- The distinction between burial in one common tomb and being gathered unto his people is also made prominent by the separation of the two events by a considerable interval of time—Jacob for instance.
- The phrase is employed concerning those who were not deposited in the same tombs of their ancestors. For example: Abraham, Moses, and Aaron were not buried in the same tomb. The phrase, "gathered unto his fathers," can mean only one thing—that they joined them in an existence beyond this life. It is a gracious expression for a life after death—an association with ancestors in the spirit-world which takes place, not at interment, but in the moment of death.

Hence, the soul does not go into the tomb, and the spirit is no part of that which is placed in the grave. The spirit does not die with the body; it lives on even though the body crumbles back to dust. One's spirit is the real man, never his body. Man merely moves into another phase of life when the body dies. This life (in the body) is but the morning of man's existence.

The Sacred Scriptures indicate that those left on earth did not consider their dead loved ones as out of existence, but only separated from the body and living in another place. David, for instance, ceased to weep and fast when he learned that his beloved child was dead; and when asked about his conduct, he replied:

> While the child was yet alive, I fasted and wept: for I said, Who knoweth whether Jehovah will not be gracious to me, that the child may live? But now he is dead, wherefore should I fast? can I bring him back again? I shall go to him, but he will not return to me (2 Samuel 12:22–23).

David's language plainly shows his belief that while his child had gone from him and could not return, he himself expected to depart this life some day and go to the child. Thus David in no uncertain language expressed his belief that he would one day be reunited with his child.

Other expressions in the Scriptures show that God's saints in the Old Testament believed in a continuation of life after death. In one of the most beautiful and best known psalms ever written, David expressed the thought that he could look forward to the journey through the valley of death without fear, for the Divine Guide would be with him there. "Yea, though I walk through the valley of the shadow of death, I will fear no evil: for thou art with me; thy rod and thy staff, they comfort me" (Psalm 23:4). David again expressed his faith in life after death when he said: "I shall be satisfied, when I awake, with beholding thy form" (Psalm 17:15). Job said: "But as for me I know that my Redeemer liveth, and at last he will stand up upon the earth: and after my skin, even this body, is destroyed, then without my flesh shall I see God" (Job 19:25–26). In this passage is one of the most triumphant expressions of confidence in God to be found anywhere in all the Holy Scriptures.

Death Cannot Kill the Soul

That the spirit survives the death of the body is plainly taught by Christ when He said that the soul cannot be killed. "Be not afraid of them that kill the body, and after that have no more that they can do" (Luke 12:4). "And be not afraid of them that kill the body, but are not able to kill the soul: but rather fear him who is able to destroy both soul and body in hell" (Matthew 10:28). This language proves that the soul is not the body, nor the body the soul. The soul and the body are clearly distinguishable; one is susceptible to destruction (death) at the hands of men; the other, only by the Lord. Although men may kill (destroy) the body, they cannot kill (destroy) the soul. The body of man, therefore, is not the whole of man, but only one part of his nature. If the body were the entirety of man, then killing it would also be killing the spirit. But if man were composed merely of dust and animal life, then whoever killed the body would at the same time kill the soul. Nevertheless, Jesus taught that the death of the body is not the death of the soul or the real man.

In view of these facts, how can some say that the body and natural life is all there is to a man and that to kill the one part is also to kill the other? Christ definitely affirmed in these passages that the soul does not die when the body dies and that the soul, which man cannot kill, continues to live after death. Nothing can ever happen to man on earth that has the power in itself to destroy the soul. At death, the soul does not die. It shall live on forever.

The fact that the dead continue to live was further taught by Christ while on the cross. After the thief said to Christ: "Jesus, remember me when thou comest in thy kingdom," the Savior answered in these words: "Verily I say unto thee, Today shalt thou be with me in Paradise" (Luke 23:42–43). This statement cannot mean that the robber was to cease to be at death; rather he was to enter at once after death into a realm with Christ. The promise of the Lord was that the robber should be with Him in Paradise that day. No time delay is permitted.

Materialists say of this passage that Christ was asking the robber a question like this: "Verily I say unto thee today, Shalt thou be with me in Paradise [at some distant future]?" This is absurd! Consider Moffatt's translation of the passage: "'I tell you truly,' said Jesus, 'you will be in paradise with me this very day.'"[1] This is correct. One thing is certain: neither the spirit of the thief nor Christ's Spirit went out of existence that day when he died on the cross.

Personal existence in the disembodied state between death and the resurrection is also taught in the account of the transfiguration of Christ (Matthew 17:1–8; Luke 9:28–36; 2 Peter 1:17–18). Jesus took Peter, James, and John to a mountain, and while there He was transfigured before them. "And behold, there appeared unto them Moses and Elijah talking with him." At the time of the transfiguration, Moses had been dead about fifteen hundred years and his body buried in some unknown place at Mount Nebo (Deuteronomy 34:5–6). Elijah had been gone from this earth a long time (2 Kings 2:1–11). Yet Moses and Elijah were still in existence, retaining their personal identity and individuality.

This incident proves that the soul lives, even for ages after its earthly house has crumbled back to dust. Moses and Elijah are not now reduced to complete non-existence. The dead are yet alive, out of their physical bodies, as they wait for the day of resurrection. This is true of all those who have died. There is personal existence between death and the resurrection in the disembodied state.

The Doctrine of the Sadducees Was Materialism

Two major religious parties among the Jews in the first century were the Pharisees and Sadducees. Their differences were keenly marked on future existence. Note this significant statement made by Luke concerning these parties: "For the Sadducees say that there is no resurrection, neither angel, nor spirit: but the Pharisees confess both" (Acts 23:8). The Pharisees believed in a state of endless rewards and sufferings after death; they believed in the existence of the soul after death and in the existence of angels. For this reason they taught the resurrection of the dead. The Sadducees discarded this doctrine.

Josephus' testimony concerning these sects is in harmony with the Scriptures. This historian affirmed a number of times that the Jewish people were divided into three sects: Pharisees, Sadducees, and Essenes. Of the Pharisees he said: "They also believe that souls have an Immortal vigor in them, and that under the earth there will be rewards or punishments according as they have lived virtuously or viciously in this life."[2] Concerning the Essenes, he said: "They teach the immortality of souls, and esteem that the rewards of righteousness are to be earnestly striven for."[3] Of the Sadducees, he wrote: "The doc-

---

1 The New World Translation of the Christian Greek Scriptures (Brooklyn, 1961), incorrectly renders the passage: "And he said to him: 'Truly I tell you today, You will be with me in Paradise.' "

2 Flavius Josephus, *Antiquities of the Jews,* Book 18, Chapter 1, Section 3 (Philadelphia: J. Grigg, 1831).

3 Ibid., Section 4.

trine of the Sadducees is this: That souls die with the bodies."[1] "They take away the belief of immortality, and the punishments and rewards in Hades."[2]

Further, Martha's reply to the Savior showed that she believed in a future existence: "I know that he [Lazarus] shall rise again in the resurrection at the last day" (John 11:24). Martha, in this respect at least, agreed with the Pharisees. But there were even some Christians in the first century who denied the resurrection at the last day. Paul mentioned two by name, Hymenaeus and Philetus, and said they had erred from the truth and overthrown the faith of some (2 Timothy 2:17–18).

The Sadducees denied the existence of angels, spirits, and the resurrection. Since they maintained the soul died with the body (like materialists today), they said there could be no conscious existence of man after death, the existence of any merely spiritual beings, or a resurrection. To them, death meant total annihilation. Indeed, if man at death passes entirely out of existence and is then recreated at the resurrection, this would not be a resurrection of the dead but a new creation. The ancient Sadducees could see this, so they logically denied any future resurrection. In their system of doctrine, they said a person ceased to exist at death. In this respect they were more consistent in their teaching than present-day materialists who claim to believe in a future resurrection; for if man ceases to exist at death, as the materialists teach, then logically there can be no resurrection. God cannot resurrect that which does not exist—unless He first creates it.

In regard to the difference in this point of doctrine between the Sadducees and the Pharisees, the apostle Paul agreed with the Pharisees, since he believed in the existence of spirits after death and in the resurrection of the dead. In Paul's defense of himself before Felix, he most distinctly declared the doctrine of the resurrection of the dead. He stated that this doctrine was held by him and his Jewish accusers in common: "having hope toward God, which these also themselves look for, that there shall be a resurrection both of the just and unjust" (Acts 24:15). Before the Sanhedrin, as Luke recorded:

> But when Paul perceived that the one part were Sadducees and the other Pharisees, he cried out in the council, Brethren, I am a Pharisee, a son of Pharisees: touching the hope and resurrection of the dead [i.e., all the dead, not merely the righteous dead, PBC] I am called in question. [He testified that this was his own belief and that of his Jewish opponents, PBC.] And when he had so said, there arose a dissension between the Pharisees and Sadducees: and the assembly was divided. For the Sadducees say that there is no resurrection, neither angel, nor spirit; but the Pharisees confess both (Acts 23:6–8).

---

1 Flavius Josephus, *Antiquities of the Jews*, Book 18, Chapter 1, Section 3.

2 Flavius Josephus, *The Wars of the Jews*, Book 2, Section 8, p. 14.

Moreover, the Sadducees believed that they were invincible in their arguments for their creed of the extinction of the soul at death. They liked to debate the question with the Pharisees. Since Jesus during His personal ministry had endorsed the position of their opponents, insofar as the resurrection was concerned, they approached Christ during the last week of His public ministry with what they considered an unanswerable argument for their belief. They presented the case of the woman who had married seven men in succession; all of the men had died, and the woman also had died. They then inquired of Jesus as to which one of the seven men would be her husband in the resurrection. "Jesus answered and said unto them, Ye do err, not knowing the scriptures, nor the power of God. For in the resurrection they neither marry, nor are given in marriage, but are as angels in heaven" (Matthew 22:29–30). Christ simply solved their difficult problem with a brief statement. The Sadducees merely assumed that marriage would exist after the resurrection and in the future state, if there were a resurrection, but they were ignorant of the teaching of the Scriptures and of the power of God.

Following this statement, Jesus gave them a further lesson in proof of the existence of the soul after death and of the resurrection of the body. He said:

> But that the dead are raised, even Moses showed in the place concerning the Bush, when he calleth the Lord the God of Abraham, and the God of Isaac, and the God of Jacob. Now he is not the God of the dead, but of the living: for all live unto him (Luke 20:37–38).

Since this argument that Jesus used to refute the Sadducees is so very important, one should note carefully what Christ said: "God said to Moses, at the burning bush, I am the God of Abraham, the God of Isaac, and the God of Jacob." The relationship was not a past but a present one. I am—not, I was—the God of Abraham, Isaac, and Jacob when they were alive on earth. Jesus then added: "God is not the God of the dead, but of the living" (Matthew 22:32). Christ interpreted God's statement to Moses to mean that Abraham, Isaac, and Jacob were still alive, that individual and personal life remained for all three of them, even though they had been gone from the earth several centuries.

The major premise of Christ's argument is the fact that God is not the God of the dead, but of the living. (Here Jesus used the word *dead* in the sense attached to it by the Sadducees; that is, one who had ceased to exist, who was nothing.) The minor premise is that hundreds of years after the death of those three patriarchs, God said to Moses at the burning bush: "I am [present tense] the God of thy father, the God of Abraham, the God of Isaac, and the God of Jacob" (Exodus 3:6). The conclusion, as the Lord affirmed, was that those Old Testament men were not dead in the sense that the Sadducees thought of death. God's statement made to Moses proved that they were not extinct; neither does God stand in such relations to extinct beings.

To put the syllogism in outline form:

1. Major premise: God is not the God of the dead (in the sense of those extinct), but is the God of the living.
2. Minor premise: God was at the time of Moses the God of Abraham, Isaac, and Jacob (although their bodies had been dead many years).
3. Conclusion: Abraham, Isaac, and Jacob were still alive (their spirits were not dead: they lived unto God).

Abraham, Isaac, and Jacob were still living then and they are still living now. They are still in existence, and living, too, in the fellowship of God. If God had said to Moses, "I was the God of Abraham 330 years ago, and I was the God of Isaac 225 years ago, and I was the God of Jacob 198 years ago before they died," using the past tense "was," then there is no resurrection. But God used the present tense, "am." (Exodus 3:6). If Abraham, Isaac, and Jacob are still alive, so are all others who have died. The departed are separated from their bodies and from those now living on earth, but they are alive to God. Jesus declared that the dead, as they are called, are still living; only their bodies have perished. He affirmed that all people are living souls to Jehovah, whether alive on earth or in the realm beyond (that is, whether the spirit is in the body or out). Why? Because "all live unto him."

One may ask, "How did Christ's statement, proving that the spirits are still alive after death, affect the subject under discussion with the Sadducees concerning the resurrection of the dead?" Bear in mind that the Sadducees' basic error consisted of believing that there are no spirits out of physical bodies (and that there can be no such things as angels, who are spirits). So they concluded that since the spirit of man has ceased to exist at death, there is no need of the resurrection of the body, for there would be no soul to inhabit the raised body. Hence, they denied a future state. If it could be proved that spirits do exist, that the spirits survive the separation from the bodies, then there can be an order of beings called angels, and there is a demand for the resurrection of the bodies in order that the disembodied spirits may again dwell in them. Or, to say it another way, if there is a resurrection of the dead, then there is the greatest proof of the fact that the spirit lives after it is separated from the body. When the Savior, therefore, proved by their Scriptures that spirits apart from bodies do continue to live after death, He also proved the resurrection of the dead. His argument was conclusive, for He silenced the Sadducees forever, and the bystanders who knew the views of the party "were astonished at his teaching" (Matthew 22:33).

If death means becoming extinct, as the ancient Sadducees taught (and as the materialists now teach), then Jesus lost His existence when He died on the cross; that is, Christ went to nothing. If this were true, then there was no spirit to be reunited with His body, and His resurrection was a fabrication. Who can believe this? Again, the material (that is, the dust) existed before God created Adam. Why then did not God resurrect Adam? Materialistic doctrine, logically, demands a re-creation of man out of the dust at the end of time in order to have man living again. Thus, those who now affirm that no part of man survives death are only reproducing the oft-refuted doctrine of the ancient Sadducees. For this reason the answer of Jesus to their question forever refutes the doctrine of materialism. Hence, this simple but glorious fact establishes the dead are still living—with their own individual personalities. It is not a case of "they have been," but "they are."

God Took Enoch

An existence beyond this life is recognized at the very threshold of the Bible. "By faith Enoch was translated that he should not see death" (Hebrews 11:5). He "walked with God," then he "was not; for God took him" (Genesis 5:24). Took him where? To annihilation? The thought is ridiculous! God called him to a closer walk, a dearer fellowship than that experienced during his earthly life. He was never subjected to death. Together here, they are still together in yonder world. The writer of Hebrews said that Abraham and others looked for a heavenly country (Hebrews 11:10–16). They believed that this life was not all there was to living.

The Souls of the Martyrs Were Still Living

John wrote: "I saw underneath the altar the souls of them that had been slain for the word of God" (Revelation 6:9). He did not see Christians in their bodies but their souls, for they had already been slain. Their souls were alive. They remembered how they had met death, and, knowing that God would render punishment on their persecutors, they asked: "How long, O Master, the holy and true, dost thou not judge and avenge our blood on them that dwell on the earth?" (v. 10). This passage definitely shows that the soul or spirit of man does exist after it leaves the body. How can such language be harmonized with the theory that man has no metaphysical spirit that will survive the shock of death?

Spirits Have Returned to Their Bodies

The miracle of bringing a person back to life was simply the returning of the spirit into the body. Note these examples: Elijah prayed that the son of the widow of Zarephath might be restored to life after he died.

> And he stretched himself upon the child three times, and cried unto Jehovah, and said, O Jehovah my God, I pray thee, let this child's soul come into him again. And Jehovah hearkened unto the voice of Elijah; and the soul of the child came into him again, and he revived (1 Kings 17:21–22).

Death came to the child when the soul became separated from the body; the child lived when "the soul of the child came into him [i.e., into the body] again." The prophet did not pray that the child's lungs be inflated again with air or that his heart commence beating again, but that his soul might re-enter the lifeless body. Although out of the body for some time, the soul was returned to re-inhabit his mortal house, and the child lived again. The spirit left the body and later returned to it.

When the ruler's daughter was raised to life by Christ, it is said: "And her spirit returned, and she rose up immediately" (Luke 8:55). This language clearly proves that, in dying, her spirit left the body, and that it had to come again into the body before she could be restored to life. God caused the spirit to return from the place to which it had gone. The disembodied spirit continued to exist.

Other such resurrections are mentioned in the Scriptures in addition to these (cf. 2 Kings 4:18–37; 13:20–21; Luke 7:11–15; John 11:17–44; Acts 9:36–41; 20:9–10). These resurrections, however, can mean but one thing, namely, the spirit returned to the earthly body that the spirit had once lived in and then had departed from that body. All of these passages of Scripture irrefutably prove that spirits exist after they leave the bodies. The dissolution of the body does not necessarily involve the end of the existence of the spirit. There is no reason to believe from any statement of Scripture that the spirit, which is a distinct entity from the body, cannot exist apart from the body after death. Man's spirit is a non-material and incorporeal being; it may or may not be associated with a physical body. These resurrections to physical life again, then serve to demonstrate the power of God and prove that the life-processes are more than the working of physical materials in complex combinations.

Hence, the fact is that the soul is an essence, which differs from the body, and is not dissolved by death. This is proved by the miracles performed which brought spirits back into their bodies after death. Evidently, the spirit survived the shock of death and remained in a separate state of existence following its departure from the body, else it could not have been called back into its house of clay.

Here is a very simple, yet a very apt illustration. A preacher, illustrating this point, took a watch, and said:

"Children, what is this I hold in my hand?"

"A watch, sir," was the answer.

"How do you know it is a watch?"

"We can hear it tick, sir," they replied.

"Correct," said the minister. "Now I'll remove the works from the case, hold the works in my right hand, the empty case in my left."

He did so, and asked, "In which hand do I now hold the watch?"

"In the right hand," they agreed.

"How do you know?"

"Because we can hear it tick."

"Now," said the speaker, "I will put the case over there under my hat, and ask you to tell me where the watch is."

The children observed him as he placed the case under the hat and returned to the stand. "Now tell me where the watch is," he said, holding the works in his right hand.

"In your right hand," came the answer.

"Can the watch tick, tell time, and keep moving without being in the case?"

"Yes, sir," replied the children.

"Well," said the minister, "so it is with the soul. It lives, feels, thinks, remembers, and goes on existing long after the body which encased it has been put into the grave. Man's body is but the tent in which the soul dwells. Someday the soul will move out of its house. This is death. So, as the works can be either in or out of the watchcase or returned to the case, the spirit can be in or out of the body or returned to the body, as it was in the miracles recorded in the Scriptures. Were new spirits created and put in those dead bodies? Certainly not! They simply returned to the bodies. As the parts of the watch which were removed from the case continued to run or keep time, even so a person's spirit will continue to live after it leaves the body. There is a man inside the outer man, and this inner man survives the perishing of the outer man."

Paul May Have Been Out of the Body

Paul said he knew a man who went to the third heaven, whether in the body or whether out of the body he did not know (2 Corinthians 12:2). Now if materialists are correct in saying that man does not possess a spirit distinct from the body, what could the writer have meant in this passage by being in the body and out of the body? Apparently Paul spoke of himself in this experience (v. 7). Had he not believed man was a dual being and the spirit could exist out of the body, he surely would have known that he was not out of the body, if such a thing is utterly impossible for man. But Paul knew that man in this life is a spirit in a body and that when one is out of the body, he is called dead. Paul also knew that life continues when the spirit is separated from the body. He knew it was possible for such visions and revelations of the Lord to take place out of the body. In which of these two states he was in when he was caught up to the third heaven, into Paradise, when he "heard unspeakable words, which it is not lawful for a man to utter," he did not know and could not tell. He could have been out of the body. At least, Paul was not a materialist. The passage proves that man can go out of the body.

Christians Depart to Be with Christ

The apostle Paul expressed a desire in the later part of his life to be absent from the body and present with the Lord. He knew that his personal existence would continue after the dissolution of the body, so he said: "To die is gain." Again, "having the desire to depart and be with Christ; for it is very far better" (Philippians 1:21–23). But how could it be far better if death meant ceasing to exist? Or if soul and body should go down together in the tomb?

Again, Paul concluded in Romans 8:38–39 that nothing—not even death—can separate the righteous from the love of God.

> For I am persuaded that neither death, nor life, nor angels, nor principalities, nor things present, nor things to come, nor powers, nor height, nor depth, nor any other creature, shall be able to separate us from the love of God, which is in Christ Jesus our Lord.

God loves that which exists. The part of man that cannot be separated from God's love—either in life or in death, in time and in eternity—continues to exist after death. So the spirit of the righteous must exist after the death of the body that it may not be separated from the love of God. How wonderful to know that the power of death does not put an end to the Christian's relationship with God, and that it can never snatch him from His love! Death cannot do him any real harm. Death kills the body, but it cannot touch the soul. Why, then, should it be dreaded when there is nothing in it that is harmful? "The righteous hath a refuge in his death" (Proverbs 14:32); to be absent from the body is to be at home with the Lord (2 Corinthians 5:8).

The conclusion derived from this investigation of the Scriptures is that in all the stages of man's existence there is no such death as materialists teach. We further conclude that the Bible teaches man can exist outside his body. Death is not cessation of personal existence. Death is not the end. Death is simply a transition or change—change into another state of existence.

When people teach that man differs from the brute only in his superior organization and that the end of man and brute is precisely alike, they are miserably wrong. Think of it! According to materialists, man in death is no more than a dead dog. Note: The body of man came from the dust of the ground; so also came the body of the dog. Man breathes the air, so also does the dog. The man dies, and his breath leaves his body; so dies the dog. Man's body returns to the dust as it was; so does the body of the dog. Thus, according to the theory of materialists, when man dies, he dies like the little dog Rover—all over! And after death he no more exists than the dog does after it dies. If this is true, it is as much a sin to kill a dog as it is to kill a man. The doctrine of materialism is the doctrine of infidelity and borders on atheism. The above doctrine, comparing man and the dog, denies man as being created in the image of God.

Summarizing this study at this point, these facts have been established:

1. Man is a spirit-being, created in the image of God.
2. The spirit becomes separated from the body at death and occupies a separate state of existence. Whether one is a believer or an unbeliever, when he dies his spirit and body are separated, and his spirit continues to exist.
3. Death—the event which arrests the functions and brings dissolution to the parts of the body—is powerless over the indwelling spirit.
4. The spirit continues to exist out of the body, in the interval between death and the resurrection; there is life between death and the resurrection. (It shall be demonstrated in future chapters that after the resurrection the souls, dislodged at death, shall be reunited with their raised and immortal bodies, never again to be separated from them.)

Since God breathed into man something of Himself, man is endowed with capacity to exist forever. Neither the spirits of the wicked nor of the righteous cease to exist at death. Is it any wonder then that the great mass of men have in all ages and in all nations believed in the continued existence of the soul after death? The immortality of man is a doctrine firmly established in God's eternal Word.

Questions for Discussion

1. What happens to the spirit at death?
2. Is there any part of man that survives death? What do materialists teach in this respect? Is the grave the destination of each person entirely, upon his death?
3. Can spirit beings exist outside of physical (material) bodies? Does God dwell in a physical body?
4. Do angels exist out of physical bodies? From whence did angels come?
5. Do evil spirits exist in physical bodies?
6. Give reasons for believing in the survival of the spirit (soul) of man after death. If one says that man ceases to exist in his entirety at death, is that a necessary conclusion?
7. When the Old Testament speaks of the departed saints being gathered to their people at death, are the references made to their gathering together in the tombs or to the concourse of departed spirits?
8. What did David say about his child when he died?
9. How did Job express his belief in life after death? How did David?
10. Where did the thief on the cross go the day he died?

11. Can one kill the body and not the soul?
12. What lesson is learned from the transfiguration of Christ concerning life after death?
13. What was the peculiar doctrine of the ancient Sadducees? How did Jesus meet their argument?
14. Can there logically be a resurrection in the doctrine of the materialists?
15. Where did God take Enoch?
16. Were the souls of the martyrs (whom John saw in vision) still living? What does that tell us about the ability of men's spirits to exist apart from physical bodies?
17. Give Biblical examples of spirits leaving their bodies and returning to them. What happened when the spirits returned to their bodies?
18. Name the resurrections mentioned in the Bible (excluding Christ's).
19. What was the preacher's illustration of the watch and its case?
20. What is taught by Paul's trip to Paradise?
21. What did Paul mean when he said the Christian's departure to be with Christ was far better than living on this earth?
22. Can death separate the Christian from God's love?
23. Does the Bible contain any statement which endorses or encourages suicide? Where are these mentioned in the Bible?
24. Show clearly how the doctrine of materialism fails to teach the true meaning of death and the survival of the soul afterwards?
25. Summarize what has been learned thus far in this study from the Bible on the origin and nature of man, the meaning of death, and the survival of the spirit following it.
26. Does the Bible teach that man will continue to exist (live) forever?
27. Show from the Scriptures that the word *soul* is generic and is used in four ways: (1) the whole person (Acts 2:41,43); (2) physical life (Psalm 78:50); (3) intellectual nature (1 Corinthians 2:14, margin, ASV); (4) spirit (Daniel 7:15; Hebrews 12:9).

THE WEAVER

Not till the loom is silent
    And the shuttles cease to fly
Shall God unroll the canvas
    And explain the reason why.

The dark threads are as needful
    In the weaver's skillful hand
As the threads of gold and silver
    In the pattern He has planned.

—from *235 Precious Poems*

The boast of heraldry, the pomp of power,
    And all that beauty, and all that wealth e'er gave,
Await alike the inevitable hour:
    The paths of glory lead but to the grave.

—Thomas Grey

When I go down to the grave I can say, like many others, "I have finished my day's work." But I cannot say, "I have finished my life." My day's work will begin again the next morning. The tomb is not a blind alley; it is a thoroughfare. It closes on the twilight, opens on the dawn.

—Victor Hugo

I shall grow old, but never lose life's zest,
Because the road's last turn will be the best.

—Henry Van Dyke

The time has never been in any period of man's history of which we have a record when he was not interested in questions concerning the world beyond and the inhabitants of that world.

—M. C. Kurfees

Truly there needs to be another life to come!
If this be all
And another life awaits us not for one,
I say 'tis poor cheat, a stupid bungle,
A wretched failure. I for one protest
Against, and I hurl it back with scorn.

—Browning

THE ROSE STILL GROWS BEYOND THE WALL

Near a shady wall a rose once grew,
    Budded and blossomed in God's free light,
Watered and fed by morning dew,
    Shedding its sweetness day and night.

As it grew and blossomed fair and tall,
    Slowly rising to loftier height,
It came to a crevice in the wall,
    Through which there shone a beam of light.

Onward it crept with added strength,
    With never a thought of fear or pride.
It followed the light through the crevice's length
    And unfolded itself on the other side.

The light, the dew, the broadening view,
    Were found the same as they were before;
And it lost itself in beauties new,
    Breathing its fragrance more and more.

Shall claim of death cause us to grieve,
    And make our courage faint and fall?
Nay! Let us faith and hope receive:
    The rose still grows beyond the wall.

Scattering fragrance far and wide,
    Just as it did in days of yore,
Just as it did on the other side,
    Just as it will for evermore.

—A. L. Frink

– 6 –

Is the Spirit Immortal?

". . . your heart shall live forever"
Psalm 22:26 (KJV)

What the Scriptures teach about the origin and nature of man has been established: man was created in the image of God (Genesis 1:27). Man is composed of body, natural life, and spirit; God gave to man His spirit: "Jehovah . . . formeth the spirit of man within him" (Zechariah 12:1). "God is a Spirit" (John 4:24). Man, therefore, having been created in God's image, who is Spirit, must be a person possessing a spirit. Man on earth is a body in personal union with a rational spirit. But what is the spirit? What are some of its characteristics? Is the spirit of man immortal? Is the soul the same as the spirit? This chapter and the one following give answers to these questions.

The first grand division of the universe is made up of matter and spirit. Matter (substance) and spirit (essence) differ. The spirit of man is not material, nor the body of man spirit. The word *spirit* is derived from the Greek word *pneuma* and refers to the essence of life that animates the body and is as invisible as the wind.

The body of man is corporeal matter. Chemists have analyzed the component parts of man's body and found that its elements are identical with those found in the earth. Scientifically, the average man's body contains some twenty-six elements including ten gallons of water, twenty-four pounds of carbon, seven pounds of lime, one and one-fourth pounds of phosphorous, one-half teaspoonful of sugar, four and one-fourth teaspoonfuls of salt, some oxygen, hydrogen, nitrogen, calcium, and enough iron for one large nail. With inflation as it is today, man's bodily materials are worth about four dollars. How small is the worth of man on the material side. But man's mental and spiritual worth is immeasurable! (cf. Matthew 16:26). It would be absurd for one to judge the worth of his fellowman by the chemical contents of his body or in terms of his financial standing. Nevertheless, the material analysis does prove the truth of the Bible's statement that the body of man was made from the dust of the earth

(Genesis 2:7). Thus, the word *matter* is a general term applied to all substances of which one has knowledge by natural senses.

The spirit of man is a non-material essence. It is wholly intellectual and forms no part of the human body. Among the definitions Thayer gives to the word *spirit* (Hebrew, *ruach;* Greek, *pneuma),* such as "wind, breath of the nostrils and mouth, the vital principle by which the body is animated, etc." is the following: "A simple essence, devoid of all or at least grosser matter, and possessed of the power of knowing, desiring, deciding, and acting . . . a human soul that has left the body"[1]

The spirit cannot be seen, weighed, or analyzed by chemical action. It would be incorrect to say that the fleshly body of man was patterned after Jehovah, because God, being an incorporeal, immortal Spirit, does not possess a material body. Jesus said: "A spirit hath not flesh and bones [i.e., a body with parts like human beings]" (Luke 24:39). (The Bible speaks of God's hands, eyes, ears, and such like, but these are figures of speech called *anthropomorphisms*—God's actions represented in human terms—and are employed for pedagogical purposes.) The essence, which is called spirit, being non-material, has none of the properties of matter. The substance, which is called body, on the other hand, is material; that is, it has the properties of matter and none of the properties of spirit. The spirit is as real and true as matter, although it does not possess the characteristics of matter. Matter is known by its qualities; spirit by its activities. The existence of the spirit of man must be admitted because of the manifestations of spiritual properties. The life of the body is its power to digest and assimilate food and build up tissue; the life of the spirit is its power to feel, to think, to will. So one learns from its manifestations what the spirit of man is. One sees that there are qualities or attributes which are not matter in any of its existing forms, namely, intelligence, reason, judgment, memory, and consciousness. To the essence that exhibits consciousness, memory, and such like is given the name spirit. The spirit of man is susceptible to love, hate, joy, and grief, and these properties are not inherent in matter. Hence, matter and spirit are distinct and different.

Material objects and spiritual personalities could only have originated from sources where the qualities are found. Since man has an intellectual and moral nature, these spiritual qualities must have come from an intelligent and moral being, a spiritual source. To illustrate, the manifestation of the power of electricity proves its existence. Hence, moral deeds can spring only from moral attributes. This, then, is why Elihu declared: "But there is a spirit in man; and the breath of the Almighty giveth them understanding" (Job 32:8). It is the

---

1 Joseph Henry Thayer, *A Greek-English Lexicon of the New Testament* (New York: American Book Co., 1889), p. 88.

spirit, and the spirit alone, which is made after the likeness of God's Spirit (Acts 17:29; Hebrews 12:9). Thus, in a unique way, man is like God. For this reason, the Scriptures teach that the spirit of man came from God, and not from the dust (Ecclesiastes 12:7).

The theory of evolution errs when it says all man is came solely from the earth, water, and air and came only by natural law. Man's body with its features came from the earth, water, and air, but his spirit with all of its features came from another source, namely, God. Scientists cannot take water and lime and the other chemicals found in man's body and create man in his fullness. Man possesses a body composed of matter and also possesses a spirit or soul which is different in its origin and distinct in its character from the body. Man on earth is both matter and spirit; he consists of two distinct components, body and spirit. Man is spirit in body. Body and spirit constitute one human being.

A person may say that he cannot understand how one is composed of two distinct parts. Neither can he understand how spirit can be connected with a material body. But one's inability to comprehend the mode is no argument against the fact. Divine revelation teaches that the spirit and the body are inseparably connected for man's existence here upon the earth.

As a result of this union of spirit and body, the person is the possessor of all the attributes both of spirit and of the body. It may be predicated of the man whatever may be predicated of his spirit. It may also be predicated of him whatever may be predicated of the body. For instance, it can be affirmed of a man that he is tall or short; sick or well. In like manner, it can be said that he is wise, good, or learned. Whatever is true of either element of his constitution is true of the man. Whatever is true of the one, however, is not necessarily true of the other. For example, when the body is wounded or burned, it is not the spirit that is subject of these accidents, and when the spirit is enlightened or penitent, the body is not the subject of change. Each has its properties and changes, but the man is subject of them all. Hence, apparently contradictory affirmations may be made of the same person. One may say that he is dust, that he is immortal and mortal. It would depend upon which part of man was meant.

The Spirit Is the Heart

The inward part of man which is patterned after his Maker is often referred to as the mind or heart. Scripture makes the heart to include the whole innerman, that is, the intellect, the emotions, the will, and the conscience. The heart thinks: "For as he thinketh within himself, so is he" (Proverbs 23:7; cf. Genesis 6:5; Hebrews 4:12). It is the spirit—the inward man, not the body—that does the thinking. Jesus taught that every sin man commits comes from the spirit and not the body (Matthew 15:19; Mark 7:21–23). The heart understands: ". . . and understand with their heart" (Matthew 13:15). The heart believes:

"For with the heart man believeth unto righteousness" (Romans 10:10; cf. Acts 8:37). The heart reasons: "Why reason ye these things in your hearts?" (Mark 2:8). These are acts of intellectual processes. The heart loves: "Thou shalt love the Lord thy God with all thy heart" (Matthew 22:37). The heart desires: "Brethren, my heart's desire and my supplication to God is for them, that they may be saved" (Romans 10:1). The heart despises: "And she despised him in her heart" (2 Samuel 6:16). The heart may be stolen: "So Absalom stole the hearts of the men of Israel" (2 Samuel 15:6). The heart trusts: "Trust in Jehovah with all thy heart" (Proverbs 3:5).

These words describe emotional processes. The heart purposes: "Let each man do according as he hath purposed in his heart" (2 Corinthians 9:7). The heart determines: "He that standeth stedfast [determined] in his heart . . . shall do well" (1 Corinthians 7:37). The heart obeys: "Ye became obedient from the heart to that form of teaching whereunto ye were delivered" (Romans 6:17). These words show volitional processes or acts of the will. Every act of acceptable obedience to God comes from the heart or spirit. The heart may be pricked: "Now when they heard this, they were pricked in their heart" (Acts 2:37; cf. 5:33). The heart may either condemn or approve: "If our heart condemn us, God is greater than our heart, and knoweth all things. Beloved, if our heart condemn us not, we have boldness toward God" (1 John 3:20–21).

These words describe processes of the conscience. Solomon said that out of the heart are the issues of life (Proverbs 4:23; cf. Matthew 12:34–35; 15:18–19). Again, "The spirit of man is the lamp of Jehovah, searching all his innermost parts" (Proverbs 20:27). Perhaps, then, the word *mind* is the closest modern term to the Biblical usage of *heart*. This is what is meant by the heart or spirit of man.

Other passages of Scripture teach that the spirit of man is intellectual and moral. "For who among men knoweth the things of a man, save the spirit of the man, which is in him? even so the things of God none knoweth, save the Spirit of God" (1 Corinthians 2:11). Here the spirit of man and the Spirit of God are introduced as intelligent spirits, each knowing the things of the person to whom he belongs. The verse affirms that it is the spirit that is the knowing, conscious, intellectual part of man. The spirit of man knows the things of man, the body does not. Paul said he served God with his spirit: "For God is my witness, whom I serve in my spirit in the gospel of his Son" (Romans 1:9). Later in the same letter he declared he served God with the mind: "So then I of myself with the mind, indeed, serve the law of God" (Romans 7:25). The mind and the spirit are different from the flesh, yet very closely related, being the moral part of man. This thought is upheld by Paul in Ephesians 4:23: "And that ye be renewed in the spirit of your mind"; also in Romans 7:22, "I delight in the law of God after the inward man." To the Christians at Ephesus Paul expressed his desire "that Christ may dwell in your hearts through faith" (Ephesians 3:17; cf. Romans 10:17). Hence, these Biblical terms—*spirit, mind, inward man, soul,* and *heart*—help us to understand what the spirit of man is. This is explained in the following way: I inhabit my body and use it, but my body is not me. I look out through my eyes, I work with my hands, I speak with my lips; but neither eyes nor hands nor lips, not all of them together, are me. The real "I" is within; that which thinks and directs and controls and governs my physical frame. This thinking, feeling, willing, "something" is the real "I." So then, what am I? I am not a mere body. That "I" or "myself" is different from the body. "I" live in "my" body. So "I" is the spiritual and intangible part of the man.

Scientists say the body is continually changing, and that the body renews itself every seven years. If this is true, then not one particle of the material of my body that I possessed as a child exists in my body today. Now if the body were "I," "I" should be an entirely different "I" from the "I" of forty years ago; but the "I" remains essentially the same, and "I" am not a different "I." There is an awareness and memory within me of that youth of forty years ago so that the "I" of today and the "I" of then are the same. The "I," therefore, cannot be this changing body.

Some believe that this thinking essence is just a function of the brain. Indeed, the brain is the instrument of thought, but the question that needs to be considered is: Are the physical brain movements the cause or source of thought? The brain is not the origin of thought; the brain is not the soul. If it were, the destruction of part of the brain would be partial destruction of the soul. The real relation between "I" and the brain is something like that between an organist and his organ. For example, the organist uses the organ to express the harmonies of some great piece of music; the organ produces at the organist's bidding. Likewise, the brain is not the "I"; it is the instrument. My brain is mine to use, but it is not "I." The real "I" is something within which thinks and feels and wills. In a word, this physical body is not "I." It is the house where the "I" lives. The real "I" is found in what the Bible calls the spirit of man, the soul. The brain is the organ; the man is the organist. Although it is important to remember that the real "I" is this invisible, spiritual "something" within the body, one does not usually think of a man without a body. To all, man is an embodied spirit, but man can be a disembodied spirit. Even though the spirit exists in a body here, there is no reason to believe that the spirit cannot exist apart from the body hereafter. Paul taught that after death the spirit is in an unclothed and therefore incomplete state until after the resurrection (2 Corinthians 5:1–6). But if our earthly house be dissolved by death, we are still in existence; our spirits still live. But the body is this ole house, as one poet put it. David said, "The Lord is my shepherd . . . and I shall dwell in the house of the Lord forever" (Psalm 23 KJV).

The Spirit Is Immortal

One asks, "Does the Bible teach that the spirit of man is immortal?" Indeed, it does. *Immortality* literally means "deathlessness or interminable existence (undyingness)." That which is immortal will not, indeed cannot, die; it is free from the power of death. That which is mortal is subject to death; it must die. Immortality is the exact opposite of mortality. *Mortal* means "subject to death"; *immortal* means "not subject to death." Immortality represents undying existence. Hence, immortality, as used in this study concerning the soul of man, means endless continuation of man's personality—the thing he calls "I."

Materialists challenge those who believe in the immortality of the soul to find a passage of Scripture that says that the spirit of man now dwelling in the physical body is immortal. Believers in man's immortality challenge materialists to find a passage that says that the spirit of man now dwelling in his body is mortal. Although this is their doctrine, materialists cannot do this. Accepting the Bible as divinely inspired, believers in the immortality of the soul can produce the passages of Holy Writ that teach very clearly that the spirit or soul of man is immortal, that the spirit, even now dwelling in a mortal body, is in its very nature immortal. In other words, you have not always been, but you always will be.

To draw right conclusions from a study of the Scriptures, one must apply correct principles of reasoning. Since God is an immortal Spirit, it can be said of Him that He begets immortal spirits. That like produces like is self-evident. As already noted in this study, man's spirit is derived from the Lord. "There is a spirit in man" (Job 32:8), distinct from the body it inhabits (cf. Zechariah 12:1; Acts 17:29; Hebrews 12:9). Hence, the spirit of man, being the offspring of God, is like its Father and is immortal. The body is not the offspring of God; the spirit is. Furthermore, the Bible nowhere says beasts are the offspring of Jehovah, nor created in His image; but man is, so immortality applies only to man. Now test this reasoning in the form of a syllogism:

1. Major premise: God is an immortal Spirit (John 4:24; 1 Timothy 1:17).
2. Minor premise: Man is the offspring of God, being created in the image of God (Acts 17:29; Genesis 1:27).
3. Conclusion: Man's image, that of an offspring, is that of an immortal spirit.

This conclusion can be refuted in only two ways: (1) by proving the syllogism is not a proper way of reasoning; (2) by proving one or both of the premises are not true. All logicians recognize the syllogism as a valid way of reasoning. So, if both premises are true, the conclusion must be true. Both premises are true, for they contain exactly what the Bible says. "God is a Spirit" and man's spirit is the offspring of God. Therefore, the spirit of man is now immortal and incorruptible, and man's existence will never end. Indeed, one cannot conceive of man's spirit being in the image of God, yet not immortal. "The spirit of man is the lamp of Jehovah" (Proverbs 20:27).

In addition to the many passages already introduced in this study on the nature of man, consider still other statements of Scripture which teach the immortality of the spirit. The psalmist declared: "Your heart shall live forever" (Psalm 22:26 KJV). The heart, as already noted, is the seat of the inner life, the fountain of man's thoughts, desires, purposes, and affections. This passage says the heart shall live forever. This surely is immortality! Solomon declared that God has put eternity into man's mind (RSV) or heart (KJV, ASV) (Ecclesiastes 3:11). Therefore, the mind or heart of man must be immortal. Man, then, is not a creature of time; he belongs to eternity.

The apostle Peter affirmed that man's spirit is immortal when he admonished Christian wives regarding their conduct before their unbelieving husbands. Among other things he said:

> Whose adorning let it not be the outward adorning of braiding the hair, and of wearing jewels of gold, or of putting on apparel; but let it be the hidden man of the heart, in the incorruptible apparel of a meek and quiet spirit, which is in the sight of God of great price (1 Peter 3:3–4).

Here the hidden man of the heart is not corruptible. That which is incorruptible is likewise immortal. The hidden man of the heart is the same in meaning as the inward man of Paul's statement in 2 Corinthians 4:16 and Romans 7:22. As the soul is immortal, so all that tends to adorn that spirit will likewise be immortal.

The adornment of the soul should take precedence over the dress of the body. This inward adornment comes by keeping the heart right with God and in practicing all the Christian graces. Saints of God possess the beauty of holiness (Psalm 96:9 KJV). "Man looketh on the outward appearance, but Jehovah looketh on the heart" (1 Samuel 16:7). Peter wanted the Christian women to realize that the attributes of inner beauty that radiate in life are not something which can be put on as jewels, but are inner qualities when Christ is in the heart.

Notice, then, these facts from this passage: (1) The hidden man is the same as the inner man—the heart, spirit, or mind. (2) The word *incorruptible* is from the Greek word *aphthartos,* which is rendered "immortal" in 1 Timothy 1:17: "Now unto the King eternal, immortal, invisible, the only God, be honor and glory forever and ever. Amen." Thayer defines *aphthartos* as "not liable to corruption or decay, imperishable."[1] So 1 Timothy 1:17 says that God is immortal, and 1 Peter 3:4 says that the hidden man of the heart is incorruptible. A footnote in the American Standard Version on 1 Timothy 1:17 has "incorruptible" for "immortal"; this shows that "incorruptible" in 1 Peter 3:4 is the same as "incorruptible" or "immortal" in 1 Timothy 1:17. What is said of God's

1 Thayer, *A Greek-English Lexicon,* p. 88.

eternal nature, therefore, is also said of the spirits of human beings: God is immortal and the spirit of man is immortal. Immortality or incorruptibility is declared also of (a) the Christian's inheritance (1 Peter 1:4), (b) the word of God (1 Peter 1:23), and (c) the crown of life (1 Corinthians 9:25). The same word—*incorruptible (aphthartos)*—is used in all three of these passages. (3) The inward adorning or ornament is to be of the inner man which is incorruptible, while the outward adorning is of the outward man.

There are at least three things mentioned in 1 Peter 3:3–4 which are very important to the study of the immortality of the spirit of man, namely: (1) the outward adorning of the outward man, (2) the inward adorning of the inward man—the hidden man of the heart, and (3) the outward adorning that is put on the outward man and the inward adorning that is put in (not on) that which is incorruptible or immortal. Since this adornment, which is related to the hidden man of the heart, is the inner man or the spirit of man and is incorruptible, the Bible, therefore, teaches that the spirit is immortal.

Angels Immortal

Christ likewise affirmed deathlessness of the angels; they cannot die (Luke 20:36). Why not? Because not only are they angels (heavenly messengers) but they are also spirits. The same is true of man's spirit; it cannot die or cease to exist. In the Scriptures, mortality is never assigned to any spirit, good or bad. Immortality is an inherent part of the nature of all spirits; they do not belong to the realm of mortality. The Bible teaches that man's spirit is everlasting; that man has (or is) an incorruptible, imperishable, immortal spirit, and all men, being endowed with immortality, will have an eternal existence beyond the grave.

God Only Has Immortality

Materialists believe that the only being who has immortality is God. They, therefore, conclude that man does not have immortality. They give 1Timothy 6:15–16 as their proof-text: " . . . who is the blessed and only Potentate, the King of kings, and Lord of lords; who only hath immortality, dwelling in light unapproachable." The context shows that the passage has reference to Jesus Christ (God the Son) (v. 14). As Christ is now in heaven in His resurrected immortal body, in His present kingly glory, He is "KING OF KINGS, AND LORD OF LORDS" (Revelation 19:16; cf. Revelation 17:14). Furthermore, Christ is the first to be raised from the dead to die no more. All others who were raised passed again through the gate of death. Christ, then, is the firstborn from the dead (Colossians 1:18), and "being raised from the dead dieth no more; death no more hath dominion over him" (Romans 6:9). When Christ appeared to John on the Isle of Patmos, He said to him: "I am the Alpha and the Omega, saith the Lord God, who is and who was and who is to come, the Almighty" (Revelation 1:8). Hence, insofar as Christ's body is concerned, He is the only one who now has an immortal, resurrected body. (The Christian will receive his immortal body at the last day [1 Corinthians 15].) When Christ came to this earth He emptied himself, and took upon Himself "the form of a servant, being made in the likeness of men [i.e., in His body]; and being found in fashion as a man, he humbled himself, becoming obedient even unto death, yea, the death of the cross" (Philippians 2:7–8). Now Christ does not have any mortality, for there is nothing about Him in glory but immortality. He was co-equal with God the Father before He came to this earth (John 1:1–4; Colossians 1:16–17; Micah 5:2), and by His resurrection He put on immortality in His body, being the firstfruits of the resurrection. For this reason He could say to John on Patmos: "I am the first and the last, and the Living one; and I was dead, and behold, I am alive for evermore" (Revelation 1:17–18).

The Bible, indeed, teaches that God only is the eternal, immortal, self-existent One (Psalm 90:2; Habakkuk 1:12; Exodus 3:14). He is the only source of immortality; He is the fountain of life (Psalm 36:9). So does Christ, like the Father, and unlike man, possess life underived and without beginning (cf. John 5:21, 26). This makes Deity differ from man in that God's life or immortality is underived, unoriginated, uncreated; He alone in His own essence is deathless. In this sense, God is life's original owner and never-failing source. This fact, however, does not mean that God alone is immortal in the sense that no being has immortality. Other beings have immortality bestowed upon them. God only has life without beginning and ending. Men and angels, created by Him, have their life by His gift; for immortality flows out of God to generate other spirit-beings. This explains why men and angels cannot die; they, created by Jehovah, have derived their immortality from God. This is an acquired immortality, because all life is from God. Man is both mortal (body) and immortal (spirit), but God has nothing mortal about Him. God does not have a mortal body. God "only hath [and is the keeper of] immortality." Thus, God, being from everlasting to everlasting, has immortality and has imparted immortality (perpetuity of conscious existence) to man's rational spirit, having created man in His own image.

So, when properly examined with all other passages of Scripture on the subject, and not isolated, nothing is said in 1 Timothy 6:16 to indicate man does not now possess an immortal spirit. The passage does not teach the essence of immortality in man. The verse simply says: "Who [God] only hath immortality." He only is immortal in Himself, and has immortality as He is the fountain of it. The immortality of angels and spirit is derived from Him. Hence, notice carefully the words: "Who [God] only hath immortality." There is nothing mortal about Him; all of His being is deathless; nothing about God is mortal. He alone can confer it. This is what the Bible says and this is what it means. But the passage does not say that no one else is immortal (in any sense); it says that God (or Christ) only has immortality. There are times when a change in the position of this word *only* in a sentence may change the meaning. Note some examples of how the word *only* can be used and the meaning changed in the following sentences:

1. Only the men smoked. (None but the men did any smoking.)
2. The men only smoked. (The men did nothing but smoke.)

or

1. He works only at night. (He does not work except at night.)
2. He works only on Saturday night. (He works only at that time.)
3. He only works on Saturday night. (He does nothing else on Saturday night; he does not play games or attend movies.)

or

1. Only John invited us to take the trip. (John, and nobody else, invited us.)
2. John only invited us to take the trip. (John invited us, but didn't urge us.)
3. John invited only us to take the trip. (John invited us, and nobody else.)
4. John invited us only to take the trip. (John invited us to take, but not to pay for, the trip.)
5. John invited us to take only the trip. (John invited us to take the trip, but to take nothing else.)

or

1. Only he lost his hat.
2. He only lost his hat.
3. He lost only his hat.
4. He lost his only hat.
5. He lost his hat only.

Now, look at 1 Timothy 6:16 again.

1. Only God has immortality. (No one but God or Christ has immortality.)
2. "Who [God] only hath immortality." (God does not have anything but immortality; He does not have mortality but man has now a mortal body, and his soul is immortal.)

Ecclesiastes 3:11

Speaking of God, note this statement from Ecclesiastes 3:11: "He hath made everything beautiful in its time: also he hath set eternity in their heart, yet so that man cannot find out the work that God hath done from the beginning even to the end." "He has also set eternity in their heart" (NASB). The heart of man shall live forever. Man in this life is dwelling in a mortal body; his soul is immortal; but after the resurrection and the final Day of Judgment he will be in an immortal body.

The righteous will possess immortal bodies at the resurrection: "This mortal must put on immortality" (1 Corinthians 15:53). But man's spirit is now immortal. The angels are immortal beings (Matthew 22:30; Mark 12:25; Luke 20:35–36). However, God is the source from whence there comes to man immortality.

David Lipscomb wrote: "Jesus Christ in the bosom of the Father only hath immortality with God."[1] Matthew Henry wrote concerning Christ: "He only has immortality."[2]

So the American Standard Version reads, "who only hath immortality" (1 Timothy 6:16), the King James Version reads also, "who only hath immortality," and The Living Oracles reads, "who only has immortality."

However, some of the later translations read a little differently. Note:

1. "who alone has immortality" (The Amplified New Testament).
2. "who alone possesses immortality" (Goodspeed).
3. "who alone has immortality" (Moffett).
4. "who alone possesses immortality" (Weymouth).
5. "who alone has immortality" (Revised Standard Version).
6. "who alone can never die" (The Living Bible).
7. "He alone is immortal" (Good News for Modern Man).
8. "Only God never dies" (The Simple English Bible).
9. "who alone has immortality" (Challoner-Rheims Version).
10. "who alone has immortality" (The New King James Version).
11. "who alone is immortal" (New International Version).
12. "who alone possesses immortality" (New American Standard Version).

Christ existed in the form of God in eternity (John 1:1–3, 14). He came to this earth, lived in a human body, died on the cross for our sins, was buried, and raised from the dead. He now lives on high, at the Father's right hand, in an immortal body. He was the first to rise from the dead to die no more (Colossians 1:18). There is nothing now mortal about Him; He "only hath immortality."

But some argue that since God alone possesses immortality, then man cannot possess it. That conclusion is false. Paul wrote of God as "the incorruptible God" (Romans 1:23), and again he wrote of God, "Now unto the King eternal, immortal, invisible, the only God, be honor and glory for ever and ever" (1 Timothy 1:17). We human beings have immortality derived from God because we are created by Him in His own image (Genesis 1:27). God has

---

1 *Commentary on 1 Timothy,* p.186.

2 *Commentary on the Bible, Volume VI,* p. 831

immortality underived; He has always been and always will be. He alone can confer it. Hence, all human beings, and angels as well, have immortal spirits by God's gift. Man has (is) a spirit which does not die as does his body; his spirit, derived from God, is immortal, incorruptible. God alone can impart immortality to others. The spirit and body are two distinct substances, and the dissolution of the latter does not also involve the end of the conscious existence of the former. The spirit lives on when man dies, though the brain remains in the body. The mind (spirit) does not cease to exist when the brain (matter) is inactivated. Mind and brains, therefore, are indeed connected in some mysterious way with man here on this earth. Since there can be no thought without a thinker, and since the brain cannot think, nor can matter in any form think, one is forced to conclude that there must be something non-material in man which thinks and which is capacitated to survive the death of man. The Holy Scriptures have clearly spoken on the origin and nature of man. Man was created in the image and likeness of God, He has a non-material spirit distinct from the material body in which it dwells, and the union of body and spirit constitute the one entire being on earth. The Bible teaches the compound or dual nature of man—a being consisting of both animated matter and spirit; his body being formed of the dust and his spirit having been divinely in-breathed. The body is material, but the spirit is a distinct entity and capable of existence separate from the body. Man is a created spirit in vital union with an organized, animated body. After death the spirit continues to exist. The spirit of man is immortal. Following death there is an afterlife. All men are created in "the image of God."

Questions for Discussion

1. What does the Bible teach concerning the origin and nature of man?
2. What are the two main divisions of the universe?
3. What is the difference between matter and spirit?
4. Does God possess a physical (material) body?
5. Where did the spirit of man originate? Do matter and spirit come from the same source? How are matter and spirit united in man on earth?
6. Where does thinking originate within man?
7. In what sense can the body of man be spoken of as the man?
8. What is the Biblical heart? Name some things the heart does.
9. What part of man knows the things of a man?
10. What is the real "I" of a person?
11. Does the brain think, remember, or reason?
12. If part of the material (body) of man is destroyed, why does that not necessarily destroy the other part (spirit)?
13. How can the body be to the spirit what the musical instrument is to the musician?
14. Which is better to say: "I have a spirit" or "I am a spirit"? Why?
15. How does one know there is a spirit dwelling inside the body of man?
16. Give reasons for believing the invisible "I" can survive the shock of death.
17. What is the doctrine of materialists?
18. In Romans 12:1 the writer draws a distinction between "you" and "your bodies." What is meant by the "you" in this statement? How should the Christian use his body? (cf. v. 13).
19. What does *mortal* mean? *Immortal?*
20. What did the psalmist say about the heart?
21. How did Solomon speak of man's mind?
22. What was Peter's statement about the hidden man of the heart?
23. Compare and discuss 1 Timothy 1:17, in reference to God, with 1 Peter 3:4.
24. Why do angels not die?
25. In what sense can it be said that "God only has immortality"?
26. How did man derive his immortality? The angels?
27. Discuss the argument that since God is immortal, and since man is created in God's image, this proves man's spirit is immortal.
28. Discuss Ecclesiastes 3:11.

–7–

What Is the Soul?

". . . may your spirit and soul and body be preserved entire"
1 Thessalonians 5:23

Materialists make their greatest doctrinal argument on the nature of man and the meaning of death by a play on the word *soul*. Here they deceive many, for they strive to make the soul in every passage of the Bible equal to the natural life, and never to the immortal spirit. But it is impossible to assign a limited meaning to the word *soul* which will apply in every occurrence in the Scriptures. Hence, to understand properly the meaning of the word, it must be studied in its context.

Soul is derived from the Greek word *psyche*. As already mentioned, it is used in the Bible to refer to at least three different things:

(1) The word *soul* sometimes expresses the animating principle which man possesses in common with beasts, the physical life which ends in death. For example, "He spared not their soul [lives] from death" (Psalm 78:50; cf. 1 Samuel 24:11). Only in this sense do animals have souls, and only in this sense does the life of the flesh (man's soul) die at death. In several statements of Scripture, *soul* describes the mortal life of man (cf. Ezekiel 18:20; 1 Corinthians 15:45). Literally, *psyche* means "the breath of living creatures" (Acts 20:10). This breath is a symbol for life itself (Matthew 6:25). The Hebrew word *nephesh,* rendered "creature" in Genesis 1:20, and sometimes rendered "soul," is assigned to fish, birds, and creeping things. "God said, Let the waters swarm with swarms of living creatures [i.e., souls]. Here the word signifies a creature that breathes or a creature which lives by breathing. The words *living creature* are applied to the entire lower creation (cf. Genesis 1:20, 24, 30; 2:19; 6:17; 7:15, 22; 9:10, 12, 15–16). In this sense only do man and beast have a likeness in life: they breathe or possess physical life in general; man is a breathing being. Thus, at creation God breathed into man the breath of life [lives] and man became a living soul (Genesis 2:7). However, as already noted, Scripture teaches that in addition to man's physical life is the immortal soul

(spirit); that between man and all living creatures is this gulf—man alone was created in the divine image, with something higher than animal life. Furthermore, at times *nephesh* is used of human beings as distinct from lower creation (cf. Numbers 31:35).

(2) Sometimes the word *soul* means the individual or person—a human being, the entire animated person. In such instances in Scripture, the soul, a part of man, is put for the whole man. For example, "eight souls, were saved through water" (1 Peter 3:20); "there were added unto them in that day about three thousand souls" (Acts 2:41).

(3) In addition, the word *soul* in Scripture specifically means the human spirit (although the word *psyche* is never translated "spirit" in the New Testament). The two words are used interchangeably in Luke 23:46 (where it is said that Christ commended His spirit to God at His death) and Acts 2:27, 31 (where Peter said Christ's soul was not left in Hades). Among the definitions Thayer gives to *soul (psyche)* such as "breath, a living being, the seat of feelings, desires, affections, etc." is the following: "The soul as an essence which differs from the body and is not dissolved by death."[1] Regarding the immortal part of man, in several passages of Scripture it is taught that man can kill both the body and the natural life of the body, but he cannot kill the soul. A man's soul has not been killed when his body has been killed. In such instances it refers to man alone, and to that immortal part of man which survives the death of the body. For example, "And be not afraid of them that kill the body, but are not able to kill the soul: but rather fear him who is able to destroy both soul and body in hell" (Matthew 10:28); "I saw underneath the altar the souls of them that had been slain for the word of God" (Revelation 6:9; cf. Hebrews 12:23, where the word *spirits* is used).

Thus, the word *soul* is sometimes used to mean the spirit; but it sometimes refers to the entire person, and sometimes it means the same kind of life as found in animals. So it can be said that in one sense beasts do have a soul (Genesis 1:20; 7:15; Ecclesiastes 3:19–21), but beasts are not created in God's image; they do not have an immortal spirit. When the word *soul* refers to the natural life of man in contradistinction to the word *spirit* (Hebrews 4:12), it might be called the connecting link between the body and the spirit or that which binds body and spirit together.

Usually Two-Fold Division

The Bible commonly speaks of man as constituted of body and soul, or body and spirit. The two-fold division is often affirmed by Paul: for example:

---

1 Thayer, *A Greek-English Lexicon*, p. 677.

- Body and spirit: "And if Christ is in you, the body is dead because of sin; but the spirit is life because of righteousness" (Romans 8:10); "So also the woman that is unmarried and the virgin is careful for the things of the Lord, that she may be holy both in body and in spirit" (1 Corinthians 7:34).
- Flesh and spirit: "To deliver such a one unto Satan for the destruction of the flesh, that the spirit may be saved in the day of the Lord Jesus" (1 Corinthians 5:5); "Having therefore these promises, beloved, let us cleanse ourselves from all defilement of flesh and spirit, perfecting holiness in the fear of God" (2 Corinthians 7:1); "For though I am absent in the flesh, yet am I with you in the spirit" (Colossians 2:5).
- Flesh and mind (heart): "Among whom we also all once lived in the lusts of our flesh, doing the desires of the flesh and of the mind" (Ephesians 2:3); "To the end he may establish your hearts unblameable in holiness" (1 Thessalonians 3:13).

The Human Spirit Is Not Breath

Scripture teaches, therefore, that the word *soul* is sometimes used to mean "breath of life"—the physical life, as materialists contend, but it is also defined as that immortal part of man, that "essence which differs from the body and is not dissolved by death." The word *soul* is a much broader word than *spirit*. Thayer also states: "Although for most parts the words *pneuma* and *psyche* are used indiscriminately, and so *soma* [body] and *psyche* put in contrast . . . there is also recognized a three-fold distinction . . .1 Thessalonians 5:23."[1] Thus, the words *soul* (*psyche*) and *spirit* (*pneuma*) can be variously defined, but they are often used indiscriminately, as can be noted by the context. The same is true regarding the usages of their Hebrew equivalents, *nephesh* and *ruach,* in the Old Testament. *Soul* and *spirit* are used synonymously by Mary in her song of praise to Elizabeth, the future mother of John the Baptist: "My soul doth magnify the Lord, and my spirit hath rejoiced in God my Saviour" (Luke 1:46–47). However, materialists teach that the spirit of man signifies wind, air, or breath; so the spirit which returns to God at death is but the air or breath which God gave. But man and breath are not equivalent terms; neither are spirit and breath in every instance. Substitute the word *breath* in passages where the word *spirit* occurs and see how fallacious the idea: for example,

- "Father, into thy hands I commend my *breath*" (Luke 23:46).
- "Watch and pray, that ye enter not into temptation: the *breath* indeed is willing, but the flesh is weak" (Matthew 26:41).
- "My *breath* hath rejoiced in God my Saviour" (Luke 1:47).

---

1 Ibid., p. 520.

- "The Spirit himself beareth witness with our *breath*, that we are the children of God" (Romans 8:16).
- "Let us cleanse ourselves from all defilement of flesh and *breath,* perfecting holiness in the fear of God" (2 Corinthians 7:1).
- "May your *breath* and soul and body be preserved entire, without blame at the coming of our Lord Jesus Christ" (1 Thessalonians 5:23).

Ridiculous? Certainly!

In Job 34:14, notice the distinction between *spirit* and *breath* where the passage speaks of his spirit and his breath. Without doubt the spirit of man and the breath of a person are distinct things. It is true, as materialists say, that sometimes the word *spirit* is used to mean air, wind, or breath, but not always. The air, wind, or breath does not have intellect, but the Bible teaches that the spirit in man has intellect. Paul asked: "For what man knoweth the things of a man, save the spirit of man which is in him?" (1 Corinthians 2:11 KJV). Many passages have already been given in this treatise which abundantly show that man has an immortal spirit which dwells in the body and manifests itself through the body, but is no part of the body, and can live consciously apart from the body after it leaves the body. Hence, the Word of God definitely teaches that there is a part of man, described Biblically as *soul* or *spirit,* which differs from the body and is not dissolved by death.

The spirit represents only the rational and moral part of man. In the New Testament, when a person has died, he is said to have given up or commended himself to the Lord, the word soul (Greek, *psyche*) is never used, but rather the word spirit (Greek, *pneuma*). For example: "Father, into thy hands I commend my spirit [*pneuma*]" (Luke 23:46); "And he bowed his head, and gave up his spirit [*pneuma*]" (John 19:30). At death, man's earthly life ceases to be, but his spirit continues to live. Death comes to the mortal man (his body), but his spirit (soul) lives on. The body returns to the dust; the spirit returns to God who gave it. "And the dust returneth to the earth as it was, and the spirit returneth unto God who gave it" (Ecclesiastes 12:7). Therefore, when anyone speaks of the immortality of the soul, he is employing the word as equivalent to the spirit, not as it is used at times to indicate mere earthly life or living creature. When the word *soul* is used to refer to the inward man, it means the same as spirit, the immortal nature of man—the undying spirit—and not the dying soul (cf. Luke 23:46; Hebrews 12:9).

As sometimes used in the Scriptures, then, the soul of man is the life principle common to men and animals; it has the capacity on one side for union with a physical body which the soul of animals have, and on the other side the capacity for union with the immortal spirit which animals do not have. Yet the words *soul* and *spirit* are often used interchangeably (Luke 1:46–47). In such instances where *soul* is used generically to embrace the non-material part of man—as when one sings, "Where the Soul Never Dies"—it is used figuratively. For this reason, when referring to man's invisible, intellectual element (essence), it is permissible to call it either soul or spirit. In this study the words are used synonymously while recognizing some distinction, for the Bible shows there is a difference—the dividing of soul and spirit (Hebrews 4:12).

The sophistry of materialists can be seen, as they select one meaning for the word *soul* as its universal and immutable meaning. Because in certain passages of Scripture, *soul* denotes earthly life in general, which is mortal, they assume that all souls are mortal. But *man* and *soul* are not always used interchangeably. They are not exactly the same. The word soul does not always denote animal life; the word *man* does not always mean soul. The word *soul* is often used synonymously with the word *spirit; soul* and *spirit* can be interchangeable.

Man Dies Like a Beast

Materialists use a few passages of Scripture to argue that man is like the brute beast, having no spirit to outlive the body.

> For that which befalleth the sons of men befalleth beasts; even one thing befalleth them: as the one dieth, so dieth the other; yea, they have all one breath; and man hath no preeminence above the beasts; for all is vanity. All go into one place; all are of the dust, and all turn to dust again (Ecclesiastes 3:19–20).

Two things are to be observed regarding this Scripture: (1) It is said to be the meditation of the writer: "I said in mine heart . . ." (v. 18). Solomon thought of it more like a temptation to unbelief respecting a future state than anything else. (2) It is said in the next verse, "Who knoweth the spirit of man, whether it goeth upward, and the spirit of the beast, whether it goeth downward to the earth?" (v. 21).

Thus, the passage shows that the deaths of men and beasts are alike only as to their bodies. The bodies of both die and return to the dust from whence they came; but they are very unlike in other ways. There is perfect harmony, therefore, of this statement and the one which says the spirit of man returns to God at death (Ecclesiastes 12:7).

Too, recall another passage in this book: "[God] hath set eternity in their heart" (Ecclesiastes 3:11). So Ecclesiastes 3:19–20, viewed in the light of all other statements in the same book, affirms that man's physical body is like the lower animals. His death is just as inevitable, and both go to the dust. Nevertheless, man has a spirit; the beasts do not. At death man's immortal spirit returns to God—to the place God has prepared for it.

What Part of Man Is Mortal?

Materialists also refer to Job 4:17 as proof of their belief that man is wholly mortal: "Shall mortal man be more just than God?" The context of this passage shows that this question was asked by Eliphaz, a man who opposed Job in his reasoning. What people said is many times recorded in the Bible, even if it is not the truth (cf. Matthew 12:24).

But, from the physical standpoint when a man dies, as the psalmist said, "His breath goeth forth, he returneth to his earth; in that very day his thoughts [his plans, purposes, as in Job 17:11] perish" (Psalm 146:4).

Wicked men said of Jesus, "This man doth not cast out demons, but by Beelzebub the prince of the demons" (Matthew 12:24). This was not true. So when the Scriptures refer to man's body, it is always called mortal, and "Let not sin therefore reign in your mortal body" (Romans 6:12); again: "your mortal bodies" (Romans 8:11); still again: "our mortal flesh" (2 Corinthians 4:11). But where does the Bible say "our mortal spirit"? or "man is wholly mortal"? It never does! The Bible does teach that man was created with a mortal body and an immortal spirit, but never that the spirit of man is mortal.

Simply stated, the outward man is perishable; the inward man, imperishable (2 Corinthians 4:16; 1 Peter 3:4). Only the body is mortal—its immortality will occur at the resurrection (1 Corinthians 15:51–54). Then God will present immortal, incorruptible bodies for all spirits to inhabit eternally. The spirit by its very nature is now immortal; but man's body, being mortal, is presently unfit as the spirit's eternal dwelling.

Materialists err in saying that man has no form of immortality now and that only the righteous will be made immortal after the resurrection. True, God has promised eternal life unto all who obey Him (Hebrews 5:9); but materialists fail to see that man has an immortal spirit now and will have an immortal body after the resurrection.

As already noted, the Greek word *aphthartos,* which means "incorruptible," is translated "immortal" once in the New Testament. "Now unto the King eternal, immortal . . . " (1 Timothy 1:17). The Greek word *athanasia,* which means "deathlessness," is translated "immortality" three times in the New Testament in the American Standard Version. These passages are as follows:

- "this mortal must put on immortality" (1 Corinthians 15:53).
- "this mortal shall have put on immortality" (1 Corinthians 15:54).
- "Who only hath immortality" (1 Timothy 6:16).

The Greek word *aphtharsia,* which means "incorruption," is also translated "immortality" in two places in the King James Version:

- "Seek for glory and honor and immortality" (Romans 2:7 KJV).
- "and brought life and immortality to light through the gospel" (2 Timothy 1:10 KJV).

However, in the American Standard Version, the word *aphtharsia* is translated "incorruption" in Romans 2:7 and is given in the footnote on 2 Timothy 1:10. So the word *immortality* or *incorruption* in these two passages of Scripture (Romans 2:7 and 2 Timothy 1:10) is used only in reference to the body. Not until the resurrection will the body become immortal, for then it becomes incorruptible (1 Corinthians 15:53–54).

The immortality that the Bible contemplates as yet future is the immortality of the body or the whole person—body and spirit—together. The body—and not the spirit—puts on immortality at the resurrection. In the Scriptures, corruptibility is not once taught concerning the spirit.

Hence, the Bible teaches that man has an immortal spirit now and will have an immortal body after the resurrection. However, an eternal existence does not always exhaust the meaning of the term *immortality* as used in the Bible. To seek incorruption or immortality is to seek freedom from suffering, decay, and corruption in this present state—to seek a glorified body. (See Romans 8:18–23.) Eternal life and immortality or incorruption are used in apposition, in Romans 2:7. To put on immortality is to put on a body free from suffering, decay, and corruption of this present life.

Immortality for man's body, therefore, is yet in prospect. For this reason, the Scriptures speak of Christians seeking immortality: "Who [God] will render to every man according to his works: to them that by patience in well-doing seek for glory and honor and incorruption, eternal life" (Romans 2:6–7). The reference here is to the life of glory and honor in an immortal body to which the believer aspires. The Christian realizes that his future happiness depends upon a change in his body when it shall become immortal. Thus, immortality for the child of God involves the resurrection, and it is not fully attained until after the resurrection.

In the Scriptures, resurrection refers to the body. The spirit, not subject to death, cannot be resurrected. Paul's hope was for the redemption of the body and eternal life in heaven with the Lord: "Even we ourselves groan within ourselves, waiting for our adoption, to wit, the redemption of our body" (Romans 8:23). The immortality of the body is an object of hope to Christians (Romans 8:20–25); they are awaiting the resurrection of their bodies at the last day. So both mortality and immortality are affirmed of the body, but only immortality is taught concerning the soul or spirit. The Bible nowhere says that in this life a person should seek for immortality of the spirit, because the spirit is already immortal.

It is important in this study to notice what part of man is referred to in any Biblical statement. Is it the body or is it the spirit? Luke 16:23 and John 19:42 are examples of Biblical usage of the whole for a part: "And in Hades he lifted up his eyes, being in torments" refers to only the spirit of the rich man: "There then . . . they laid Jesus" refers to only the body of Christ. Man is mortal. Indeed, but what part of man is mortal? Man is immortal. Indeed, but what part of man is now immortal? Man shall become immortal. Indeed, but what part of man shall one day be made immortal? It can be clearly seen that it was resurrection of the body and not immortality of the soul that the apostle Paul proclaimed to early Christians. Man in his fleshly state is not equipped for heaven: "flesh and blood cannot inherit the kingdom of God . . . this mortal must put on immortality" (1 Corinthians 15:50–53).

In heaven, the redeemed will have both an immortal spirit and an immortal body, dwelling in union with God eternally. In hell, the damned will also possess imperishable bodies for their immortal spirit, and they will exist forever in torment, away from God. In the very nature of the case, man cannot experience eternal life or eternal punishment, unless he is an eternal being. Hence, immortality of the body is not a conditional gift bestowed upon a certain class; for all men, both wicked and righteous, will be raised with undying bodies when Jesus comes. Jesus said:

> Marvel not at this: for the hour is coming, in the which all that are in the graves shall hear his voice, and shall come forth; they that have done good, unto the resurrection of life; and they that have done evil, unto the resurrection of damnation (John 5:28–29 KJV).

Christ also said that God was "able to destroy both soul and body in hell" (Matthew 10:28). The resurrection of the body will not impart immortality to the spirit, for the spirit is already immortal; but at that time immortality will only be to the body.

Furthermore, Christians living at Christ's return will be changed; their bodies will become immortal ones. Paul stressed this when he said Christ "shall change our vile body, that it may be fashioned like unto his glorious body" (Philippians 3:21 KJV). "We all shall not sleep [i.e. die], but we shall all be changed" (1 Corinthians 15:51). The Holy Scriptures teach Christians that both those who have died and those who are alive upon the earth at the end of time will receive a body like the resurrection-body of Christ. Hence, all men will either experience, by death or change, the putting off of mortality and the putting on of immortality. The general resurrection of all bodies is without doubt the New Testament teaching with respect to future life. How glorious the thought that at the resurrection, an incorruptible body shall house an immortal spirit, and the whole man shall become immortal! (Further study on the resurrection of the body will be given later.)

All Men Are Immortal

The spirit of man is immortal. The Holy Scriptures teach that all men shall live on and on forever. Each one must say, "There was a time when I was not, but there shall never be a time when I shall cease to be." How comforting to know that it will not be into extinction and nothingness that all shall pass when the spirit leaves the body. There is a life beyond; there is a hereafter. God is! This fact assures those in fellowship with Him of a blessed life beyond the horizon of death. This He pledges. The entire Bible is built upon this background. All spirits are immortal. The Scriptures do not teach conditional immortality. The Bible teaches that all spirits—God, angels, Satan, demons, and human spirits—cannot cease to exist. Physical death, however, is the separation of the spirit from the body, but it is not the extinction of the spirit. One can be separated from God, but he cannot be annihilated. Man has no reason, therefore, to suppose that after having started his existence here on earth, he shall ever cease to be. An immortal being cannot be destroyed. It is the characteristic of spirit to be deathless. The Bible nowhere teaches that the spirit dies or that the rational mind of man will ever cease to exist. In the Scriptures, the spirit is never said to be destroyed, to die, or cease to be. The spirit is not subject to death. Materialists are challenged to find a single verse of Scripture that intimates the extinction of a human spirit.

A belief in the doctrine that at the end of this life a man and his dog fare alike can only result in present relaxation and dimming of hope. One of the greatest calamities which could befall the human race would be a serious decline in faith of the doctrine of life after death, a doctrine manifested by teaching that man is wholly mortal. Man would rapidly revert to the bestial level, and lose eternal life.

Man shall not always live in a mortal body, but always he shall live. Man is an immortal being. Death cannot destroy him. He shall exist when the stars grow dim with age. The advancing and retreating eons shall not fade his eternal existence. Immortality in the sense of endless existence is an inalienable endowment of mankind. The Bible affirms the endless existence of every human being, whether saved or lost. Eternal life, as shall be noted later, is a particular quality of life which emanates from God; it is more than endless existence. Likewise, as shall be seen from the Scriptures, the second death is not mere annihilation, but everlasting existence while separated from God forever.

Questions for Discussion

1. How do materialists confuse people over the meaning of the word *soul?*
2. How is *soul* used in the Bible?
3. In what sense do animals have souls but not spirits?
4. What part of man is mortal? What part immortal?
5. Does the word *spirit* mean wind or breath or life? Discuss examples.
6. When will man have an immortal body? When will all bodies be changed?
7. In what sense does man seek immortality?
8. What does the Bible teach about the eternal existence of all men, both good and bad?
9. In what sense does a man die like a beast? In what sense is his death unlike a beast? How are many of the statements about death used in the book of Ecclesiastes and in the Psalms?
10. What finally happens to the morals of a nation of people when they cease to believe in the immortality of the soul?

HE IS JUST AWAY

I cannot say, and I will not say
    That he is dead. He is just away.
With a cheerful smile and a wave of the hand,
    He has wandered into an unknown land,
And left us dreaming how very fair
    It needs must be since he lingers there.

And you—O you, who the wildest yearn
    For the old-time step and the glad return—
Think of him faring on, as dear
    In the love of There as the love of Here.
Think of him still as the same, I say;
    He is not dead—he is just away.

—James Whitcomb Riley

This, do you tell me, is the end of all?
    This silence deep, this shroud and pall?
These folded hands on a pulseless breast?
    This fallen form in grave clothes dressed?
Here was a man with a mind and heart,
    Wrought by a strange, mysterious art.
Onward through years of toil and strife
    He suffered the pangs and pain of the years,
And bathed himself in blood and tears.
    Why did he buffet the ocean of Time,
If he saw not a destiny sublime?

Oh, tell me not, thou foolish one
    That for toil like this no guerdon's won.
Something assures me this is true:
    Those eyes shall wake to visions new;
Those hands shall reach for nobler deeds,
    And love shall rule above all creeds.
Life is no futile, fading thing;
    It is an angel on whose wing
We fly from regions of the sod
    To radiant heights of home and God.

—Samples

– 8 –

Does Death Mean Annihilation?

"For the wages of sin is death"
Romans 6:23

The doctrine of materialism alleges that man is wholly matter, without an immortal spirit, and hence ceases to exist at physical death. Materialists insist that death means annihilation and complete cessation of the whole person. This idea of the materialists is based upon the false assumption that the soul is merely the result of physical organization and can have no separate existence. But death is not the destruction of the spirit; the soul does not die with the body. The human soul revolts against the doctrine of annihilation; man instinctively refuses to believe that God made the soul to destroy it when the body of man expires.

As previously noted, the word *death* in the Holy Scriptures always means separation, not cessation of being or absolute non-existence. Death is not the end. One must go to the Bible for the true meaning of death. Here it is noted that there is a deeper life than physical living and a deeper death than physical dying, but never annihilation of the person. The word *life* always means union with or united to, while *death* means separation.

Three Senses

In the Scriptures, both the words *death* and *life* are applied to man in three different senses. First, death is used in three different senses:

1. Physical death—the separation of the spirit of man from his body. This has been learned in a previous chapter from a number of passages, e.g., "as her soul was in departing (for she died)" (Genesis 35:18). The departure of the immortal spirit, or soul of man, from the body is physical death (Ecclesiastes 12:7; James 2:26).
2. Spiritual death—the separation of the spirit of man from the Spirit of God while one is living in trespasses and sins in the body. Paul said to Christians, "And you did he make alive, when ye were dead through your trespasses and sins" (Ephesians 2:1). Sin breaks one's communion

with God: "Your iniquities have separated between you and your God" (Isaiah 59:2). Spiritual death is the result of sin in this life. So one may be alive (physically) and dead (spiritually) at the same time.
3. Eternal death—the separation of the soul of man from the Spirit of God for all eternity. "For the wages of sin is death" (Romans 6:23). This is not physical death, but eternal death or the second death, when the soul is separated from God forever. "And death and Hades were cast into the lake of fire. This is the second death, even the lake of fire. And if any was not found written in the book of life, he was cast into the lake of fire" (Revelation 20:14–15). Those who are condemned to everlasting punishment will experience eternal separation from God. Sin, the most dreadful fact in the universe, separates one from God both now and forever.

Second, the word *life* is used in three different senses:

1. Physical life—the union of the spirit of man with his body. The miracle of bringing persons back to life in Biblical times was simply the returning of the spirit to the body. Elijah prayed that the son of the widow of Zarephath might be restored to life. "I pray thee, let this child's soul come into him again . . . and the soul of the child came into him again, and he revived" (1 Kings 17:21–22). Death came when the soul became separated from the body; the child lived when "the soul of the child came into him [i.e., into the body] again." When the ruler's daughter was raised by Christ, "her spirit returned" (Luke 8:55). The same was true concerning Dorcas, raised by Peter (Acts 9:36–41). In dying, her spirit had left the body; in coming to life again, her spirit had to return.
2. Spiritual life—the union of the spirit of man with the Spirit of Christ which includes membership in His spiritual body, the church. "He that hath the Son hath the life" (1 John 5:12). He not only has physical life but also spiritual life: namely that spiritual state in union with God, the fountain of life.
3. Eternal life—the union of the spirit of man with the Spirit of God in heaven forever. "And these [the wicked] shall go away into eternal punishment: but the righteous into eternal life" (Matthew 25:46). Other Biblical references illustrate these senses of the words *life* and *death*.

Many Other References

Adam Died That Day

When God placed Adam in the Garden of Eden, He told him he could eat of the fruit of every tree except one—the tree of the knowledge of good and evil. Jehovah said: "For in the day that thou eatest thereof thou shalt surely die [or, more literally, 'dying, thou shalt die']" (Genesis 2:17). Later, Satan, in tempting Eve to eat of the fruit, said: "Ye shall not surely die" (Genesis 3:4). Materialists are bold to say that the theory of immorality is founded upon a lie told by the devil; that Satan said, "Ye shall not die," even though God said, "Ye shall die." They ask, Which one told the truth, God or Satan? Of course, the materialists' definition of death is "to cease to exist," but this is not God's definition. With the Lord, death means "separation."

God said, "In the day you eat of it you will die." Adam sinned by eating of the forbidden fruit. Did he die that day? Surely Adam died some kind of death that day, for God declared that he would. Materialists say Adam did not die that day. But in the very day he ate the forbidden fruit, he did die. God told the truth! However, Adam did not die physically that day. His death was not a cessation of being or the mere dissolution of the body, yet he died the day he disobeyed God. How? He died in the sense that he became separated from God. Adam sinned, and sin separated his spirit from God (Isaiah 59:2; James 1:15). It was a spiritual death that he died.

Here is a question materialists cannot answer: What part of man died the very day Adam ate the forbidden fruit? It is easy to see that he died spiritually the day he disobeyed—that there was a change in his relationship with God, and his spirit was separated from the Spirit of God, the source of spiritual life. In this sense only could Adam have died the day he violated the divine precept, for afterwards he lived in the flesh several hundred years. Mortal Adam began to die physically when God drove him out of the Garden; he became separated from the tree of life (Genesis 3:22–24). Physical death, then, followed as a necessary consequence of his transgression, but not until many years later; Adam was 930 years old when he died (Genesis 5:3–5). That Adam could have remained in Eden after he sinned and continued to eat of the tree of life which bestowed physical life and immortality is evident from the fact that after he sinned, God put him out of the Garden "lest he put forth his hand, and take also of the tree of life, and eat, and live for ever" (Genesis 3:22).

The Dead Hear and Live

Christ recognized a spiritual death—an alienation of the inner man from God—in that there is a spiritual resurrection. He said: "Verily, verily, I say unto you, The hour cometh, and now is, when the dead shall hear the voice of the Son of God; and they that hear shall live" (John 5:25). This actually happened on Pentecost, when the church was established, when three thousand people heard the gospel, believed, repented, and were baptized for the remission of their sins (Acts 2). They died to sin, were buried in water as Jesus was buried in the earth, and were raised in the likeness of His resurrection to walk in newness of life (Romans 6:3–4). In apostolic days, this experience was multiplied over and over again. Hence, regeneration is a resurrection to "newness of life." In other words, spiritual life is begun in true conversion to Christ when the sinner turns to the Lord.

In contrast to John 5:25, the language of Jesus in John 5:28–29 refers to the bodies of those who die a physical death as being quickened (made alive) in the resurrection.

> Marvel not at this: for the hour cometh, in which all that are in the tombs [i.e., all the physically dead] shall hear his voice, and shall come forth; they that have done good, unto the resurrection of life; and they that have done evil, unto the resurrection of judgment.

In harmony with Christ's statement in John 5:25 is another addressed to those in the flesh. Now let *life* in this passage mean "existence" and see how ridiculous the reading is: "He that hath the Son hath 'existence'; and he that hath not the Son of God hath not 'existence.'" A strange "he" who has not existence! The individual outside of Christ is dead in sin, separated from God; he hath not life. So separation from God is death, whether here or hereafter. But the spiritually dead who are physically alive can hear the voice of the Son of God and live, and the physically dead will one day hear His voice and be raised from the dead. Therefore, death—physical or spiritual—does not mean annihilation or cessation of existence. It always means separation. There must be three sorts of death as well as three sorts of life, for there is a death for each life. Further, if death reduces a man to nothingness, as materialists claim, then how can there be a second death, as mentioned by John in Revelation 20:14?

The Believer Passes from Death to Life

Another verse showing that life and existence are not synonymous is the language of Christ describing the spiritual condition of the man of this world: "Verily, verily, I say unto you, He that heareth my word, and believeth on him that sent me, hath everlasting life, and shall not come into condemnation; but is passed from death unto life" (John 5:24 KJV). Is it not plain that the believer here spoken of possessed physical life while being dead in the sense in which he is now made alive? Such a one was dead but is now alive. A new and different kind of life was added to his former physical life, namely, a spiritual life. So the life which Christ is talking about is not the same as that which is the product of physical birth. According to the Savior, here is a living man passing from death to life. Therefore, the one who possesses human life may at the same time be dead in some sense.

To this, add the language of the apostle John to Christians: "We know that we have passed out of death into life, because we love the brethren. He that loveth not abideth in death" (1 John 3:14). Here are those living who have passed from spiritual death to spiritual life, while possessing, before and since, human life. *Life* and *death,* as applied here, then, are terms used to designate a spiritual state, a moral or spiritual condition of the soul. Hence, he who lives in sin is called "dead."

The Dead Can Bury the Dead

Again, Christ once said to a man, "Follow me; and leave the dead to bury their own dead" (Matthew 8:22; cf. Luke 9:60). Here the word *dead* is used in two different senses. Here was a man physically dead who was to be buried; but those who were to bury the dead (physically) were dead in another sense, that is, dead to God by sin. Otherwise, how would a dead man bury a dead man? This proves that a person can be alive in one sense while dead in another, or that an individual may possess human life and at the same time be as dead to God, as a man void of human life is dead to the world. So, Christ surely meant by these words that they who are not alive to God may bury those who are literally dead. Definitely, He could not have meant that the non-existent must bury the non-existent. Hence, some are represented in the Scriptures as being dead spiritually. The expression describes the present state of certain live men. They may desire to be the Lord's disciples but are unable to depart from earthly things.

Certain Widows Are Dead While They Live

Paul used the term *dead* with double meaning when he referred to a young widow who would give herself to pleasure: "But she that giveth herself to pleasure is dead while she liveth" (1 Timothy 5:6). This condition would certainly be impossible if materialists are correct about death, for that would mean that a person is in existence and out of existence at the same time. Paul clearly means that the woman living in pleasure is dead in a spiritual sense and separated from God because of her sins. Yet, at the same time, she is alive physically; she is neither extinct nor deceased. Hence, a person may be dead in one sense and alive in another, at one and the same time. This passage certainly proves that death cannot mean ceasing to exist.

Believers May Be Dead to the World Yet Alive

Moreover, Jesus taught that believers may be dead to the passions of this world and at the same time alive to God, for He said to Martha at the tomb of Lazarus: "I am the resurrection, and the life: he that believeth in me, though he die [i.e. die physically], yet shall he live; and whosoever liveth and believeth on me shall never die [i.e., die spiritually]" (John 11:25–26). Although the soul becomes separated from the body—for when one is dead physically, his spirit has left his body—the spirit (soul) of the believer will never be separated from God. The believer shall live though he dies; he shall never die. "Believest thou this?" (v. 26).

It is clear then in this passage that to die is used in two different senses, referring in the former case to physical death, in the latter to separation from God and the true life of the soul. Spiritual death, caused by the individual's own sin, brings separation from God in this life and also in eternity. Physical death, which brings severing of physical ties, has no effect upon spiritual ties. The death of the body does not separate the obedient soul from fellowship with the Lord. The faithful may die physically and yet be alive spiritually. Of course, in regard to physical death the man who believes in Jesus dies exactly as any other man dies. Death stays his course for no man, believer or unbeliever. Christ did not promise the believer any immunity from physical death. He meant that physical death is powerless to destroy the believer's spiritual life.

The Believer Never Dies

Upon another occasion Jesus said: "Verily, verily, I say unto you, If a man keep my word, he shall never see death" (John 8:51). Again, in this statement Christ affirmed that the life of the faithful man of God never ends, that the faithful may die physically and yet be alive spiritually. How did the people react to the truth? "The Jews said unto him, Now we know that thou hast a demon. Abraham died, and the prophets; and thou sayest, If a man keep my word, he shall never taste of death" (v. 52). Jesus knew Abraham was dead (if the body is all that is involved in death). Yet, He also knew that Abraham lives, for God is the God of the living. Thus, when materialists say a man dies entirely when physical death comes, they also, in effect, accuse Christ of having a devil, as the Jews did then.

The Old Testament declares: "In the way of righteousness is life; and in the pathway thereof there is no death" (Proverbs 12:28). This passage says that the righteous do not die. But what kind of death does this mean? The righteous do die physically, but not spiritually. Hence, the believer never dies spiritually.

Man Can Eat and Live Forever

In His wonderful discourse about the Bread of Life, Jesus affirmed the same truth. He said "a man may eat thereof, and not die" or "he shall live for ever" (John 6:50–51, cf. v. 58). Thus eternal life designates the reward of the righteous, the life of perfect happiness in the world to come. So Christ came to bring life to man (John 10:10).

In the afore-mentioned passages, the Savior spoke of spiritual life, begun here, as flowing on uninterrupted forever—physical death being a mere incident scarcely worthy of thought as compared with that deeper death of the spirit. If a person who is dead in sin in this life is not converted to Christ before physical death comes, then said spiritual death becomes the second death—eternal separation of the spirit of man from God. Only by obedience to the Lord's teaching can the second death be avoided. So, in the deepest sense of the word, the believer in Christ does not die at all. The living have no advantage over the dead insofar as spiritual life and communion with God are concerned—for believers.

Hence, death for the believer does not destroy the soul's relationship to God and Christ. The soul is without body after physical death while awaiting the resurrection; but it, being united to Christ, still lives, and living, never dies. Natural death does not interrupt continuity of the true life begun here. The believer remains in union with God. The true believer never dies spiritually.

Further, just as the person who continues faithful to the Lord shall never see that which is truly death (i.e., the death of the soul), so the person who remains in unbelief and disobedience to God shall never experience true life (i.e., life with God). Note again the language of Jesus which affirms that those who do not find life by faith in Him will perish: "He that believeth on the Son hath eternal life; but he that obeyeth not the Son shall not see life, but the wrath of God abideth on him" (John 3:36). In this verse eternal life is regarded as a present possession for believers (as in John 5:24 and 1 John 5:13); but in other passages, in regard to its consummation, eternal life is spoken of as an object of hope: "in hope of eternal life" (Titus 1:2). Christians, united with Christ, who is that "eternal life" (1 John 1:2), have life, and they have eternal life eternally in prospect! Likewise, Christians are in the kingdom of Christ now (Colossians 1:13; Revelation 1:9; Hebrews 12:28), yet there is the eternal phase of the kingdom of God which is future and awaiting those who remain faithful (Acts 14:22; 2 Peter 1:4–11; Revelation 2:10). So long as the believer is faithful, nothing can separate him from the Lord: but one must continue to hold fast the beginning of his confidence steadfast to the end (Hebrews 3:14; 10:38).

Thus, *life* and *existence* cannot mean the same; the words cannot be used interchangeably. There is a marked difference between simple *existence* and *life* as the Bible uses the terms. Life means union with God. Hence, man is only alive to that to which he is united; he is dead to that from which he is separated, for death always results from separation.

The Second Death Is Eternal Separation from God

The lake of fire, the place of eternal punishment for the wicked, is described as the second death (Revelation 20:14). "But for the fearful, and unbelieving, and abominable, and murderers, and fornicators, and sorcerers, and idolaters, and all liars, their part shall be in the lake that burneth with fire and brimstone; which is the second death" (Revelation 21:8). Here, in the lake of fire, the soul is eternally separated from God. In the Scriptures, *second death* designates the eternal punishment of the wicked, the eternal separation of man from fellowship with God. Man has been so made by his Creator that he cannot truly live unless he is in the right relationship to God, in this life and in eternity. So the wicked will exist forever—away from God. This is the second death. But eternal destruction—the second death (2 Thessalonians 1:7–9)—is not eternal extinction or oblivion.

Man Can Save and Lose His Life

Again, Christ proclaimed: "Whosoever would save his life shall lose it; and whosoever shall lose his life for my sake and the gospel's shall save it" (Mark 8:35). The plain meaning is that he who will lose his life in the lower sense for Christ shall save it in the higher sense. There is a play on the two meanings of the word *life*. By failing to follow Jesus, a person might save his physical life, but in so doing he would lose the eternal life. Hence, spiritual life is a vital union with God, and spiritual death is a separation from God.

Spiritual Life Is in Christ

Jesus once said to the carping Pharisees: "Ye will not come to me, that ye may have life" (John 5:40). The Pharisees were dead spiritually; because of their sin, they were severed from God. They had no spiritual life, but they refused to come to Christ that they might have life. The same condition is true now of all those who are out of Christ and refuse to come to Him. Life is in the Son: "And this is the record, that God hath given to us eternal life, and this life is in his Son. He that hath the Son hath life; and he that hath not the Son of God hath not life" (1 John 5:11–12 KJV).

According to the Sacred Scriptures, life must come from a source outside of man, namely, from Jesus Christ (cf. John 1:4; 6:33, 35; 10:10). The Savior did not come and die on the cross to give man continuous existence, for this he already had by nature, being a creature in the image of God. Christ came to be the means of man's securing eternal life. Jesus affirmed: "And this is eternal life, that they should know thee the only true God, and him whom thou didst send, even Jesus Christ" (John 17:3 KJV). An obedient faith in Christ is the source of life, both here and hereafter. In this respect man has a choice, but only in the deeper dimension of the spirit can man choose between life and death (Deuteronomy 30:15, 19, 20; Jeremiah 21:8). The Bible teaches that all men will exist forever. However, those faithfully obedient to the Savior to the end of this earthly life will exist in fullness of life in union with God in heaven; those who disobey the Lord will exist forever away from God in eternal punishment (Hebrews 5:9; Revelation 22:14–15; Matthew 25:46; 2 Thessalonians 1:7–9).

Therefore, when eternal life is promised to those who believe in the Lord and do His will, it is not mere immortal existence that is meant, but rather eternal happiness with God and all the redeemed. Future happiness alone is conditioned upon one's faith in the Lord, and not future being. Immortal existence is not made dependent upon the reception or rejection of the Savior; all men shall exist forever—some in happiness, because of a holy life; others in torment, because of a sinful life. Christ is man's only Redeemer, and to reject Him and His offer of grace and mercy is to be damned eternally.

In this world, then, life for man is found in vital union with Christ. The Bible affirms that all spiritual blessings are in Christ, that salvation is in Christ Jesus (Ephesians 1:3; 2 Timothy 2:10), that life is in Him (John 1:4; 1 John 4:9).

A Christian's spiritual life is very beautifully set forth by Jesus under the likeness of the vine and its branches (John 15:1–8). By a connection with the vine, the branch has life; separated from it, there is death. The same is true of the Christian. Everyone who has the Son or is connected with Christ has also the life that is in Christ; but if he lets go of the Son, then he is himself cast off as a branch. Christ, then, is the source of life; union with Him is as necessary as the union of a branch to the vine; apart from Him one does not have life. Abiding in Him, the True Vine, is the secret of fruit bearing (Galatians 5:22–23). Thus, spiritual life is in or through Christ, because in Him only is life.

Sardis Was a Dead Church

In the letter to the church at Sardis, there is a perfectly clear case in which the word *dead* neither designates a corpse nor a deceased person. "I know thy works, that thou hast a name that thou livest, and thou art dead" (Revelation 3:1). The church was spiritually dead. "Your iniquities have separated between you and your God, and your sins have hid his face from you" (Isaiah 59:2).

The Prodigal Son Was Dead

Similarly, the prodigal son, while away from home and separated from his father, was dead; yet he was alive (i.e., in physical existence) all the time. This explains why, upon his return, the father said: "For this my son was dead, and is alive again; he was lost, and is found" (Luke 15:24). This is a perfect parallel to man's being dead to God and holiness. A sinner alienated from God is lost; his repentance leads to his recovery. Hence, the word *dead* can describe the spiritual condition of a person. Although a sinner is living in the world, he is dead; but when he becomes a Christian, he is made alive—he lives! The teaching of the Sacred Writings on the meaning of life and death is too clear to be misunderstood.

Christians Have Been Made Alive

Paul wrote to the Ephesians: "And you did he make alive, when ye were dead through your trespasses and sins" (Ephesians 2:1). People, prior to their conversion to Christianity, are described as being dead through their sins; but they are at the same time physically alive. A person, therefore, is dead spiritually when he is giving himself to sin. "Dead in sin" cannot mean one is non-existent. So the words *life* and *death,* or *dead* and *alive,* are used both literally and metaphorically in the Scriptures.

Christians Are Also Dead

Moreover, the Bible teaches that Christians are dead, even though still living in this world. "For ye died, and your life is hid with Christ in God" (Colossians 3:3). Although alive physically, believers are dead to the world; that is, they are "dead unto sin, but alive [spiritually] unto God" because they have put on the new man (Romans 6:11; cf. Romans 6: 4, 7; Colossians 3). Christians become dead to sin by their obedience to the gospel; at this time they also become alive to God. They are alive in one sense, yet dead in another. These Colossian saints, addressed by Paul, were not non-existent, even though the writer said they were dead. To the rich young ruler, in the prime of life, Jesus said: "If thou wouldst enter into life, keep the commandments" (Matthew 19:17). Here again, life denotes a spiritual state.

Christians May Die Spiritually

Hear Paul again: "For if ye live after the flesh, ye must die" (Romans 8:13). Die how? Will not all Christians, both good and bad, die physically? Whether they live after the flesh or Spirit, they die physically. This is true of all. It is obvious, therefore, that Paul had reference to their spiritual and eternal death.

In addition James says, "My brethren, if any among you err from the truth, and one convert him; let him know, that he who converteth a sinner from the error of his way shall save a soul from death, and shall cover a multitude of sins" (James 5:19–20). What kind of death is the soul saved from? This is not death of the body, for all, whether converted or not, shall die physically. To convert a man is to save his soul from death, the second death.

Thus, in every instance where the word *death* or any of its equivalents are found in the Scriptures, the word *separation* may be used without doing violence to the meaning. But to use the word *annihilation* or any of its equivalents, as materialists do, is to destroy the meaning of the Word of God. In the Sacred Scriptures, death never means ceasing to exist when used relative to man. Hence, the statement, "The soul that sinneth, it shall die" (Ezekiel 18:20), is not a proof that souls become extinct.

The True Meaning

Summarizing the passages, these truths become very clear: death does not literally mean, nor does it include, extinction of being, cessation of existence, or even dissolution. Life and death do not mean simple existence and simple non-existence. Life is a condition of existence; it is not existence itself; it is something more—something super-added. Existence can be where life is not. For example, rocks exist, but they do not have life. Death is a condition of existence but also a condition opposite to life. Eternal life does not mean eternal existence, neither does the second death mean eternal non-existence. Rather, life and death have reference to two states or conditions of existence, or union and separation. Hence, immortality and eternal life are not the same in the Scriptures.

Physical life is a connection with God through nature; physical death is disseverance with that system. This is true, whether a person is referring to a man or a tree. God produces all three kinds of life in this world—animal, vegetable, and spiritual. Hence, in all three are three kinds of death—animal, vegetable, and spiritual. A man may have connection with God in one sense, and not in another. A man can die in just as many senses as he can be separated from God. What people call death does not involve extinction, only change. Dissolution of the body after death does not mean annihilation of the spirit. Since man has a connection with his Maker through physical and spiritual natures, he may die either physically or spiritually. As already learned, God is the only original, ever-enduring fountain of life: He "giveth to all life, and breath, and all things" (Acts 17:25). Union with God in some way is essential to all life; separation from Him is always death. Definitely, death does not ever mean annihilation in the Bible. Materialists are wrong on the meaning of death. Annihilation is a name for what never yet occurred to any spirit of man and never can.

Further, if materialists could show that the soul is a material substance, it would not disprove its immortality. For science teaches that matter is never destroyed; it merely changes form. A house may burn to the ground, but in all this transformation of matter, there is no annihilation. Not a single atom has ceased to be. This principle is known as the law of the Conservation of Energy. The fact is, there is no evidence from either the Bible or science that a single atom of matter that God has created has ever been or ever shall be annihilated. Man has no power over matter to destroy it. He can only change its form.

Thus, the materialistic contention of annihilation of man at death, or at the judgment, is purely hypothetical. Satan told Mother Eve that she would not surely die (Genesis 3:4). He is still preaching the same damnable doctrine. Man can die—become separated from God—both in time and in eternity. Having once brought a soul into existence, God will not let it disappear into nothingness. Annihilation of created beings is not a part of God's plan, and no created being has the power to annihilate any other being.

Therefore, the word *death* in the Bible always means separation, not annihilation, and every physically living person accountable to God is both dead and alive. If he is a Christian, he is dead to sin and alive to Christ; if he is not a Christian, he is alive to sin and dead to Christ.

At death—the separation of the spirit from the body—people often grieve; and yet this is not the death over which one should be most concerned. The awful death is the death of the soul. "The soul that sinneth, it shall die" (Ezekiel 18:20). At the final judgment every person whom the Lord places on the left hand will be cast into the lake of fire, and that soul (in the resurrected body) will be eternally separated from God. And for all those who are lost, no cessation of being will come to relieve the soul of its agony, but it must continue to writhe amid the agonies of the eternal torment while the unending ages roll on.

Moreover, remember, too, that eternal life is not primarily everlasting existence, though the popular concept of eternal life is merely the continuation of being, mere future existence. But all men will have eternal existence; the lost sinner will exist forever. Immortality assures all men of unending existence, but eternal life and eternal existence are two different things. Everlasting existence is a part of eternal life, but not the main part. It is the kind of life (the quality), not the length of life (the quantity), that predominates the Scriptural conception of eternal life.

The word *immortality* in these Scriptures describes the imperishable existence of the soul, regardless of the quality of living which is associated with it here on earth. The Bible nowhere speaks of annihilation, which means the complete extinction of being. All men will have eternal existence—some in happiness, because of a holy life; others in torment, because of a sinful life.

The truth is, the physically dead are still living—with their own individual personalities. It is not a case of "they have been," but "they are." The dead are alive, out of their bodies. They wait for the day of the resurrection of their bodies. All mankind will have a future eternal existence—some in happiness, because of a holy life; others in torment, because of a sinful life. Therefore, if one is born but once (physically), he will die twice (physically and the second death), but if he is born twice (physically and spiritually) and faithfully lives the Christian life, he will die but once (physically).

Questions for Discussion

1. How do materialists define death?
2. In what three senses is the word *death* used in the Bible?
3. In what three senses is the word *life* used in the Bible?
4. What is the Scriptural meaning of the terms *life* and *death?* Give several passages to support the Biblical definition of each.
5. In what sense did Adam die the day he ate the forbidden fruit?
6. In what sense can the dead in sin hear and live?
7. How does the believer pass from death to life?
8. How can the dead bury the dead?
9. Can a person be both dead and alive at the same time? Can he be both in existence and out of existence at the same time?
10. How can living Christians be dead? How can dead Christians be alive?
11. In what sense does the obedient believer never die?
12. Does life mean mere existence? Does death mean mere non-existence?
13. What is the Scriptural meaning of the second death?
14. What is the Biblical meaning of eternal life? In what sense does the believer now have eternal life?
15. Who will receive the punishment in the lake of fire? Who will receive eternal life?
16. Where (in what sphere) is spiritual life located?
17. In what way is a church mentioned in the Bible as a dead, yet living, church?
18. Why was the prodigal son dead while still living?
19. How are living people who are sinners called dead?
20. What does *annihilate* mean? Is the word found in the Bible?
21. Does physical death and/or the second death mean annihilation of the spirit?
22. Will any soul ever be annihilated? Defend your answer.

– 9 –

Are the Dead Conscious?

"Son, remember . . ."
Luke 16:25

Death, as proved in Scripture, is not an extinction or annihilation, but separation of the soul from the physical body. Friends and loved ones have already gone from this life, and all now living will soon be called to leave this world. So man seeks a scriptural answer to the questions, "Is the spirit in its disembodied state conscious or unconscious?" "What is the condition of the departed soul after death and before the resurrection of the body?" It is natural to ask, "What shall be on the other side of death?" These questions will now be considered. In this chapter several statements of Scripture that clearly teach that the departed soul is conscious between death and the resurrection shall be noticed.

The Rich Man and Lazarus Were Conscious

Christ taught the conscious existence of both righteous and wicked souls after death in His narrative of the rich man and Lazarus:

> Now there was a certain rich man, and he was clothed in purple and fine linen, faring sumptuously every day: and a certain beggar named Lazarus was laid at his gate, full of sores, and desiring to be fed with the crumbs that fell from the rich man's table; yea, even the dogs came and licked his sores. And it came to pass, that the beggar died, and that he was carried away by the angels into Abraham's bosom: and the rich man also died, and was buried. And in Hades he lifted up his eyes, being in torments, and seeth Abraham afar off, and Lazarus in his bosom. And he cried and said, Father Abraham, have mercy on me, and send Lazarus, that he may dip the tip of his finger in water, and cool my tongue: for I am in anguish in this flame. But Abraham said, Son, remember that thou in thy lifetime receivedst thy good things, and Lazarus in like manner evil things: but now here he is comforted, and thou art in anguish. And besides all this, between us and you there is a great gulf fixed, that they that would pass from hence to you may not be able, and that none may cross over from thence to us. And he said, I pray thee therefore, father, that thou wouldest

> send him to my father's house; for I have five brethren; that he may testify unto them, lest they also come into this place of torment. But Abraham saith, They have Moses and the prophets; let them hear them. And he said, Nay, father Abraham: but if one go to them from the dead, they will repent. And he said unto him, If they hear not Moses and the prophets, neither will they be persuaded, if one rise from the dead (Luke 16:19–31).

In this narrative, Christ gives complete proof of conscious existence after death. Were this the only reference in Scripture concerning this subject it would be wholly sufficient.

Jesus knew whereof He spoke when He talked of life beyond the grave. He told of the fact and something of the nature of the life beyond death. This narrative teaches that the soul lives after the body dies, in bliss or misery, according to the life lived upon this earth. The rich man died and entered immediately into a state of misery; he was in torments. Not only did he know of his misery, but also he remembered his five brothers, still alive on earth, and wished to keep them from coming to his place of torment. He was told to remember his life back on earth. This no doubt would help him to understand why he was now tormented.

Lazarus died and entered immediately into a state of blessedness; he was comforted and knew it. Hence, both the rich man and Lazarus were in a state of conscious existence, for such could not be true if they had not been. They not only were in another state of existence, but they also could still remember things as they knew them on earth. Memory is one of man's unique endowments.

Further, Lazarus recognized himself as Lazarus, and the rich man recognized himself as the rich man, and he recognized Lazarus in Abraham's bosom. Although out of their bodies, the rich man and Lazarus were the same mental, spiritual beings they were on earth. Here is taught also the preservation and perpetuation of personal identity in the life beyond the grave.

Although this is plain, materialists seek to evade the force of the language of Jesus by saying that this is just a parable. Many ask, "Is this a parable or history?" This is not a parable. But even if we say it is, the narrative is still true. The Scripture teaches truth, not falsehood. Sometimes Christ used historical facts to illustrate spiritual truth. At other times, He used parables to teach things that did, or could, occur. At all times, the parables were founded upon facts. Not one of the Lord's parables is without real fact for its foundation. Christ stated facts in His parables and then compared the things to be taught by these facts. Were there not literal vineyards, sheepfolds, and wedding feasts? Were there not literal prodigal sons, lost money, and straying sheep? As, for example, a man has a hundred sheep, and one of them goes astray. The shepherd searches for it until he finds it, and then rejoices. This fact illustrated, so Jesus taught the love and interest of God for lost souls. So, if the account of the rich man and Lazarus is history or a parable, the facts are the same. The parables of the Lord never teach falsehoods. A parable is true in every particular, never false or unreal, as is a fable. Hence, Christ's statements about the rich man and Lazarus, recorded by Inspiration, must all be facts, or the narrative is false. Jesus, being divine, surely knew conditions as they existed in the other world, and He could speak of them. Such a state of things as the Lord described in this narrative did exist, and He gave an accurate description of realities there. In fact, there never was and never can be a more emphatic historic record of matters of fact than that of the rich man and Lazarus. Christ said, "There was a certain rich man." Was there? He also said there was "a certain beggar named Lazarus." Was there, or did Jesus lie about it? Christ also said that Lazarus died. Did he? Christ also said that the rich man also died. Did he? Even a casual reading of the story will reveal these were statements of an actual case, given for the purpose of teaching spiritual truth. The story relates to particular persons, one named.

Furthermore, the parables recorded by Luke which were given by Christ usually begin as follows: "And he spake a parable unto them, saying . . ." (See Luke 12:16; 5:36; 6:39; 8:4; 13:6; 15:3; 18:1,9; 19:11; 20:9; 21:29.) The account of the rich man and Lazarus does not begin in such fashion; the word *parable* is not in the text. Christ did not say anything is like unto these two men, so why call it a parable? Just say Jesus was describing the conditions both of the good and bad spirits (souls) in the state between death and the resurrection; He was simply stating facts; He told what happened immediately after the deaths of the rich man and Lazarus. They were living and they were in Hades.

Jesus, therefore, lifted the curtain dividing this world from the next and permitted man a glimpse of the conditions beyond the grave. Some lessons taught by the Savior regarding conditions hereafter are:

- There is a future life after physical death, an existence beyond the grave.
- The dead still have a conscious existence. Souls are represented as living, talking, remembering, and being comforted or tormented after death. The rich man and Lazarus had such experiences.
- The identity of self is preserved in the disembodied state. Every man who has died is at this instant in full possession of all his faculties.
- The doctrine of universal salvation is also shown to be false. The righteous and the unrighteous are forever separated with no change after death. (This point will be discussed more fully in a later chapter.)
- Those who will not believe the testimony of Scripture would not be convinced by one if he returned from the dead. No power was at that time equal to the writing of Moses and the prophets (the Old Testament) to bring men to repentance, and surely none can now be equal to the teach-

ing of Christ and the apostles to bring sinners to repentance (the New Testament). The gospel is the power of God unto salvation (Romans 1:16). God's way of influencing men is through the gospel.

- The wicked in conscious torment remember friends and loved ones on earth, are concerned about them, and would send missionaries to them if they could.
- Those who live lives devoted to earthly riches and pleasures and then die in their sins will go to torment, as it was with the rich man. His sin was not in having riches, but the misuse of those riches. Similarly, the righteousness of Lazarus was not in being poor, but in pleasing God. Thus, the narrative not only teaches the right and wrong use of riches but also teaches the consequences hereafter of their use. The condition of the men involved was determined by the manner in which they had conducted themselves on earth. The Bible teaches that there is no arbitrary arrangement of election and reprobation on God's part, but each individual is the arbiter of his own destiny.

While all matters related in this narrative were facts, it was necessary for man's understanding for the Lord to use some figurative language. It was impossible for the Lord to speak and for man to comprehend, other than in human language. The Scriptures speak of God as having human form—ears, hands, eyes, etc., as already noted. So, figurative language is used to describe the things that are real. The Holy Spirit uses man's language with which to speak of God (a bodiless spirit), heaven, hell, and disembodied spirit-beings. There may be little reason to conclude there was or is any literal flame of fire or water or gulf in the spirit realm, but there is something real and certain represented by the terms in the narrative.

Many illustrations of this point could be given from the Bible. Take, for instance, the description of heaven, represented to man's mind in images, symbols, and figures by the aid of which he gains a faint conception of the eternal city of the redeemed. The Bible says a river flows through it, and upon the banks of which trees grow. It is a city of pure gold, with foundations and walls of precious stones. To interpret these literally would only detract from the beauty of that blessed home. They are symbols of spiritual realities. Indeed, it does not yet appear what the righteous shall be, nor what heaven shall be like (1 John 3:2). Man in the flesh cannot comprehend those joys because there is no language that can adequately describe them. The joys of heaven will exceed one's fondest anticipation. John could not find language to describe what he saw without using words—figures for the real thing—and the thing itself is far more beautiful than the figure used to describe it. The principle of rhetoric is that a figure of speech is used only when it is impossible to convey the thought through ordinary language; a figure of speech conveys the thought as far as is possible.

The same can be said of the descriptions of hell or eternal punishment. People ask, "Is it literal fire in hell, or is this a figure of speech?" If a figure of speech, the thing figured is far worse than the figure itself, and what is the real thing like?

Again, consider the book of life in heaven (Revelation 20:12). Surely no one supposes it to be a literal book, but something is there that answers to a book and is best illustrated by a book. Hence, the account of the rich man and Lazarus, even if by figurative language—fire, flame, water, gulf—prove reality; the facts are real, and the meaning is real. The conscious joys and torments of these persons in the disembodied spirit-world are true facts, though described in figurative language.

What further proof is needed to show the use of figurative language to describe that which is real? Concerning wicked Herod Antipas, Christ said: "Go and say to that fox . . ." (Luke 13:32). Was not Herod a literal man? Indeed. *Fox* was figurative language forcibly describing him as a crafty man, like a fox. So also of the words in this story of the rich man and the beggar: the conscious joys and torments of these persons in the disembodied spirit-world are true facts, though described in figurative language.

Jesus said, "My sheep hear my voice, and I know them, and they follow me" (John 10:27). In this text our Lord used metaphorical language. He literally meant: "My followers listen to me and I know who they are and they obey me." No one should have difficulty in understanding this. People use figures of speech every day in their conversation. One often says of a mean, crafty man: "He is a snake in the grass," but he does not intend to be understood that the man is not a man but a literal snake in the grass.

Summarizing these statements of Christ about the rich man and Lazarus, two great truths can be learned pertaining to life in the hereafter: (1) To die is not extinction, as already shown. The spirit survives the dissolution of the body and lives after the body has returned to the dust. The soul of man does not die or cease to exist with the death of the body. (2) Disembodied spirits are in a state of consciousness, happy or miserable, depending upon the life they have lived while in the body. They are not only conscious of existence, but they also retain memories of earthly life. The Sacred Writings, therefore, teach that man's spirit, created by Jehovah and in His image, is distinct from the body in which it dwells and is capable of a separate and conscious existence when the body is dissolved. This is true both of the righteous and the wicked during the period after death and before the resurrection of the immortal body. Personal joys follow immediately after death for the righteous and retributions follow for the wicked. Since the disembodied spirits of the righteous and the unrighteous are now either happy or miserable, they are in a state of conscious existence, and Jesus mentioned the name of a person.

At the separation of the spirit from the body, the spirit does not take away anything that is essential to the body; neither does the body retain anything that is essential to the spirit. At death, the body with all of its essential material elements goes to the grave, while at the same time the spirit with all of its essential non-material elements goes back to God. The body goes to the grave and is unconscious. The spirit with its consciousness goes to God, for consciousness is a quality of the spirit. Physical death does not destroy the spirit and its powers. Man will be conscious and his mind active and his memory vivid though he has passed into the other world. Abraham said to the rich man: "Son, remember . . ." How could he remember if he did not have a memory? It is evident that man's memory will never be blotted out. Throughout all eternity every person will be fully conscious that he is himself and be able to say, "I am the same identical person who lived on earth." Each shall exist as himself.

Man's prayer should be like that of Balaam's: "Let me die the death of the righteous, and let my last end be like his!" (Numbers 23:10). Surely such a joyful, peaceful end is desired. Who does not desire that his death be full of peace and hope? The sweetest of all consolation in the hour of bereavement is the assurance that the spirit of the departed is at rest in the bosom of God. It takes the sting out of death to know that one's righteous loved ones whom he has given up are still alive and fully conscious in God's care and keeping on "the other side." So when we die, we do not go to heaven but to Hades. But the Lord is in heaven now (Acts 1:9–11; 2:31–33). And one day death and Hades will be no more (Revelation 20:14).

The Wicked Are Now under Punishment

That the souls of the wicked and righteous are in conscious existence after death is taught in Scripture other than the narrative of the rich man and Lazarus. The apostle Peter affirmed: "The Lord knoweth how to deliver the godly out of temptation, and to keep the unrighteous under punishment unto the day of judgment" (2 Peter 2:9). Since the disembodied souls of the unrighteous are now suffering punishment, they are in a state of conscious existence.

To Depart and Be with Christ Is Far Better

The apostle Paul viewed death not as a loss but as a gain, a departure to be with Christ. "But I am in a strait betwixt the two, having the desire to depart and be with Christ; for it is very far better: yet to abide in the flesh is more needful for your sake" (Philippians 1:23–24). The words in the original, here translated "very far better," are very emphatic. They mean "better beyond all expression," "by much far better."

To Paul there was an advantage in dying over living. It would be far better for him, in the midst of hardships and imprisonment, to depart and to be with Christ. He did not think of death as cessation of life or unconscious existence. If this had been true, how could this condition after death have been far better than living in this world? One cannot imagine that he meant he preferred the total blank of unconscious existence—not to mention annihilation!—to the mingled joys and sorrows of this wonderful life on earth serving the Lord.

Paul desired two things: (1) to be released from the difficulties of this life and enjoy the rest provided by the Lord for the righteous, and (2) to remain in the flesh and benefit the church and the world in labors as an apostle. He could not do both, so he was in a strait between two desires. To him, personally, to depart this life for the rest was a condition greatly preferred. His soul would have been immediately with the Lord, and he would have been conscious of the fact. In the face of death he could say, "To die is gain" (Philippians 1:21). This passage teaches that the soul of the believer is made happy when separated from the body at death. If, like Paul, the Christian can say, "To me to live is Christ," then he can say, "To die is gain." Thus, for the faithful child of God, death holds no pangs of remorse. He goes to be comforted, which is far better than living in his earthly body here.

Paul's Account of the Third Heaven Is Recorded

Paul argued distinction of spirit and body and taught that spirits are in conscious existence in or out of the body. He said:

> I know a man in Christ, fourteen years ago (whether in the body, I know not; or whether out of the body, I know not; God knoweth), such a one caught up even to the third heaven. And I know such a man (whether in the body, or apart from the body, I know not; God knoweth), how that he was caught up into Paradise, and heard unspeakable words, which it is not lawful for a man to utter (2 Corinthians 12:2–4).

The context shows that Paul was defending his apostleship by citing his visions and revelations (cf. vv. 1, 6, 7). At the time of the happening, and even later when Paul wrote this, only God knew whether Paul was in or out of the body. If out of the body, Paul's spirit continued to exist in consciousness while in the third heaven. If in the body, his spirit and fleshly body together experienced things in Paradise. At least Paul knew it was possible to have been out of the body while he experienced things unlawful to be told about Paradise. Paul's visions and revelations permitted him to know that the soul could continue to exist in consciousness, whether in or out of the body. But since he did not know whether he was in the body or out, it follows that he may have had such an experience out of the body, which is certainly possible.

Hence, the spirit in man and life after death are both clearly established. Paul realized the spirit might be taken to Paradise without the body and so be in a state of separate existence and consciousness. What was true in this case is likewise true in every other case of separation of body and spirit—the spirit continues in conscious existence after departure. The departed are consciously alive on the other side.

Regardless of when this experience occurred, the truth is the same. The passage plainly establishes the fact of conscious life in and out of the body and refutes every phase of the doctrine of materialism. As already learned, this system of infidelity teaches that man is all matter, that when man dies all of him ceases to exist, and that there is no conscious existence apart from the body. This passage teaches that man is more than a body with physical life. It proves that man may see, hear, and know, although out of the body.

Souls under the Altar Were Conscious

Another passage equally conclusive in proving that disembodied spirits are conscious and aware of past experiences upon earth is this:

> And when he opened the fifth seal, I saw underneath the altar the souls of them that had been slain for the word of God, and for the testimony which they held: and they cried with a great voice, saying, How long, O Master, the holy and true, dost thou not judge and avenge our blood on them that dwell on the earth? And there was given them to each one a white robe; and it was said unto them, that they should rest yet for a little time, until their fellow-servants also and their brethren, who should be killed even as they were, should have fulfilled their course (Revelation 6:9–11).

The souls under the altar were people who had suffered for righteousness, even to death. The bodies of these first-century martyrs had been slain, but their spirits, although in a disembodied state, were alive, conscious, and aware of the means by which they were killed. Furthermore, these spirits knew their blood had not yet been avenged—their murderers were still unpunished. Hence, these disembodied souls knew why they were there: they had been murdered. They inquired when judgment would be exercised on those who had been guilty of their murder. These individuals in the spirit realm were conscious.

For these souls underneath the altar, the period between their martyrdom and the resurrection at the last day is called "a little season" (KJV), a period of time. They are still waiting the day of judgment, at which time God will avenge the blood of all Christians who have died for Him (cf. Romans 12:19–21). The righteous should never forget that the Lord is on His throne. And then, no matter what the outward fortunes, they will be victorious at last. He that is with His church is mightier than they that are with her foes.

The Thief Was "Today" in Paradise

That the believer enters into a conscious state at once upon the death of the body is indicated by Christ in His statement to the thief on the cross: "Today shalt thou be with me in Paradise" (Luke 23:43). By this Jesus simply meant that He and the thief were both going to die and their spirits would be together that very day in Paradise. In Paradise with Christ did not and could not mean either a state of blank unconsciousness or non-existence. Some try to make the verse read: "I say to you today, you will be with me in Paradise," meaning at some distant time in the future. But this is not true because we know from Psalm 16:10 and Peter's quote in Acts 2:27 that Jesus died and went to Hades the very same day. But He was not left in Hades because of the resurrection. So, just as in the narrative concerning Lazarus, Jesus also died and went to Paradise in Hades, and the thief went with Him the same day. Jesus returned from Hades and Paradise three days later, on the day of His resurrection, after which He ascended to the Father (John 20:17).

As for Lazarus, Abraham, and the thief on the cross, they are in Hades even until this very day. They are awaiting the second coming of Christ when death and Hades will be cast into the lake of fire and they will then be transported into heaven forever (Revelation 20:13–14).

Stephen Had Faith in the Hereafter

Almost equally decisive proof of consciousness after death is the case of Stephen (Acts 7:55–60). As the mob rushed upon him, "he . . . looked up stedfastly into heaven, and saw the glory of God, and Jesus standing on the right hand of God, and said, Behold, I see the heavens opened, and the Son of man standing on the right hand of God." Immediately the mob stoned Stephen, calling upon the Lord, and saying, Lord Jesus, receive my spirit. Now who can doubt what was this first Christian martyr's expectation? After saying, "Lord Jesus, receive my spirit," even as his Lord had said on the cross, "Father, into thy hands I commend my spirit" (Luke 23:46), it is not reasonable to think that Stephen thought his spirit would become either extinct or unconscious. "And when he had said this, he fell asleep"; that is, he died, and his spirit went to be with the Lord.

The Righteous Dead Are Happy

Another proof of immediate blessedness of the dying saint is found in Revelation: "Blessed are the dead who die in the Lord from henceforth: yea, saith the Spirit, that they may rest from their labors; for their works follow with them" (Revelation 14:13). The word *blessed* may also be translated "happy." "Happy are the dead who die in the Lord." "Blessed [happy] . . . from henceforth" suggests the promise of immediate blessedness. This passage, therefore, does not describe a state of unconsciousness but active enjoyment. One lost to all consciousness is not happy, yet the verse says those who die in the Lord are happy. It does not say they will be happy, but that they are happy now. The righteous dead are happy after they die, and a person cannot be happy while unconscious. Hence, the righteous dead must be conscious.

Moreover, the blessing here pronounced is upon a certain class of the dead—those who die in the Lord. This implies two things as necessary to secure this blessing: (1) to come into the Lord, for no one can die in the Lord who does not first come into Him; (2) to live faithfully in Christ till death, for no one can die in the Lord and receive Christ's mercy unless he is faithful unto death (cf. Romans 6:3–4; Galatians 3:27; Revelation 2:10; John 15:1–8).

The uniform teaching of the New Testament is that salvation comes to men through Christ alone (Acts 4:12). People err when they say all is well with all men at death, because all is not well with the disobedient. To speak, as some do, as if all men at death enter the blessed life is contrary to the Scriptures. Two ways of dying are described in the Bible: (1) dying in sin and (2) dying in Christ. "Except ye believe that I am he, ye shall die in your sins," said Jesus (John 8:24); and "whither I go, ye cannot come" (John 8:21). "Blessed [happy] are the dead who die in the Lord" (Revelation 14:13; cf. Psalm 116:15). There are the dead in Christ (1 Thessalonians 4:16) as well as the dead out of Christ. "Say ye of the righteous, that it shall be well with him: . . . Woe unto the wicked!" (Isaiah 3:10–11). God never pronounces the wicked who die as blessed or happy, but it is a blessed thing to die in the Lord. Hence, the closing scenes of life have two aspects, bright or dark, calm or terrible, according to the character of him who dies. For the Christian, heaven's peace descends at the close of life on earth. Blair said:

> The last end of the good man is peace.
> How calm his exit!

There Is Hope in Death

The wise man stated: "The righteous hath hope in his death" (Proverbs 14:32 KJV). Hope is made up of desire and expectation. A person who is unconscious cannot have any desire or expectation in his death. The passage does not say that the righteous hath hope at his death or before his death, but in his death. The righteous, therefore, are conscious and able to hope in death. The people of God have always believed in conscious existence beyond the grave. Such is the teaching of the Holy Scriptures.

The Righteous Are Carried By the Angels to Rest

Note again the language of Christ concerning the death of Lazarus: "And it came to pass, that the beggar died, and that he was carried away by the angels into Abraham's bosom" (Luke 16:22). Carried away by the angels! What a wonderful, comforting thought! Perhaps the beggar had no one to care for him in his hour of death. His body might have been buried in the potter's field. He did not have a big funeral as the rich man had. Yet Lazarus did not die alone, because he had the companionship of angels when his soul departed its earthly house. He had heavenly pallbearers.

God will see that the righteous here on this earth shall not be left alone in death. How comforting to know that the Christian does not go alone when he exchanges worlds, and no harm can come to him in the dark valley. "I will be with thee," says the Good Shepherd, and the believer replies, "I will fear no evil; for thou art with me" (Psalm 23:4). The child of God approaches death with sweet assurance that death is the gateway to endless joy. Who can deny that ministering angels, unseen by human eyes, are sent from heaven to watch around the bed of the dying Christian and to convey his ransomed spirit home to rest, like they gathered around the dying Lazarus and carried him to rest in Abraham's bosom? Some sing about the angels coming for the souls of the righteous at their death.

My latest sun is sinking fast,
My race is nearly run;
My strongest trials now are past,
My triumph is begun.

I've almost gained my heav'nly home,
My spirit loudly sings;
Thy holy ones, behold, they come!
I hear the noise of wings.

O come, angel band,
Come, and around me stand;
O bear me away on your snowy wings
To my immortal home.
—Wm. B. Bradbury

Then when one shall have crossed the Jordan of Death, his dear friends and loved ones who have gone on before shall meet and greet him on the other side.

He will keep me till the river
Rolls its waters at my feet;
Then He'll bear me safely over,
Where the loved ones I shall meet.
—P. P. Bilhorn

Although these poems were written by men, they suggest the Biblical teaching of the righteous being conveyed to a place of rest at death. Nearly three thousand years ago David wrote: "Yea, though I walk through the valley of the shadow of death, I will fear no evil: for thou art with me" (Psalm 23:4 KJV). O the bliss of the redeemed spirits when the dawn of eternal blessedness begins to break upon their enraptured vision!

Not Soul-Sleeping

Some believe in soul-sleeping, that is, that the spirit exists after death in a state of total unconsciousness. This doctrine is referred to as soul-sleeping, and those who hold this view assert that the Holy Scriptures so teach. Inasmuch as the Bible is the only reliable source of information regarding the state of the dead, passages most commonly used to argue the theory of soul-sleeping should be examined. The question is: "Does the soul, apart from the body, sleep in unconscious existence until the resurrection?" Keep in mind, the Bible does not contradict itself.

Death Is a Sleep

Passages of Scripture which speak of death as a sleep are used by the adherents of this belief to teach that the soul is unconscious between death and the resurrection. Jesus often referred to death as a kind of sleep. Concerning the daughter of Jairus, He said: "The damsel is not dead, but sleepeth" (Matthew 9:24; cf. Mark 5:39; Luke 8:52). After Lazarus died, Jesus said to the apostles: "Our friend Lazarus is fallen asleep; but I go, that I may awake him out of sleep" (John 11:11). They understood the word *sleep* literally. His disciples asked why they should go if Lazarus was merely asleep, and then Christ told them in plain terms: "Lazarus is dead" (v. 14; cf. Deuteronomy 31:16; 1 Corinthians 15:6, 18; 2 Peter 3:4).

However, note that the word sleep is used figuratively in the Bible; there is a resemblance between a dead body and the body of one asleep. A dead person looks as though he were asleep. Sleep is applied to death, then, because in some respects it is like sleep. Although there is repose in sleep, sleep does not suggest extinction of existence or unconsciousness in one who sleeps, for the mind of a sleeping man may be active in dreams. The mind never sleeps. One still lives, even in sleep.

In the Scriptures, therefore, the word *sleep,* when used concerning physical death, always refers only to the body of a person, not to the spirit. Now note some passages which clearly show this.

- "And many of them that sleep in the dust of the earth shall awake, some to everlasting life, and some to shame and everlasting contempt" (Daniel 12:2). Asleep where? In the dust! It has already been learned that only the body goes to the dust, since only the body came from the dust; the spirit does not go to the dust but to God who gave it (Ecclesiastes 12:7). The bodies which sleep in the dust of the earth till the resurrection shall rise when Christ comes again (1 Corinthians 15). As to his material, bodily form, man sleeps in the dust at death.

- When Christ arose from the dead, the Bible says "many bodies of the saints that had fallen asleep were raised; and coming forth out of the tombs after his resurrection they entered into the holy city" (Matthew 27:52–53). They came out of what? The graves! Where, then, were these saints asleep? In the tombs. But what part was in the tomb? The body.

- When Stephen, the first Christian martyr, was being stoned, "he kneeled down, and cried with a loud voice, Lord, lay not this sin to their charge. And when he had said this, he fell asleep" (Acts 7:60). Later devout men came and buried him—that is, they buried his body (Acts 8:2). It was Stephen's body then that fell asleep.

- Paul clearly stated that David's body was in the grave sleeping: "For David, after he had in his own generation served the counsel of God, fell asleep, and was laid unto his fathers [i.e., in the grave], and saw corruption" (Acts 13:36; cf. 2 Samuel 7:12).

  But when the body (the outer man) sleeps in the grave, the real man (the inner man) will not go to sleep with the body. It will leave the body at death and go to some other sphere in conscious existence. James states, "The body apart from the spirit is dead" (James 2:26).

- To the Corinthians, Paul wrote: "Behold, I tell you a mystery: We all shall not sleep [i.e., die], but we shall all be changed [i.e., in our bodies, both the living and the dead, when the Lord comes again], in a moment, in the twinkling of an eye, at the last trump: for the trumpet shall sound, and the dead shall be raised incorruptible, and we [who are living] shall be changed" (1 Corinthians 15:51–52).

- To the Thessalonians, Paul also wrote: "But we would not have you ignorant, brethren, concerning them that fall asleep [i.e., those who die]; that ye sorrow not, even as the rest, who have no hope. For if we believe that Jesus died and rose again, even so them also that are fallen asleep in Jesus [i.e., the disembodied spirits of the righteous] will God bring with him. For this we say unto you by the word of the Lord, that we that are alive, that are left unto the coming of the Lord, shall in no wise precede them that are fallen asleep" (1 Thessalonians 4:13–15). Here again, sleep refers to bodies in the graves of the departed saints.

The word *cemetery,* the burial place of the dead, literally means a sleeping chamber or burial place. However, it is a sleeping place only for dead bodies as they await the resurrection. The spirits are not in the burying places; only fleshly bodies are there. The souls are not asleep anywhere, but alive. God "is not the God of the dead, but of the living: for all live unto him" (Luke 20:38).

Because of false teaching on soul-sleeping, it must be emphasized that it is the body, and only this part of man, that sleeps in death. The Bible does not say the soul falls asleep. Although the body sleeps in the dust of the earth, the spirit by no means sleeps after death—the soul does not return to the ground. Hence, in the Holy Scriptures, sleep is a metaphorical way of speaking of the death of the body. In the Bible, death does not mean either unconsciousness or extinction.

Man's spirit retains its consciousness and intellectual quality in death. God does not give man an unconscious spirit, but a conscious soul (1 Corinthians 2:11). Since the spirit of man knows, it retains its knowledge when it returns to God. The Bible view of death carries nothing to suggest the error of the doctrine of soul-sleeping.

However, death is not comparable to sleep in every respect, yet it is like sleep in some respects. Death, like sleep, is a cessation from activity; and, like sleep, it brings quiet and rest. But sleep also implies an awakening. As the sleeping person awakes in the morning to activities of a new day, so will the bodies that sleep in the graves, after a season of rest, be raised up to live another life at the general resurrection. What a beautiful picture of death! Christians fall asleep in death. That is the word! It is a case of "good night," the closing of a person's eyes on one scene to open them on a fairer scene. Death is only a sleep until the time when God shall awake them. Hence, sleep refers to the body, not to the soul.

The Dead Know Nothing

The Scripture most used as proof-text that the dead are unconscious is Ecclesiastes 9:5: "For the living know that they shall die: but the dead know not anything, neither have they any more a reward; for the memory of them is forgotten." The next verse should also be read: "As well their love, as their hatred and their envy, is perished long ago; neither have they any more a portion for ever in anything that is done under the sun." This passage has reference solely to what the dead can know, or do, "under the sun"; that is, the dead are cut off from the active, busy world in which they once lived.

Furthermore, if one reads opinions into this passage, why not say it means soul-death, for if the dead know not anything, the soul may cease to exist rather than sleep. Neither is true. The passage affirms that, after death, man's activity ceases on earth. Also, this passage, without qualifications, and all-inclusive, would deny rewards after the resurrection to the righteous, for it says, "Neither have they any more a reward" (KJV). Are the righteous dead cut off from rewards? Abraham, Isaac, and Jacob are dead. Do they have any more a reward? It must be apparent that the two phrases, "the dead know not anything" and "neither have they any more a reward," are qualified by "under the sun." "The dead know not anything . . . under the sun," "neither have they any more a reward [under the sun]."

Too, similar statements in the Bible, which use the expression "know not anything" show that the phrase is limited in its context. For example: "Jonathan's lad gathered up the arrows, and came to his master. But the lad knew not anything" (1 Samuel 20:38–39). Was the lad unconscious while running after the arrows? Surely not. Again: "And with Absalom went two hundred men out of Jerusalem, that were invited and went in their simplicity; and they knew not anything" (2 Samuel 15:11). Were these two hundred men unconscious as they marched? Of course not! This is an adapted expression and means they did not know anything about the plans of Absalom.

Similarly, Paul said of a certain person: "He is puffed up, knowing nothing" (1 Timothy 6:4). Did he mean that the man was unconscious? Again, "If any man thinketh that he knoweth anything, he knoweth not yet as he ought to know" (1 Corinthians 8:2). If "know not" means the person is unconscious, then we have an unconscious man thinking. One often says, "He knows nothing" or "He does not know what it is all about." He means the individual is either uneducated or lacks information on some particular subject. No man knows everything about everything. In some matters at least, it may be said of the best-informed man, "He knows nothing."

The same idea, then, is in Ecclesiastes 9:5. The passage states that the dead know nothing of what is going on here on earth after they die. That is all that it teaches. The Scripture has no reference whatsoever to the spirit after death being unconscious. "Under the sun" or "on the earth" is the limiting clause. Thus, insofar as this world is concerned, the dead have neither knowledge, reward, nor portion.

Solomon also stated that the body only goes to the grave, but the spirit goes to God (Ecclesiastes 12:7). He again said, "There is no work, nor device, nor knowledge, nor wisdom, in Sheol, whither thou goest" (Ecclesiastes 9:10). The body which goes into the grave does not work nor have knowledge; but the spirit does not go into the grave. "The dead know not anything," but what part of man is dead? It is the body. Only the dead bodies in their graves know not anything—the spirit that knows is not in the grave. There is no contradiction, therefore, of this verse with any statement of the Bible that teaches that the spirits of the departed are conscious. However, the dead do not know what is happening in this world since they departed. Thus, one cannot pray to one's deceased mother and expect her to hear. This does not mean she is in an unconscious state; she does not know what is going on in this world. So prayers to saints are to no avail.

Man's Thoughts Perish

Another verse is used in an attempt to prove that man's soul is unconscious in death: "His breath goeth forth, he returneth to his earth; in that very day his thoughts perish" (Psalm 146:4). The footnote says "purposes" for thoughts. The purposes of one's mind are his thoughts: "My days are past, my purposes are broken off, even the thoughts of my heart" (Job 17:11). Man's unaccomplished purposes perish when he dies, but he does not cease to exist at that time. The Bible teaches that the unrighteous must forsake his thoughts to be converted (Isaiah 55:7). But this does not mean he must die physically or that he must stop thinking. So, man's thoughts, intentions, and purposes come to naught on earth the day he dies. But the mind of man is one thing; his plans another.

Other Scriptures Are Used

Other passages are used to bolster the theory that the spirit of man has no conscious existence from death to the resurrection:

- "But the wicked shall perish, and the enemies of Jehovah shall be as the fat of lambs: they shall consume; in smoke shall they consume away" (Psalm 37:20).
- "For Sheol cannot praise thee, death cannot celebrate thee: they that go down into the pit cannot hope for thy truth" (Isaiah 38:18);
- "For in death there is no remembrance of thee: in Sheol who shall give thee thanks?" (Psalm 6:5).
- "The dead praise not Jehovah, neither any that go down into silence" (Psalm 115:17).

The evident meaning of these passages is that here man can and should praise the Lord. But one is in a praiseless condition in death, for the dead are separated from earthly scenes and employment. The part of man that goes to the grave does not praise God, for the spirit goes to God who gave it; and the righteous spirit of man praises God.

By reading the works of materialists, it will be observed that nearly all the texts offered to prove the unconsciousness of souls between death and the resurrection are taken from the Old Testament, and particularly from the poetical books. To ignore the plain and clear teachings of the New Testament Scriptures and to adopt as a basis of doctrine the highly poetical and figurative utterances of a former dispensation certainly does not indicate the highest wisdom on the part of those who follow this course. Yet this is what materialists do. The passage in Isaiah 14:9–10 represents the dead as awake and conscious.

Thus, all the passages used by materialists to support their theory of the soul's being unconscious after death fail to prove their doctrine when properly understood. As it was only the body that was formed of the dust, it is only the body that is to return to the dust. The idea of soul-sleeping is not taught in the Scriptures.

The Bible teaches conclusively that the human soul is alive and conscious after death; that the spirit, in returning to God, does not become absorbed by the divine Spirit but passes into a state of personal conscious existence. The passages cited (e.g., Luke 16:19–31; 23:43; Philippians 1:23–24; 2 Corinthians 12:2–4; Revelation 6:9–11; 14:13) establish a conscious existence between death and the resurrection, both of the wicked and the righteous. During this period spirits live unto God and are happy with the Lord, or they are tormented, although their bodies slumber in the grave. In this faith the early Christians lived; in this hope they died. God is the God of the spirits of all flesh [i.e., all mankind] (Numbers 27:16). Whether a Christian lives or dies, he is the Lord's, for the Lord is "Lord of both the dead and the living" (Romans 14:9). Physical death is not extinction—the spirit has conscious existence after death for every person. Each person will continue to be himself in the life beyond the grave, the very same self after death as before, though not in the physical body. A person cannot commit suicide and end it all. Death does not blow out the candle. This personality—this "I"—will survive the decay of the body. This being true, each person on earth can say, "I am an immortal soul and 'I' shall never cease to exist as a conscious being." All that a man has he leaves at death, but all that he is he takes with him into the life beyond. What a sobering thought to know that man was created with the power of an endless, conscious existence!

Conclusion

So there is one truth which is as sure and clear as Revelation can make it: those called dead are not dead, as materialists say, but alive. Death is not a state; it is an act. It is not a condition; it is a transition. Those who die do not cease to be; the righteous person in dying enters immediately upon a larger and richer life. Lay hold of this great fact: souls do not spend the long years and ages that may lapse between death and the resurrection in some state of coma or unconsciousness. Nowhere does the Bible teach that the dead are unconscious. The departed are consciously alive on the other side.

The idea of soul-sleeping is not taught in the Bible. Souls do not spend the long intervening years between death and the resurrection in some comatose state. In the Bible, death is neither extinction nor unconsciousness of the soul. The departed spirits are living and conscious.

Questions for Discussion

1. In what state can a man be conscious?
2. What does the narrative of the rich man and Lazarus teach concerning departed spirits?
3. Do you think this story is a parable? Defend your answer.
4. What is the difference between a parable and a fable?
5. Give examples of figures of speech used in teaching spiritual truths.
6. What are some of the figures of speech in the narrative of the rich man and Lazarus? Give their meanings.
7. What are some of the lessons clearly taught in the narrative of the rich man and Lazarus? Why could the rich man remember?
8. Are the departed wicked not under a kind of punishment?
9. Why did Paul think death would be far better than living on earth?
10. Give Paul's statement about his experience in Paradise. What does this incident prove about the departed spirits?
11. How are the souls of the early martyred saints described?
12. What was Christ's promise to the dying thief?
13. What happens to those who die in the Lord?
14. What did Stephen expect when about to leave his body?
15. Who carried the soul of Lazarus to Abraham's bosom?
16. What should be one's desire about how he dies?
17. What is the doctrine of unconsciousness after death often called?
18. Why is death spoken of in the Scriptures as sleep? Give some passages.
19. In what sense are the dead asleep? What part of man sleeps? Where?
20. What does the word *cemetery* mean?
21. In what sense do the dead know not anything?
22. In what sense does man die like a beast? In what sense is he unlike a beast?
23. In what sense, or what viewpoint, are many of the statements used in the book of Ecclesiastes? In the Psalms?
24. What are man's thoughts that perish at death?
25. Is man's life all over when he departs this life? Prove your answer from the Scriptures.
26. What are some of the passages of Scripture which teach that man's spirit is conscious between death and the resurrection?
27. Do our departed loved ones and friends see us today and know what we are saying and doing?

– 10 –

Where Are the Dead?

". . . neither was he left unto Hades, nor did his flesh see corruption"
Acts 2:31

It has been shown that (1) man is a compound being: body, physical life, and spirit; (2) death is separation of spirit and body; (3) the soul neither ceases to exist nor becomes unconscious between death and the resurrection; (4) the souls of the righteous are happy immediately following death; and (5) the souls of the wicked are miserable immediately following death. Since at death the human spirit leaves the body and maintains a separate, conscious existence, there must be a place for departed souls to dwell.

This question now arises: Where do souls go at death to await the resurrection? Is it the final heaven or hell that shall be theirs after judgment, or is it an intermediate abode? At death, the spirit lives on; but where?

Although it is generally agreed that there is an intermediate state for disembodied souls between death and the resurrection, there is some misunderstanding as to the place where departed spirits dwell. The Holy Scriptures do shed light upon the subject.

It has been shown that the spirit at death returns unto God who gave it. The soul is neither asleep with the body in the grave, nor has it gone into some other body, as some religionists suppose.

The place prepared by the Lord where all disembodied spirits dwell between death and the resurrection is an intermediate abode called Hades. Two passages in the New Testament state this fact. (1) The spirits of both the rich man and Lazarus after they died were in Hades. Of the rich man Jesus said: "And in Hades he lifted up his eyes" (Luke 16:23). (2) The spirit of Jesus went to Hades when He died. Peter, on Pentecost, referred to a prophecy of David, and said: "For David saith concerning him . . . thou wilt not leave my soul unto Hades . . . neither was he left unto Hades" (Acts 2:25–31). When man dies, the spirit goes to Hades, and the body goes to the tomb. Hades is divided into two compartments: Paradise, the abode of the righteous, and Tartarus, the abode of the wicked. After the resurrection and the judgment, righteous souls will leave Paradise and dwell in heaven; wicked souls will leave Tartarus and dwell in hell or Gehenna. This will become clear as this discussion progresses.

The original Greek word, *Hades,* is translated "hell" in the King James or Authorized Version of the New Testament (A.D.1611) in the above passages (Luke 16:23; Acts 2:27, 31). Three distinct words are translated "hell" in this version: *Hades, Gehenna,* and *Tartarus*. For proper understanding, it is necessary to know what each word is and how it is used in the Bible.

Hades Is the Realm of Disembodied Spirits

First, *Hades* primarily means, "the unseen, or invisible world." According to Thayer, it is "the common receptacle of disembodied spirits"[1] The place of departed souls is not unseen to God; but it is unseen to those on earth. Hades designates the place to which all spirits go, without reference to their moral character. It is the realm of all disembodied spirits, both righteous and wicked, between death and the resurrection. The grave denotes only the receptacle of the body. Hades never means the grave, cemetery, or the tomb. Always, in the New Testament, Hades only signifies the region of disembodied spirits. In the American Standard Version (A.D.1901, commonly called "The Revised Version") the Greek word *Hades* is never translated "hell" but "Hades." The word *Hades* occurs ten times in the American Standard Version of the New Testament Scriptures. The passages where Hades appears are:

1. Matthew 11:23—"thou shalt go down unto Hades."
2. Matthew 16:18—"and the gates of Hades shall not prevail against it."
3. Luke 10:15—"thou shalt be brought down unto Hades."
4. Luke 16:23—"And in Hades he lifted up his eyes."
5. Acts 2:27—"Because thou wilt not leave my soul unto Hades."
6. Acts 2:31—"neither was he [Christ] left unto Hades."
7. Revelation 1:18—"and I have the keys of death and of Hades."
8. Revelation 6:8—"and Hades followed with him."
9. Revelation 20:13—"and death and Hades gave up the dead that were in them."
10. Revelation 20:14—"And death and Hades were cast into the lake of fire."

In Matthew 11:23, Matthew 16:18, and Luke 10:15, Hades is used by Christ metaphorically. Many ancient Greek manuscripts use Hades in 1 Corinthians 15:55: "O death, where is thy sting? O grave [Hades], where is thy victory?" (KJV).

---

1 Thayer, *A Greek-English Lexicon,* p. 11.

Gehenna Is the Final Abode of the Wicked

Gehenna is the Greek word used to denote the final abode of the wicked, the hell of fire. It is always translated "hell" in the King James and American Standard versions. The American Standard Version gives *Gehenna* in the footnote every time the word occurs in the original text and is translated "hell." While in the American Standard Version, the word *Hades* is never translated "hell," the word *Gehenna* is uniformly translated "hell." Hence, Gehenna is the designation of the place and state of just retribution reserved for impenitent sinners after the judgment . . . the place of final punishment.

The word *Gehenna* occurs twelve times in the Greek New Testament Scriptures—seven times in Matthew, three times in Mark, once in Luke, and once in the epistle of James. In every one of these passages, except that of James, the word is used by Christ, and each passage it refers to the final abode of the wicked. From the American Standard Version, these verses, in their order, are as follows:

1. Matthew 5:22—"in danger of the hell of fire."
2. Matthew 5:29—"thy whole body be cast into hell."
3. Matthew 5:30—"thy whole body go into hell."
4. Matthew 10:28—"destroy both soul and body in hell."
5. Matthew 18:9—"be cast into the hell of fire."
6. Matthew 23:15—"a son of hell than yourselves."
7. Matthew 23:33—"how shall ye escape the judgment of hell?"
8. Mark 9:43—"go into hell, into the unquenchable fire."
9. Mark 9:45—"be cast into hell."
10. Mark 9:47—"be cast into hell."
11. Luke 12:5—"to cast into hell."
12. James 3:6—"is set on fire by hell."

Tartarus Is the Temporary Abode of the Wicked

The word *Tartarus* occurs only one time in the Greek New Testament Scriptures. It is translated "hell" in both the King James and American Standard versions. It is found in 2 Peter 2:4: "For if God spared not angels when they sinned, but cast them down to hell, and committed them to pits of darkness, to be reserved unto judgment." The American Standard Version has a footnote on this verse to explain that the Greek word in this passage translated "hell" is not *Hades* or *Gehenna,* but *Tartarus*.

Similar to Peter's statement concerning fallen angels is the one made by Jude: "And angels that kept not their own principality, but left their proper habitation, he hath kept in everlasting bonds under darkness unto the judgment of the great day" (Jude 6). Peter and Jude state that the fallen angels are now awaiting judgment. Hence, Tartarus is the compartment of the Hadean world occupied by wicked spirits between death and the resurrection as they await final judgment. It is that part of Hades maintained for the wicked dead during the intermediate state—the realm where the disobedient are held in bonds of darkness, only until the Day of Judgment. It is a dark place, a prison, for punishment of the souls of the unrighteous after death, prior to the time of resurrection and eternity. Tartarus is the "deep" where demons begged not be sent to be tormented before their time when Christ was about to cast them into the swine (Luke 8:31). Thayer says Tartarus was "regarded by the ancient Greeks as the abode of the wicked dead, where they suffer punishment for their wicked deeds."[1]

People ask, "Why did scholars at the time they made the King James Version in A.D.1611, translate all three Greek words—*Hades, Gehenna,* and *Tartarus*—as hell, since they do not mean the same?" When the King James translation was made, the English word conveyed both the idea of a worldly place—the realm of the dead and the place of eternal punishment—and the world of the dead generally. Hence, the King James translators put the word *hell,* meaning an unseen place, for *Hades, Gehenna,* and *Tartarus,* since all three were in reality unseen to the people on the earth. However, since there are three different words in the Greek language, and since hell in this present day means exclusively the final place of punishment of the wicked, the translators of the American Standard Version made Hades into an English word without translating it. They translated *Gehenna* "hell," and translated *Tartarus* "hell." So today the word *hell* is correctly applied to Gehenna, but not to Hades. The New Testament never uses *Hades* to portray the final abode of punishment after the judgment. *Gehenna* always signifies the place of eternal punishment. *Hades* refers to the intermediate state of disembodied spirits between death and the resurrection, and the word *Tartarus* refers to that part of Hades where the wicked are during this intermediate state awaiting their eternal destiny. Tartarus is not Gehenna. Tartarus is only the place of painful restraint, where the souls of the wicked are reserved to the final judgment.

Although the Scriptures teach that the good and bad go alike to Hades at death, their condition is not the same. Some are in a state of happiness; others are in a state of misery. There are two divisions in Hades: Paradise and Tartarus.

There Is a Place of Rest in Hades

Paradise is for the good spirits in Hades. The word *Paradise* has always implied a state of happiness and comfort wherever it is used. Christ used this term to refer to the abode of righteous spirits in Hades. While both the rich man and Lazarus were in Hades, they were not both in the same compartment; for

1 Thayer, *A Greek-English Lexicon,* p. 615.

one was comforted, the other tormented. In the disembodied state the blessed dead are separate in some sense from the ungodly. Jesus said a great gulf is between them (Luke 16:26). Thus, Christ taught that Hades is divided into two compartments or conditions—one for the righteous, the other for the wicked.

The term *Abraham's bosom,* where Lazarus was, is a name referring to the place of bliss, where the wicked cease from troubling and the weary are at rest (Job 3:17). It is a figurative phrase expressing innermost communion. Abraham's bosom is not heaven, the eternal home of the soul for the righteous, but the place of rest in Hades.

Similarly, the Scriptures affirm that Christ went to Paradise when He died—said He to the penitent robber: "Today shalt thou be with me in Paradise" (Luke 23:43). Thus, the following facts are evident from this passage:

1. The Lord and the thief were together somewhere that day.
2. They were not together in the tomb, but in Paradise.
3. Therefore, reference is made to their spirits, i.e., their souls were together that day; their bodies were not. Hades is the place where the spirit goes at death to await the day of resurrection of the body. Hades is not hell, the place of eternal punishment after the judgment. Paradise in Luke 23:43 is a part of Hades, a place of bliss and comfort for the righteous.

By contrasting Christ's statement to the thief (Luke 23:43) and Peter's statement about Christ on Pentecost ("neither was he left unto Hades," Acts 2:31), it must be understood that Paradise is a compartment of Hades. Note again these facts:

1. Christ went to Hades (Acts 2:27, 31).
2. Christ also went to Paradise (Luke 23:43).
3. Therefore, Paradise is in Hades; Jesus and the thief were together in Hades while they were together in Paradise.

Thayer defines Paradise as "that part of Hades which was thought by the later Jews to be the abode of the pious until the resurrection."[1] Hence, Hades is not in heaven, nor any part of the final abode of the righteous.

Although the spirit of Christ came from Hades when His body arose from the tomb, the soul of the thief yet remains in Hades, and will continue there until the resurrection of all the dead at the last day. The thief 's body did see corruption.

The word *Paradise,* therefore, as here used by Christ in Luke 23:43, refers to that part of Hades which is the abode of the disembodied spirits of the righteous, the blessed dead (Revelation 14:13).

---

1 Ibid., p. 480.

In an effort to prove that Paradise means the grave, materialists parallel the language of Christ to the thief with that of Samuel to King Saul: "Tomorrow shalt thou and thy sons be with me" (1 Samuel 28:19). They claim that the only difference between the two statements is in point of time—one was to occur "today," the other "tomorrow." In other words, they think that Samuel, the prophet of God, simply told Saul that he and his sons would die and be buried "tomorrow." But in relating the burying of the bodies of Saul and his sons, it was not "tomorrow" from the time Samuel made his statement to King Saul. Although they did die the next day in battle with the Philistines, their bodies were not buried until several days later (1 Samuel 31). For this reason the statement, "Tomorrow shalt thou and thy sons be with me," had no reference to the burial of their bodies. The passage means that Saul and his sons were going to be with Samuel the next day in the Hadean world—and on the morrow they did die. Yet they (their bodies) were not with Samuel (his body) in the grave. Similarly, when Jesus told the thief that both of them would be in Paradise that day, He was not referring to the grave but to that portion of the Hadean realm called Paradise. Christ's body went to the grave, but His spirit did not go to the grave. The word *Paradise* never refers to the grave; it is the abode of the righteous spirits until the resurrection. (The word is also used to refer to the eternal home of the soul called heaven in Revelation 2:7, which will be noted later.)

There Is a Place of Torment in Hades

Just as there is a place of bliss for the righteous, there is a place or condition of torment in Hades for those who have not lived according to God's will on earth. The rich man went to Hades at death, and in that state he suffered torment. Although in a place of anguish, he was not in Gehenna, the final abode of lost souls, but in Hades (Luke 16:23). Jesus described the condition of both good and bad spirits in Hades, the state between death and the resurrection, for the rich man was in Hades immediately after his death.

The rich man and Lazarus were not in their final destinations, hell and heaven, but in Hades during the interval between death and the resurrection. This narrative does not speak of conditions after the Day of Judgment, for the rich man still had five brothers on this earth. The brothers continued to live on earth where opportunities for obeying the Lord had not ceased. The rich man was in Hades in torments, but Lazarus was comforted. The resurrection and judgment had not yet occurred, and will not occur until the end of time when Christ comes again.

Jesus did not say that the rich man lifted up his eyes in Gehenna, and Peter did not say that Christ's soul was not left in Gehenna. Christ's spirit did not go to hell (Gehenna) when He died on the cross. His spirit was in Hades while His body was in the tomb. When the Savior entered Hades, the thief also entered it.

Christ's spirit came out of Hades on the third day, and His body was raised from the dead. The spirit of the thief, on the other hand, did not come from Hades, and his body did not arise but remained in the grave. His spirit will remain in Hades and his body in the grave until the day of resurrection. The same is true of all disembodied spirits. To affirm, therefore, as many do, that at death the departing spirit goes immediately to heaven (if righteous) or to hell (if wicked) rules out an intermediate state of souls (Hades, the disembodied realm) between death and the judgment, and renders many plain passages of the Bible meaningless. The Scriptures have no such teaching.

While both the rich man and Lazarus were in Hades, they were not both in the same compartment; for one was comforted, the other tormented, and a great gulf was between them (Luke 16:23–26). Lazarus was in Abraham's bosom. This surely means a place of rest and is equivalent to Paradise in Luke 23:43, for the souls of believers at death pass into a state of blessedness. They will remain in that state until the resurrection, at which time they will be greatly exalted to a higher state of being, their final bliss. However, just as there is a place of bliss for the righteous, there is a place or condition of anguish in Hades for those who have not lived according to God's will on earth. The rich man went to Hades at death, and in that state he suffered anguish. Although in a state of anguish, he was not in Gehenna, the final abode of lost souls, but in Hades. Jesus described the condition of both good and bad spirits in Hades, in the state between death and the resurrection, for the rich man was in Hades and his five brothers continued in this present life. Since there was a gulf between the rich man and Lazarus, the rich man was, of course, in another part of Hades, different from Abraham's bosom or Paradise.

Moreover, since the nature of the place where fallen angels are said to be (2 Peter 2:4; Jude 6) is the same as that which characterized the rich man in torments in Hades (while separated by a great gulf from the righteous who were likewise in Hades), it seems logical to say that the places are in the same realm (Hades). It is clear then from what has been studied that Tartarus is in Hades and is that part of the spirit-realm in which the disobedient are confined until the judgment. The rich man in Tartarus and Lazarus in Abraham's bosom were both in Hades.

In Hades, the receptacle of all disembodied spirits, there are joys and torments. The souls of departed saints are in Paradise, in the bosom of Abraham, not in the highest rewards of heaven, but joyfully awaiting them. The souls of the wicked are in Tartarus, not suffering the eternal fire of Gehenna.

Hence, the Scriptures teach that the punishment of the ungodly precedes as well as follows the final judgment. Observing the deliverance of Noah and Lot, and having knowledge of the angels who sinned, Peter further said: "The Lord knoweth how to deliver the godly out of temptation, and to keep the unrighteous under punishment unto the day of judgment" (2 Peter 2:9). So the unrighteous dead are now enduring punishment. This punishment for sinners begins immediately after death and continues in this intermediate state until the final judgment. At the judgment the unrighteous will receive their final punishment. The Bible teaches that at the time the godly are out of temptation, the ungodly are under punishment, and this is prior to the Day of Judgment. This punishment is both severe and continuous in Tartarus. The Scriptures also teach that there is a difference in the mode and degree of punishment of Tartarus and Gehenna. The punishment of Tartarus is the punishment of the disobedient spirit, whereas the punishment of Gehenna is that of both soul and the resurrected body (Matthew 10:28). Although there is a degree of happiness and a degree of misery that comes to obedient and disobedient spirits in Hades, that happiness or that misery, as the case might be, in its highest degree does not commence until after the reunion of the spirits with their raised bodies at the resurrection and after the final judgment.

The Scriptures teach, therefore, that the righteous dead are now in a state of happiness; the wicked dead are in a state of suffering. The full degree of their joy or misery will come in eternity. These shall be augmented to perfection after the resurrection when the righteous shall be welcomed into heaven and the unrighteous shall be cast into hell (Matthew 25:46). Whatever, then, the state of the good and bad may be while their spirits are in Hades and their bodies are sleeping in the dust of the earth, that state will certainly close and be exchanged for another at the resurrection and final judgment.

The New Testament Greek word *Hades* parallels the Old Testament Hebrew word *Sheol*. Both words mean the unseen realm of departed spirits, the place of the dead. William Gesenius says of Sheol: "The underworld . . . where dwell the shades of the dead . . . whither men descend at death."[1]

In the Scriptures, *Sheol* never refers to the grave. Neither does the word refer to hell (i.e., Gehenna), the final and eternal place of punishment for the wicked. Sheol refers only to the place of departed (disembodied) spirits—both the righteous and the wicked. It is true that in the Old Testament Scriptures Sheol is often described poetically as having gates and bars, and the dying are said to go there. But Sheol is never spoken of as a place where the spirits are without consciousness, nor is it used in the plural, Sheols, which would be true if it could mean graves. Further, to see that Sheol has exactly the same meaning as the Greek word *Hades,* compare Psalm 16:10 with Acts 2:27: "Thou wilt

---

1 William Gesenius, *A Hebrew and English Lexicon of the Old Testament,* 982–983. (Note: Originally written in Latin and later translated by others. Houghton Mifflin Co. published a translation by Edward Robinson, 1906. Translator and publisher of the material referenced here is unknown.)

not leave my soul to Sheol" (Psalm 16:10); "Because thou wilt not leave my soul unto Hades" (Acts 2:27).

When Hebrew scholars translated the Old Testament Scriptures from Hebrew into Greek about 270 B.C., they commonly translated *Sheol* into the Greek word *Hades*. This version, the Septuagint, was in use among the Jews during the personal ministry of Christ. *Sheol* and *Hades* are identical, meaning the same place. *Sheol* is Hebrew; *Hades* is Greek. The grave receives only the material part of man; Sheol (Hades) is where the spirit goes.

The first time the word *Sheol* is found in the Bible is where Jacob, grieving over his beloved son Joseph whom he thought to be dead, said: "I will go down to Sheol to my son mourning" (Genesis 37:35; cf. 42:38). Jacob anticipated death and thought he would soon go where his son's spirit had gone. Jacob understood that Sheol was the place where all disembodied spirits go at death. But—and here is the astonishing thing—the King James Version has the word Sheol in the passage translated "grave."

The American Standard Version merely anglicizes the Hebrew word *Sheol,* as it does the Greek word *Hades*. There is no word in the English which conforms to the Hebrew *Sheol*. Thus, wherever the word occurs in the original language, the American Standard Version has the word *Sheol* throughout the entire Old Testament. The reader of only the King James Version may not know whether the word refers to the body or to the spirit of the deceased person, for this version translates *Sheol* "the grave," "hell," and "the pit" in the Old Testament.

Now notice the translations as they occur in the King James Version of the Old Testament.

A. *Sheol* is translated "the grave" thirty-one times.

Genesis 37:35
Genesis 42:38
Genesis 44:29
Genesis 44:31
1 Samuel 2:6
1 Kings 2:6
1 Kings 2:9
Job 7:9
Job 14:13
Job 17:13
Job 21:13
Job 24:19
Psalm 6:5
Psalm 30:3
Psalm 31:17
Psalm 49:14 (twice)
Psalm 49:15
Psalm 88:3
Psalm 89:48
Psalm 141:7
Proverbs 1:12
Proverbs 30:16
Ecclesiastes 9:10
Song of Solomon 8:6
Isaiah 14:11
Isaiah 38:10
Isaiah 38:18
Ezekiel 31:15
Hosea 13:14 (twice)

B. *Sheol* is translated "hell" thirty-one times.

Deuteronomy 32:22
2 Samuel 22:6
Job 11:8
Job 26:6
Psalm 9:17
Psalm 16:10
Psalm 18:5
Psalm 55:15
Psalm 86:13
Psalm 116:3
Psalm 139:8
Proverbs 5:5
Proverbs 7:27
Proverbs 9:18
Proverbs 15:11
Proverbs 15:24
Proverbs 23:14
Proverbs 27:20
Isaiah 5:14
Isaiah 14:9
Isaiah 14:15
Isaiah 28:15
Isaiah 28:18
Isaiah 57:9
Ezekiel 31:16
Ezekiel 31:17
Ezekiel 32:21
Ezekiel 32:27
Amos 9:2
Jonah 2:2
Habakkuk 2:5

C. *Sheol* is translated "the pit" three times.

Numbers 16:30
Numbers 16:33
Job 17:16

In all the Old Testament, *Sheol* occurs sixty-five times. The American Standard Version in all places retains the Hebrew word *Sheol*. Thus, in the Scriptures, *Sheol* invariably refers to the abode of disembodied spirits. Therefore, it becomes apparent that all students of God's Word should obtain a copy of the American Standard Version and use it freely in the study of the Scriptures. As observed in the American Standard Version, *Sheol* replaces "hell" in the Old Testament, and *Hades* replaces "hell" in the New Testament in all places where the original word refers to the intermediate or disembodied state of the dead. Likewise, in this version (as in the King James) the word *Gehenna*—the place of punishment for the wicked beyond the judgment—is always translated "hell." The version certainly makes the meaning of these words much clearer.

Hence, the dwelling place of departed spirits is called Sheol in the Old Testament and Hades in the New Testament. How foolish, then, for one to think that Sheol or Hades means the grave! The spirits go to Sheol or Hades when they become separated from their bodies. Neither *Sheol* nor *Hades* means the grave, which receives only the body.

Much error could be avoided in the religious world with the proper understanding of the words *Sheol, Hades, Paradise, Tartarus,* and *Gehenna*. The following sentences will serve as good examples of this, taken from J. F. Rutherford's book, *Where Are the Dead?* "Hell means the grave . . . The word sheol, translated "hell," means the grave, the tomb, the condition of silence."[1]

The Apostles' Creed—so-called, although the apostles of Christ had nothing to do with it—states that Christ at His death descended into hell. This statement has confused many people. They often ask, "Did Christ really go to hell when He died?" He did not! His spirit went to Sheol or Hades . . . His body went to the tomb.

If the word *hell* means the grave, as materialists teach, then why is it that only the wicked go there, as the Bible affirms? (Matthew 5:22; 25:46; 2 Thessalonians 1:8–9). Do not the righteous also go to the grave?

One can avoid such incorrect ideas and statements as listed above if he will but remember that *Sheol, Hades, Tartarus, Paradise,* and *Gehenna* never refer to the grave, and that the spirit at death does not go to the grave. Sheol, Hades, grave, and hell are not one and the same. Understanding Sheol or Hades, one can now see why the good spirit of Samuel said to the wicked King Saul who was soon to die, "Tomorrow shalt thou and thy sons be with me [i.e., in Sheol, where all spirits go at death]" (1 Samuel 28:19). For Samuel knew that all spirits in departing from their bodies went to Sheol, and were in a state of consciousness; some in a state of misery, others in a state of happiness.

Summarizing, note again the meaning of the words *Hades, Sheol, Paradise, Tartarus,* and *Gehenna*. *Hades* and *Sheol* refer to the intermediate state of disembodied spirits between death and the resurrection. Paradise and Tartarus are compartments in the Hadean realm, for all who await their eternal destiny; Paradise is for the righteous; Tartarus is for the wicked. Gehenna is the place of eternal punishment for the wicked after the judgment. *Hell* does not mean Hades. Scripture never uses *Hades* to portray the final state of punishment; the word is always *Gehenna*. Gehenna is not Tartarus—the place of wicked spirits in Sheol or Hades while awaiting judgment. How foolish to teach, as some do, that *Sheol* or *Hades* or *Gehenna* means the grave! Learning that disembodied spirits go to Hades or Sheol, many naturally ask, "Where is that invisible world or spirit-land called Sheol in the Old Testament and Hades in the New Testament?"

Many seem to have the idea that souls of the departed are near their graves. Hence, less intelligent people fear the cemetery. Others think the ghost (spirit) of a murdered man lingers near the place of the crime, even appearing at times to people. But the spirits are not in the cemetery; only the dead bodies are there. Souls are not in the graves, nor hovering around the spot where the bodies

1 J. F. Rutherford, *Where Are the Dead?* (Brooklyn: Watchtower Bible and Tract Society, 1932), pp. 21, 24.

sleep. Neither has the soul entered into some other body. The old idea of transmigration of souls is not taught in the Scriptures. The pious dead are in the Lord's care and keeping, in Paradise, while the wicked dead are in Tartarus.

Several expressions concerning the departed going to Sheol or Hades might be noticed with profit. Very often the dying are spoken of as going down, as a descent into some lower place. For instance: "Jehovah killeth, and maketh alive: He bringeth down to Sheol, and bringeth up" (1 Samuel 2:6). Some think the realm of the dead is a place under the earth, and cite: "That in the name of Jesus every knee should bow, of things in heaven and things on earth and things under the earth [i.e., Hades, the underworld]" (Philippians 2:10).

Certainly, God knows where Sheol is and the condition of all those in the Hadean realm. He is omniscient. The spirit-world is open to His all-seeing eye. Job affirmed: "Sheol is naked before God, and Abaddon [i.e., the grave, the place of corruption] hath no covering" (Job 26:6). Again, Solomon said: "Sheol and Abaddon are before Jehovah: how much more then the hearts of the children of men!" (Proverbs 15:11). But as to where Hades or Sheol is located no one knows; it has not pleased God to reveal this to man. Hence, all speculations about where this disembodied realm is located are useless and vain. Besides, it must not be of any practical value to man to know the exact location of the place or the Lord would have revealed it in His Word. In the long ago, Moses made a very important statement which is pertinent today: "The secret things belong unto Jehovah our God; but the things that are revealed belong unto us and to our children for ever, that we may do all the words of this law" (Deuteronomy 29:29).

Some say one should not be concerned about the state of the dead, for it is all pure speculation. While it is true that the secret things belong unto the Lord, one must not forget that the other part of the verse says also that the "things which are revealed belong unto us." What God has been pleased to reveal in His Sacred Word is surely a subject for man's knowledge and comfort and edification. So one is not presumptuous when he makes inquiry about the dead and seeks out what God has said in the Holy Scriptures concerning them. Surely, one is free to study and discuss what the Bible teaches on this or any other subject. Although no one knows the location of Hades or Sheol, it does no violence to the Scriptures for one to think of his departed loved ones and friends as being just beyond the horizon, living in another room.

Paradise

The word *Paradise* is also applied to the eternal home of the redeemed which they will inherit in their resurrected immortal bodies after the Day of Judgment. The Lord said to the church in Ephesus: "To him that overcometh, to him will I give to eat of the tree of life, which is in the Paradise of God" (Revelation 2:7). The word *Paradise* is used three times in the New Testament: Luke 23:43; 2 Corinthians 12:4; and Revelation 2:7.

Paradise primarily means "a pleasure garden, a place of delight." It is used in the Scriptures in the following senses: (1) the Garden of Eden (see the Septuagint Version in Genesis 2 and 3), (2) the place of rest for the righteous spirits after death (Luke 23:43), and (3) heaven, the place of bliss for the righteous after the judgment (Revelation 21; 22:1–5; Matthew 25:46).

So Paradise is any place prepared for enjoyment. It also signifies a condition. The place where the condition exists must be learned from the context. For example, Dallas, Texas, is a city, but so are New York City and Tokyo, Japan. The word *city* does not mean in itself just which particular city. Paradise can be a proper description of the place for man's original home, also a place where righteous spirits go at death to await the resurrection, or a place where the righteous go after the judgment (heaven). Therefore, the three times the word *Paradise* occurs in the New Testament do not always refer to the same place.

When Christ said to the thief on the cross that they were both going to die and their spirits would be together that day in Paradise, He had reference to the place of rest for disembodied spirits in the Hadean world (cf. Revelation 14:13). To be in Paradise with Christ did not and could not mean being in a state of unconsciousness or non-existence, as already seen, neither the grave nor heaven. Christ did not go to heaven when He died; He did not ascend to heaven until forty days after His resurrection (Luke 24:50–51; Acts 1:3–11). Paradise, in Hades, is not heaven, the eternal home of the soul for the righteous. Hades is not part of the final abode. Jesus and the penitent robber were together in Hades while they were together in Paradise. Therefore, *Paradise,* in Luke 23:43 does not refer to heaven, the eternal abode of the saved. Christ went to Hades when He died on the cross. Definitely, Christ's spirit did not go to hell in the generally accepted meaning of that word. His spirit was in Hades while His body was in the tomb; but His soul was not in hell. Furthermore, the body of Jesus was not left in the grave to undergo corruption (in contrast with David's body, as Peter stated, Acts 2:29–31, 34), but was gloriously raised on the third day; neither was His spirit left in Hades.

The body and soul of Christ were not the same. The soul went to Hades; the body was carried to the grave. Later, Christ's spirit came from Hades; the body came from the grave. The spirit of Christ was in Hades, the place of departed spirits during the interval when His body lay in the grave, and not in the final abode of the righteous.

The Final Judgment

At the day of final judgment, when Christ comes again, the Lord will say to the redeemed: "Come, ye blessed of my Father, inherit the kingdom prepared for you from the foundation of the world." To the wicked He will say: "Depart from me, ye cursed, into the eternal fire which is prepared for the devil and his angels . . . And these shall go away [i.e., not go back away] into eternal punishment: but the righteous into eternal life" (Matthew 25:34–46).

So on that day the followers of Christ will receive their crown of righteousness (2 Timothy 4:8; 1 Peter 5:4; Luke 14:14), and the wicked will be cast into Gehenna, but not before. Then Hades will be no more. Hence, souls do not enter their eternal state, either heaven or hell, at the moment of death. When a man dies, the spirit goes to Hades, and the body goes to the tomb.

IN MY FATHER'S HOUSE

No, not dead beneath the grasses,
Not closed-walled within the tomb;
Rather, in my Father's mansion,
Living in another room.
Living, like the man who loves me,
Like yon child with cheeks a-bloom;
Out of sight, at desk or school-books,
Busy in another room.
Nearer than the youth whom fortune
Beckons where the strange lands loom;
Just behind the hanging curtain,
Serving in another room.
Shall I doubt my Father's mercy?
Shall I think of death as doom,
Or the stepping o'er the threshold
To a bigger, brighter room?
Shall I blame my Father's wisdom?
Shall I sit enswathed in gloom,
When I know my love is happy,
Waiting in another room?

—Robert Freeman

Questions for Discussion

1. What is the word used in the Greek New Testament to describe the place where spirits go after death to await the resurrection?
2. Discuss Hades.
3. Name the three Greek words translated "hell" in the King James Version.
4. How did the translators of the American Standard Version translate *Hades?*
5. According to Psalm 16:10 and Acts 2:27, 31, where did Jesus go when He died? Compare the reading of Acts 2:27, 31 in the King James Version and American Standard Version.
6. When did Jesus go to heaven?
7. Who alone has come from the realm of the dead to die no more?
8. Where were the rich man and Lazarus after death?
9. Are both good and bad spirits in Hades?
10. How many times does *Hades* occur in the Greek New Testament?
11. What does the word *Gehenna* mean? How many times is it found in the New Testament?
12. Has the punishment of Gehenna yet come in the history of humanity?
13. What does the word *Tartarus* mean? Where does it occur in Scripture?
14. What does the word *Paradise,* as used in Luke 23:43, mean?
15. Do the words *Hades, Paradise, Tartarus,* and *Gehenna* ever refer to the grave?
16. At death, what goes to the grave? What goes to Hades?
17. What does the Hebrew word *Sheol* mean? Does it ever mean the grave?
18. How did the scholars of the Septuagint Version translate *Sheol* into Greek?
19. What did the translators of the King James Version do with the word *Sheol?* How many times is *Sheol* translated in the King James Version "the grave"? "hell"? "the pit"?
20. How did the scholars of the American Standard Version translate *Sheol?* Will a careful study of the American Standard Version help remove some of the errors about where spirits go at death?
21. How do materialists use the words *Hades, Sheol, Gehenna, hell,* and *grave?*
22. What did the writers of "The Apostles' Creed" mean when they said Christ descended into hell at His death?
23. Does God reveal in His Word where Hades or Sheol is located? Does He know?
24. What is the statement of Scripture about the things that have been revealed and the things not revealed?

25. Is it presumptuous on man's part to want to know all that God has revealed about death and the hereafter? Is there a benefit in studying the Bible on this, and all subjects?
26. According to Scripture, where do all souls go at death? What are the two compartments of this realm?
27. Some have the idea that all the righteous spirits came out of Hades at the resurrection, or the ascension, of Christ and now they go directly to God in heaven at death. Others teach that the Hadean realm was emptied in A.D.70, and since then the righteous at death go immediately to heaven, avoiding Hades, but the wicked spirits go to Hades (Tartarus) and there await the resurrection of their bodies. Evaluate these ideas in the light of what has been studied in this chapter. Who goes to Hades at death, and for how long?
28. We need to note also the error and false teaching of the New International Version of Acts 2:27, 31 in regard to Christ's body being in the grave and His spirit being in Hades prior to His resurrection; "because you will not abandon me to the grave, nor will you let your Holy One see decay . . . he was not abandoned to the grave, nor did his body see decay." Christ's spirit was not in the grave, only His body, and only His body came from the grave in His resurrection, having not seen corruption. His spirit did not go to the grave. Discuss this point in our study very carefully, for the New International Version has Christ going to the grave and not to Paradise in Hades.
29. "O death, where is thy victory?" "O death, where is thy sting?" Since many translations give the word "Hades" in 1 Corinthians 15:55 instead of "death," ("grave" KJV) in this passage of Scripture, we note a few translations using the word "Hades":
    - "O Hades, where is your victory?" (NKJV). (cf. Hosea 13:14).
    - "Hades! where is thy victory?" (Living Oracles, 1878).
    - "Where, O Hades! is thy victory?" (MacKnight).
    - ". . . the Hades of departed spirits" (Ellicott).
    - "where of thee, O Hades, the victory" (Berry's Interlinear Greek-English New Testament).

    Some Greek teachers may prefer to use the word "Hades" instead of the words "death" or "grave," in this passage. What are your views regarding this translation which is also found in the New King James Version?
30. Has David gone to heaven yet? See Acts 2:34.
31. What do you think is the time the righteous enter their eternal home? Note Christ's language concerning the final judgment and all being sent

either to "eternal punishment" or "into eternal life" (Matthew 25:31–46). Does this not refer to the end of time?

32. Discuss also Paul's statement about being "caught up even to the third heaven" and being "caught up into paradise" and hearing "unspeakable words" (2 Corinthians 12:2–4; cf. Acts 14:19).
33. Does not the Bible at times refer to the eternal part of man made in the image of God as soul? (Cf. Matthew 10:28.)

– 11 –

WHAT IS THE STATE OF SPIRITS IN HADES?

"I am in anguish in this flame"
Luke 16:24

Scripture teaches that man is endowed with an intelligent soul and bodily organization, including physical life. The Divine Being has made the soul indestructible and immortal; immortality is the heritage of the whole human race. Too, the Holy Scriptures teach that death is a separation of the spirit from the body and that the place of dwelling for all disembodied spirits between death and the resurrection is Hades or Sheol, the exact location of which has not been revealed. Attention now shall be given to several questions frequently asked concerning spirits in Hades. The answers to them will be in the light of God's revealed will to man, the only source of reliable information regarding life in the hereafter.

The Bible does not tell all one would like to know concerning the condition of souls in the spirit-realm. The Bible does assure that life continues after death, and considers the completion of human destiny as taking place when soul and body are re-united in a future world, eternity after the judgment. Therefore, the Bible says comparatively little about the interim of disembodied spirits after death, prior to the resurrection. However, there is probably much more to be learned from the Scriptures about the intermediate state than most people think.

Although the Bible may not answer all our questions on life beyond the grave, the Scriptures are emphatic on the intermediate condition of disembodied spirits, good and bad. One may not know just how the spirit lives and acts apart from the body (or how the soul is united to the body), yet the soul does live and act in Hades. Hence, one should be content with what the Lord has revealed, realizing that all things need not be made clear and plain. One should avoid speculation and be content with things recorded. Some ask, "Why did not the Lord tell man more about that life?" and one may wonder why those raised from the dead did not tell what they saw. Lazarus was raised from the dead after four days in Hades, but there is no intimation that he communicated anything experienced by him while there. If he had, God would have had that information recorded for the benefit of all. Many people may have asked Lazarus questions about what happened to him after he died. Surely some inquired, "Where were you?" "Did you see what we were doing on earth?" "Were you happy?" Lazarus, however, left no word of what he saw, heard, or felt while his body was in the grave. Thus Tennyson, speaking of Lazarus, said:

> Behold a man raised up by Christ!
> The rest remaineth unrevealed;
> He told it not; or something sealed
> The lips of that Evangelist.

There is no record of any report which anyone ever gave whom Christ or the apostles brought back to life from the spirit-land. Paul did not mention what he saw in "the third heaven" (2 Corinthians 12:2–4); it was not lawful for him to reveal the things he had experienced in that hour; Paul knew that what was seen could not be told. So one must abide by what God has seen best to reveal unto him and be content therewith.

A few people have pretended journeys to heaven and have attempted to describe what they saw. For example, the prophet of Mecca, Muhammad, claimed a visit to heaven. Mrs. Ellen G. White more recently claimed a visit to heaven and a vision like Paul's. This so-called prophetess said she saw the ark of God and the tables of stone; there was a halo of glory around the fourth commandment, and she learned the "Sabbath was not nailed to the cross."[1] Now, if Mrs. White made a trip to heaven, and if God did tell her to tell it, why would He not permit Paul to tell what he had seen and heard? What a lecture Paul could have given! My Trip to Paradise and Return: What I Experienced While in the Third Heaven. What a theme for the sensational preacher of modern times!

Furthermore, God has not told man more about Hades, as already indicated, because it is difficult to describe in a way that our earth-bound minds can understand a mode of life so different from earthly experiences. Man does not have the faculties to understand fully either the realm of disembodied spirits or the eternal destinies of man after judgment. For example, a blind person cannot behold the glories of a sunset. Imagine trying to describe to a deaf man the harmony of a piece of grand music. Can a father answer a child the same

---

1 D. M. Canright, *Seventh-Day Adventism Renounced*, reprint of Fourteenth Edition (Nashville: Gospel Advocate Co., nd), p. 217.

way as he would an adult? Things connected with the life hereafter are as far beyond the ken of man's poor, finite senses as the life of the butterfly is beyond the imagination of the chrysalis. However, man is assured that wonders and blessings of the beyond for the righteous will throughout all eternity far surpass the greatest imaginations of the greatest minds on earth.

But, what about those who claim to have special revelations from God? The Bible is authoritative, complete, and final (2 Timothy 3:16–17; Jude 3; Revelation 22:18–19); no more revelation will be given from any source. The whole story of those who have claimed to have made a trip to heaven and then talked about it is a delusion and the work of Satan (2 Thessalonians 2:11–12). Since no one raised from the dead in the Bible story related what he had seen or heard while his spirit was out of the body, why should one think that several hundred years later God has seen fit to reveal to man through certain "latter-day prophets" information not found in the Scriptures?

The important thing for us is to accept only the truths that the Lord has given in His inspired Word concerning Sheol or Hades, the intermediate state, and the condition of the spirits in that realm. Surely this is enough. God has not wished to reveal much in the Scriptures regarding spirits in the Hadean realm.

Mysteries will emerge from God's revelation just as there is always a degree of mystery in any revelation given by a higher to a lower intelligence. For example, a child asks for an explanation of something which has puzzled him. His father gives him an answer suited to his comprehension. The result is that his reply, though perfectly correct and intelligible from his standpoint, has started in the child's mind a whole series of perplexities which the parent cannot enable him to understand. So, it may be just as impossible for man, compounded of flesh and spirit as he is, to understand some things about the life of beings who are pure spirits, as it is for the child to understand his father. But one can take all that God has revealed to him in childlike faith. Beneath all these questions lies one principle: one should not let the difficulty of questions, for the solution of which he is not responsible, keep him from doing the plain duty that is at his hand.

On the other hand, one should not let the unbeliefs on the part of so-called religious people keep him from believing what the Bible teaches concerning life in the hereafter. In *Christianity Today* there appeared an article entitled "The NCC Elite: A Breakdown of Beliefs," in which thirty-one percent had doubts about a life beyond the grave. Excerpts from the article follow:

> One-third of the delegates at last December's National Council of Churches assembly in Miami Beach could not affirm unqualified belief in the reality of God, the divinity of Jesus, or life after death. This startling evidence of the inroads of liberal theology on the leadership of major Protestant denomina-

> tions comes from the first study of beliefs ever included in the customary poll made at NCC assemblies.
>
> On God, 33 percent were unable to choose the response, "I know that God really exists and I have no doubts about it" . . . The statement, "Jesus is the Divine Son of God and I have no doubts about it," was rejected by 36 percent of the NCC delegates...
>
> Thirty-one percent of the delegates could not say with complete certainty that "there is a life beyond death."
>
> . . . Questionnaires were filled out by 223 voting delegates, as well as a larger number of observers from church councils, local churches, or denominations. The delegate group was quite representative of the geographical and denominational make-up of the NCC. And those who responded were mostly professionals: 70 percent had attended previous NCC assemblies, two-thirds were ordained clergymen, and 42 percent were on denominational staffs. Three-fourths were from major metropolitan centers (somewhat over the national average); and only 4 percent were black, compared to 11 percent in the U. S. population. Nine out of ten NCC delegates were college graduates. Only 6 percent were under 40 years of age.[1]

No wonder the faith of millions of people has been shipwrecked! Their moorings have been cut by modernism. Drifting out into the uncertain seas of human philosophy and rationalism and being unable to see through the fogs of intellectualism must surely give a feeling of hopelessness! Let all reaffirm their faith in the existence of God, the divine Sonship of Jesus Christ, the Bible as the inspired Word of God and the one standard of authority in matters religious, and in a life beyond the grave.

Do the Dead See Us?

The first question people usually ask about departed spirits is: "Do those in Hades know anything about human affairs that are now going on among those who are still living on this earth?" People wonder if the dead see people in this life; or, if they do know all about man, are they made happy or sorrowful by the conduct of earthly loved ones and friends.

God has not wished to reveal much in the Scriptures regarding such matters. It is true that the rich man in Hades remembered that he still had five unfaithful brothers living on earth, but nothing is said about his knowledge as to their activities after he died. The rich man knew only of the state of his brothers when he left them; this he remembered. Of course, the rich man was thinking of his brothers and was deeply concerned about their souls' welfare.

From Ecclesiastes 9:5–6, which was noted earlier in this study, the conclusion can be reached that the dead do not know what is now happening on earth. Solomon said: "The dead know not anything . . . under the sun." Thus, death

---

1 *Christianity Today,* July 21, 1967, Vol. XI, no. 21, p. 46.

breaks all ties between the living and the dead. The dead no longer have any knowledge of what goes on here.

Too, Josiah, king of Judah, was told that God was going to bring evil upon Jerusalem because of their sins, but that the king would be taken away by death before it occurred. "Behold, I will gather thee to thy fathers, and thou shalt be gathered to thy grave in peace, neither shall thine eyes see all the evil that I will bring upon this place, and upon the inhabitants thereof" (2 Chronicles 34:28).

The conclusion is, the Bible does not teach that the spirits of the dead see what is now going on in this earth. It seems foolish for people to reprove some disobedient child, for instance, by saying to him that his deceased father "is watching from heaven" and knows just what the wayward child is doing and is grieved by his conduct.

What Is the Form of Disembodied Spirits?

People ask: "What is the form or shape of the soul in Hades, and how can it exist in a disembodied state?" Concerning the mode of existence and the form of the soul when disembodied, one's conception can only be vague and inadequate because God has not spoken on these matters. The heathen poets and philosophers thought and wrote of the manes or spirits of the dead as still retaining their human form. The Scriptures represent the dead, in some respects at least, as retaining their appropriate form. For instance, this was true of Moses and Elijah when they appeared with Christ on the Mount of Transfiguration (Matthew 17:3–4). In some way Peter recognized them as Moses and Elijah. Christ represented the rich man recognizing Lazarus in Hades. At least, people shall be the same individuals in Hades as they were here on earth. They shall feel themselves to be a living continuation of the past. They shall be conscious that they are themselves and not another. One's distinct individuality will survive in Hades and throughout all eternity.

Why Is There Suffering in Hades?

Many are puzzled about the rich man's torment, so they ask: "If the rich man was in Hades and not in hell (*Gehenna*), and this was before the final judgment, why, then, was he suffering? And in what way was he suffering since he was not in his resurrected body?"

The Bible plainly says the rich man was in Hades and that he was in anguish (Luke 16:24). Hence, the spirit does not go to its final place of reward at death. All disembodied souls go to the same place, but are in different states, while awaiting their final reward.

For an example of suffering, prior to the resurrection and judgment, consider this simple illustration: A man is murdered in the community. Two men are arrested and jailed as the possible suspects. One man is innocent, and he knows it; the other one is guilty, and he knows it. The guilty man is tormented in mind, and dreads for the court to convene. It will mean his condemnation. The poet Milton expressed a well-known truth when he said:

> The mind cannot be changed by place or time;
> The mind is its own place, and in itself
> Can make a heaven of hell, or a hell of heaven.
> —Paradise Lost

So, in jail with the innocent, the murderer recalls the crime committed, and experiences torments. He fears all the facts of the murder will be uncovered, made known, and he, being found guilty, will be sentenced to life imprisonment or death for his crime. Not so with the innocent man. His conscience does not bother him. Immediately after the crime, while both men are in the same place, the jail, side by side, one man is in misery or tormented in mind, while the other man is at peace. Though the trial has not been held, and the judge has not delivered the sentence, it might be said of these men: One is in Paradise, the other in Tartarus.

In this analogy, Hades represents the jail and Tartarus the miserable state of mind of the guilty man (for it has been shown that Tartarus is the condition where culprits who have despised their Creator in this life are held awaiting the final judgment). The trial represents the day of judgment (and at God's trial, the disobedient will be sentenced to serve an eternity of time in God's penitentiary, which is Gehenna).

This illustration also answers the objection so often made: "If some are in Paradise and some in Tartarus, they already know where they are going after the judgment, having already been judged." They judged themselves. Would it not be better to think of the two compartments of the Hadean realm as states or conditions, as well as places? Even on earth people may have Paradise or Tartarus in their hearts, for the righteous experience a foretaste of heaven to come, the wicked the pains of hell.

Here is a man with an undiscovered crime upon his conscience; this man, though no earthly court has ever passed sentence upon him, lives in constant dread and fear . . . tormented. Many a man, indeed, unable to bear the torment of fear any longer, has given himself up to justice. Better the handcuffs, the prison cell, or the very worst punishment the law can give than the enslavement to a ceaseless dread. As an example of this, just recently there appeared in the newspapers an article about a man in Los Angeles, California, who had confessed "to the 1965 slaying of the Grime sisters in Chicago." He stated to the officers, according to the news article, that he had been running ever since the crime. He was quoted as saying to the police: "I see visions of those two girls all the time. All I think about lately is how I let them die, stripped and naked on that snow bank in the woods . . . I just had to tell somebody." He was tormented by the flames of a guilty conscience.

Illustrations of this idea could be multiplied. For instance, when the works of Jesus were attracting wide attention, Herod Antipas, who had put John the Baptist to death, dismissed all other explanations of the mighty miracles of Christ. He said it was "John, whom I beheaded, he is risen" (Mark 6:16). The guilty conscience of Herod, who had murdered an innocent man of God to please his wife, thought that Jesus was John come back to life. He was already in torment. Again, the story is told of Tiberias, who, while issuing slaughter and torture orders from his island retreat at Capri, commenced a letter to a friend in these words: "How shall I write, or what shall I write? May the gods and goddesses destroy me worse than I daily feel myself punishing if I know." This statement shows that already this ruler was in a Tartarus he had made for himself. So, for some people, even now in this life, the flames of torment are kindled in their hearts; and that memory will be retained in Hades in Tartarus. O memories that bless and burn.

Or, as another poet so well expressed it:

> The moving finger writes; and, having writ,
> Moves on; nor all your piety nor wit
> Shall lure it back to cancel half a line,
> Nor all your tears wash out a word of it.
> —Omar Khayyam

Thus, the rich man was alone with himself; and the memory of his misdeeds, lost opportunities, and the terrible condition of his brothers all brought torment. Although men often put themselves in a hell of anguish in this life—and suffer torment after death in Hades in Tartarus—this is not to be confused with future, final punishment in hell (*Gehenna*).

Too, the day will never come, in this world or the next, when sins, once pardoned by the grace of God through the blood of Christ, will again be brought to light or hurled by the Lord into the sinner's face (cf. Ephesians 2:8–9; Hebrews 8:12; Acts 2:38; 3:19). Memory, therefore, which is absolutely indestructible, is one great element in future retribution. Although one may forget some things momentarily, nothing is completely lost by the soul. At the final judgment one will remember his past life (Matthew 25:34–45). Memory retains things acquired in life; and in Hades, at the judgment, and in eternity, nothing will be forgotten.

> Painted on the eternal wall
> The past shall re-appear.

Memory, then, will be a part of the sinner's punishment in Hades and in Gehenna; each act of wickedness will stand out before him as it really was—rebellion against God. This accounts in part for the agony of the lost in Hades; it is a natural and necessary result of violating the law of God. Since memory remains with the wicked in Hades, it must be a part of the flame, which is surely not literal but symbolic of a spiritual anguish, as intense to the soul as the pain of material fire is to the quivering flesh. Nevertheless, the suffering is real; the figure denotes the intensity of agony. The sacred Scriptures describe both the happiness of the righteous and the torments of the wicked in Hades in symbols and figures; yet they are real conditions. Happiness, or misery, depends upon the character of the individual of whom it is a part. Tartarus must be a state (as well as a place) of unspeakable sadness, even though it is in Hades. This torment is not an angry God meting out punishment, but rather the consequence of living sinfully in a moral universe, one in which laws operate as certainly as the law of gravitation. Men never break law; they violate it. The man who walks over the cliff does not break the law of gravitation; he proves it! He breaks himself!

So there was no angry denunciation from Abraham when he said to the rich man, "Son, remember that thou in thy lifetime receivedst thy good things, and likewise Lazarus evil things: but now he is comforted, and thou art tormented" (Luke 16:25 KJV). There were both comforts and torments—and each with exact justice. What the rich man had chosen by the life he lived, now he received in Hades. Each one kindles his own flame, if such will be his after death. No need of literal flame and sulphur that some speak of being in Hades. Souls cannot be burned with that kind of flame; but souls can be burned with the flame of memory. Hence, the disobedient, aware that future punishment is deserved and awaiting, begin suffering before entering into Gehenna. Sheol in the Old Testament and Hades in the New Testament refer to the place of departed spirits, and there is a compartment there for the wicked where there will be suffering.

Yet some men go on in sin, treasuring up wrath of "the righteous judgment of God" (Romans 2:5). When one passes from this life in a sinful condition, no escape is possible from the bitterness of memory, the flames of remorse, and the stings of conscience that shall be his forever. Oh, what a mass of fuel some are gathering now to feed the fires of hell! Just think how some souls now in Hades must be in torment with the memories still clinging to them! What they would give to be able to forget! Hence, the Scriptures teach there are torments in Hades; the anguish of the rich man was punishment endured in Tartarus. Abraham said to the rich man, "Son, remember . . ."

Does Death Change One's Condition?

Again, people ask: "Can death work any change in a person's life?" Indeed not! Death cannot make saints out of sinners. If men love spiritual things and have been obedient to God's will on earth, they will be in Paradise when they die. The person who will find happiness in the hereafter is the one who has developed a delight in spiritual values during his earthly existence, and this development of spiritual character requires effort. The one prepared to enjoy the things God has promised the righteous is the one who now, in this life, enjoys the worship of God, the study of His will, and all things holy and righteous. If a person does not enjoy these things now, how can he suddenly begin to enjoy them when he dies? He will be the same person after he dies as he was before. Hence, those who do not love and serve the Lord on earth will not become changed in death and be happy in Hades.

Some people seem to think that when they die, delights and desires will undergo complete change—no longer will they find pleasure in the evil things which interest them now. They seem to think that spiritual values, that mean so little now, will then become precious. However, if a person is sinful and carnal, no profitable spiritual change will begin suddenly and mysteriously when the body dies, since the real self continues to live, unaffected in character by death. No power in death can transform a Nero into a Paul. The old maxim, "Heaven is a prepared place for a prepared people," has much truth in it. The Scriptures speak of Judas Iscariot after his death as having gone "to his own place" (Acts 1:25)—to the surroundings and company that were appropriate to his conduct and interests on earth. That is where all will go. Man's future condition depends upon what he is, not on what he has or where he lived, for men do not stray accidentally into the blessedness of heaven. They prepare for it, and for it they are prepared. Heaven gets into them here before they get into heaven there. Tartarus, just like heaven and hell, is a condition as well as a place. Each one, when this life is over, will go to his own place, whether it be a place of joy or one of pain. And at the judgment, as it was said of Judas, every man shall go to his own place, the place that he himself has made certain by the choices and deeds of his life. In this place—either heaven or hell—he will continue to exist forever.

The objection is heard: "God decides where a person will spend eternity." True, but only in one sense. It is no arbitrary decision on the part of God whether or not one will enter into heaven or hell. It is not like that. To try to live in heaven with God in the hereafter without the spiritual qualities of the soul would be as disastrous as a fish trying to live out of water. It is not that God arbitrarily excludes people from heaven. Man does that himself. The Bible is emphatic in that eternal life is conditional (cf. Hebrews 5:9).

Therefore, one carries in death the character he has formed in life. It is a very common, but mistaken notion, that in death one somehow takes upon himself a new and different character (if he be wicked). But Scripture teaches that one dies as he lives; he goes to the intermediate state with the character, habits, and feelings formed in this life; each person in Hades possesses the same moral characteristics he had in this life. "The wicked is thrust down in his evil-doing" (Proverbs 14:32); he does not leave his guilt behind him; he departs with it. The decrees of the Lord touching the character and destiny of all men after death and the judgment are given in these words: "He that is unrighteous, let him do unrighteousness still: and he that is filthy, let him be made filthy still: and he that is righteous, let him do righteousness still: and he that is holy, let him be made holy still" (Revelation 22:11). ". . . in the place where the tree falleth, there shall it be" (Ecclesiastes 11:3). Death is simply passing from one state of existence to another. All that the soul is at death, it will be after death—nothing more, nothing less. It loses nothing of itself. It only goes. The unjust will remain unjust forever; the holy will remain holy to all eternity. The destiny of the soul is decided at death.

What Is the Gulf in Hades?

Still others ask, "What is the gulf in the hadean world mentioned by Christ?" The gulf is not a chasm to be measured in feet or yards. It is a moral separation—a division in character. A like gulf exists in this life. The two men in jail, referred to previously, were separated by a gulf—one was guilty, one was innocent. Two people may sit side by side, yet have a gulf between them—one may be righteous, the other wicked.

Consider another illustration. Two men go to a concert of classical music. One is a trained musician and has given hours to studying and practicing music. Every phase of the concert gives him delight to the utmost of his capacity. By his side is his friend who has never liked music, never taken any interest in it, and never studied it. His friend is bored by the entire program; in fact, he longs for the intermission and its delights. Between these two men there is a great, fixed gulf, as far as that program is concerned. The musician cannot bring his friend into the bliss that his appreciation of music has made for him. The two men, though good friends and together during the concert, listen to the recital in two different ways, according to their capacity for music, and this capacity depends to a great extent on their previous training.

Now, apply this to the spirits in Hades. Their condition, whatever it may be, will depend upon their character, a character in which they have developed or failed to develop in their capacity for God and for things spiritual. Since the ego (self) continues its existence, the essential self will be the same in the life beyond the grave. Thus, what one makes of that self now will determine his condition in Hades. It is no meaningless proverb which says:

Sow an act, and reap a habit;
Sow a habit, and reap a character;
Sow a character, and reap a destiny.

Or, to express this thought in another way, each person is the captain of his soul.

I am the master of my fate:
I am the captain of my soul.

How, then, must the sinful soul in Tartarus feel? He must have a sense of deprivation as he is separated from God. It must include remorse and sorrow, a sense of the harm he has done others, a realization of the effects of sin, and a realization that continuance in sin has wrought the deterioration of character. So now he comes to hate self.

Although the idea of the sinner's suffering after death in flames of fire was perhaps caricatured in a bad way by some in former generations, people are doing this present generation a greater disservice in making light of sin and pretending that it does not matter. Some seem to think that God will pat everyone on the head at last and say, "There, there, it doesn't matter, as I am sure you didn't mean it, so enter thou into the joys divine." Men need to remind themselves that the tender lips of Jesus gave the narrative of the rich man in torment, depicting the most terrible things ever said about sin and suffering. Sin is an awful thing, the blackest thing in the universe.

Why Is Final Judgment Necessary?

Still another question is asked: "Is not the final judgment unnecessary, since long before that time the wicked know where they will spend eternity; so know the righteous? Since this is true of the souls in Hades, separated in either Paradise or Tartarus, why a final judgment?" The judgment is necessary for several reasons:

1. Those still living when time ends have not been assigned to bliss or misery; hence, they must be judged. The degree of weal or woe everyone will receive in soul and body for eternity has not yet been designated, for up to the moment of the judgment day, all the dead are in Hades, either Paradise or Tartarus, with respect to their souls only.

2. Righteousness must be publicly displayed that God may be glorified and Christ and the honor of His people vindicated. When the world last saw Jesus, He was on a cross dying as a criminal. (He was seen only by His

followers after His resurrection.) This estimate must be reversed. All men, even those who pierced Him, must see Him in all of His glory. At the judgment, then, the justice of God will become evident. The righteousness of Christ, of His cause, and of His people will be made manifest, and even the wicked will be made to admit it.

3. Too, the essence of judgment is exposure. The true nature of each person will then be made clear, the hidden revealed, and all deeds will face their consequences. The exact sentence affecting each person will be pronounced at the judgment, and the reason for it will be given. Every deed which a man has ever performed, every word he has ever spoken, every thought he has ever conceived, every ambition ever cherished, must be laid bare for himself and all to see. The Bible says, therefore, that at the judgment the books will be opened (Revelation 20:12); that is, the complete record of each person's life, which exists in God's omniscience, will then be made manifest.

4. Further, note that the consequences of one's works on earth follow him to the judgment. "The evil that men do lives after them," Shakespeare said. So lives also the good that men do; their works do not stop when they die. Of Christians, the Bible says after their death: "Their works follow with them" (Revelation 14:13). Who can measure, for example, the good influence of the life of the apostle Paul or the bad influence of Tom Paine? Both have been dead for generations, yet they are still influencing individuals through their writings. Both men are as potent for good or evil now as when they were living, with some people probably more so. Who, then, can measure the good of righteousness or the guilt of sin? Only the final day of God's judgment can determine what the full extent of one's life has been. The Lord at that time will hold men responsible not only for the commission of their own deeds, but also for the consequences resulting from their deeds. The Scriptures tell of Abel's obedience to God and affirm that "he being dead yet speaketh" (Hebrews 11:4). The influence of one's life was also affirmed by Jehovah through the prophet Jeremiah: "I, Jehovah, search the mind, I try the heart, even to give to every man according to his ways, according to the fruit of his doings" (Jeremiah 17:10; cf. 32:19).

Each person, therefore, should realize that he is living not only for time but also for eternity. Hence, the Scriptures definitely declare that there shall be a judgment for all at the end of time (cf. Matthew 25:31–46; Romans 14:10, 12; 2 Corinthians 5:10). The holiness of God demands that the sinner be fairly judged and punished.

Questions for Discussion

1. Has God revealed to men in His Word all things about spirits in Hades?
2. Why has God not revealed more?
3. Did Lazarus tell anything about what he (his spirit) saw and heard while his body was in the grave for four days?
4. Did the apostle Paul tell what he saw and heard in Paradise? Why not?
5. What about those who have claimed latter and special revelations from God?
6. What is the Lord's final, complete, and authoritative revelation to man?
7. What should always be man's first concern? If he does this, what will God do for him? What about those who reject much of the Bible? What of the liberal trend in religion today?
8. What does the Bible teach about the dead seeing and knowing what people are now doing on earth?
9. Do the dead remember things about their loved ones and friends as they were when they left this earth? Are they concerned about their spiritual welfare?
10. Does the Bible give a description of the form of disembodied spirits or relate how they live out of the bodies?
11. What are the two subdivisions of Hades? In what part was the rich man? In what part was Lazarus?
12. Explain the difference in Tartarus and Gehenna.
13. Is Abraham's bosom the same as Paradise in Luke 23:43?
14. How did Jesus describe the suffering of the lost in Tartarus? How can there be suffering for the lost before the final judgment?
15. Is the suffering in Hades as complete as it shall be in Gehenna?
16. How can memory cause torment even here on earth?
17. How are the joys of the righteous described in Hades? Will their delights be increased in the eternal state beyond the judgment?
18. When will the full punishment of the wicked and the full reward of the righteous begin? How long will these last?
19. When will the lost go into Gehenna? Have any been sent to hell yet?
20. Will the damned ever be able to get away from himself or change his condition in Hades? Is Hades a state, a place, or both?
21. What is meant by the gulf? Is the destiny of every soul fixed at death?
22. Does death make any change in character of the one who dies?
23. Do all the dead know immediately after death that they are in either Paradise or Tartarus? Do they all know what their eternal destiny is going to be? Will there be any surprises at the day of judgment? (cf. Matthew 7:22–23.) Can a faithful Bible student deceive himself into believing that

all is well with his soul and then be disappointed at the judgment (cf. 1 Corinthians 13:1–3; 2 Thessalonians 2:11–12)? Does the Bible give conclusive answers to these questions?

24. Why is the final judgment necessary?
25. Does the influence of one's life, for good or for evil, continue after death? If so, for how long?
26. Why will not the final judgment be held until the end of time?

– 12 –

What about Purgatory?

"And besides all this, between us and you there is a great gulf fixed"
Luke 16:26

This chapter relates to the idea of the theory of purgatory. Much misunderstanding has occurred concerning souls in Hades because of the erroneous Roman teaching during the Reformation in order to support their doctrine of purgatory and because of the usage of the word *hell* for both Hades and Gehenna in the King James Version.

The Theory Explained

The theory of purgatory is that in Hades the souls make satisfaction by suffering for sins committed after baptism, the period of time depending on the degree of their guilt. Once they are purged, they go then to heaven. Those who hold to this theory believe the "Church" on earth has power by her prayers and the sacrifices of mass to shorten these sufferings or to remit them altogether.

Webster's New Collegiate Dictionary defines purgatory as: "1. An intermediate state after death for expiatory purification. 2. A place or state of temporary punishment." Hence, the doctrine of purgatory is that at death man goes to an intermediate state for temporary punishment, after which he is released and goes on to heaven.

Cardinal Gibbons said concerning purgatory:

> The Catholic Church teaches that, besides a place of eternal torments for the wicked and of everlasting rest for the righteous, there exists in the next life a middle state of temporary punishment, allotted for those who have died in venial sin, or who have not satisfied the justice of God for sins already forgiven. She also teaches that, although the souls consigned to this intermediate state, commonly called purgatory, cannot help themselves, they may be aided by the suffrages of the faithful on earth.[1]

---

1 Charles Chiniquy, *Fifty Years in the Church of Rome* (Grand Raptids: Baker Book House, reprint ed., 1960), p. 247.

So the doctrine of purgatory teaches that the spirit goes into his place, Hades, there to suffer for sins committed in life on earth. When enough is done, the spirit is released from purgatory and finally enters heaven. It teaches that prayers, money, and good works done by the living in behalf of those dead who are in purgatory will expedite their release.

The doctrine of purgatory does not offer a second chance to those who have refused Christ here; it rather is the place in which the true child of the "Church," who died at peace, but whose soul was not yet perfect, can have expiation made for "venial" sin by suffering and thus escape the bonds of guilt. In purgatory, according to the theory of said Church, the souls make satisfaction for sins committed after baptism by suffering for a while—a longer or shorter period of time, according to the degree of their guilt—and are purged after death, before they go to heaven.

Those who hold to the theory of purgatory believe the Church on earth has power by her prayers and the sacrifices of mass to shorten these sufferings, or to remit them altogether. But does the Bible teach that satisfaction can be rendered in the future life for the sins done in the body? Biblically, purgatory is an unknown. There is no such place.

The Scriptures teach that there is conscious suffering in Hades for the wicked in the condition called Tartarus; this suffering is not borne by the righteous, for their condition is one of conscious bliss and joy. But neither the rich man nor Lazarus went to purgatory; neither made a change. Then how can it be said that by the prayers and money paid to certain ones on earth, a disobedient soul may pass from Tartarus to Paradise? This idea of purgatory has no foundation in the Scriptures. The intermediate state is not a place of purgatory—for anybody. Christ said in the story of the rich man and Lazarus that the rich man in Hades was told "between us and you there is a great gulf fixed, that they that would pass from hence to you may not be able, and that none may cross over from thence to us" (Luke 16:26). According to this passage, the Scriptures teach that the condition of all those who die in sin is fixed and can never be changed. In Hades no opportunity is given the wicked to make a change.

Regardless of how much men's feelings may incline them to wish the theory of purgatory to be true, it is false. God's Holy Word alone is man's sole and absolute authority, and it forbids a purgatory. What the Bible teaches is the truth—on this as on all other subjects—whether men agree or not. Purgatory is an invention of men, of pagan origin.

Several other objections can be urged against the doctrine of purgatory, showing it to be neither Scriptural nor reasonable. For instance:

1. The theory of purgatory is opposed to the truth that men's sins are purged by the blood of Christ, not by some pain inflicted in Hades. "The blood

of Jesus his Son cleanseth us from all sin" (1 John 1:7; cf. Hebrews 9:22–28).

2. The theory of purgatory attributes to human works the power to shorten one's sufferings in torment; but the rich man in torment was not told his brothers might pray and pay in order to remove the pangs of his torment. All the masses the rich man's brothers might have offered for him, with all the money he may have left them, could have availed nothing. There is no hint in all of God's Word that the state of the dead can be altered by those who live on the earth. On the other hand, the Scriptures teach that at death the condition of all is fixed; there is no further opportunity for anyone to be saved (Luke 16:26).

3. The belief of purgatory attributes to people on earth a certain power to forgive sins, while the Bible teaches that only God can forgive sins (Mark 2:7; Hebrews 8:12).

4. The doctrine of purgatory is against good judgment. Take this illustration as an example: Let us suppose that my mother dies as a very wicked person, although a member of the "Church"; your mother dies as a very upright, but erring, person. As per the theory, they will both go to purgatory. I have plenty of money; many prayers are said in behalf of my mother, so according to the theory, she will soon pass from purgatory to heaven. However, your mother, who has a son lacking means to pay for prayers in her behalf, must remain in purgatory and suffer a long time. Is God so unjust? One cannot believe it!

Two passages from the Bible, besides tradition and the authority of the Church, are often used in an effort to support the idea of purgatory.

Some Works Will Be Burned Up

Paul said,

> But if any man buildeth on the foundation gold, silver, costly stones, wood, hay, stubble; each man's work shall be made manifest: for the day shall declare it, because it is revealed in fire; and the fire itself shall prove each man's work of what sort it is. If any man's work shall abide which he built thereon, he shall receive a reward. If any man's work shall be burned, he shall suffer loss: but he himself shall be saved; yet so as through fire (1 Corinthians 3:12–15).

There is nothing here about purgatory, punishment, or souls purified. Paul used an illustration. In the example, the church is compared to a building into which may be placed both good and bad materials. The foundation is Christ (v. 11). The materials are the converts; the one who builds on the foundation is each

Christian who teaches God's Word. Some members are good, metaphorically represented by gold, silver, and valuable stones; some converts may turn out bad, represented by wood, hay, and stubble. The fire is the testing that comes to all converts to try their faith. If some converts are lost, it does not follow that the Christian teacher will be lost. His life will be tested just as other members' lives are tried. If the converts—the material built into the church—are like gold and silver, they will stand the test and endure; but if some are like wood and hay, they will not endure. If some converts do turn back to the world and are finally lost, the teacher's work will thereby be lost. Note that the passage also says that the day (singular, one day) shall declare each man's work. The day of judgment will reveal the true character of all in and out of the church; purgatory will not do so. Purgatory involves many days. Christ wanted the church to be built of true, sincere Christians—the proper material—and not of hypocrites. Too, the passage says, "The fire itself shall prove each man's work of what sort it is." It does not say every Christian will be subjected to the fire of purgatory. The fire in verse 13 is applied to man's work (product), and not to man himself. The passage emphasized "each man's work." Assuming the doctrine of purgatory there to be true, all must go to purgatory, and if so, what about Lazarus? Did Lazarus go to Paradise without first going to purgatory? If Lazarus could pass from this life as a righteous person, undefiled, and go to Abraham's bosom, so can others.

Furthermore, what about those living when Christ comes again? Will they first go to purgatory to have sin burned out of them? They will go before the Lord in judgment and from there be assigned to either heaven or hell. The passage in 1 Corinthians 3 teaches that the Christian's works which may be burned are the persons he converted who become unfaithful. This would be a loss, but he himself could still be saved; yet he too would be tested. The people at Corinth were Paul's work, and he feared some might be lost.

One Sin Hath Never Forgiveness

The other verse used in support of purgatory is Christ's statement concerning the sin of blasphemy against the Holy Spirit. Jesus said this sin would not be "forgiven him, neither in this world, nor in that which is to come" (Matthew 12:32; cf. Mark 3:28–30). Those who believe in purgatory say this implies that other sins can be forgiven in the world to come. The words of Christ contain no such implication. Christ did not say some sins will be forgiven in the world to come; he used an emphatic never—that there is absolutely no pardon for this sin, ever. Those who blaspheme against the Holy Spirit have no pardon in this world or the one to come; forgiveness can never happen under any circumstances; this sin is unpardonable. This is all that Christ affirmed.

Some affirm that since "world" comes from the Greek word *aion,* often translated "age" (see margin of the American Standard Version), and since at that time the people were living in the Jewish age, this age meant the Jewish dispensation and the age to come, the Christian age. Although this word is sometimes translated "age," as in Hebrews 9:26, it is not always so rendered; as, for instance, in Mark 10:30, where the word refers to heaven, the eternal state (cf. Luke 20:35. Are there any marriages in the Christian age?) Luke 16:25 shows that at death the gulf is fixed. From the context (Matthew 12:36), the two phrases, "this world" and "that which is to come," must cover the whole present and future. By any fair interpretation, Christ certainly implied a continued existence in the world to come as much as in this world, and declared that in that world, as in this, the sinner shall forever remain under the displeasure of God, never forgiven. Mark 3:29 expresses both: "But whosoever shall blaspheme against the Holy Spirit hath never forgiveness, but is guilty of an eternal sin"; that is, the condemnation of God will rest upon him eternally; he will be forever in the state of condemnation. The wicked shall remain forever sinful and never forgiven.

No sins will be forgiven after death. If one obtains forgiveness for any sin, the pardoning from God will have to come while the person lives in this world, for there is no forgiveness in the world to come. If then the spirit of man is separated by sin from the Spirit of God in this life, and a person dies in this condition, that separation becomes an eternal, unending separation from God. So Matthew 12:32 cannot be used in support of the theory of purgatory, as it contradicts the plain teaching of Luke 16:25, which says that at death the gulf is fixed.

Purgatory is just another scheme invented to obtain more money from deluded souls. No one who knows the history of those who have been deceived by it can deny that it has proved to be most lucrative. The amount of money from this single doctrine of purgatory is beyond human computation! Men began teaching purgatory about A.D.588. Tetzel, the famous seller of indulgences, made much of this teaching prior to the Reformation. Cardinal Gibbons called the doctrine of purgatory a cherished doctrine.[1]

Charles Chiniquy was a member of the Church of Rome for fifty years and functioned as a priest for half of that time. After his conversion to Protestantism he wrote:

> How long, O Lord, shall that insolent enemy of the gospel, the Church of Rome, be permitted to fatten herself upon the tears of the widow and of the orphan by means of that cruel and impious invention of paganism—purgatory? Wilt thou not be merciful unto so many nations which are still the vic-

---

1 Charles Chiniquy, *Fifty Years in the Church of Rome*, p. 247.

> tims of that great imposture? Oh, do remove the veil which covers the eyes of the priests and people of Rome, as Thou hast removed it from mine![1]

The doctrine of purgatory: a "cherished doctrine" or a "cruel and impious invention of paganism." Which is it? However cherished or lucrative, it forms no part of the teaching of Christ, the apostles, or any other truly inspired man. Let no one, therefore, be deceived into paying money in order that souls of their loved ones might be prayed out of purgatory. By this doctrine, the possessions of grieving loved ones are seized upon and used by these religionists. It is a cruel and vicious racket, a monstrous fraud.

It is claimed by said Church that Peter was the vicar of Christ on earth and had power to forgive sins; it is also claimed that it is the prerogative of the authorities of the said Church, at their discretion, to remit entirely or partially the penalty of sins under which the souls there detained are suffering. This is why the practice connected with the theory of purgatory is a lucrative business. Yet, how absurd the idea that the Pope and his subordinates have power over the unseen world: power to retain or remit the sins of departed spirits or power to deliver souls from purgatorial fire or allow them to remain under its torments!

But appeal, in support of the doctrine, is made to the express declarations of Christ. First, the language of Christ to Peter: "I will give unto thee the keys of the kingdom of heaven: and whatsoever thou shalt bind on earth shall be bound in heaven: and whatsoever thou shalt loose on earth shall be loosed in heaven" (Matthew 16:19 KJV). The same promise of binding and loosing was later given to all the apostles (Matthew 18:18). The primacy of Peter cannot be sustained by the Scriptures. Christ has all authority (Matthew 28:18). He is the head of the church, and the church is subject unto Him (Colossians 1:18; Ephesians 5:23–24). Peter never spoke of himself as the head of the church on earth nor exercised any authority over the other apostles. The apostles never referred to Peter as their head or the head of the church. No individual on earth has ever been granted the privilege of exercising authority over Christ's church. Neither has God given to any man or any set of men the right to make laws for His church. Christ is the only universal head of the church, and He lives forever. Furthermore, Christ did not promise to build His church upon Peter but upon the truth of Peter's confession—that is, upon His divinity. Literally translated, the promise of Christ to Peter was, "Whatever you bind will have already been bound in heaven." That means the apostles announced to the world what had already been bound or loosed in heaven. Whatever Peter and the other apostles bound or loosed on earth was also bound or loosed or ratified in heaven; namely, the terms of salvation and all matters pertaining to the church.

---

1 Charles Chiniquy, *Fifty Years in the Church of Rome*, p. 29.

The second passage used are the words of Christ to all the apostles: "Receive ye the Holy Spirit: whose soever sins ye forgive, they are forgiven unto them; whose soever sins ye retain, they are retained" (John 20:22–23). This means that in their preaching the apostles were guided infallibly into all truth by the Holy Spirit (John 14:26; 16:13). They announced the conditions upon which the Lord would forgive sins. Their power, therefore, was simply declarative. Beginning at Jerusalem on the day of Pentecost, the apostles declared Christ's terms of pardon, guided by the Holy Spirit, in their public ministry (Acts 2:36–38). In this way only did the apostles remit and retain sins, that is, by declaring the conditions of salvation. Had they undertaken to bind or loose, to remit or retain sin on any other conditions than those prescribed by the Savior, their preaching would have amounted to nothing and brought upon them the curse of heaven (Galatians 1:8–9). Moreover, the apostles had no successors. Today, man does not have access to inspired men but to the inspired Book, and he can find in it the Lord's terms of forgiveness. Faithful ministers of God's Word now declare what God has revealed in the Scriptures (cf. 2 Timothy 3:16–17).

Thus, the power to forgive sins is the exclusive prerogative of God (Mark 2:7). For this reason, the apostles never claimed, never possessed, and never pretended to exercise, the power assumed by said Church, in regard to the remission of sins. They never presumed to pronounce the absolution of any sinner in the sight of God. They had no authority to do this, but they could declare the terms upon which God alone had promised to forgive sins. One man has no more power to forgive sins than another. No such power has ever been committed to the hands of sinful men.

The Protestant Reformation had its origin in a righteous protest against abuses then existing in the Roman Catholic Church. Chief among those that evoked the theses of Martin Luther was that of the doctrine of indulgences. The Pope was trying to raise money to complete St. Peter's Cathedral in Rome, and one of the ways of securing it was by the sale of these indulgences. Those who had the sale of these indulgences taught that by the purchase of them with money designated for so holy a cause, men might buy pardon from sin for themselves or for their dead friends and loved ones. Against this doctrine the Reformers protested with all their might. They emphasized that no Christian has priestly powers over other Christians. Through Jesus Christ every Christian is a priest and can address himself directly to God on his own behalf.

And so should it be done now. The whole fabric of priestly power—the most absolute and the most dreaded ever exercised over man—should be exposed by the teaching of God's Word. The belief of the people that the priests have power to forgive sins and to save or destroy souls at will is founded on "lying wonders." The "miracles" wrought as proof of their doctrines are frauds (cf. 2 Thessalonians 2:7–12; Revelation 13:14).

What about Praying to the Departed?

Closely associated with the doctrine of purgatory is the invocation of saints. People ask, "What does the Bible teach on the subject of praying to the dead?" Really, the subject of prayer between those on earth and those in the other world can be divided into three parts: (1) prayer for the dead, (2) prayer to the dead, and (3) the dead praying for the living. Some teach that the souls in purgatory are relieved by the prayers of certain ones on earth. Prayers for the living are enjoined in the Scriptures (e.g., James 5:16; Acts 8:24), but nowhere in the Bible did Christ or any inspired man tell the living they should pray for the dead, the souls in Hades. The Scriptures give no sanction to prayers on behalf of the dead. Neither do they give sanction to prayers through or to anyone who has departed this life.

Man's access to God in prayer is through Jesus Christ (Ephesians 2:18; John 14:6); Christians are to pray in the name of Christ (John 16:23–26). Christ makes intercession for God's children at the right hand of the Father. "It is Christ Jesus that died, yea rather, that was raised from the dead, who is at the right hand of God, who also maketh intercession for us" (Romans 8:34). "Wherefore also he is able to save to the uttermost them that draw near unto God through him, seeing he ever liveth to make intercession for them" (Hebrews 7:25). Further, Jesus is man's only mediator. "For there is one God, one mediator also between God and men, himself man, Christ Jesus" (1 Timothy 2:5). No person—living or dead—can qualify as man's mediator. Only Jesus can qualify as a perfect mediator, for He is the only one who is equally related to both sides, God and man. Too, man does not need another mediator in addition to Christ anymore than he needs another God other than Jehovah. Moreover, according to the Bible, every Christian needs no mediator other than Jesus, his High Priest (Hebrews 8:1). Christians pray to God through Christ, not to or through saints. Praying for the dead is a superstitious practice, having no support from the Bible.

Likewise, the dead cannot benefit those on earth when the living pray to them for help; nothing is said in the Scriptures about fellowship of the living with the dead. The request of the rich man in anguish is the only invocation whereof the Bible speaks, and this case is far from being a satisfactory example —his pleading availed nothing (Luke 16:27–31).

Some religionists think they should pray to Mary. Although it was an honor for Mary to have been the mother of Jesus, the Scriptures do not sanction prayer or worship to Mary. She is not a Christian's intercessor. On the contrary, the Bible strictly forbids man to worship any being but God (Exodus 34:14;

20:4–5; Deuteronomy 6:13–14; Isaiah 45:20). The Scriptures teach it is idolatry to worship or pray to any creature; in fact, no idolatry is more gross than the worship of the creature more than the Creator (Romans 1:25). Man is to worship God (John 4:24; 1 John 5:21; Revelation 22:8–9). Abraham was highly honored as the father of a people through whom the Messiah would come, Paul was chosen to be an apostle to the Gentiles, Peter was honored in preaching the gospel first to the Israelites and to the Gentiles, but one dare not worship Abraham, Paul, or Peter because of these things. The Bible has no statement that would even intimate that man is to pray to Mary, or any departed saint, as his mediator or intercessor; such practice, since it violates divine teaching, is wrong. The last time Mary, the mother of Jesus, is mentioned in Scripture is Acts 1:14; this was a few days before the church of the Lord Jesus Christ was established in Jerusalem on the day of Pentecost (Acts 2). The conclusion, then, is that praying for the dead, like the doctrine of purgatory, is an invention of men without a single reference in the Holy Scriptures which sanctions the practice, and such practice has no value whatsoever. "Thou shalt worship the Lord thy God, and him only shalt thou serve" (Matthew 4:10).

Speaking about praying for the dead, Cardinal Gibbons further said:

> The existence of purgatory naturally implies the correlative dogma, the utility of praying for the dead . . .
>
> How consoling is it to the Catholic, to think that, in praying thus for his departed friend, his prayers are not in violation of, but in accordance with, the voice of the Church . . .
>
> Oh, it is this thought that robs death of its sting and makes the separation of friends endurable.[1]

One can agree with the cardinal that "the existence of purgatory naturally implies the correlative dogma, the utility of praying for the dead," but we must also affirm there is no teaching in the Bible instructing Christians to pray for the dead. Nothing can now be done, either by those who have died or by those who are living, to change the condition of the departed, because the gulf is fixed.

Secular history records the doctrine of purgatory:

> The first decree on this subject is found in connection with the councils of Florence, 1439. The 25th session of the Council of Trent declares that there is a purgatory and that the souls there detained are helped by the suffrages of the faithful.[2]

May all, therefore, avoid this evil doctrine of men. However, let no one in rejecting this invention of men denounce anything that the Scriptures teach on

---

1 Charles Chiniquy, *Fifty Years in the Church of Rome*, pp. 247, 262, 263.

2 Nelson's Encyclopedia, Vol. 10, p. 114.

the subject of the Hadean world. The Bible just does not teach that the spirit goes at death into purgatory. There is no Scripture that teaches men to pray to Mary or any departed saint as his mediator or intercessor. Christians need no other mediator than Christ.

Summary

To summarize, these important facts have been established in this study about human souls in the intermediate or disembodied state:

1. The soul or spirit of man lives on after the body dies.
2. Souls out of their earthly bodies are conscious; they do not sleep.
3. Obedient souls are happy in Hades.
4. Disobedient spirits are in anguish in Hades.
5. Souls are not on probation in the intermediate state. Tartarus is not a place to prepare for the judgment and heaven.
6. The Bible affirms that judgment, not probation, will be the next great event after death. "And inasmuch as it is appointed unto men once to die, and after this cometh judgment" (Hebrews 9:27). Furthermore, nothing is said in Scripture about any probation after death and before the judgment. The resurrection will be either unto life or unto death (John 5:28–29).
7. Now is the time to prepare for life after death. This life alone is decisive for eternity. People need to realize that this life is the time for a person to obey the Lord and be saved and that each person must act for himself. When one dies, the day of grace is gone forever; opportunity is gone; the gates are shut. The departed one is now in the hands of a just and merciful God, and there each individual must be left, knowing that the Judge of all the earth will do right (cf. Genesis 18:25). Although the "second chance" doctrines of men may attempt to bridge the great gulf that Christ said was fixed and impassable, those theories are all without Scriptural foundation. At death the gulf is fixed.
8. These Scripture passages should serve as a beacon light to warn all those who are now living in disobedience to God to turn to Him in faith and obedience before it is forever too late. Some day it will be too late. Let no one put any trust in the future, for there is no pardon after death (cf. Proverbs 27:1; James 4:13–17; Luke 12:19–20). Probation ends with this life, and the Bible does not teach that sinners will have a chance to be saved after death. It is on this side, and on this side only, that men can believe in and obey Christ their Savior and, through the grace of God, be saved from their sins.

As a tree falls, so must it lie;
As a man lives, so must he die;

As a man dies, so must he be
Through the ages of eternity.

9. Whatever condition the soul enters into at death, that condition is changeless as to moral character. So shall it remain in Hades, so shall it be at the resurrection, and so shall it be in eternity. Hear and heed these words of warning to all: "Behold, now is the acceptable time; behold, now is the day of salvation . . . Wherefore even as the Holy Spirit saith, Today, if ye shall hear his voice, harden not your hearts" (Hebrews 3:7). The apostles preached this as the true teaching of God's Word. In Hades, no one changes his state. The day of salvation is now—not some future time, whether that be in the disembodied state or at the end of the world. Of course, the lost after death will desire to exchange their state of pain for a place of blessedness, but it will be too late; the chasm will be fixed, and there will be no escape from anguish—there is no post-mortem gospel for them. According to the Scriptures, the probation of man ends at death.
10. In view of these facts, one must insist that the Bible offers no hope of the possibility of a change for the better for those who have died in their sins; the "second chance" idea is false. Cries for help in yonder's world will do no good, for then the last door of opportunity will have been closed. Hence, let each so live that when this life is over, he will not be found on the wrong side of the impassable gulf.

God's Word, the Power to Save

Another lesson that Jesus taught in the narrative of the rich man and Lazarus was that the Lord's way of warning people on earth is the Word of God and that this message is sufficient to lead men to repentance. God will not, at the request of anyone, perform a miracle that someone may be converted. Not only do people now have Moses and the prophets (the Old Testament), but they also have Christ and the apostles (the New Testament) for their instruction and warning (Romans 1:16). If they will not heed this teaching, "neither will they be persuaded, though one rose from the dead" (Luke 16:31 KJV). God, therefore, gives to all sufficient warning through His Word; He urges all men to prepare for death, and nothing beyond His Word will be given to warn men of their needs. So, with the Bible as man's infallible and all-sufficient guide in religion, there is no excuse for anyone to live and die impenitent and be forever lost! But if one should die impenitent and in disobedience to the Lord, then the anguish will be indescribably great, as represented by the torment in flames of fire, torment from which there is no escape. No changing of character and no possibility of salvation is in the future world, so if one secures salvation at all, he must secure it in this life. It is a fearful thing to die in sin. A person cannot live wrong and die right. The only hope for human redemption is while people live. It is too late when they are dead. There is nowhere in Scripture any support for the doctrine of a chance to hear the gospel after death.

This, then, is the teaching of the Scriptures concerning souls in Hades. Hades is the place where departed spirits, both good and bad, remain until the resurrection. This is a conscious state, one in which the spiritual quality of each person is fixed, and not the final state. Hades is limited. In the intermediate state the moral distinctions are clearly defined, and man begins to gather the moral harvests of his earthly life. Here righteous spirits begin to reap their moral harvest in conscious bliss, being "with Christ, which is far better" (Philippians 1:23 KJV). even though their final heaven has not been reached. Here, too, unrighteous souls begin to reap the harvest of sin, in mental anguish, remorse, suffering, and distress. These results, of course, are not forced upon them by an arbitrary God, but are the beginning of the fulfillment of His great moral law that a man reaps as he sows. Although happy or miserable in Hades, as the case might be, the souls have not yet attained ultimate glory or the full degree of punishment.

Everlasting punishment of the wicked in hell (*Gehenna*) and everlasting life in heaven will be studied in later chapters. Other interesting questions about souls in Hades will be considered in the next few chapters. Thus, existence in Hades is an unbroken continuance of the life begun on earth—only the environment is changed. The righteous are happy; the wicked are miserable.

Questions for Discussion

1. What is the meaning of the doctrine of purgatory?
2. Do the wicked in Hades (Tartarus) change? If so, how?
3. Can the gulf that divides the wicked from the righteous be crossed?
4. What are some Biblical reasons for not believing in the doctrine of purgatory?
5. What is the meaning of Paul's language about some works being burned?
6. What does Christ's statement about blasphemy against the Holy Spirit say about sins being forgiven in the world to come?
7. What is the unpardonable sin? Can a person ever become incapable of turning to God in genuine repentance? Do those who harden themselves irrevocably against the Lord on earth close the door of mercy against themselves? (Study Hebrews 6:4–6.)
8. How has the doctrine of purgatory been used by some for gain?
9. In what sense did Peter have the keys of the kingdom? Do any today possess this power? In what sense could the apostles bind and loose?
10. Does the Bible mention anything about invocation of saints?
11. Who in heaven intercedes for the child of God? Does Mary?
12. Who alone should be worshipped? (Use passages of Scripture.)
13. Does the doctrine of purgatory, since it is false, imply that the teaching of the Scriptures on Hades is likewise false?
14. When did the doctrine of purgatory originate? With whom?
15. To whom and through whom does the Christian pray?
16. Are Christians taught in the Scriptures to venerate Mary as the Mother of God? (cf. Luke 11:27–28; Colossians 3:17.)
17. Since Scripture condemns the worship of any save God, what about the making and adoring of images? (cf. Acts 10:26; Revelation 22:8–9; Acts 17:29).

– 13 –

Is There a Second Chance?

". . . he went and preached unto the spirits in prison"
1 Peter 3:19

Some affirm that there is a second chance for those who die impenitent. They argue that there is probation in the next life for those who fail to benefit by the probation they have had in this life. A second chance after death implies, of course, a first chance in this world. However, some have died without having heard the gospel for the first time. Will these people also have a chance after death to accept Christ? If people cannot be convinced in this life and stirred to accept their Savior, how can these impenitent and disobedient spirits obey the Lord in the next world? Nothing in the history of the soul encourages the hope that future probation, even if extended, would be accepted by all the wicked; character tends to become fixed.

If the lost were given another opportunity for repentance, would not this tend to nullify the purpose of this earthly life? Would not there be thousands, yea millions, who would continue to live in sin, since they believe they could change for salvation after death? Consider a few passages from God's Word that are offered in support of the theory that men will have another chance after death and before the judgment to hear the gospel and be saved.

Christ Preached to the Spirits in Prison

Peter wrote:

> Because Christ also suffered for sins once, the righteous for the unrighteous, that he might bring us to God; being put to death in the flesh, but made alive in the spirit; in which also he went and preached unto the spirits in prison, that aforetime were disobedient, when the longsuffering of God waited in the days of Noah, while the ark was a preparing, wherein few, that is, eight souls, were saved through water (1 Peter 3:18–20).

Those who believe in a second chance argue from this passage that Christ, while His spirit was in Hades, preached to the spirits (souls) of those who lived in Noah's day, that Christ went into Hades to preach the gospel to the lost, giving them another chance.

The theory of a second chance based upon this passage provokes a number of insurmountable obstacles, counter to plain statements of Scripture. For instance:

1. Why did Christ select the few of Noah's generation and neglect all others who had died impenitent? Why pass by multitudes of other lost souls in Hades and preach only to contemporaries of Noah, who, while still in the flesh, had every opportunity to repent? Why did Christ not give all impenitent souls in Hades another chance? Peter did not say that the preaching was to all people who had lived since the creation of the world up to Noah's time and had died impenitent; neither did he say it was to all who had lived until the death of Christ; he said it was only to those alive during the days of Noah. No other group of people was in Peter's picture.
2. If people who lived during the time of Noah were given another chance to repent, does it not follow that all mankind after Christ's death will be given another chance in Hades? And if all of these then repent, will there be any lost souls in hell (Gehenna)?
3. The passage says nothing of the content of the message that was preached, why Christ preached, the results of Christ's preaching, or whether it now continues. These matters are left untold. If Christ's offer was not salvation, why the preaching?
4. Was Peter consistent in urging fellow-Christians (his readers) to be patient under suffering, yet at the same time informing them that the antediluvians had a second chance?
5. If the message was an offer of salvation, what of the many passages which clearly state that at death one's destiny is sealed and the gulf fixed?
6. What about those who will be alive on the earth when Christ returns? Will they be brought unto judgment without probation, or will they too be given another chance to obey?
7. Finally, since God is no respecter of persons (Acts 10:34), if the Lord gives a post-mortem gospel for some, will He not have to give all disobedient people another chance? In fact, can He be a "no respecter of persons" and not give this opportunity to all?

A close examination of the passage about Christ's preaching to the spirits in prison will reveal its true meaning and show that it offers no proof of probation after death. First Peter 3:18–20 teaches that Christ was put to death in the flesh and quickened (made alive) by (in) the spirit, and that by (in) this spirit, He (long before His incarnation on earth) had preached to the disobedient of Noah's day; that the preaching was done by Christ through Noah, who was inspired by the Holy Spirit, and He preached to the people who were living at the time the ark was being prepared. Please note:

1. The "which" in verse 19 refers to "spirit." The word *spirit* here does not refer to the Holy Spirit—the second person of the Godhead—but the inner principle of life not subject to death. (Compare reading of ASV and RSV with KJV.) "in which [i.e., in this spirit, His pre-existent and divine nature] also he [Christ] went and preached."

   Already Peter in this epistle had spoken of "the Spirit of Christ" as once active in the prophets: "Searching what time or what manner of time the Spirit of Christ which was in them did point unto, when it testified beforehand the sufferings of Christ, and the glories that would follow them" (1 Peter 1:11). So Christ preached through the prophets long before His own personal ministry. Since Jesus has existed from all eternity (John 1:1–3, 14; 17:1–5), He certainly could have done this preaching through the Holy Spirit just as the prophets of the Old Testament spoke as they were moved by the Holy Spirit (2 Peter 1:21; cf. 1 Peter 1:10–11). Furthermore, the Bible contains a direct reference to the work of the Spirit in the days of Noah: "And Jehovah said, My spirit shall not strive with man for ever" (Genesis 6:3). So God's Spirit strove with men through Noah, who, according to Scripture, was a "preacher of righteousness" (2 Peter 2:5; cf. Hebrews 11:7). The Spirit in Noah, appealing to the people, was also the Spirit of Christ warning that sinful generation. Christ did not go in person; He went by the Spirit in the person of Noah. Christ by the Spirit, in Noah, preached unto the spirits in prison. In that manner the Holy Spirit was striving with them. The spirits were in prison at the time when Christ preached to them through Noah.

2. The preaching was done, the passage asserts, "When the long suffering of God waited in the days of Noah, while the ark was a preparing." *When* and *while* are adverbs; they denote the time that the preaching was done by Christ through Noah. That is when the souls (spirits) "were disobedient," during the time of Noah, before the flood, while the ark was being built. So, instead of the preaching being done by Christ in person when His Spirit was in Hades and His body in the tomb, the going, the preaching, and the disobeying were all events of that time when the long suffering of God waited in the days of Noah's preaching, while the ark was being built during the 120 years of his preaching. Therefore, Christ Himself preached before the flood to the antediluvians, in and through Noah,

who was guided by the Holy Spirit; the preaching was done in the days of Noah, during the probation of a hundred and twenty years (Genesis 6:3). Christ, by the Holy Spirit in Noah, preached to those lost in sin during the time that the ark was being prepared. But neither this passage nor any other verse of Scripture tells of Christ's Spirit preaching to anyone for any purpose while His body lay in the grave.

In harmony with Peter's statement in this connection is Paul's reference in which he said that Christ "came and preached peace to you that were far off [i.e., the Gentiles], and peace to them that were nigh [i.e., the Jews]" (Ephesians 2:17). However, Christ never, during His death or following it, preached in person to the Gentiles to whom Paul wrote at Ephesus (Ephesians 2:14). How, then, did Christ preach to them? It was through the inspired apostles, Paul being one of them. Thus if Christ could come and preach to the Gentiles through Paul after His personal ministry, He could also go and preach to the people before the flood through Noah before His personal ministry. What one does through an authorized agent, he is said to do himself. For example, the Bible says Jesus made and baptized more disciples than John during His personal ministry, but He did it through His disciples (John 4:1–2). The actual work was done by others, that is, by His authority; Jesus baptized not at all. Hence, Christ, in the person of Noah, preached to the people before the flood. The preaching was not done while Christ's body was in the tomb and His spirit in Hades, nor after His resurrection. It was during the time of Noah.

3. The spirits were in prison at the time when Christ went and preached to them through Noah. By "in prison" is meant the bondage of sin. "Every one that committeth sin is the bondservant of sin" (John 8:34). Sinners are often referred to in the Scriptures as being captives in Satan's prison until made free from sin (cf. Luke 4:18; Isaiah 61:1–2; 42:7; Romans 6:16; 2 Timothy 2:26). Christ addressed the message through Noah to the intelligence of men, their spirits (cf. 1 Corinthians 2:11). Those antediluvians then were shut up under sentence of death, in sin, awaiting the day of execution; their time and opportunity for accepting the Lord's plea to enter the ark was limited. However, the contemporaries of Noah were obstinate—only eight people were saved from the flood. The prison was the imprisonment in sin, in bondage to Satan.

   There are those who teach that the spirits in prison were the disembodied souls in Tartarus of the people to whom Noah preached—now in prison, in a state of confinement and under restraint as wicked beings, like the fallen angels (2 Peter 2:4; Jude 6). Illustrative of this idea, take the following sentence: The minister said to me, "I married that couple standing there on the corner of the street." Now, did the minister mean by the statement that he married the couple while they were standing there on the corner of the street and that they are now standing there, or did he mean that he married the couple at some previous time and that there they now stand, the same couple, on the corner of the street? Either interpretation is possible, yet the latter meaning is the one that would most likely be given to the above sentence. However, the word *spirits,* used by Peter in the passage under review, does not have to mean disembodied spirits. The word *spirits* can refer to men (1 John 4:1). Of course, when Peter wrote they were dead as to their bodies, yet alive unto God as to their spirits in a disembodied state. Nevertheless, Peter definitely does not say that those who were preached to were in a disembodied state when the preaching was done. Christ did not preach to people when He was dead and in the tomb. *When* and *while* are adverbs of time.

There should be no difficulty in understanding the passage if one will keep in mind these four questions: (1) When did Christ preach to those spirits in prison? (2) How did Christ preach to them? (3) Who were the spirits in prison? (4) What was the prison in which the spirits were held? Christ preached in the days of Noah through Noah to those antediluvians in sin. The Bible plainly declares when they lived on the earth and when the preaching was done. The passage, therefore, affords no evidence of an offer of salvation to ungodly men after death; it lends no support to the theory of a second chance. Note that the little word *now* is not in verse 19 in the King James and the American Standard versions: "the spirits [now] in prison." Why was it put there in some translations unless they wanted to favor the "second chance" theory?

The Gospel Was Preached to the Dead

Another passage incorrectly used to teach the second chance theory is also from Peter's writing: "For unto this end was the gospel preached even to the dead, that they might be judged indeed according to men in the flesh, but live according to God in the spirit" (1 Peter 4:6). The preaching in this verse relates to the present life, rather than to the intermediate state—between death and the judgment. The people said to be dead were alive in the world at the time the gospel was preached to them, but dead when Peter wrote the epistle. Note the tense of the verse in the passage: the gospel was (past tense) preached to them that are (present tense) dead. The passage does not say the gospel was preached to spirits or to any in the disembodied state. The gospel was preached to them while they lived, and they are now dead. This was done that they might be judged by the gospel, that is, judged by the same gospel as those in the flesh (or alive) when Jesus comes. The gospel is for the living and not for the dead (except for those dead in their trespasses and sins). This verse does not teach the doctrine of a second chance. The gospel "was preached" (past tense) to those who "are dead" (present tense). The gospel was not preached to them after they were dead, but they were dead when Peter was writing this.

What about Baptism for the Dead?

Closely associated with "second chance" theories is the belief held to by some on baptism for the dead, the practice of baptizing living people on behalf of dead people, usually referred to as vicarious baptism. If a person dies unbaptized, some living person may be baptized in his stead. Hence, this doctrine and practice claims to offer some assistance from the living on the earth to those who have died. But can people today be baptized for one who has died not having received New Testament baptism? The Bible does not sustain this belief.

First Corinthians 15:29 Does Not Teach It.

The advocates of this doctrine claim support of the practice from Paul's question in 1 Corinthians 15:29: "Else what shall they do that are baptized for the dead? If the dead are not raised at all, why then are they baptized for them?" This passage has its difficulties, but most Bible scholars are agreed that it does not teach vicarious baptism. What, then, does it mean?

The whole chapter to the Christians at Corinth was for the purpose of assuring them that their dead loved ones will be raised in the resurrection of all mankind at the last day. The apostle presented unanswerable arguments to prove Christ's resurrection and the general resurrection of all men to future life. Paul reasoned that if the dead be not raised, several conditions would necessarily follow. The argument is that if the dead do not arise (as some in Corinth were being taught and were believing), then Christ did not arise; therefore, no one else will arise. Consequently, when one dies he is dead never to live again.

In verse 29, Paul simply made the argument that if the dead are not raised, why be baptized in preparation for death, since there is no resurrection to life after death? Baptism prepares one for life after death, but if there is no life after death, then why be baptized? In effect Paul said, "What shall they do who are baptized with the view to the resurrection of their dead bodies if there is no resurrection?" "Why be baptized for the remission of sins unless it be with reference to the resurrection and life beyond the grave?" (The preposition *for* carries the meaning here of "with reference to" or "with a view to.") If there be no resurrection, then one is baptized in behalf of a dead man—one who will never live again.

This explanation fits perfectly into the line of argument for the resurrection—the very thing Paul was trying to prove in the chapter. There is nothing in this passage that remotely suggests the doctrine of one person being baptized in behalf of another person, either while that person is dead or living. All Christians at Corinth had been baptized. Acts has this brief statement of their conversion: "And many of the Corinthians hearing believed, and were baptized" (Acts 18:8). Their baptism was in the likeness of the death, burial, and resurrection of Christ (Romans 6:3–4). But why were they baptized in view of death or in preparation for it if the dead rise not? Why obey Christ if He is still in the tomb, and if there is no general resurrection? This is Paul's reasoning—why be baptized for the dead, if the dead rise not? The explanation that seems most natural is this: if the dead ones will not be raised up from the dead, then why should one be baptized in view of the state of the dead one? Baptism itself is a declaration of one's faith in a resurrection. However, there is no sense in the act of baptism if the dead ones are not to be raised. Why, then, be baptized for the dead, that is, with the state of the dead in one's mind, if there is no resurrection of the dead? This interpretation supports the argument of Paul on the resurrection. The Bible does not teach proxy baptism; only those who personally believe and repent are proper subjects of baptism (cf. Mark 16:16; Acts 2:36–39; 8:35–39).

The passage is dealing with the doctrine of the resurrection, not baptism per se. Some in the Corinthian church, influenced by others, denied the doctrine of the resurrection of the body from the grave (15:12). Thus Paul, by use of an ad hominem argument (i.e., an argument designed to highlight the inconsistency of another's position), urges them to abandon this false idea.

Definitely, the verse is not authorizing the practice of some person in the church being baptized so that some dead person can be saved. This would contradict the many plain passages that teach personal responsibility for one's conduct, be it good or bad, at the day of judgment (2 Corinthians 5:10). One can no more obey God and have the blessing transferred to the dead, than he could disobey the Lord and have that condemnation imputed to some deceased person. Proxy baptism is not in view at all.

Today, all who understand New Testament teaching regarding salvation in Christ and the resurrection from the dead, and who thus obey the Lord, are baptized for the dead, that is, for the resurrection of their dead bodies. They know that "if we have become united with him in the likeness of his death, we shall be also in the likeness of his resurrection" (Romans 6:5), and if people do not obey the gospel, everlasting punishment awaits them (2 Thessalonians 1:7–9). So Paul is asking why a person should be baptized in hope of the resurrection, if the dead will not be raised. The Bible does not teach vicarious baptism—the practice of baptizing living people on behalf of dead people.

Paul's statement in 1 Corinthians 15 is that man's resurrection is dependent upon Christ's resurrection. There can be no doubt that baptism here is to be taken in its natural sense. So why be baptized for the resurrection of the dead if there is no resurrection?

David Lipscomb, a nineteenth century gospel preacher, in commenting on this difficult passage, said,

> The purpose, scope, and connection will admit of but one meaning—if the dead rise not, what shall they do who are baptized in the hope of the resurrection? Men are "baptized into Christ," that they may live in him, die in him, and finally be justified and saved in him . . . In view of their dying they are baptized in order to their well-being after death. If they are not to be raised from the dead, why are they baptized to fit them for the resurrection?[1]

So what is to become of those who, on being baptized, do so knowing their lives will probably be taken, if the dead rise not? There were persecutions of Christians in that day, but many obeyed the Lord anyway.

The Practice of Vicarious Baptism Came Years Later.

Church historians agree that the practice of living persons being baptized in the place of those dead cannot be found until the fifth century. For instance, Conybeare and Howson, in their great work on the apostle Paul, say: "The practice was never adopted except by some obscure sects of Gnostics, who seem to have founded their custom on this very passage."[2]

The wrong interpretation of Paul's statement, then, is the thing that gave rise to the practice. The Bible does not mention an example of anyone being baptized for another, dead or alive. The idea of one person being baptized for another is not taught in either 1 Corinthians 15:29 or any other passage in the Bible. Each person must be baptized for himself. If he fails to do this, no one else can do it for him, either while he lives or after he dies.

While people live on earth they should "fear God, and keep his commandments; for this is the whole duty of man" (Ecclesiastes 12:13). "Therefore to him that knoweth to do good, and doeth it not, to him it is sin" (James 4:17 KJV).

Baptism Applies Only to a Penitent Believer.

The Scriptures teach that baptism is a command of the Lord to be obeyed by a responsible, taught individual. (See the Great Commission as given by Christ in Matthew 28:18–20 and Mark 16:15–16.) Further, the Bible teaches that faith is an essential prerequisite to baptism after one has heard the gospel;

---

1 David Lipscomb, *Commentary on 1 Corinthians* (Nashville: Gospel Advocate Co., 1989), p. 234.

2 *Life and Epistles of St. Paul*, p. 413.

no one but a believer is qualified to be baptized (Acts 8:36–38; Galatians 3:26–27; Romans 1:16). Repentance is likewise a necessary condition of pardon and an essential prerequisite of baptism; no one but a truly penitent believer can be Scripturally baptized (Acts 2:36–38; Luke 13:3, 5; 24:46–47; 2 Peter 3:9). The confession of one's faith in the Lord as the Son of God also precedes baptism (Acts 8:37; Matthew 10:32–33; Romans 10:10). The whole teaching of the Scriptures and the nature of baptism make it impossible, therefore, for one to even countenance the idea that Paul taught vicarious baptism in 1 Corinthians 15:29. Now consider some reasons why the theories of both a second chance and baptism for the dead cannot be true.

The Theories Are Out of Harmony with the General Teaching of the Scriptures

In the narrative that Jesus gave of the rich man and Lazarus (Luke 16:19–31), Abraham reminded the rich man, who was in Hades, that there was a great gulf fixed between the righteous and the wicked, and that there was no crossing from one place to the other (v. 26). This alone refutes the notion that eternal destiny may be changed after death by some message to the disembodied spirits or through baptism by proxy—or in any other way. At death the gulf between the saved and lost is fixed, and there can be no crossing. In this life the gulf is not fixed. The sinner can, while yet living, become a Christian; he can, by obedience to the gospel, cross the dividing line between the lost and the saved. But should death come to him while in an unsaved condition, the gulf will then be set, and none can cross it. Hence, the moral and spiritual quality of each person is a decided matter at death.

Jesus said to unbelievers, "I go away, and ye shall seek me, and shall die in your sin: whither I go, ye cannot come" (John 8:21). If a message of salvation can be preached to the souls of the departed offering pardon, or if one on earth can be baptized for a dead person, why did not Jesus say, "Ye cannot come to me, unless you accept the other chance which will be given to you, or unless someone is baptized for you"?

It is true that the beginning of one's condition originates in this life. The chasm between the rich man and Lazarus in Hades had its beginning on earth, and it could have been bridged by the rich man in this world before his death. But failing to do this, the rich man found it was impossible to cross the gulf after his death. The rich man made the chasm by selfishness. His covetousness hardened into character. Then after death the gulf was impassable—thus to remain so eternally for no change of place, no probation will then be provided or possible. Indeed, death does not change the bent of one's life and character; it fixes it. One's character here determines his destiny there. God has ordained man to be a free moral agent. Thus, man actually chooses his own destiny;

death is the fixing time. The issues of eternity are settled for each one in this life. O, how solemn is life!

The Bible teaches that each individual is accountable to God. "So then each one of us shall give account of himself to God" (Romans 14:12). If one can be baptized for another, that makes him responsible for another. Many Scriptures clearly teach that each person shall answer to God for himself and no one can borrow oil or righteousness from another human being (cf. Ezekiel 18:20–24; Matthew 25:1–13; Romans 14:7–15; Galatians 6:4–5; Matthew 3:9–10; 2 Corinthians 13:5; 1 Timothy 4:16; Romans 2:6–11). So the doctrine of baptism for the dead is contrary to the principle of individual accountability upon which God deals with man.

Again, another reason one cannot accept the idea of a second chance or of vicarious baptism is that the wicked are kept under punishment until the final judgment, and there is no change for them.

> For if God spared not angels when they sinned, but cast them down to hell [Tartarus], and committed them to pits of darkness, to be reserved unto judgment . . . the Lord knoweth how to deliver the godly out of temptation, and to keep the unrighteous under punishment unto the day of judgment (2 Peter 2:4–9).

The conduct of people in this life, in the body, will furnish material for the final sentence at the judgment; what was done for them while they were in the intermediate state will have no effect on their sentence. "For we must all be made manifest before the judgment-seat of Christ; that each one may receive the things done in the body, according to what he hath done, whether it be good or bad" (2 Corinthians 5:10). Each individual, therefore, must be judged according to what he has done while in the body.

When Christ described the final judgment, He spoke of some things done and some things not done in this life, such as feeding the poor and visiting the sick (Matthew 25:31–46); He did not speak of anything that was done or not done by the person or for the person while the soul was in Hades. A person's eternal destiny, therefore, is determined by the deeds done in the body while on earth. The following passages clearly teach that each will be so judged—that at death probation ends, doom is sealed, and destiny is fixed (Ezekiel 18:26; Luke 12:13–21; 13:22–27; John 8:21–24; Titus 2:11–12). The Bible teaches that each one must obey the gospel to be saved and that salvation is a personal, individual responsibility (2 Thessalonians 1:7–10; Hebrews 5:9; 1 Peter 1:22; Romans 6:17; Matthew 7:21–27).

The "Second Chance" Idea Is False

To summarize, these important facts have been established in this study about human souls in the intermediate, or disembodied, state:

1. The soul, or spirit, of man lives on after the body dies.
2. Souls are conscious after death; they do not sleep.
3. Obedient souls are happy in the Hadean realm.
4. Disobedient spirits are in torment in Hades, in Tartarus.
5. Souls are not on probation in the intermediate state; Tartarus is not a place to prepare for the judgment and heaven.
6. After death all that remains is the judgment.
7. Proxy baptism, like purgatory, is a product of the mind of man.

Does the Bible Teach Reincarnation?

Another question concerns some people regarding the departed, namely, "Does the Bible teach reincarnation?" The word means a rebirth of the departed soul in another body; it could be in the body of a baby, or even in an animal. Will people live on earth again?

The Old Testament closes with the promise of the coming of Elijah the prophet: "Behold, I will send you Elijah the prophet before the great and terrible day of Jehovah come" (Malachi 4:5). The Jews knew this prophecy, so when Peter, James, and John were on the mount and saw Jesus transfigured, they also saw Moses and Elijah talking with Him, and they were reminded of this prophecy. They asked Jesus about it, and the Lord replied, "Elijah is come already" (Matthew 17:12). "Then understood the disciples that he spake unto them of John the Baptist" (v. 13). John the Baptist came in the spirit and power of Elijah; he was like Elijah. But he was still John and not Elijah living in a new body again on the earth. So Jesus said of him, "This is Elijah, that is to come" (Matthew 11:14). The Bible does not teach reincarnation, although this has been taught by many religious groups in various parts of the world for many centuries. No one will come back to live in another human body before the final day of judgment. (But Shirley MacLaine's book, *Out on a Limb,* has influenced some in our nation to believe in reincarnation.)

The Bible plainly teaches a resurrection of all the bodies for all people. Paul wrote, "For as in Adam all die, so also in Christ shall all be made alive" (1 Corinthians 15:22). And Jesus said, "The hour cometh, in which all that are in the tombs shall hear his voice, and shall come forth; they that have done good, unto the resurrection of life; and they that have done evil, unto the resurrection of judgment" (John 5:28–29). But there is a great difference between a resurrection of the bodies and a reincarnation of the spirits. Resurrection means being raised from the dead, but reincarnation means living again on earth in a different physical body. The whole idea of reincarnation is based upon idolatry and superstition, thinking that when the spirit departs it comes again into some living thing. It could even be a dog or a cow or a cockroach. But the Scriptures teach that God gives each one a life to live, one body in which to live it, and that judgment comes after this life, and then eternity, either heaven or hell. The order is life, death, judgment, and eternity. The resurrection and a new body are certainly promised, but reincarnation is not taught anywhere in the Bible. Does one remember having lived on this earth in another body, maybe years or centuries ago, and now as the same person living in this present body? Of course not. Reincarnation contradicts Hebrews 9:27: "And as it is appointed unto men once to die, but after this the judgment" (KJV). The Bible does not teach that the dead are reborn into other bodies many times and die many times. Reincarnation is a chief doctrine of Hinduism; it is also an important part of witchcraft. Witchcraft is condemned as a work of the flesh (Galatians 5:20). According to Exodus 20:5, some people, even children and grandchildren, receive the consequences of other persons' sins. For example, if a woman took LSD a few years ago and then gave birth to a deformed child, maybe with AIDS, it would not be correct to say that the child bore the mother's guilt; rather, the child received the consequences of the mother's sins. The Bible does teach that actions have consequences, but the Bible does not teach the doctrine of reincarnation.

The Bible urges one to obey God today (2 Corinthians 6:2; Hebrews 3:7–8), but if a sinner expects to be reborn in another body, he believes he will have many more chances to have his sins forgiven. Hence, it is not urgent for him to obey God now. So this fantasy must be rejected as another imaginative doctrine of men. Reincarnation cannot possibly be true. Wisdom would suggest that man read his Bible and accept and obey the truth so that he can go to Paradise when he dies, and then go on to heaven after the final resurrection and the judgment.

Questions for Discussion

1. What is the theory of a second chance?
2. Does 1 Peter 3:18–20 offer proof that the impenitent will be given chance to repent and be saved after death?
3. What does this passage of Scripture teach?
4. In what sense did Peter mean that the gospel was preached to those now dead?
5. What is meant by the theory of baptism for the dead?
6. Which religious body practices baptism for the dead?
7. What was Paul discussing in the whole of 1 Corinthians 15?
8. Give reasons for saying that the theory of vicarious baptism is contrary to the whole of the Scriptures.
9. What did Jesus say about the gulf that separates the saved and the lost in Hades?
10. What warning should the unsaved heed while he lives? Why?
11. What is sufficient to warn the unsaved and lead him to repentance?
12. Review what has now been learned concerning souls in Hades.
13. Discuss the idea of reincarnation of souls in another body after death?
14. Did Peter's expression "spirits in prison" refer to those who were then in the prison of sin, or did it refer to those who were then in prison in Hades in Tartarus, and were preached to by Noah before their death? Or, did it refer to Christ preaching to the spirits in Hades while His spirit was in Hades? The New American Standard Bible reads "to the spirits now in prison" in 1 Peter 3:19; the King James Version and the American Standard Version do not have the word *now* added to it, just "to the spirits in prison," and so does the New King James Version. The Living Bible reads, "And it was in the spirit that he visited the spirits in prison, and preached to them." Today's English Version reads, "and in his spiritual existence he went and preached to the imprisoned spirits." The Simple English Bible reads, "In the spirit, Christ went and preached to the spirits in prison. They did not obey in the past." The Challoner-Rheims Version reads, "in which also he went and preached to those spirits that were in prison. Those in times past had been disobedient when the ark was building." But nowhere in the Bible is the doctrine of purgatory or a second chance theory to be found. This should be made clear in the minds of all. The New International Version has, "through whom also he went and preached to the spirits in prison who disobeyed long ago when God waited patiently in the days of Noah while the ark was being built." Besides, the New International Version has David conceived and born in sin (Psalm 51:5). It also has Jesus going to the grave, and not to Paradise in Hades

(Acts 2:27, 31). The New International Version aids Calvinism, and we cannot recommend it entirely, for it teaches some errors.

– 14 –

Can the Living Communicate with the Dead?

". . . should not a people seek unto their God? . . . To the law and to the testimony!"
Isaiah 8:19–20

According to the Holy Scriptures there is a spirit world where the disembodied spirits are conscious. "Can the dead speak?" "Can one communicate with the spirits of those who have passed from this life?"

Some seek to peer beyond the grave out of idle curiosity; others because their hearts are grieved due to the death of a loved one or friend. And yet others search desiring to know the condition or state of spirits in Hades. They want assurance that their loved ones are alive and happy in the next phase of life. Having heard that psychic experience is possible, those bereaved by the death of dear ones long for comfort from the realm of the supernatural. The parting caused by death leaves hearts burdened and sorrowful. To know that the departed are happy or to hear their voices again would bring unspeakable comfort to the bereaved. This desire is natural. After a great cataclysm there is usually a revival of interest in the idea. Some human parasites, under the guise of commercialized spiritualism, take advantage of the sorrowing—and grow rich on the tragedy of death. This work was never more popular in the world than it is today, due perhaps to widespread bereavement from the wars. Too, there is a yearning of the human mind for the knowledge of the future, especially before some momentous event. The unknown frightens man. So, regardless of the reasons, there are those who are eager to talk with departed spirits, to lift the curtain and see things yet to come.

The practice of invocations of the dead comes from the belief in the continual existence of disembodied spirits still living. Witchcraft and sorcery have long been practiced among ignorant and degraded people. The claim that contacts can be made with the spirit-world is as old as human nature itself, perhaps. Pretended communication with the spirits of the dead has been common in paganism from the earliest times; the heathen nations were practicing it when the children of Israel came to Canaan; the Israelites learned it from them. There were magicians, sorcerers, and diviners in those days. So this is not some new question; it is not modern. In olden times it was called witchcraft, sorcery, wizardry, necromancy, or consulting with those who had familiar spirits; now it is spiritualism.

What is spiritualism? It is the theory that spirits of the dead can and do communicate with those still living in this world in a direct, audible manner. Spiritualists say that by sitting in a circle, holding hands, and being passive, the spirits will talk with them. Their meetings, called séances, are usually held at night.

Of course, once convinced of communication, a deluded person is ready to attend the meetings and talk to the dead. But is this possible? And is the Christian to indulge in spiritualistic practices? Although some have found comfort in this system of religion, their belief that such can be done has nothing to do with proof. Thus, in this chapter search is made for the Scriptural and scientific answer to the ever fascinating question: "Can the living and the dead communicate?"

The Bible sheds light on this problem of spiritualism. In it the attempt to hold consultation with the dead is strictly forbidden and emphatically condemned. As shall be noted even in the long ago God forbade man to enter into this sphere.

In the Old Testament a variety of words designating spiritualistic phenomena is found. Notice some of these words and their meanings, with some warnings of Jehovah concerning spiritualism.

Divination

The practice of divination was an attempt to obtain secret knowledge and foretell future events by means of signs, augurs, or the claimed influence of some spirit. Many methods of divination were used, but all were feeble efforts to forge the word of God in divine utterances.

"But as for you, hearken ye not to your prophets, nor to your diviners, nor to your dreams, nor to your soothsayers . . . for they prophesy a lie unto you" (Jeremiah 27:9–10). One of the claims of spiritualism, ancient and modern, is its ability to foretell the future and provide certain knowledge desired by men. But remember, God alone knows all things and can reveal the future. Man has sought in various ways and in vain to penetrate the dark veil that hides the future.

The Bible contains predictions of future events which have come to pass long after the predictions were made. This surely proves the existence of God and the inspiration of the Scriptures, for only the Lord could communicate such things to men through inspired writers (2 Peter 1:21; 1 Corinthians 2:10–13). In conversation with heathen nations concerning false gods, the Lord challenged, "Let them . . . declare unto us what shall happen . . . Declare the things that are to come hereafter, that we may know that ye are gods" (Isaiah 41:22–23). Again,

> I am God, and there is none else; I am God, and there is none like me, declaring the end from the beginning, and from ancient times things that are not yet done; saying, My counsel shall stand, and I will do all my pleasure (Isaiah 46:9–10).

For this reason wise philosophers and historians do not attempt to foretell the future—they deal with the past, draw what lessons they can for the future, but make no attempt to lift the veil that hides tomorrow. Furthermore, no inspired man ever was a fortune-teller or spiritualist for any individual.

Witchcraft

The person who claimed to possess supernatural or magical powers by contact with evil spirits was called a witch. The person, usually a woman, was thought to have formed a compact with the devil or with evil spirits, by whose aid she was able to perform all sorts of injury to people. In every form of witchcraft there was an appeal to a power not acting in subordination to divine law. This explains why witchcraft and divination are acts of rebellion against God, and why they were strictly forbidden in Israel and punishable by death. Moses commanded, "Thou shalt not suffer a witch to live" (Exodus 22:18 KJV).

Sorcery

The Hebrew and Greek words for *witch* and *witchcraft* are sometimes rendered "sorcerer" and "sorcery" in the English versions. Sorcery was a pretended familiarity with the spirits of the dead and was originally an attempt to foresee and foretell the future by using incantations or magical formulas.

Wizardry

The wizard was a soothsayer, magician, or one possessed with a spirit of divination who claimed to know the secrets of the unseen world and pretended to have ability to converse with the spirits of the dead. The wizard was the old-time counterpart of one today who is called a spirit medium. Wizards pried into forbidden things, and the children of Israel were strongly commanded to put all such to death. "A man also or a woman . . . that is a wizard, shall surely be put to death" (Leviticus 20:27 KJV). Wizards persist among heathen and degraded peoples who follow the witch doctors of voodooism and kindred cults.

Familiar Spirits

In order to do business according to the theory, disembodied spirits had to find a person or medium whom they controlled and through whom they worked. Mediums, then, were supposed to have an invisible spirit, subject to their call, who would inspire them when they sought his direction. The practice of consulting familiar spirits was forbidden: "Turn ye not unto them that have familiar spirits, nor unto the wizards; seek them not out, to be defiled by them: I am Jehovah your God" (Leviticus 19:31).

Too, not only the medium was condemned to die, but the dupe as well: "And the soul that turneth after such as have familiar spirits, and after wizards, to go a whoring after them, I will even set my face against that soul, and will cut him off from among his people" (Leviticus 20:6 KJV).

Every trance medium of the twentieth century has a familiar spirit. Each relies upon its particular control. The control is always the same; it is called by name and is the familiar spirit or the spirit medium.

Necromancy

This word is found in the following passage:

> There shalt not be found with thee any one that maketh his son or his daughter to pass through the fire, one that useth divination, one that practiseth augury, or an enchanter, or a sorcerer, or a charmer, or a consulter with a familiar spirit, or a wizard, or a necromancer. For whosoever doeth these things is an abomination unto Jehovah (Deuteronomy 18:10–12).

The necromancer was one who had a familiar spirit, a person who was supposed to have power to call up the spirits of the dead to learn of them things respecting future events. Thus a necromancer pretended to consult the dead. God's people in the Old Testament were not to turn to, nor seek one who sought to communicate with the dead. Paul says that they who practice such or seek witchcraft shall not inherit the kingdom of God (Galatians 5:19–21).

Under these names (divination, witchcraft, sorcery, wizardry, familiar spirits, necromancy), spiritualism is referred to and strongly condemned in the Old Testament. Although Jehovah forbade His people from going to these, often they went to them instead of appealing to the Lord. There were those in Israel who pretended to summon the dead into communication with the living. God's people in times of trouble seemed always to have been inclined to consult those claiming supernatural powers. For example, Manasseh, king of Judah, when threatened by Assyria, looked to enchanters and familiar spirits.

> And he did that which was evil in the sight of Jehovah, after the abominations of the nations . . . And he made his son to pass through the fire, and practiced augury, and used enchantments, and dealt with them that had familiar spirits,

> and with wizards: he wrought much evil in the sight of Jehovah, to provoke him to anger (2 Kings 21:2– 6).

On the other hand, King Josiah put those who dealt with familiar spirits out of the land; this pleased the Lord (2 Kings 23:24–25). God's people in the Old Testament were not to turn to or seek one who sought to communicate with the dead.

Sorcery in the New Testament

Early in the history of Christianity, Philip the evangelist went "to the city of Samaria, and preached Christ unto them" (Acts 8:5 KJV). Miracles were performed to confirm the word preached, causing great joy in the city. Prior to Philip's work, there had been a great sorcerer by the name of Simon, who had bewitched the people, giving out that he was some great one. His fraudulent claims being exposed, later Simon himself believed also and was baptized (Acts 8:5–24).

Note Paul's list of the works of the flesh, which, if practiced, will keep a person out of heaven:

> Now the works of the flesh are manifest, which are these: fornication, uncleanness, lasciviousness, idolatry, sorcery, enmities, strife, jealousies, wraths, factions, divisions, parties, envyings, drunkenness, revellings, and such like; of which I forewarn you, even as I did forewarn you, that they who practise such things shall not inherit the kingdom of God (Galatians 5:19–21).

Note again the destiny of those who practice sorcery: "But for the fearful, and unbelieving, and abominable, and murderers, and fornicators, and sorcerers, and idolaters, and all liars, their part shall be in the lake of fire and brimstone; which is the second death" (Revelation 21:8). Again: "Without are the dogs, and the sorcerers, and the fornicators, and the murderers, and the idolaters, and every one that loveth and maketh a lie" (Revelation 22:15). Some practiced sorcery in apostolic times. Simon, called Magus, and Bar-jesus were prominent ones (Acts 8:9–11; 13:6–8).

In no city was sorcery so much practiced as in Ephesus. This city was a stronghold of paganism with the magnificent temple of Diana, one of the seven wonders of the world and the most notable of all temples of the pagan world. The worship of this goddess and the pursuit of magic were deeply imbedded in the lives of the people of Ephesus. Professors of the black art practiced their incantations openly, while all sorts of fakirs, impostors, sorcerers, and fortune-tellers swarmed in the city. Into the midst of this magic and sorcery came the apostle Paul on his third missionary journey. Here he labored faithfully for three years, striving to turn the city of a half million souls to the teachings of the Savior.

The miracles wrought by the power of God through the apostle were for the purpose of confirming the Word preached. They constrained the magicians themselves to acknowledge that the power accompanying Paul was divine. Soon many came and confessed their evil-doings, and sorcerers brought their expensive books on curious arts and burned them in the presence of the people. The people were amazed at the sacrifice. "And they counted the price of them," adds Luke the historian, "and found it fifty thousand pieces of silver. So mightily grew the word of the Lord and prevailed" (Acts 19:18–20).

Here is an illustration of the power of the gospel. These men truly repented and did not flinch at the cost. They were determined to cease the practice of their evil calling. They did not try to sell to others that which they felt was wrong for them to keep, but they utterly destroyed their books and relied on the Lord to take care of them. Of course, when people sincerely repent of any sin, the evil practice will be abandoned at any sacrifice. The only question will be, "What is right?" not, "What will it cost?"

From these passages in both Testaments, it must be reasoned that Satan is the author of this unholy system of sorcery. The Bible teaches that the devil uses two methods to ruin people's faith: one, keeping them in ignorance of the truth; the other, using religious fanaticism to which the theory of spiritualism belongs. From an examination of the Scriptures, spiritualism is in contradiction to the statements of the Bible.

Thus, the words of Isaiah are appropriate even today:

> And when they shall say unto you, Seek unto them that have familiar spirits, and unto the wizards, that chirp and that mutter: should not a people seek unto their God? on behalf of the living should they seek unto the dead? To the law and to the testimony! if they speak not according to this word, surely there is no morning for them (Isaiah 8:19–20).

In effect the prophet said, "When people say unto you, 'Let us go to them that have familiar spirits to inquire about the dead,' you should say, 'No, we should go to the law of God, and whatever it says is sufficient.'" Then, should the living seek the dead? Isaiah answers the question. He says men should seek God and not pretend to hold consultation with the dead; they should go to "the law and to the testimony"—that is, to the revelation which God has given. The prophet issues a call to try the practice by the revealed will of the living God, and if the necromancers "speak not according to this word [i.e., the revealed will of God, the Holy Scriptures]" it is proof positive that "there is no light [i.e., no true teaching] in them" (KJV). They are in utter ignorance and are not to be followed.

The "chirp" and "mutter" mentioned in this passage were claimed to be the low whisperings and feeble sighs of the departed, the voices of the spirits.

By making these imitative noises necromancers feigned to converse with the departed souls; thus they imposed upon the ignorant people and led them to believe that they had supernatural powers. The art of the modern ventriloquist, often practiced today, seems to have been connected with the practice of necromancy.

Too, incidentally, in this statement of Isaiah, there is affirmed the unfailing and infallible standard by which all doctrines, as well as spiritualism, are to be tested. If the doctrines are not in harmony with God's Word, they are false. Today, "the law and the testimony" determines whether the teaching is right or wrong. What the Bible says is absolutely true, and man can depend upon it. Therein is revealed all, that the man of God may be complete, "perfectly equipped for every good work" (2 Timothy 3:16–17 Weymouth). Jude exhorted Christians to "contend earnestly for the faith which was once for all delivered unto the saints" (Jude 3). Now, since God has given His Word, which is sufficient for instruction, man ought not to seek more knowledge by forbidden methods.

Moreover, the Bible's last amen of the book of Revelation demands that nothing is to be added to or changed in God's Word by any so-called new revelation. All one needs to know for his own glory, honor, or happiness is in the Holy Scriptures. Thus, if anyone claims to speak with authority of inspiration, or presents additional information to the Scriptures, people should refuse to listen to him. God, the only author of supernatural information, has given all the teaching in the Bible. The Scriptures are complete. Let not man, therefore, seek the dead for help or enlightenment, for he has already all the knowledge that is essential for his present guidance and everlasting happiness.

When spiritualists claim to foretell future events, it is mere pretension; they neither know the future, nor can they foretell it. They may hazard a guess, which may be fulfilled in part, but anyone can surmise what may come to pass, reasoning from cause to effect, and may be right part of the time. If spiritualists and fortune-tellers could know what is going to happen in the future, they undoubtedly would be the most successful traders in the stock market, for they would know in advance whether stocks were going up or down. Every candid person surely must admit then that the phenomenon of spiritualism is fraud, pure and simple—nothing but deception and imposture. Thus, when examined in the light of the Scriptures, the words of spiritualists manifest their origin—Satan.

Demon Possession Today?

Are men demon possessed today? Most of the cases of demon possession were in the period of Christ's earthly ministry. There was a great conflict between Christ and Satan. The devil was allowed to exhibit an unusual amount of influence, but Jesus would destroy the works of the devil (Luke 10:17–19); Satan would lose his power in the area of demon possession. When the Lord ascended to heaven He gave the necessary gifts for the early church to deal with cases of demon possession (Acts 19:13–16). So with the passing of the apostles, passed also the age of demon possession. Hence, demons were the spirits of wicked men whom God permitted to exit the Hadean realm in order to possess some people on earth. No demons possess anyone today (1 John 3:8). All the claims about demon possession today are false (Zechariah 13:2). The age of miracles has passed. Yet Satan tempts people to sin today (1 Peter 5:8). But one day Satan will be cast into hell (Revelation (20:10).

Spiritualism in the Scientific World

Now examine the system of spiritualism from the scientific standpoint. Christianity has never had anything to fear from any true science of body, soul, or spirit. But there is now, as well as in former ages, much that is called science, which is "science falsely so called" (1 Timothy 6:20 KJV).

If in all the range of so-called spiritualist's phenomena there can be proved one single instance of genuine spirit manifestation, then the fact of spiritualism might be established. But this has never been done.

In recent years, claims of spiritualism have been examined by scientists, and positive proof of spirit communication still rests with the spiritualists. For several years an award of five thousand dollars has been offered by the *Scientific American* to any medium who can produce a demonstrated case of undoubted trance communication; that is, the medium must present a case that cannot be duplicated by natural and scientific means. The money still remains in the treasury of the magazine.

Any well-trained stage magician or sleight-of-hand performer can reproduce any of the so-called proofs of spirit communication produced at séances, the exception being that the magicians say that they can reproduce the same tricks in the light before a large audience that any medium can do in the dark in their meetings. Yet the so-called spirits of the medium séance are all afraid of the light and will perform only in the dark. One wonders why! The late, world famous magician, Harry Houdini, was an avid student of spiritualism, and perhaps did more than any other man to expose phony mediums. He challenged them in these words: "I offer ten thousand dollars to any man or woman who provides proof of psychic powers, or produces any effect I cannot duplicate." His reward was never accepted.

Houdini was determined to pry out the riddles of the next world. He entrusted some family secrets to his wife Bessie and told her, "After I die, I will try to repeat these words to you on the anniversary of my death. Be watchful." Mr. Houdini died in October, 1926, and for the next decade his grieving widow attended hundreds of séances, always hoping that her departed husband would give some message in some way. For years she kept a light burning in front of his portrait, thinking she would ultimately hear his voice repeating the sentences he had revealed to her before his death. But no message ever came.

On the tenth anniversary of his death, Bessie Houdini attended her final séance, received no word, and went home to switch off the light which had burned so long for the magician who never answered from the other world. She died aboard a train at Needles, California, at the age of sixty-nine, doubtful of immortality because no message came from her late husband. According to the Associated Press news article which announced her death, prior to her passing she said, "Whoever says they have communicated with my spirit after my death will be lying. I will not come back, even if I have the power."

In Headrick, Oklahoma, August, 1907, J. W. Chism, a gospel preacher, met John W. Ring, a spiritualist minister, in a public discussion on the subject of spiritualism. All during the debate Mr. Chism asked his opponent to try some work, to produce some sign as done in the spiritualist séances, and Mr. Chism promised Mr. Ring that he would do the same thing there before the people gathered for the discussion. Needless to say, Mr. Ring never did undertake to perform any of the things spiritualists claim to do in their meetings. Doubtless he knew that Mr. Chism was capable of doing the same tricks as an act of magic and would thus expose his fraudulent claims. In his closing speech on the negative, Mr. Chism said:

> I challenge him [Mr. Ring] to produce a spiritual photograph. He refused to even try. When he makes a spiritual photograph, I am ready to make them right out there in the open sunlight, before this people, and you cannot tell how it is done either. I am ready to do it. Again, when he gets into his cabinet and sews himself up in a sack, and the spirit comes out and walks across the floor, I am ready to go into the cabinet and be sewed up in a sack and walk out in person, and yet you will find me still sewed up in a sack. I am ready to go to the test when he is.[1]

Evidently, Mr. Chism knew something of the tricks of magic and sleight-of-hand performances or he could not have issued to Mr. Ring this challenge.

Man is indebted to masters of magic such as Houdini, Blackstone, and many others who have done so much to discredit fraudulent seers and clairvoyants, even many mediums who have been found fakers after much so-called bona fide evidence! Furthermore, tests have actually been made in the séances by those who wanted to know the truth about spiritualism—and they

---

1 J. W. Chism, John Ring, *The Great Debate,* p. 139. (After many years out of print (1907), the book has been reprinted by The Old Paths Book Club, Rosemead, California.)

have learned it! Individuals have gone to their meetings, requested to speak with the spirit of some loved one, received a message all right, and then left the meeting convinced, but not converted, because the particular person talked to was not even dead. So, from the scientific viewpoint, spiritualism is a fake system, and the organizations of some who claim such powers are nothing but cults.

Some think an element of supernatural power exists in the phenomena of spiritualism. From what sources can the supernatural come? There are only two: God or Satan, heaven or hell. The power could not come from God; He would not contradict His Word. Satan is still trying to deceive mankind just as he has done in days past (2 Thessalonians 2:9–12). Just as there is counterfeit money, there are also counterfeit acts and false doctrines in religion made possible by the influence of Satan and his emissaries (2 Corinthians 11:13–15). So, what of table-tipping, slate-writing, and many other remarkable demonstrations? It is trickery. Magicians do sleight-of-hand tricks, things wholly inexplicable to the uninitiated, but this does not prove they do them by supernatural power. In fact, they say it is by their own power—the hand is quicker than the eye! So it is with the spiritualists.

King Saul became the victim of this delusion, and spiritualists sometime refer to his visit with the witch of Endor and Samuel's talking to the king as an example of medium communication with the dead. Now examine the narrative (1 Samuel 28:3–25).

After having forsaken God, Saul was abandoned by the Lord because of his transgressions; Samuel, who had often rebuked the king and admonished him, was dead. The Philistines, long-time enemy of the Israelites, were encamped near Shunem, ready for battle the next day with Saul and the army of Israel. The king was apprehensive of the outcome; furthermore, the Lord answered him not. So in desperation he decided to seek a spiritualist. He knew full well that necromancy was in direct disobedience to God's will, for early in Saul's reign he had ordered witches to be killed. Apparently, this one at Endor had escaped. The despondent and worried king, having learned of a woman who had a familiar spirit, sought knowledge of future events by going that night to the witch at Endor. The town was near the camp of Israel, so it was convenient for the disguised king to make the visit. In so doing, he sinned against the Lord and did the very thing he had before punished others for doing.

At first the witch was rather reluctant, thinking that her visitor was King Saul. But after being assured no harm would befall her, she was persuaded to do her job. The king asked to speak to Samuel. Even if Saul must hear words of doom, he would hear them from a friend and counselor of his youth. So he said, "Bring me up Samuel." Then, Lo! Samuel appeared! And he announced the king's doom. The spirit of this holy man revisited earth and delivered a final and awful prediction. With that, the soul of Samuel vanished again. Saul immediately fell prostrate in the witch's den. An important question that presents itself is: Did the spiritualist at Endor cause the spirit of Samuel to appear and speak to Saul?

The inspired record affirms that Saul's apparition was real, but it also says the woman was frightened and utterly unprepared for what happened. This certainly would not have been the case had she been in the habit of doing what she claimed to do. The Bible says, "When the woman saw Samuel, she cried with a loud voice" (1 Samuel 28:12). Nothing is more clear from the narration than that the woman at Endor saw something she never dreamed of seeing. Else, why did she cry out with a loud voice? It is evident from the context, to put it in simple words, that the witch was scared out of her wits when she saw Samuel. Yes, this time the person actually returned in spirit from the unseen world. (God later caused Moses and Elijah to return, though not in physical bodies [Matthew 17:1–5].) Samuel, therefore, did not come in response to the medium's call; God sent him. The record clearly states that Samuel talked with Saul, but not through the medium. Samuel came and talked, but not by any power of the sorceress. The witch did not palm off the counterfeit on Saul as she had been in the habit of doing. At this séance she was not the medium of communication; she was just an ordinary, scared observer. This story, properly studied, falls far short of proving to be a real case of spiritualistic communication.

It is, however, the only case on record where God ever so acted, and He did so in this instance to show the utter fallacy of this type of business. Why, then, should spiritualists today point triumphantly to the narrative as a striking example of a successful, spiritistic séance? After all, it is God's exposé of the deception of spiritualistic meetings. That night scene at Endor makes one's flesh creep. However, the re-appearance of Samuel upon the above-mentioned occasion is just another portion of Scripture in evidence of the fact that life continues after death.

Furthermore, according to the Scriptures, Saul's sin of visiting the witch at Endor provoked his punishment. "So Saul died for his trespass which he committed against Jehovah, because of the word of Jehovah, which he kept not; and also for that he asked counsel of one that had a familiar spirit, to inquire thereby" (1 Chronicles 10:13). Saul went from this spirit-medium's séance to a suicide's grave. The next day he and his sons died in battle on Mount Gilboa and their spirits went to Sheol, just as Samuel said they would. What a sad story of a man who fell away from God and wrecked his life! The road to Endor is, and always will remain, the way of death.

Rudyard Kipling's words are very appropriate:

Oh, the road to Endor is the oldest road,
And the craziest road of all.
Straight it runs to the witch's abode
As it did in the days of Saul,
And nothing has changed of the sorrow in store
For such as go down on the road to Endor.

"The tree is known by its fruits." This is a true adage, based upon the language of Christ (Matthew 12:33; cf. 7:15–20); this is the invincible test. Everything good in society originates in and issues forth from true religion (Christianity), while everything bad originates in and issues from false religion. What, then, shall be said of spiritualism?[1]

Spiritualism is ruinous to the nervous system of the mediums, often beginning with seemingly innocent table-turning and ending by death in a mad house. Spiritualism is likewise ruinous to the mental health of its disciples. It has swept into mental midnight some of the most intellectual people of the world. The fascination of the system of consulting the spirits of the dead has a tendency to lead people away from their right judgment into fanaticism that is revolting to the natural mind.

Many have been physically, mentally, financially, and spiritually hurt by this satanic system called spiritualism. A person succumbing to the blight of insanity corresponds identically with that of a medium going into the trance condition, according to tests that have been made. A violent maniac corresponds with that of a medium while in the trance condition. This does not mean that the spirit medium is insane, but it does demonstrate that while the medium is in the trance state, the mental powers are greatly disturbed. Some have even taken their own lives, thinking that the spirits told them to do so to join the spirits in the other world.

The mediums today are often of low moral character. Any system that advocates free love, and says that every person has an affinity who will be his or her spouse throughout eternity, is so blasphemous of the Scriptures that it can produce nothing else but immorality as its natural outgrowth. God told His ancient people that if they became familiar with the system of spiritualism they would become defiled thereby (Leviticus 19:31). Observation clearly reveals that this is as true of modern spiritualism as it was of ancient spiritualism.

Furthermore, spiritualism hurls its shafts of criticism into practically every vital truth of the Christian faith. For example: the system denies the inspiration

---

1 William, B. Biederwolf, in his booklet "Spiritualism," lists three black I's of this soul-destroying religion: insanity, immorality, and infidelity. (Wm. B. Biederwolf, "Spiritualism," Grand Rapids: Wm. B. Eerdmans Pub. Co., nd, 23–26.) Many of the statements which follow in this chapter are adopted from this booklet.

of the Holy Scriptures, the atonement, the personality of the Holy Spirit, and the deity of Jesus—just to name a few. Spiritualism has been known to shipwreck one's faith and to take away from one the fear of death and of hell.

Thus, one has sufficient information, both in the Bible and from scientific tests, to warrant him in saying that the claim of spiritualism to communicate with the spirits of the departed is false. Therefore, all are warned of the danger of this dark religion. Leave it alone! If a person enters the road to Endor, it may possibly lead to a wrecked and ruined nervous system, destruction of his faith in the Bible as God's Word, and finally damnation of his soul in the eternal fires of torment. From such a system let every man and woman of self-respect, good sense, and sound discretion turn away with scorn and contempt. For verily, the system of spiritualism leads to moral degradation and destruction of the soul. Many who are currently trifling with spiritualism have no idea where its pernicious teachings and practices will finally lead them. It is a system of lies, a damnable soul-destroying religion.

> What fellowship hath righteousness with unrighteousness? and what communion hath light with darkness? And what concord hath Christ with Belial? or what part hath he that believeth with an infidel? . . . Wherefore come out from among them, and be ye separate, saith the Lord, and touch not the unclean thing (2 Corinthians 6:14–17 KJV).

Surely, consulting those with familiar spirits cannot be pleasing to God now when anciently it was an abomination to Him. Modern spiritualism is magic or sorcery under a different name, and Christians should have nothing to do with it. Spiritism is a system of satanic delusion.

Conclusion

Realizing that Scripture teaches the continued conscious existence of the departed, some claim that they can talk to the dead, but the Bible does not teach that the living can communicate with the spirits of those who have passed from this life. The practice of spiritualism, or spiritism, is severely condemned in the Scriptures. By tricks of magic and sleight-of-hand performances, mediums deceive people into thinking they are receiving messages from their departed friends and loved ones. Spiritualism is of the devil and utterly false in its claims. Men should seek God and not pretend to hold consultation with the dead.

Questions for Discussion

1. Why do people want to communicate with the dead?
2. Define the doctrine of spiritualism.
3. What terms were used in the Old Testament to describe this system?
4. What did King Manasseh do? King Josiah?
5. What is related about Simon in Samaria?
6. Give some passages from the New Testament which condemn spiritualism.
7. What city, noted for its magical arts, was visited by Paul? With what results?
8. What is Isaiah's admonition respecting seeking those who claim to practice this fraud?
9. What is able to furnish one completely unto every good work?
10. Have modern-day sleight-of-hand performers studied the claims of the spiritualist cult?
11. Relate some things about Houdini and the spiritualists.
12. How did J. W. Chism challenge John W. Ring?
13. Relate the interesting experience of King Saul with the witch at Endor. What does this narrative prove about spiritualism?
14. What are the three black "I's" of spiritualism?
15. From the teaching of Scripture, is it right for one to patronize those who practice spiritualism?
16. Do you know of anyone who has been severely hurt, either mentally or physically, by attending their meetings?

– 15 –

Will Jesus Come Again?

"I will come again"
John 14:3 KJV

Having studied the origin and nature of man, the meaning of death, and the state of disembodied spirits in Hades, let us now note the teaching of the Scriptures concerning the end of time and the eternal state of man's existence.

The world had a beginning, and, according to Scripture, the world and the present state of things will come to an end. When will this earth pass out of existence? According to the Bible, as it shall be shown in this chapter, this earth will cease to exist when Jesus comes again. Yet, people ask, "Will the Lord come again?" Many doubt it, but Christ will come again. This fact is clearly stated numerous times in the New Testament, with more than three hundred passages either mentioning or alluding to it. Unfortunately, however, there have been so many theories concerning Jesus' second coming (and so many controversies) that many Christians have neglected to give this Scriptural theme proper attention.

Will the Lord Come Again?

The second coming of Christ is an unquestionably established promise of the Bible. At the ascension of Jesus, the angels said to the apostles as they looked up toward heaven, "Ye men of Galilee, why stand ye looking into heaven? this Jesus, who was received from you into heaven shall so come in like manner as ye beheld him going into heaven" (Acts 1:11). Jesus Himself said He would come again. Prior to His leaving the disciples, Jesus said to them, "I go to prepare a place for you. And if I go and prepare a place for you, I will come again, and receive you unto myself" (John 14:2–3 KJV). The apostles declared that Christ would come again. Paul wrote, "For the Lord himself shall descend from heaven" (1 Thessalonians 4:16). The writer of the book of Hebrews said that Christ "shall appear the second time" (Hebrews 9:28), and John wrote, "He shall appear" (1 John 3:2 KJV).

Even now, as in early days, some doubt the Lord's return.

> Knowing this first, that in the last days mockers shall come with mockery, walking after their own lusts, and saying, Where is the promise of his coming? for, from the day that the fathers fell asleep, all things continue as they were from the beginning of the creation (2 Peter 3:3–4).

Although skeptics doubt and mockers scoff at the idea, Christians believe this promise also, for they believe the Holy Scriptures. The promised deluge was long delayed, but God kept His promise. As far as the fulfillment of this promise is concerned, a thousand years is no more than one day with God (v. 8). Time is not with God as it is with man.

> The Lord is not slack concerning his promise, as some count slackness; but is longsuffering to you-ward, not wishing that any should perish, but that all should come to repentance. But the day of the Lord will come as a thief; in the which the heavens shall pass away with a great noise, and the elements shall be dissolved with fervent heat, and the earth and the works that are therein shall be burned up (2 Peter 3:9–10).

When He does come again, "then cometh the end" (1 Corinthians 15:24).

How Will the Lord Return?

The manner of Christ's personal coming is described in the Scriptures. His coming will not be hidden and concealed but open and manifest. He is coming "in the clouds" (Acts 1:9, 11; Matthew 26:64), "in flaming fire" (2 Thessalonians 1:7), with His mighty angels (Matthew 13:40–43; 16:27; 25:31; Mark 13:26–27; 2 Thessalonians 1:7), "with ten thousands of his holy ones" (Jude 14), "with a shout, with the voice of the archangel, and with the trump of God" (1 Thessalonians 4:16).

Christ's return will also be visible to all. "Behold, he cometh with the clouds; and every eye shall see him, and they that pierced him [the actual participants of the crucifixion]; and all the tribes of the earth shall mourn over him" (Revelation 1:7). No one need go to Jerusalem, Salt Lake City, or anywhere else in order to see the Lord when He comes. Regardless of where they may be, all nations of the earth shall witness His return.

The Scriptures also teach that Christ will come suddenly, without immediate warning (Matthew 24:36; Mark 13:32–36; 1 Thessalonians 5:1). He will come unexpectedly and unannounced, even as a thief in the night (2 Peter 3:10; 1 Thessalonians 5:2). Undoubtedly, Christ's certain coming will be visible, audible, glorious, and sudden. Unquestionably, the Lord's wonderful and unexpected appearance will be an awesome spectacle to unbelievers, but what a wonderful day it will be for the righteous when He comes!

When Will He Come?

The time of His coming is something that is hidden in the mind of God, one of the secret things which belongs to God (Deuteronomy 29:29). God alone knows the day of Christ's second coming (Acts 17:31), but He has not revealed the date to any man, so the time of that event is not a subject for man's speculation.

Jesus said concerning His coming: "But of that day or that hour knoweth no one, not even the angels in heaven, neither the Son, but the Father" (Mark 13:32; cf. Matthew 24:36). Christ's second coming may be at midnight or early morning. He may appear at any moment; it could be today.

When Jesus comes, business will be going on as usual, even as it was before the flood, and many will be unprepared. Jesus again said,

> And as were the days of Noah, so shall be the coming of the Son of man. For as in these days which were before the flood they were eating and drinking, marrying and giving in marriage, until the day that Noah entered into the ark, and they knew not until the flood came, and took them all away; so shall be the coming of the Son of man ((Matthew 24:37–39).

Hence, since one does not know the time of Christ's second coming, this solemn warning is meaningful: "Therefore be ye also ready; for in an hour that ye think not the Son of man cometh" (Matthew 24:44). "Watch therefore . . . lest coming suddenly he find you sleeping. And what I say unto you I say unto all, Watch" (Mark 13:35–37).

Date-Setters Are Deceiving

In view of these facts, it is ridiculous for anyone to set dates for Christ's return. Yet this has been done, and is still being done. Honest people are still being deceived by the date-setters.

As an example of those who have been mistaken as to the date of the Lord's return, William Miller, the founder of the Adventist movement, predicted that Christ would come in October, 1843.[1] He seemed to have been a rabble-rousing preacher who converted many people to his belief. At least many of his followers disposed of their property, prepared for themselves white ascension robes, and joyously awaited the Lord's appearance. The date came, but Jesus did not come. Although disappointed, Miller would not be outdone, so he told his followers he had missed his calculations in prophecy by one year, and that the Lord would come the next year at that time. Again the date came, but Christ did not come in 1844.

---

1 D. M. Canright, *Seventh-Day Adventism Renounced*, reprint of Fourteenth Edition, pp. 68–80.

Later, Charles T. Russell, founder of the religious group now known as Jehovah's Witnesses, wrote about Christ's return. He said the Lord came in October, 1874, but only certain ones (his followers) were aware of it—that to all others He was invisible.[1] This view directly contradicts Revelation 1:7.

"Pastor" Russell, as he was often called, made many predictions about the "Golden Age" that was to commence in connection with the second coming of Christ; but all of his predictions in this respect proved him a false prophet. "When a prophet speaketh in the name of Jehovah, if the thing follow not, nor come to pass, that is the thing which Jehovah hath not spoken: the prophet hath spoken it presumptuously" (Deuteronomy 18:22).

Following Russell's death in 1916, "Judge" Rutherford fell heir to the "throne" and he, too, made predictions. In 1920, Rutherford published a small book entitled *Millions Now Living Will Never Die,* in which he predicted that in 1925 the righteous who accepted the Ransomer would return to the days of their youth and "live on the earth forever and never see death."[2] This meant that elderly people with wooden legs would get new limbs, all with false teeth would get new teeth, and all bald-headed men would get a new suit of hair . . . in 1925! He further predicted that Abraham, Isaac, Jacob, and David, along with other Old Testament worthies, would be living on earth, and visible, after 1925. Indeed, 1925 would be the beginning of the "Golden Age." All of that sounded good to many people before 1925, but 1925 came and Rutherford's predictions failed. Even the "Judge" himself died after 1925! He was one of the millions living when 1925 came, but he died. He, too, was a false prophet. Of more recent date, one said that Christ would come in 1982. So, on and on the date-setters continue to deceive those who are ignorant of God's Word.

It surely becomes evident that man knows absolutely nothing about that phase of the subject. In view of these facts, why is it that some will continue to set dates for Christ's return? And stranger still, why do some still believe that the so-called prophets know what they are talking about when they tell people a time of Christ's coming? How gullible can human beings be? Could it be that they do not study the Scriptures? That date has not been revealed to any one. Yet the date-setters continue to deceive those who are ignorant of God's Word.

Modified Date-Setters Are Deceiving

Some do not set any particular day for the Savior's return but stress the idea that His coming is imminent, that it will be during "this year" or "this

---

1 Charles T. Russell, *Studies in the Scriptures,* Series III, Thy Kingdom Come (Brooklyn: Watch Tower Bible and Tract Society, 1891), pp. 124–125, 127, 133.

2 J. F. Rutherford, *Millions Now Living Shall Never Die,* (Brooklyn: International Bible Students Association, 1920), pp. 12, 88–89, 90. 97–28, 100.

generation." Although this is possible, the Bible does not teach it. The Scriptures did not teach in the first century that Christ's return was very near (cf. 2 Thessalonians 2:1–3), and they do not teach that the Lord's second coming is imminent now. Perhaps as never before in history, men are thinking of the end of the world. While some have been influenced by the sensational type of preaching and writing, others, perchance, have become indifferent, due to false prophets, to any Biblical teaching of the last things. In view of this fact, since the Bible does not say when Christ will come, no one should say the Lord is coming soon. We do not need to sing "Jesus is coming soon." Just say He is coming again.

John, in closing the book of Revelation, wrote, "He who testifieth these things saith, Yea: I come quickly" (Revelation 22:20). His coming will be quick when He does come. He did not mean He would come soon after talking to John, for centuries have passed and He has not come yet. But it is certain that He will come. Regardless of the actual time, He will come again.

Christ's Language in Matthew 24 Is Misapplied

Those who talk much about signs, the fulfillment of prophecy, and the imminence of Christ's coming usually refer to the first part of Matthew 24 for proof of their interpretations of the times. These words of Jesus, herein recorded, have caused many students to study the Bible concerning the Lord's appearance at the end of time.

Jesus uttered these words immediately following His last public discourse, just prior to His crucifixion. He had closed His speech with the solemn words: "Behold, your house is left unto you desolate" (Matthew 23:38). As Jesus and His disciples were leaving the temple grounds to go to the Mount of Olives, they pointed out to Him the buildings of the temple (Matthew 24:1). Christ then said to His apostles, "There shall not be left here one stone upon another, that shall not be thrown down" (v. 2). Then later as he sat on the Mount of Olives, the disciples came unto him privately, saying, "Tell us, when shall these things be? and what shall be the sign of thy coming, and of the end of the world?" (v. 3). Then Jesus, in answering their questions, gave to the four apostles the prophecy concerning the destruction of the temple and His second coming. Note that Christ carefully answered two questions, namely: (1) "When shall these things be [i.e., the overthrowing of Jerusalem and the destruction of the temple which He had just predicted]?" and (2) "What shall be the sign of thy coming, and of the end of the world?" The apostles had the mistaken assumption that all these events would be simultaneous. Some divide the passage into three questions: (1) when the destruction of the temple and of Jerusalem was to occur; (2) what was to be the sign of His coming; and (3) when the end of the world was to take place (cf. Mark 13:4 and Luke 21:7).

Jesus answered their questions in the same order as they were asked. Matthew 24:4–28 contains Christ's answer to the first question; verses 29–35 seem to be transitional, and verses 36–51 contain His answer to the second question (with further teaching about His coming and the final judgment in chapter 25). First He taught concerning the destruction of Jerusalem. Second He taught regarding His second coming. In the passing from one question to the other, Jesus in effect said, "The Son of man personally will come at the end of the world, but He will not come in person when Jerusalem is destroyed. However, when you see all these things come to pass, you will know that the destruction of Jerusalem is near, just as you know that summer is nigh when you see the fig tree putting forth leaves. Of my second coming at the end of the world, no one knows the day or the hour when this will occur; it will not be preceded by any sign whatever."

The destruction of Jerusalem occurred in A.D.70 under the Roman emperor Titus. This was just forty years after Jesus spoke these words. A Muslim mosque stands today on the spot where the temple once stood. Christ's Olivet prophecy was literally fulfilled—not one stone of the temple building was left upon another. Furthermore, in interpreting the passage, Matthew 24 should always be studied in connection with the parallel accounts in Mark 13 and Luke 21:5–28. Luke 21:20 contains a clear wording of the statement of Matthew 24:15 about the soldiers' encompassing Jerusalem: "But when ye see Jerusalem compassed with armies, then know that her desolation is at hand." The presence of the Roman army in Judea would be a sure sign of the nearness of the destruction of the city. Hence, when the disciples saw the soldiers around Jerusalem, they knew with certainty that the hour had come for them to flee Jerusalem and Judea. So completely were the early disciples taught these things about the destruction of the city, and so well-warned were they, that history does not record that a single Christian lost his life in the terrible catastrophe.[1]

Further note that Jesus said in Matthew 24:34 that all the events previously mentioned would be fulfilled in the lifetime of that generation, the people living at that time. "This generation shall not pass away, till all these things be accomplished." Thus, every sign mentioned in Matthew 24, except those at the very time of the second coming of Christ, has been fulfilled; that present generation did not pass away till all these things spoken about the destruction of Jerusalem were fulfilled. These signs, then, being fulfilled before that genera-

---

1 H. Leo Boles wrote: "It is a matter of history that the Roman army, first under Cestius Callus, besieged Jerusalem about A.D.66, and then withdrew from it; again, the city was besieged by Vespasian about A.D.68; the devastation continued until the final overthrow and destruction by Titus in A.D.70." *(Commentary on Luke* [Nashville: Gospel Advocate Co., 1940], p. 398.)

tion passed away, could not have referred to the second advent of Christ, but must refer to His previous prediction of the destruction of Jerusalem. To make those things signs leading up to the second coming of Christ and the end of the world would contradict His positive statement that no signs would precede and give warning of His second advent. Jesus clearly told His disciples that they should not regard such events as wars, famines, pestilences, and earthquakes as the signs of His return. It is surprising, then, that people now will persistently take these things to be signs of His coming, even though Jesus said that these very things were not to be regarded as such. Yet, unfortunately, some teachings now used are taken from statements which Christ made in regard to the destruction of Jerusalem and the end of the Jewish state from Matthew 24:4–22, and are applied to His second coming and the end of the world. Jesus emphasized that no one knows the day or the hour when this great event shall take place, but that it will be at a time when people think not (Matthew 24:44). Yet, in spite of this plain warning which the Lord gave to His disciples, many present-day religionists are filled with admiration for the minister who speaks learnedly about the signs of the times. Such a one strives to show to his audience that this or that terrible war, serious earthquake, or devastating famine is according to prophecy, a sure sign of Christ's imminent coming. Let all beware of those who do not know how to rightly divide the Word of truth.

The purpose, then, of the Lord's Olivet discourse was not to give to His disciples signs of His second coming, but was to warn that generation of believers of the approaching destruction of Jerusalem and to give to them a sure sign whereby they might secure their safety by fleeing from the city.

So the "false christs" (Matthew 24:5), the "wars and rumors of wars" (v. 6), the "false prophets" (vv. 11, 24), and the gospel being preached "unto all the nations" (v. 14; Mark 13:10) had reference to that period of time before the destruction of Jerusalem. Too, this event in which the Roman army brought an end to the Jewish nation was a time, according to Josephus, a Jewish historian, of "great tribulation" (Matthew 24:21). This great act of divine judgment, which Moses had foretold (Deuteronomy 28:49–64), was such as had not been "from the beginning of the world" (Matthew 24:21), and if God's mercy had not interposed for the sake of the followers of Christ, the whole Jewish nation that inhabited the land would have been swept away; there would have been no flesh saved (v. 22; cf. Daniel 12:1; 1 Thessalonians 2:16). Thus, the great tribulation, mentioned so often by some Bible students, is now a matter of the distant past, having been completely fulfilled.

Therefore, if one will carefully examine the entire discourse, he will see that the Lord divided the future into two distinct periods. The first of those extended from the time of the discourse to the destruction of Jerusalem; the second period from that event to His second coming and the end of the world. Regarding the first period, Jesus said, "But take ye heed: behold, I have told you all things beforehand" (Mark 13:23); but concerning the second period, instead of giving a sign whereby His people might be warned of the approaching end, He spoke only in general terms, and made it plain that no immediately preceding signs would be given whereby His disciples would know that His advent was near. Yet this statement from the Lord's discourse is given frequently and applied to the end of time: "And this gospel of the kingdom shall be preached in the whole world for a testimony unto all the nations; and then shall the end come" (Matthew 24:14). Here "end" refers to the destruction of Jerusalem, as in verse 6. That the gospel was "preached in all the world" before that event is declared by Paul in Colossians 1:23. This epistle was written in about A.D.63, about seven years before "the end" (cf. Colossians 1:6; Romans 10:18; 1:8; Mark 16:20).

The words, "immediately after the tribulation of those days" (Matthew 24:29), may mark the beginning of Christ's discussion of the answer to the second question—the final coming of the Son of man at the end of time. However, the word *immediately* must surely be understood as God counts time, and not as it would appear to men (cf. 2 Peter 3:8; Revelation 22:20).[1]

From these sayings of Christ, one can surely see that it is an impossibility to calculate, from any prophecies in the Bible, the year or the day of Christ's return. Furthermore, one can see how contrary to the teaching of Jesus is the idea that He will be revealed at the end of a supposed great tribulation. The only point in the discourse that Christ stressed concerning His second coming and the end of the world was that His disciples should be in a state of expectancy of His coming again and be always ready. Hence, every Christian should govern his life by the fact that Christ could return at any time.

---

1 A differing point of view by many Bible scholars is that Matthew 24:29–30 has to do with Christ's coming in the execution of judgment on the Jewish nation and the extinction of the great lights of the Jewish state based upon similar figurative language as used in Isaiah 13:10. Mark's language of this statement is: "But in those days, after that tribulation, the sun shall be darkened" (Mark 13:24). The second coming of Christ was to take place after the siege of the city and the time of its destruction; but the length of time "after that tribulation" and before the Lord's return, which will end time, Christ did not say, nor does the Bible answer. The only parables Jesus gave concerning His second coming are the ones about the servant doing his master's will at all times, lest the master should return unexpectedly and find him unprepared, plus the two parables in the next chapter, the ten virgins and the talents, which stress preparedness (Matthew 24:45–51; 25:1–30). (Definitely, Matthew 24:36 begins His second coming.)

What Will Happen When Jesus Comes?

The events associated with Christ's second coming are likewise plainly set forth in the Scriptures.

1. When Jesus comes, this will be the end of the world; the earth will be burned up and the works that are therein.

> But the heavens that now are, and the earth, by the same word have been stored up for fire, being reserved against the day of judgment and destruction of ungodly men . . . the heavens shall pass away with a great noise, and the elements shall be dissolved with fervent heat, and the earth and the works that are therein shall be burned up (2 Peter 3:7–10).

The apocalyptic language here used, describing the time wherein "the heavens being on fire shall be dissolved, and the elements shall melt with fervent heat" (v. 12), was once considered ridiculously exaggerated; but to those who now live in the days of A-bombs and H-bombs, the statement does not seem too difficult to understand because all know how literal these predictions could be.

2. When Christ returns there will be the simultaneous resurrection of all mankind, both the good and the bad.

> Marvel not at this: for the hour cometh, in which all that are in the tombs shall hear his voice, and shall come forth; they that have done good, unto the resurrection of life; and they that have done evil, unto the resurrection of judgment (John 5:28–29).

> For as in Adam all die, so also in Christ shall all be made alive. But each in his own order: Christ the firstfruits; then they that are Christ's, at his coming. Then cometh the end . . . for the trumpet shall sound, and the dead shall be raised incorruptible, and we shall be changed (1 Corinthians 15:22–52).

3. When the Lord returns there will then be the final judgment for all men, the just and the unjust.

> But when the Son of man shall come in his glory, and all the angels with him, then shall he sit on the throne of his glory: and before him shall be gathered all the nations: and he shall separate them one from another, as the shepherd separateth the sheep from the goats (Matthew 25:31–32).

> Christ Jesus . . . shall judge the living and the dead (2 Timothy 4:1).

> And I saw a great white throne, and him that sat upon it, from whose face the earth and the heaven fled away; and there was found no place for them. And I saw the dead, the great and the small, standing before the throne; and books were opened: and another book was opened, which is the book of life: and the dead were judged out of the things which were written in the books, according to their works (Revelation 20:11–12).

Thus, the Scriptures connect the end of the physical world, when the atmospherical and planetary heavens that surround this earth shall pass away, the general resurrection, and the final judgment with Christ's second coming. Let the hour of the Lord's return be when it may, the Bible is plain to the effect that the coming of Christ is a coming to end time, to raise the dead, both good and bad, and to judge the living and the dead. This will be the greatest day the world has ever seen. It will be the day when all shall then be the inhabitants of eternity.

The resurrection of the dead and final judgment will be studied more in detail in the next two chapters.

Questions for Discussion

1. What promise was made by the angels to the apostles at the ascension of Christ?
2. What promise did Jesus make to His disciples prior to His return to heaven?
3. Cite passages which show that the apostles said Christ would come again.
4. Why do some doubt this promise?
5. How will Jesus come the second time?
6. Will all see Jesus when He comes?
7. Has the date been revealed as to the time of Christ's return?
8. Does God know the time it will be?
9. How should all people be when Christ comes again? How is this possible?
10. Give some instances of date-setting for Christ's return. Why do some believe these so-called prophets?
11. Have these date-setters done harm to the Biblical theme of Christ's second coming? What do you think of the book, *The Late Great Planet Earth,* by Hal Lindsey?
12. What two events did Christ mention in Matthew 24?
13. Why do some miss the meaning of Christ's prophecy in this chapter?
14. When and by whom was Jerusalem destroyed?
15. In Matthew 24:34, was Jesus speaking of the Jewish race or of the people living at that time?
16. What does "the great tribulation" mean? Has it occurred?
17. Was the destruction of Jerusalem in A.D.70 more terrible than the world had ever experienced? (Read Deuteronomy 28 and Daniel 9.)
18. What is the meaning of "the abomination of desolation" spoken of by Daniel the prophet in Daniel 9:27?
19. What did Jesus mean by the use of the illustration of the fig tree?
20. What lessons are taught to Christians in the parables of the Ten Virgins and the Talents in Matthew 25?
21. What three events are associated with Christ's second coming?

– 16 –

WILL THE BODY BE RAISED?

". . . there shall be a resurrection of both the just and unjust"
Acts 24:15

All mankind will die except those who will be living at the time of Christ's return. Death is no respecter of persons. It comes every day to someone and someday to everyone. So the ancient and ever-returning question, as expressed by Job, is, "If a man die, shall he live again?" This question is universal.

There is an ever-constant longing in the heart of man for life beyond. The earliest histories of man indicate man's desire of a future life. In every person there is a conviction he was not made to die, that the grave is not the end, and that the Maker's plan for him is not annihilation. He believes he was made to live in a higher and nobler existence than this earth-life. Immortality has been the belief of all people of all nations of all ages. Verily, man wants to live after death.

Is man not justified in concluding that the faith in life after death is evidence of the fact? Why this sentiment, this universal longing for existence beyond the grave? Was it as surely implanted in man by his Creator as instincts were implanted in animals? Can one believe that these deep desires are to be frustrated at death? Does a good and wise God plant a hope in the soul for mockery? Where in all of nature can one find instinct falsified? The wings of the bird mean that it was meant to fly: the fins of the fish mean that it was made to swim. Surely, then, this instinct, which infidels and atheists have never been able to uproot from man's mind, is prophetic of its own fulfillment in eternity. God will not disappoint man in this respect.

Then, too, life here is so incomplete, even the longest is insufficient for the fulfillment of half of man's capabilities. He is often cut off when he is just ready to make some greater advance. A future life is needed for completeness. Life on earth is short. All of man's plans are made with the knowledge that he may not live to carry them out. Even a life of threescore years and ten is a short life, and if by reason of strength they be fourscore, yet the life is soon cut off

(Psalm 90:10 KJV). "What is your life? For ye are a vapor that appeareth for a little time, and then vanisheth away" (James 4:14). Is this yearning, then, after perfection and fullness the soul's prophecy of its own immortality? Of course, man can believe that it is, and say with Addison:

> It must be so—Plato, thou reasonest well—
> Else whence this pleasing hope, this found desire,
> This longing after immortality?
> Or whence this secret dread, and inward horror,
> Of falling into naught? Why shrinks the soul
> Back on herself and startles at destruction?
> 'Tis the divinity that stirs within us;
> 'Tis Heaven itself that points out a hereafter
> And intimates Eternity to man.

Moreover, God in His Word so declared it!

Will All the Dead Be Raised?

That the Scriptures teach a general resurrection of all the dead is admitted by all. The evidence for the resurrection of the dead, wholly Biblical, is certainly ample, clearly taught, and divinely demonstrated. And this is the excellent ground of one's faith in immortality. Hence, the expression "I believe in the resurrection of the dead" has been the language of faith in all ages of Christianity.

Jesus Taught the Resurrection of the Body

Jesus taught as one of His cardinal truths the doctrine of the resurrection of the dead. One direct affirmation is:

> Marvel not at this: for the hour cometh, in which all that are in the tombs shall hear his voice, and shall come forth; they that have done good, unto the resurrection of life; and they that have done evil, unto the resurrection of judgment (John 5:28–29).

At Capernaum, Christ repeatedly stated that the righteous would be raised at the end of time: "For this is the will of my Father, that every one that beholdeth the Son, and believeth on him, should have eternal life; and I will raise him up at the last day" (John 6:40; cf. vv. 39, 44, 54).

At the home of Martha and Mary in Bethany, Jesus said to Martha, "Thy brother shall rise again" (John 11:23). Martha then expressed a common belief when she said of her dead brother: "I know that he shall rise again in the resurrection at the last day" (v. 24). Then Christ informed, "I am the resurrection, and the life: he that believeth on me, though he die, yet shall he live" (v. 25). In effect, Jesus said to Martha, "The power that shall raise all the dead at the last day is present and can raise your brother now as well as then; I am the source of the resurrection and life." Then, following this statement, Jesus went with Martha and Mary to the tomb of Lazarus and called him forth from the dead (John 11:38–44).

The Apostles Taught the Resurrection

The doctrine of the resurrection of the dead constitutes a large portion of apostolic teaching, as clearly seen from a number of statements.

The apostle Paul asserted God would raise the dead: "And God both raised the Lord, and will raise up us through his power" (1 Corinthians 6:14); and "he that raised up the Lord Jesus shall raise up us also with Jesus" (2 Corinthians 4:14). In fact, all the apostles, beginning with Peter on Pentecost (Acts 2:24–36), gave witness to the resurrection of Christ with great power (Acts 3:15, 26; 4:10, 33; 5:30), and the consequent resurrection of all. Luke wrote that they proclaimed in Jesus the resurrection from the dead (Acts 4:2). Indeed, Christ was proclaimed to be the Prince of life (Acts 3:15), who was raised to a glorified life and is capable of imparting that life to others.

Peter preached the resurrection of Christ to Cornelius and his household (Acts 10:40); Paul, in his first sermon at Antioch in Pisidia, preached that God raised Christ from the dead (Acts 13:26–41) Later, as he continued his first missionary journey, he taught the same thing at Thessalonica and Athens (Acts 17:3, 18, 31, 32). While on trial before King Agrippa, Paul proclaimed Christ's resurrection (Acts 26:8, 23).

The Old Testament Writers Mentioned the Resurrection

The servants of God in the Old Testament Scriptures gave intimations and hopes, more or less, in regard to the resurrection and future life after death. Abraham believed God was able to raise his son Isaac from the dead if he should offer him as a sacrifice (Hebrews 11:19).

Job expressed his belief:

> So man lieth down and riseth not: till the heavens be no more, they shall not awake, nor be roused out of their sleep . . . If a man die, shall he live again? All the days of my warfare would I wait, till my release should come [i.e., till I live again]. Thou wouldest call, and I would answer thee (Job 14:12–15).

> I know that my Redeemer liveth, and at last he will stand up upon the earth: and after my skin, even this body, is destroyed, then without my flesh shall I see God [i.e., I shall see God in my resurrection-body] (Job 19:25–26).

David also believed in the resurrection: "As for me, I shall behold thy face in righteousness: I shall be satisfied, when I awake, with beholding thy form" (Psalm 17:15). Again, "But God will redeem my soul from the power of Sheol, for he will receive me" (Psalm 49:15).

The prophet Daniel spoke of the resurrection: "And many of them [i.e., the multitude] that sleep in the dust of the earth shall awake, some to everlasting life, and some to shame and everlasting contempt" (Daniel 12:2). Likewise, Isaiah: "Thy dead shall live; my dead bodies shall arise. Awake and sing, ye that dwell in dust; for thy dew is as the dew of herbs, and the earth shall cast forth the dead" (Isaiah 26:19).

Hence, revelation assures man that there shall be a resurrection.

When Will the Resurrection Occur?

As to the time of the resurrection, the Scriptures are very explicit. It will occur at the end of time—the end of the world—at Christ's return when He comes to judge all men (cf. 1 Thessalonians 4:16; 1 Corinthians 15:23, 52; 2 Timothy 4:1–2; Matthew 25:31–32; Revelation 20:12–13).

As to the extent of the resurrection, it will be universal, i.e., all will be raised at the same time (John 5:28–29). Believers will be raised, said Jesus, at the "last day" (John 6:39, 40, 44). He also said that the wicked will be judged at the "last day" (John 12:48). Hence, the wicked will be also raised at the "last day." Paul declared one general resurrection (singular, not resurrections): "There shall be a resurrection, both of the just and unjust" (Acts 24:15).

However, in one sense the resurrection of the people of God differs from that of unbelievers in its final issue, and can, therefore, be distinctive and desired above the resurrection of the wicked. Thus, when Paul expressed his desire to "attain unto the resurrection from the dead" (Philippians 3:11), he had reference to the nature of the resurrection and not to the time of it. Paul desired to participate in the full honor and glory of a resurrection of a righteous person. To be raised as a just man is a most desirable object, which must be secured by obedience to the Lord.

How Are the Dead Raised?

Further evidence that the dead are to be raised is needless. However, some questions should be considered; namely, (1) in what will the resurrection consist? (2) what does Christ's resurrection mean to man? (3) how will the body be raised? (4) what kind of body will the resurrection-body be?

The Body Only Will Be Raised

The word resurrection means "standing again." The word is derived from two Latin words: *re,* meaning "again," and *surgo,* "to rise." It is the standing again of the person in a body. The Bible emphasizes that it is the body only that is placed in the tomb, so only the body will come from the tomb. The dead will be raised, but that which is buried is that which will be raised. Hence, it is the body that dies and is raised again. There is no such thing as the resurrection of a spirit—it never enters the grave; a spirit never dies nor is buried. The spirit in death remains consciously alive after the dissolution of the body. The spirit goes to God at death (Ecclesiastes 12:7). When Jesus comes again He will bring the spirits with Him (1 Thessalonians 4:14–16) and raise their dead bodies. Spirits then will be re-united with their proper bodies. Each one will receive his own body, the resurrection-body. If that were not true, it would be foolish to talk about a resurrection at all.

There is a great difference, then, in the meaning of the expressions "resurrection of the body" and "immortality of the soul." The Scriptures do not just teach the survival of the spirit after death, but they also teach a resurrection of the body. Man on earth is body and spirit, so body as well as spirit must be restored if the complete man is to live again. For this reason, to teach the immortality of the soul without also affirming the immortality of the body would give immortality to only half the man. The Biblical doctrine includes the whole man. Death makes a division in man's compound nature; resurrection repairs that division. Disembodiment means incompleteness, and God will not leave man imperfect in this sense. As long as man is under the dominion of death and his body is in the grave, his redemption is incomplete. Neither heaven nor hell is an eternal abode of disembodied spirits only. Many of the ancient Greeks taught the immortality of the soul, but the Bible teaches the doctrine of the redemption of both soul and body.

Christ's Resurrection Is Pledge and Proof of Man's Resurrection

Christ's resurrection from the dead carries with it the certainty of the resurrection of all mankind. As Christ arose, so also He guarantees the resurrection of all bodies. Although the belief of some kind of future life has been with all peoples of earth since their earliest existence, all now have in the New Testament a much clearer revelation of that future life. Consequently, since Christ arose and since God has definitely promised the resurrection, all may be sure that the general resurrection of all mankind will occur in due time. Even though the resurrection is definitely promised, this act is not yet consummated. Nevertheless, the barriers of death have been broken, and ultimately death itself will be completely destroyed. Definitely, death's actual and total abolition is foretold and certain.

Christ said to His disciples, "Because I live, ye shall live also" (John 14:19). Suppose Christ had not been raised from the dead—how terrible to be without hope! But He was raised! He lives! And this is evidence that all shall live again.

Job's question waited long for a definite answer, but at last Christ's all-sufficient answer came. Jesus gave it by the grave of Lazarus in His words of calm assurance to all the world: "I am the resurrection, and the life: he that believeth on me, though he die, yet shall he live" (John 11:25). These precious words have brought hope to millions, but they would be worthless if Christ had not confirmed them by fact.

Man's hope, therefore, of a resurrected, immortal body is guaranteed to him by Christ's own resurrection and life in glory. Paul affirmed that Jesus has "abolished death, and brought life and immortality to light through the gospel" (2 Timothy 1:10). Christ did this in His own resurrection. This event brought the doctrine of the resurrection to the front and greatly enlarged man's hope of being resurrected. Jesus lifted the old concept out of possibility and brought it into the realm of reality. Christ's resurrection flashed an unusual light on the subject of existence beyond the grave. The ancient world had not the positive assurance of a future life; it was not so clearly revealed and proved to them as it is to people who now live under the teaching of Christianity. The wisest and best of men among the ancient heathen world, though they had some hopes and longings for a future life, were never able to reach the truth about life beyond the grave. It was not definite then as now. So Christ established the fact of the immortal life, and in this sense brought life and immortality to light. With the resurrection of Christ and the teaching of the New Testament being revealed, the doctrine of immortality was completed.

Unbelievers question the resurrection. They say it is contrary to their experience. However, to doubt the resurrection because one has never seen a resurrection from the dead is like a man in a tropical climate saying it has never snowed on earth. He has never seen it snow; he has never talked to anyone who has seen snow and ice; therefore, he says it has never snowed and such is impossible. This, nevertheless, does not prove that it has never snowed. Similarly, people today have never seen the dead raised or beheld one raised from the dead, but some saw the miraculous resurrections of Christ's personal ministry. Furthermore, many today believe the testimony of the eyewitnesses of the risen Christ—and they believe the words of the Lord Jesus that one day all shall be raised from the dead.

Paul Discussed the Resurrection Based on Christ's Resurrection

In the fifteenth chapter of 1 Corinthians, Paul furnished the most logical and sublime argument for the resurrection of the dead. Here are given both the fact of the resurrection of Christ and a summary of the evidence or proof by which that doctrine was supported. Some at Corinth denied the resurrection of the dead, but Paul insisted on the resurrection of Christ and the truth of the resurrection of all mankind.

There are two main divisions of this resurrection chapter: (1) the certainty of the resurrection (vv. 1–34), and (2) the nature of the resurrection (vv. 35–54). The first part answers the question of verse 12: "How say some among you that there is no resurrection of the dead?" The second answers the questions of verse 35: "How are the dead raised? and with what manner of body do they come?"

In the first part of the chapter (vv. 1–11), the apostle answered their first question: Is there really to be a resurrection from the dead? (cf. v. 12). This he did from the basic truth of Christianity—namely, the resurrection of the Savior from the dead. This had been set forth when he preached the gospel unto them. In this message he declared, "He hath been raised on the third day according to the scriptures" (v. 4).

The resurrection of all men and the whole structure of Christianity are based upon Christ's resurrection. In verses 13–19, the apostle showed that to deny the resurrection is to deny the entire scheme of redemption, for if there were no resurrection, then Christ did not rise and there is no hope of salvation. On the fact of Christ's resurrection rests man's assurance of being raised from the dead. If the dead do not rise, it follows that Christ has not risen; but if God raised Him, He will also raise all from the dead. If Christ has not been raised from the dead, the apostles are false witnesses, their preaching is vain, man's faith is vain, people are yet in their sins, and those who have fallen asleep have perished. A denial of the resurrection strikes at the very root of the Christian religion.

However, in verses 20–28, Paul asserted emphatically that Christ had risen. "But now hath Christ been raised from the dead." Jesus conquered death. In verses 29–34, Paul showed that to obey Christ and to sacrifice for His church would be nothing short of foolishness if there is no resurrection.

Everyone, therefore, who believes that Christ was raised from the dead should believe that all who sleep in the dust of the earth will likewise be raised; and, conversely, everyone who denies the certainty of the resurrection must, if consistent, deny the resurrection of Christ. The Scriptures supply evidence of the certainty of Christ's resurrection. After His death Jesus showed Himself alive to His apostles by many proofs (Acts 1:2–3). Indeed, there is no other fact in history sustained by such an array of evidence as the miraculous resurrection of Christ. As a fact in history, this fundamental tenet of Christianity is attested by evidence more certain than can be produced in favor of any accepted facts, ancient or modern. Christ was seen alive by trustworthy witnesses. Man's faith, therefore, in life in the hereafter is based upon that glorious event. Reason may lead one to hope, but revelation produces faith (Romans 10:17). Christ's resurrection demonstrates His deity and the existence of life beyond the grave, proving His claim to be the Son of God (Romans 1:3–4). Christ's resurrection is the guarantee that the day will come when all bodies will be raised as was His. This, then, is the foundation of the Christian's faith in a future life.

Atheists deny the resurrection of Christ and, in effect, affirm that no amount of evidence can prove that a supernatural event ever occurred. For one to make such an affirmation is ridiculous. Christianity is at stake in this controversy, for if Christ did not arise, His deity cannot be upheld and Christianity cannot be maintained. Nevertheless, if Christ be risen, how can one deny the resurrection of the dead?

How grateful all should be that the fact of Christ's resurrection serves as a pledge and proof of man's resurrection, and that one day all shall come forth from their graves to live forever and ever. Christ's resurrection, as fact, demonstrates the certainty of life after death. As Christ lives, so shall all live again. Immortality is made absolutely sure by the resurrection of Christ. The Savior suffered and died and rose again from the dead, and in His triumph over death is the assurance of man's resurrection at the last day. As surely as "in Adam all die, so also in Christ shall all be made alive" (1 Corinthians 15:22).

Christ Is the "Firstfruits" of the Resurrection

Paul also affirmed that Christ rose as "the firstfruits of them that are asleep" (1 Corinthians 15:20). If Christ rose from the dead, all His people must. In this language the apostle used a striking metaphor. Under the old law, the first sheaf of the harvest was carried into the temple on the day following the Paschal Sabbath and consecrated to God; it was the pledge and prophecy of the reaping in due season of all the miles of golden grain that waved in the sunshine (Leviticus 23:10–12). Likewise, Christ, the Antitype, has been raised before Christians; He is the first to rise from the dead to die no more and is declared to be "the firstborn from the dead" (Colossians 1:18; cf. Acts 26:23). As the devout Israelite farmer brought the first of his harvest to present before the Lord, so Jesus has now presented Himself before God as the firstfruits of the great harvest, the people of God. To the Christians at Corinth, Paul said concerning the resurrection: "But each in his own order: Christ the firstfruits; then they that are Christ's, at his coming" (v. 23). Christ arose first, then those who are His disciples shall rise at His second coming. This whole chapter deals with the resurrection of believers, not unbelievers. Other passages of Scripture teach that the wicked too will be raised at the last day, for example John 5:28–29. Hence, just as the firstfruits and the first ripe sheaf were offered to the Lord, Christ's resurrection is the pledge and promise of a coming harvest. Every reader of this fifteenth chapter of 1 Corinthians must see how much depends on the fact that Jesus Christ rose again from the dead.

God Can Raise the Dead

Resurrection is not impossible, for Divine power is able to raise the body from the grave. The resurrection is both reasonable and possible. If one has been raised from the dead by the power of God to die no more, then all can be.

That Jehovah God has the power to resurrect the body has been clearly demonstrated. Those mentioned in the Bible, in both the Old Testament and the New (besides Christ), as having been brought from the dead, are:

1. The widow's son at Zarephath, by Elijah the prophet (1 Kings 17:17–22).
2. The Shunammite's son, by the prophet Elisha (2 Kings 4:18–37).
3. The unnamed man whose body when being buried touched the bones of Elisha (2 Kings 13:20–21).
4. Jairus' daughter, by Christ (Matthew 9:18–26; Mark 5:35–42; Luke 8:49–56).
5. The widow's son at Nain, by Christ (Luke 7:11–15).
6. Lazarus, the brother of Martha and Mary, by Christ (John 11:17–44).
7. Dorcas (Tabitha), a Christian woman who lived in Joppa, by Peter (Acts 9:36–41).
8. Eutychus, the man at Troas who fell out the window, by Paul (Acts 20:5, 9–10).[1]

None of these instances of miraculous resurrections, however, were a resurrection to an immortal or incorruptible body, for they all later died again and saw corruption. They were restored to their natural bodies. These cases do, however, show that there is a power superior to death. Those eight persons, along with the reminder of mankind, will be the subjects of that final resurrection by the power of the Lord at the last day which shall completely swallow up death in victory; for this same infinite God shall awaken to life all the dead in "the resurrection at the last day." This will be a display of almighty power. Indeed, God is able to clothe the spirits of the righteous with celestial bodies, suitable for the eternal abode in heaven. If one accepts the personal existence of an omnipotent God, why not the possibility of raising the dead by a miracle of power? If in the long ago Abraham believed in the possibility of a bodily resurrection (Hebrews 11:19), it should be much easier for one who now lives under a much fuller revelation of God's will to believe the doctrine of the resurrection. The resurrection of the body is not incredible.

William Jennings Bryan once delivered a lecture and confirmed his faith in immortality in these words:

> If the Father designs to touch with divine power the cold and pulseless heart of the buried acorn and to make it burst forth from its prison walls, will He leave neglected in the earth the soul of man, made in the image of his Creator?

---

1 This list of cases of resurrection in the Bible does not include the strange event where "many bodies of the saints that had fallen asleep were raised; and coming forth out of the tombs after his [Christ's] resurrection" (Matthew 27:52–53). Neither does it include Ezekiel's vision of the valley of dry bones and their resurrection—a symbol of the restoration of Israel from Babylon (Ezekiel 37:1–14) and not a literal bodily resurrection.

> If He stoops to give to the rose-bush, whose withered blossoms float upon the autumn breeze, the sweet assurance of another springtime, will He refuse the words of hope to the sons of men when the frosts of winter come? If matter, mute and inanimate, though changed by the forces of nature into a multitude of forms, can never die, will the imperial spirit of man suffer annihilation when it has paid a brief visit like a royal quest to this tenement of clay? No. He who, notwithstanding His apparent prodigality, created nothing without a purpose, and wasted not a single atom in all His creation, has made provision for a future life in which man's universal longing for immortality will find its realization.

Although there have been many who have believed in the resurrection of the dead, others have denied it. For example, when Paul addressed the Athenians on Mars' Hill, he had an attentive audience until he spoke of the resurrection of the dead. This was too much; the sermon ended abruptly (Acts 17:22–32). Since denial of the resurrection was largely the belief of the Greeks, and since the resurrection had been denied by some at Corinth, Paul was concerned; he did not want the early Christians influenced by the heathen philosophers to doubt the possibility of a future bodily resurrection. As unbelievers in the resurrection, the heathen asked two questions: "How are the dead raised?" and "With what manner of body do they come?" (1 Corinthians 15:35).

In answering the first question raised by the objectors to the idea of a future bodily resurrection, Paul used a parable:

> Thou foolish one, that which thou thyself sowest is not quickened [made alive], except it die: and that which thou sowest, thou sowest not the body that shall be, but a bare grain, it may chance of wheat, or of some other kind; but God giveth it a body even as it pleased him, and to each seed a body of its own (1 Corinthians 15:36–38).

The common processes of nature in the vegetable world answer the question by general analogy and common sense. The seed sown is apparently lifeless, but after germination in the soil, there springs the green blade. Each year, at the beginning of spring, man witnesses the whole creation of God stirring with life and power. The planted grain comes forth with new life. The same power that causes the planted grain to come forth into a new plant will raise the body of man to a new life.

If a stalk can rise from a grain, if spring can come from winter, if a butterfly can be the after-life of a caterpillar, it is reasonable that the almighty power that made man can raise man's body from the tomb.

Thus the seed of plants of every kind is put into the ground and decays, but a new body springs therefrom. This process is so evident that no one pretends to deny it, though none is able to explain by his own reasoning how it is accomplished. "So also is the resurrection of the dead" (v. 42).

Paul's answer, then, refers the objector to a case that transpires constantly in nature. Both the resurrection of the dead and of a new plant is accomplished by Divine power. The resurrection of the dead will indeed be a miracle. As Paul once said to King Agrippa, "Why is it judged incredible with you, if God doth raise the dead?" (Acts 26:8). It is no more difficult to believe the Lord will raise the bodies than that He created the heavens, the earth, and man's body (Genesis 1). So let the doubter ask, "By what power are the dead raised?" The same power that created all things and brought Christ from the dead is able to raise all bodies from the dust. This is neither impossible nor unreasonable. If the unbeliever asks, "How can this decaying dust yield a harvest?" the believer answers, "The dust cannot; God can." It happens each springtime in nature, and the resurrection occurs in the realm of the spiritual. Jesus declared, "Except a grain of wheat fall into the earth and die, it abideth by itself alone" (John 12:24). During Christ's personal ministry the Pharisees believed in and the Sadducees denied the resurrection of the dead. To the caviling Sadducees Jesus said, "Ye do err, not knowing the scriptures, nor the power of God" (Matthew 22:29). God Almighty can raise the dead.

The Resurrection-Body Will Be Different

Since God's power shall raise all the dead, what substance or fashion will the new resurrected body be? People question both the power to effect the resurrection and the result—that is, the possibility and the accomplished fact.

Paul vindicates the doctrine of the resurrection by answering this question (1 Corinthians 15:35–50). He said the resurrection-body will be characterized by two things; namely, a change and continuity.

Paul shows that the properties of the raised bodies are not the substance of the bodies that were, nor are they a reproduction of the old bodies. Surely the word resurrection is strained when one insists that the exact body, the precise substance, is to be restored. The resurrection shall be instantaneous, "in a moment, in the twinkling of an eye" (1 Corinthians 15:52).

Paul insisted on the difference between the bodies of this life and the bodies resurrected. He emphasized this truth by reminding his readers of the difference between the various plants and animals with which they were familiar.

In answering the doubter's second question, Paul said, "All flesh is not the same flesh: but there is one flesh of men, another flesh of beasts, and another flesh of birds, and another of fishes" (1 Corinthians 15:39). There are many varieties of grain and bodies, earthly and celestial, each distinguishable from the other. The sun, moon, and stars differ one from each other. "So also is the resurrection of the dead" (v. 42). Paul intended for people to understand that God is able to raise a body suitable for the eternal realm. He said just as in the sprouting of the seed, the stalk is not of the precise substance that dies but a product from it, likewise the body of the resurrection. The result is one of processes, not products. The analogy from nature helps one to understand the kind of the resurrection-body. The sown body (in the seed) retains its identity, but it is greatly changed.

So Paul's answer first establishes that the seed of grain sown never returns, the particles perish, but a new life comes from the seed sown. Thus it will be in the resurrection. The new body will not be composed of the actual particles that were put in the grave, but a new body will come forth. Does this not answer then the objection that it would have to be the same body?

Some say the body may be lost at sea, devoured by monsters of the deep, passed into other animal bodies, and maybe back into other human bodies. Another is burned and the ashes scattered to the four winds. Or another body has gone into vegetable life. There is no need to find all the particles of a decomposed body to have a resurrection. Like seed sown, "thou sowest not the body that shall be" (v. 37). Yet the growth of the seed shows there is identity under a complete change in physical conditions. So it is an identity of character and a continuity of life in the resurrection. This is true in nature, for God gives to every seed its own body—the seed of wheat seed produces wheat, the grain of corn brings forth corn. In the buried seed there is a decomposition, yet a transformation. This transformation is a continuity. The kernel of the old body is embodied in the new, resurrected body.

Thus, every human body will retain its own identity; each man shall be himself; all that essentially belongs to the body at death will be raised to life and will constitute the resurrection-body. Only in the sense of continuity and identity, therefore, the same body that is laid in the grave shall be raised. Else the new body would be a creation, not a resurrection. A change does not destroy continuity. The ugly caterpillar is changed into a beautiful butterfly, but it is the same creature. The buried seed comes forth in a stalk, but it is the same plant, whether it be wheat or corn.

The Christian's Resurrection-Body Will Be a Glorious Body

The apostle set forth the differences between human bodies laid in the grave and resurrected bodies. According to Paul's language, the change will be fourfold; the new body will be distinguished by four great qualities, in contrast to the present earthly house of this tabernacle. Note:

> It [the physical body] is sown in corruption; it [the resurrected body] is raised in incorruption: it is sown in dishonor; it is raised in glory: it is sown in weakness; it is raised in power: it is sown a natural body; it is raised a spiritual body. If there is a natural body, there is also a spiritual body (1 Corinthians 15:42–44).

Thus, a resurrection of the body is taught in the Scriptures without any distinctions as to what constitutes the body. God, who made the body of man, knows what is and what is not essential to its glorified state. Man does not. It is enough for the Christian to know that the body shall be raised and live again. All that properly belonged to the body and is essential to its identity and integrity will be raised again to life, and will go to constitute the new or resurrection-body. The body which will be raised will not be the same in the sense that the same particles of matter shall compose it, but the same only in the sense that it will have sprung from that buried body.

For man, then, there are two kinds of bodies—one from Adam, the first parent; the other from Christ, the second Adam.

Note further the contrasts:

1. The present body is corruptible, that is, subject to death or tending to decay. The future body will be incorruptible, that is, deathless or undying; it shall never decay; it shall never die. This distinction is so important that Paul returned to it again later in the chapter and reaffirmed it positively:

   > Now this I say, brethren, that flesh and blood [i.e., a physical body] cannot inherit the kingdom of God [i.e., the eternal home of the soul]; neither doth corruption [i.e., a dying body] inherit incorruption [i.e., a place where there is no dying]. Behold, I tell you a mystery [something that has not previously been made known]: We all shall not sleep [or die], but we shall all be changed [in body, whether alive or dead when Christ comes, for at the resurrection all living and dead bodies shall be changed into immortal bodies], in a moment, in the twinkling of an eye, at the last trump: for the trumpet shall sound, and the dead [all the dead] shall be raised incorruptible, and we [who are living] shall be changed. For this corruptible must put on incorruption [i.e., the dead will be raised incorruptible and will never be subject to death], and this mortal must put on immortality [i.e., the living will be changed and put on immortality so that they will never be subject to death]. But when this corruptible shall have put on incorruption, and this mortal shall have put on immortality [i.e., when these two changes have been made], then shall come to pass [or be fulfilled] the saying that is written, Death is swallowed up in victory (1 Corinthians 15:50–54).

   So the resurrection-body will not be flesh and blood. It will be incorruptible. And the transformed bodies of the living will be the same in kind as the raised bodies. When Christ comes, all bodies will put on incorruption and immortality, for "flesh and blood [bodies] cannot inherit the [eternal] kingdom of God" (v. 50).

2. The present body is sown in dishonor, but it will be raised in glory. The resurrection-body will be a glorious body suited to command honor and

praise—the sown body deserves neither; it is subject to base and degrading uses, the seat of passions and lusts. The body that shall be raised will deserve and receive both honor and praise, being purged of all that is low and vile, and becoming a thing of beauty and joy forever.

3. The physical body is sown in weakness, but will be raised in power—with unfailing vigor, capable of great and unwearying activity; whereas the body man has now is inherently weak. The redeemed will have bodies to clothe their spirits (inner personalities) in eternity, only they will not be weak, material bodies like these, liable to disease, sickness, and death.

   The well-known commentator Albert Barnes made this fine comment concerning the transformed body:

   > The body of the worm, the chrysalis, and the butterfly is the same. It is the same animal still. Yet how different the gaudy and gay butterfly from the creeping and offensive caterpillar! So there may be a similar change in the body of the believer, and yet be still the same . . . And no infidel can prove that the one is attended with any more difficulty or absurdity than the other . . . And why should we deem it strange that between bodies adapted to live here and bodies adapted to live in heaven, there should be a difference?"[1]

4. The earthly body is sown a natural [or animal] body, but it will be raised a spiritual body. The spiritual body, however, is not a spirit. The word *spiritual* here does not refer to the substance of the renewed body, but describes the office or function of it. Notice that the word *spiritual* is not put in contrast with the word *material*. The body that is sown is not a material body, but a natural body. The natural body means the body of the natural man, made for this physical life. The spiritual body is adapted to the divine life or heaven. The spiritual, incorruptible body is but a contrast with the corruptible or mortal body. Hence, the spiritual body is the present body made incorruptible. A body of flesh will not be raised. The righteous will be given spiritual bodies, free from the frailties to which men are subjected in this life. The future body is called spiritual because it will be a body suited to the spirit, fit for the eternal realm, just as this physical body is suitable for this world.

In 1 Corinthians 15, Paul stressed the resurrection of those who would be raised to eternal life. The Bible does not describe the resurrection-body of unbelievers.

Having defined the difference between the two bodies, Paul further said, "And as we have borne the image of the earthy, we shall also bear the image of

---

1 Albert Barnes, *Commentary on 1 Corinthians,* (Grand Rapids: Baker's Book House, 1949), pp. 312–313.

the heavenly" (v. 49). As man is here on earth, he bears the image of the earthly, but in heaven he will bear the image of the heavenly. The earthly cannot pass over into the heavenly. Thus, the apostle described the difference between the body in which the Christian now lives and the body in which he shall live hereafter—a contrast of the body before death with the body after the resurrection. "It"—the body before death—is corruptible; "it"—the body at the resurrection—is incorruptible. The body placed in the tomb will be raised, though in a transformed, imperishable, glorious, powerful, spiritual condition.

> 'Twas sown in weakness here
> 'Twill then be raised in power:
> That which is sown an earthly seed
> Shall rise a heavenly flower.
> —Bonar

In one sense, the resurrection-body will be the same body as it was before death, and yet not the same body. It will be the same in whatever is necessary to personal identity and yet not the same in its material and use. Paul taught these things about the resurrection-body: the natural body will be raised a spiritual body, man's identity will be preserved, and the raised body of the righteous will be refined and glorified.

The Redeemed Will Have a Body Like Christ's

Again, Paul said to the Christians in Philippi that when Christ comes He "shall fashion [transform] anew the body of our humiliation, that it may be conformed to the body of his glory, according to the working whereby he is able even to subject all things unto himself" (Philippians 3:21).

The passage does not say that the present body will give place to another body, but that it will be changed and fashioned after the glorious resurrection-body of Christ. This verse locates the change in the body. The believer's body will be changed from the present vile flesh and be fashioned after the body of Christ which He now has in heaven. Goodspeed's translation of the passage says that Christ "will make our bodies over to resemble his glorious body." Hence, saints in heaven shall bear the image of the heavenly being, conforming to the glorified Christ.

Since Scripture says it is the image of the heavenly, not the image of the earthly, which the righteous are to put on (1 Corinthians 15:49) like the glorious body of Christ (Philippians 3:21), some claim that the resurrected body of Christ, while on earth and before His ascension, serves as the pattern of man's future resurrected body. This, however, is without scriptural foundation. Since Christ returned to life in the body that was crucified and buried, which did not see corruption, this then cannot be proof that Christians are so to be raised. If one could obtain a knowledge of Christ's present glorified body—the body He now has in heaven—he would indeed have a pattern of that resurrected body in glory. The fact, then, that because the fleshly body of Jesus was raised from the dead does not necessarily imply that He ascended in the same body; nor does it imply that His body was in the same state in which He arose and had on earth for forty days. Christ's glorified body must have been put on at or after His ascension, and no inspired writer has given any description of it. There are a few brief references to His body after His ascension: He was seen in heaven by Stephen (Acts 7:56), later in a vision by Paul (1 Corinthians 15:8; Acts 9:4, 17; 22:14; 26:16), and finally in a vision by John on the isle of Patmos (Revelation 1:10–18). All that can be said, therefore, of the resurrection-body of the believer is that it will be like the glorified body of Christ. Raised from the dead by the Lord's power, believers at the resurrection shall be transformed into His glorious image.

The nature of the immortal bodies of believers is still not fully known, for John wrote, "Beloved, now are we children of God, and it is not yet made manifest what we shall be. We know that, if he shall be manifested, we shall be like him; for we shall see him even as he is" (1 John 3:2). More than this cannot be said. It is vain to speculate on the constitution of man's future body. He shall know hereafter.

This great doctrine of the resurrection of all mankind at the last day should lead Christians to work diligently in firmness of faith, since their labor in the Lord is not in vain (1 Corinthians 15:58).

To the Christian, death is the last enemy to overcome (1 Corinthians 15:26). When all the dead will be raised to live forever, then the redeemed saints will praise the Lord and say "thanks be to God, who giveth us the victory [over death] through our Lord Jesus Christ" (v. 57).

Christians, therefore, not only expect but actually desire the Lord's return with hopeful anticipation, because at this time all the dead will be raised and their souls joined and united with their proper bodies. Those who shall be living at the end of time shall not die as the others, but be changed in the twinkling of an eye from corruptible bodies to incorruptible. The deathless spirit will be united with an incorruptible body, never again to be separated by death. All the dead will be raised, and their souls will be united with their proper resurrected bodies. It will be the same spirit or person that once dwelt in the earthly body that shall be in the raised body; but in the resurrection there will be a definite contrast of the bodies raised to the bodies that were retired by death. Christians will rejoice to re-enter their old bodies, so completely repaired and highly improved—vigorous, incorruptible, and immortal. They shall then never more fear pain or sorrow or death. This is a wonderful hope. The barriers of death have been broken, and ultimately death itself will be totally destroyed.

In the following noble passage, the apostle seems to personify death and Hades, and introduces the righteous, after the resurrection, singing a song of victory over both:

> O Death, where is your sting?
> O Hades, where is your victory?
> —1 Corinthians 15:55 (NKJV)

Hence, the fundamental truth behind our faith is the historical fact of the resurrection of Christ. If Jesus did not arise from the dead, we face dire consequences according to Paul's language in 1 Corinthians 15. Note, if Christ be not risen:

1. Then our faith is vain (v. 14).
2. Then our preaching is vain (v. 14).
3. The eye witnesses are only false witnesses (v. 15).
4. We are still in our sins (v. 17).
5. Those who have died in Christ have perished (v. 18).
6. Then we have no hope and are to be pitied above all people (v. 19).

In spite of the denial of many religious leaders today, Christ did rise from the dead. Each Lord's Day faithful Christians remember the great sacrifice of Christ at Calvary and His triumphal resurrection from the dead, as they imitate the early Christians in partaking of the communion, the Lord's Supper (Acts 20:7; cf. Hebrews 10:24–25). They remember that Christ died for their sins, "and that he was buried; and that he hath been raised on the third day according to the scriptures" (1 Corinthians 15:4).

The glorious message of the gospel of Christ, which gives the facts about the future life and immortality, has now removed much of the fear of death. By Christ's resurrection and the teaching of the New Testament Scriptures, much of death's sting and terror has been taken away, so that no longer is it a terrible monster. Christians have nothing to fear in death. With this faith Paul had no fear of dying or anxiety about moving out of his old weather-beaten tent: "For we know that if the earthly house of our tabernacle be dissolved, we have a building from God, a house not made with hands, eternal, in the heavens" (2 Corinthians 5:1).

Christians should not mourn over their dead as those who have no hope, because Christians shall meet again in a life in which parting shall be no more. The Scriptures give definite assurance of another life after death. How comforting, therefore, to know that though one's dear loved ones die, they shall live again. There is a resurrection. Man lives through death and after it. Physical death is not the termination of human life, and the grave is not the end. One's sleep will not be an eternal one. The dear, departed loved ones have not perished.

The dead shall rise. God has promised it, and He, by His own miraculous power, can make it possible. Because Christ lives in a resurrected immortal body, man also shall live again. Death does not end all. There is an existence beyond the tomb. Hence, when people ask, "Shall man go down to the grave with no promise of a hereafter?" all may answer, "There is a Beyond; though a man die, he shall live again."

"Even so, come, Lord Jesus."

Questions for Discussion

1. Why do all men desire to live again? What does this universal desire indicate?
2. What did Jesus teach concerning the resurrection?
3. Give several Biblical statements in which the resurrection is taught.
4. What did Daniel say about the resurrection?
5. What question did Job ask?
6. When will the resurrection occur? How many will be raised?
7. What will be raised? What dies and is buried? What does the spirit of man long for?
8. What is there about man in the flesh that is not immortal?
9. What fact in history serves as the proof and pledge of man's resurrection?
10. How did Christ bring life and immortality to light?
11. Discuss reasons for believing in the resurrection of Christ. Why is this such an important tenet in the Christian faith?
12. How did Paul in 1 Corinthians 15 prove the resurrection of all mankind?
13. How is Christ the "firstfruits" of the dead?
14. Name those mentioned in the Bible whom God caused to live again (besides Christ). Did these all die again? Will these, too, be raised at the last day?
15. How (by what power) will the dead be raised?
16. How many things were mentioned by Paul about the resurrection-body? Define each term.
17. Will identity of the body be preserved in the resurrection?
18. Whose body now serves as the pattern for the Christian's raised body?
19. What is the last enemy to be destroyed?
20. Does the Bible describe the resurrection-body of the wicked?
21. What had denying the future resurrection of the body done to the faith of some of the early Christians? See 2 Timothy 2:18.
22. Do any religious sects today deny the resurrection of the body?

– 17 –

What about the Judgment?

"Christ Jesus . . . shall judge the living and the dead"
2 Timothy 4:1

The Scriptures connect the end of the world, the general resurrection, and the final judgment with Christ's second appearance. Although no one is informed of the day and hour of the Lord's return, one is assured that His coming will be to raise all the dead, both good and bad, and to judge all mankind. On the lips of prophets and apostles and Christ Himself, the end of time and the final judgment for all men was one of the most frequent themes, and it should be given serious attention by all now.

Judgment for All Sure

Life is veiled with uncertainty; no one knows what the future holds, but one thing is definite: "We shall all stand before the judgment-seat of God . . . So then each one of us shall give account of himself to God" (Romans 14:10–12). All shall meet the Lord when He comes again, and all shall stand before Him in judgment. This appointment made for man is one that he cannot break. There is no escape from it. All the living and all the multitudinous hosts of the dead from every place on earth, of every age of the world from the time of Adam to that of the Lord's return, will be summoned before Christ's tribunal. For, before Him shall be gathered all nations, both the living and the dead, when Christ comes, "And he shall send forth his angels with a great sound of a trumpet, and they shall gather together his elect from the four winds, from one end of heaven to the other" (Matthew 24:31). All human beings who have ever lived—the small and the great, the good and the bad, the rich and the poor, the wise and the simple, all races and all tongues—will appear before the great white throne. None will be excluded.

The consciences of all mankind corroborate the teachings of the Scriptures with regard to the certainty and necessity of a final judgment. A few criminals may escape the officers and the courts of civil government, but none can escape the judgment day. In a certain sense, men are judged and often punished in this world, but that fact does not invalidate the future judgment; it only serves to add weight to the necessity of God's future judgment for perfect and final justice. Obviously, there is no such thing as absolute justice in this world for several reasons:

1. There are so many sins and transgressions like ingratitude, hatred, persecution, falsehood, slander, and dishonoring parents of which human laws take no cognizance.
2. The judgments of men are imperfect and inadequate. Human judges in the courts often do not know what penalty best fits the offense. In fact, sometimes right judgment is perverted and wrong triumphs.
3. The human judge is often uncertain as to the guilt or innocence of the person on trial. Surely no one would claim that human justice is infallible.
4. Judgment is necessary to rectify the inequities of this life, for sometimes the innocent are punished while the guilty often escape arrest and punishment.
5. Not only should the guilty be punished and the righteous rewarded, but their lives should be declared and uncovered to all. Sometimes that happens in this life, but so often only God knows. Hence, the bad are sometimes esteemed good, and the good bad.

Human reason, therefore, demands that a righteous judgment must come; this will be the righteous judgment of God at which time the great Judge of all the earth will do right in the last day (Genesis 18:25). Although no human being knows when the day of judgment will be, we do know that all who have ever lived, or who will ever live, will be there.

Christ Will Be the Judge

The honor of judging the living and the dead has been conferred on Christ, and before His judgment seat all men must stand. "For neither doth the Father judge any man, but he hath given all judgment unto the Son" (John 5:22). Peter said at the house of Cornelius: "And he charged us to preach unto the people, and to testify that this is he who is ordained of God to be the Judge of the living and the dead" (Acts 10:42). Paul said, "For we must all be made manifest before the judgment-seat of Christ; that each one may receive the things done in the body, according to what he hath done, whether it be good or bad" (2 Corinthians 5:10). So, by Christ, God will judge the world in righteousness in one day, of which the resurrection of Jesus is surety. Paul said to the Athenians: "He hath appointed a day in which he will judge the world in righteousness by the man whom he hath ordained; whereof he hath given assurance unto all men, in that he hath raised him from the dead" (Acts 17:31). Jesus Christ gave a picture of the judgment scene when He described Himself as a shepherd, dividing the people as sheep and goats:

> But when the Son of man shall come in his glory, and all the angels with him, then shall he sit on the throne of his glory: and before him shall be gathered all the nations: and he shall separate them one from another, as the shepherd separateth the sheep from the goats; and he shall set the sheep on his right hand, but the goats on the left. Then shall the King say unto them on his right hand, Come, ye blessed of my Father, inherit the kingdom prepared for you from the foundation of the world . . . Then shall he say also unto them on the left hand, Depart from me, ye cursed, into the eternal fire which is prepared for the devil and his angels . . . And these shall go away into eternal punishment: but the righteous into eternal life (Matthew 25:31–46).

Man Judged By Deeds, Words, Thoughts

The basis of the judgment will be one's deeds, words, and thoughts. At the judgment the books of the records of each life will be opened, all his works will be made manifest, and each individual shall then give an account of "the things done in the body, according to what he hath done, whether it be good or bad" (2 Corinthians 5:10); the Lord "then shall . . . render unto every man according to his deeds" (Matthew 16:27). Every act of life will be brought under review; even the hidden and secret things, good or bad, shall be brought to light. "For God will bring every work into judgment, with every hidden thing, whether it be good, or whether it be evil" (Ecclesiastes 12:14). Nothing can be hid from God's all-seeing eye, "All things are naked and laid open before the eyes of him with whom we have to do" (Hebrews 4:13). "The eyes of Jehovah are in every place, keeping watch upon the evil and the good" (Proverbs 15:3; cf. Psalm 139:1–12).

The world's Redeemer is perfectly qualified to be the judge at the last day of earth's history because He is Divine and has perfect knowledge of both man's deeds and motives. Christ knows what is in man (John 2:24–25). He has perfect sympathy, too, since He once lived on this earth; and He will be merciful to the full extent of mercy consistent with perfect justice and perfect truth (cf. Hebrews 2:17–18; 4:15).

Not only of overt acts will the Judge take account, but He also "will both bring to light the hidden things of darkness, and make manifest the counsels of the hearts" (1 Corinthians 4:5), thereby judging "the secrets of men" (Romans 2:16). It is possible to cover up sin and iniquity in this world—as many do—but all will be uncovered in that great day, even the secret plans made in the heart but never carried out. Everything will be made known in the day of judgment, and all men will be dealt with as individuals.

Furthermore, Jesus said, "Every idle word that men shall speak, they shall give account thereof in the day of judgment. For by thy words thou shalt be justified, and by thy words thou shalt be condemned" (Matthew 12:36–37). So not only does God keep a record of man's deeds and his thoughts, but He also keeps a record of his words as well (cf. Malachi 3:16; Ephesians 4:29). Man must give an account of his speech in the day of judgment.

In Christ's description of the judgment (Matthew 25:31–46), He commended the righteous for their deeds of charity done unto His disciples. These acts of faith and love constitute one of the conditions of acceptance in that day, for none can be finally saved without them.

In reality, the ground of man's acceptance at the final day will be his faith in Jesus Christ, man's Savior, manifested by his obedience to the Lord's will and by his discharge of this obedience in accordance to his ability and opportunities (cf. Ephesians 2:8–9; 1 John 1:7; 2:2; Matthew 7:21–27; 12:41–42; 25:15; Luke 10:12–14; 12:47–48; Revelation 22:14).

Man Judged By God's Word

The Bible also teaches that man will be judged by his life in harmony with God's Word. Not by the creeds and dogmas of men, but by the eternal Word of God will all be judged in the last day. Jesus said, "The word that I spake, the same shall judge him in the last day" (John 12:48; cf. Revelation 20:12).

Judgment Impartial

This final judgment of God's, based upon man's moral life and in accordance with His revealed law, will be impartial. The judgment-seat of Christ will not be an arbitrary trial but a sentencing. The teaching of the Bible (whether accepted or rejected by man) will determine eternal destiny. Character, formed in this life, will decide the fate of all men. Peter announced this principle in God's dealing with the world at the house of Cornelius in these words: "Of a truth I perceive that God is no respecter of persons: but in every nation he that feareth him, and worketh righteousness, is acceptable to him" (Acts 10:34–35). Paul affirmed: "For there is no distinction between Jew and Greek: for the same Lord is Lord of all, and is rich unto all that call upon him" (Romans 10:12).

Two Sentences Passed

In the language of Jesus wherein He described the judgment (Matthew 25:31–46), there is declared (1) the time of the judgment—at the second coming of Christ, (2) the Judge—Christ Jesus, (3) the subjects—all nations, and (4) the sentences passed—enter into eternal life, or enter into eternal punishment. Christ will bring both rewards and punishments with Him when He comes to judge the world: "Behold, I come quickly; and my reward is with me, to render to each man according as his work is" (Revelation 22:12). As observed earlier in this study, at Christ's second coming, not only will the righteous dead be raised from their graves but the wicked dead also. Hence, all are to be rewarded or punished at the same time—at the last day—the living and the dead, the good and the bad (cf. John 5:28–29; 6:39–40, 44; 12:48; 2 Timothy 4:1).

Thus, at the judgment, each one will hear God's final sentence upon his soul: everlasting happiness or eternal misery. Then some will pass in triumph to the company of the blessed and some in woe to the company of the condemned. At that time the good and the bad will be separated forever, and the destiny of all persons will be immediately fixed. The sentences there given will never be reversed. Those whose names are written in the Lamb's book of life—the redeemed—will enter into heaven; those whose names are not recorded in this book—the wicked—will be sent to torment (Revelation 20:15; 21:27; cf. Exodus 32:33; Philippians 4:3; Revelation 3:5). The judgment will be final.

The saddest departure will be when one is turned away with that multitude into everlasting punishment, when the Son of man shall separate the righteous from the unrighteous, and when He says to those on His left hand: "Depart from me, ye cursed, into the eternal fire which is prepared for the devil and his angels." Even families will then be divided, never to meet again. God, however, does not desire that any should perish; He wants all to come to repentance (2 Peter 3:9), and He, by His grace, has made it possible for every accountable person to have his sins forgiven through the shed blood of Christ (Ephesians 2:8–9; Hebrews 2:9; 5:9; 1 John 2:2; Mark 16:15–16; Acts 2:38; Romans 6:3–4).

Because Christ will be man's judge, He is needed now as man's Savior. Truth declares that now is the day of salvation (2 Corinthians 6:2). When Paul preached before Governor Felix and his wife Drusilla, "he reasoned of righteousness, and self-control, and the judgment to come" (Acts 24:25). The sermon was so powerful that Felix was terrified, yet he did not obey. He said, "Go thy way for this time; and when I have a convenient season, I will call thee unto me" (v. 25), but he was never again so stirred in his soul by the truth. He never did accept Christ, so far as is known, but he died as he had lived, a slave to sin. That convenient season never came.

Inasmuch as all shall stand before the judgment seat of Christ, let each person relate every duty, every decision, every temptation, every act, every human relationship to that final account. The thought of the second coming of Christ, the end of the world, and the judgment, constantly dwelt upon, should act as a powerful restraint from sin. Since all must face Christ one day as Judge, let each one resolve to face Him, not as scoffing skeptics or neglectful servants, but as faithful Christians. Peter admonished the saints to "give diligence that ye may be found in peace, without spot and blameless in his sight" (2 Peter 3:14; cf. vv. 11–12). The early disciples held the Lord's return to reward the righteous as the great object of expectation and desire; and, assuredly, belief in this great event should encourage godly living and instill comfort and hope in Christians now, as it did for those of the first century (cf. 2 Timothy 4:7–8; 1 Thessalonians 4:18; 1 Peter 1:3–9, 13; 1 John 3:2–3; Philippians 3:20–21; Romans 15:13; Titus 2:13).

All should prepare now for the judgment (Amos 4:12; 2 Corinthians 6:2). Only by being a faithful Christian can one always be prepared for this great day. Death ends probation.

Judgment at Last Day

Thus, when the Lord returns He will raise the dead, hold the final judgment of men, and establish eternal order. Man is not represented as being judged and receiving final adjudication of reward or punishment at the time of death or even immediately after it. An intermediate period elapses. The Scriptures fix the judgment after death: "It is appointed unto men once to die, and after this cometh judgment" (Hebrews 9:27). The Bible points directly to the resurrection and the judgment as the period when these great events shall take place. The day of final adjudication is not the same as that on which one dies. A careful study of the Bible will show that no allusion is made to death as being the time when the righteous shall receive their eternal reward and the wicked their final doom. When will Christ give to every man according to his deeds? (Matthew 16:27; Revelation 22:12). When He comes at the end of time and at the judgment. There can be no doubt that the future state of rewards and punishments will begin at the second coming of Christ. Jesus said again that the judgment will be "in the last day" (John 12:48). Every person, those who receive and those who reject the word, will be called to meet God in judgment, but this will be in the last day.

Here, then, two errors find their correction: The first is that the righteous are judged at death, which is not the case; both the righteous and the wicked shall be judged in the great and final day. The second error is that the saints of God enter upon the full realization of their everlasting joy immediately at death, independently of their resurrection-bodies; but this is not the case, for the Scriptures plainly show that the body must be raised incorruptible before the consummation of the bliss of the redeemed. Just as the lack of an immortal, glorified body is an imperfect condition for the righteous, he is in an imperfect state and will remain so until his body is raised from the dead. When the body of the righteous is raised in incorruption and power and glory and is re-inhabited by the spirit which was dislodged from it at death, then, and not until then, will any person be saved in the highest and fullest sense. Thus, the Bible always represents the final states of both good and evil as lying beyond the resurrection and the judgment. The resurrection of the body, its reunion with the soul, and the final judgment will not occur until the end of time, when Christ comes again. "For the Son of man shall come in the glory of his Father with his angels; and then shall he render unto every man according to his deeds" (Matthew 16:27).

All should prepare to meet the Lord in the judgment. Study the cases of Felix and Drusilla (Acts 24:24–25) and King Agrippa (Acts 26:27–29).

Many people, realizing the need in their lives to obey the Lord and become a Christian and prepare themselves for death and the judgment, keep putting off that great step in their lives until something happens and they depart this life. James wrote, "To him therefore that knoweth to do good, and doeth it not, to him it is sin" (James 4:17). Solomon declared, "Boast not thyself of tomorrow; for thou knowest not what a day may bring forth" (Proverbs 27:1). The Bible teaches that "now is the acceptable time; behold, now is the day of salvation" (2 Corinthians 6:2).

Questions for Discussion

1. What are the three great events associated with Christ's second coming?
2. Will all people be judged at the same time? How do you know?
3. Why is a final judgment after this life necessary?
4. Who will be the judge? Why?
5. What will be the basis of judgment for all men?
6. What effect will man's words have to do with the sentence passed?
7. What about man's deeds of charity?
8. How do we know the judgment will be impartial for all?
9. How will the Bible be used in judging men?
10. How many sentences will be passed? Can any appeal then be made?
11. Who trembled when told about the final judgment? Did he repent?
12. When and how should one prepare for the judgment?
13. Who will be ready when that day comes?
14. How was the hope of the Lord's second coming to reward the righteous a source of comfort to the early Christians?
15. What two errors find correction in the study of this chapter?

TOMORROW

He was going to be all that a mortal should be
    To-morrow.
No one should be kinder or braver than he
    To-morrow.
A friend who was troubled and weary he knew,
    Who'd be glad of a lift and who needed it, too;
On him he would call and see what he could do
    To-morrow.
Each morning he stacked up the letters he'd write
    To-morrow.
And thought of the folks he would fill with delight
    To-morrow.
It was too bad, indeed, he was busy to-day,
    And hadn't a minute to stop on his way;
More time he would have to give others, he'd say,
    To-morrow.
The greatest of workers this man would have been
    To-morrow.
The world would have known him, had he ever seen
    To-morrow.
But the fact is he died and he faded from view,
    And all that he left here when living was through
Was a mountain of things he intended to do
    To-morrow.

—Edgar A. Guest

PREPARE TO MEET THY GOD

Careless soul, why will you linger,
    Wand'ring from the fold of God?
Hear you not the invitation?
    O prepare to meet thy God.

Why so tho'tless are you standing
    While the fleeting years go by,
And your life is spent in folly?
    O prepare to meet thy God.

Hear you not the earnest pleadings
    Of your friends that wish you well?
And perhaps before tomorrow
    You'll be called to meet thy God.

If you spurn the invitation
    Till the Spirit shall depart,
Then you'll see your sad condition,
    Unprepared to meet thy God.

Careless soul, O heed the warning,
    For your life will soon be gone;
O how sad to face the judgment,
    Unprepared to meet thy God.

—J. H. Stanley

– 18 –

When Will the Spirits Leave Hades?

"I have the keys of death and of Hades"
Revelation 1:18

At death the spirit or soul goes to Hades or Sheol, an intermediate state or place of disembodied spirits. Christ's return will terminate Hades when the dead (bodies) will be raised. Hades will be destroyed when the dead (bodies) are raised at the last day. At that time, which ends death, all the disembodied spirits will be reunited with their resurrected bodies. This is the Scriptural answer to the questions often asked: "How long will the spirits remain in Hades?" "When will the disembodied spirits leave Hades and go to their eternal destinies?"

Christ Has the Keys

When Christ appeared to John on Patmos, He said, "I was dead, and behold, I am alive for evermore, and I have the keys of death and of Hades" (Revelation 1:18). This means that Jesus has the power over death (i.e., over the dead bodies) and of Hades (i.e., over the spirits in their disembodied state), since He was raised from the dead to die no more. He can unlock the gates of Hades and cause the spirits to come forth and the bodies to be raised. He has that power because He conquered death and Satan (2 Timothy 1:10; Colossians 1:18; 1 Corinthians 15:23). Christ will use this power (i.e., the keys) at the end of time marked by the resurrection of all mankind (John 5:28–29).

In 1 Corinthians 15, Paul, in anticipation of the termination of Hades and of the resurrection of the bodies of all saints, quoted from Hosea 13:14. The passage reads: "I will ransom them from the power of Sheol; I will redeem them from death: O death, where are thy plagues? O Sheol, where is thy destruction? repentance shall be hid from mine eyes." To appreciate this sublime prophecy, one needs only to remember what man is, what death does to him, and what the resurrection is to effect. As man is on earth, he consists of a material or mortal body and an immaterial or immortal spirit. Death separates the spirit from the body, consigning the body to the dust and the spirit to Sheol. In the resurrection the body is raised from its tomb to life and immortality, and the soul leaves Sheol, its intermediate abode, to enter its deathless, resurrected body to dwell forever. Thus, in triumphant joy at the resurrection, the redeemed soul addresses both the grave and the place of departed spirits: "O death [*maveth,* Heb.] the principle of corruption, the grave], where are thy plagues? O Sheol [the unseen realm of departed spirits], where is thy destruction?" Death, or the power to cause the bodies to die and go into the grave, shall be destroyed, for the body shall be raised incorruptible. Sheol or Hades, the place of disembodied spirits, shall also be destroyed, for it must deliver up the spirits of all the dead. So both are to cease and be succeeded by the everlasting abodes to which all mankind will be assigned at the judgment.

The inspired apostle must also have had Isaiah 25:8 in mind: "He hath swallowed up death for ever." In 1 Corinthians 15 Paul wrote passages similar to some found in Hosea and Isaiah: "O death, where is thy victory? O death, where is thy sting?" (1 Corinthians 15:55). Through the redemptive work of God, the Christian's victory over both sin and death is consummated in the resurrection "through our Lord Jesus Christ" (v. 57), and in that victory, "the saying that is written" (v. 54) shall be brought to pass. Both Hades (where the disembodied spirits were) and the grave (where the bodies were) alike are to be abolished in the resurrection at the end of time.

MacKnight gives this rendering of 1 Corinthians 15:55: "Where, O death! is thy sting with which thou killedst the saints? Where, O Hades! who has lead them captive, is thy victory, now that they are all brought out of thy dominions?" Then he adds this fine comment:

> The word *Hades,* translated the grave, literally signifies the invisible world, or the place where departed spirits, both good and bad, remain till the resurrection: Job xi. 8; Psal. cxxix. 8; Isa. xiv. 9 and especially Psal. xvi. 10 . . . The place where the spirits of the righteous abide, the Jews called Paradise; the place where the wicked are shut up, they called Tartarus, after the Greeks. There the rich man is said to have gone when he died. There also many of the fallen angels are said to be now imprisoned, 2 Pet. ii. 4. In this noble passage the apostle personifies death and the grave, and introduces the righteous, after the resurrection, singing a song of victory over both. In this sublime song, death is represented as a terrible monster, having a deadly sting, wherewith it had destroyed the bodies of the whole human race, and the invisible world as an enemy who had imprisoned their spirits. But the sting being torn from death, and the gates of the invisible world set open by Christ, the bodies of the righteous shall rise from the grave, no more liable to be destroyed by death, and their spirits being brought out of Paradise, the place of their abode, shall reanimate their bodies: and the first use of their newly recovered tongue will

> be to sing this song, in which they exult over death and Hades, as enemies utterly destroyed; and praise God who hath given them the victory over these deadly foes through Jesus Christ.[1]

So the passage literally means, "O Death, thy power to separate spirits from their bodies is no more! O Hades, thy dominion over disembodied spirits is destroyed!" Similarly, the verse may be translated this way: "O Death, where are thy plagues? Where, O Hades, is thy destruction?" The word *sting* answers to the Hebrew word *plagues,* that is, a poisoned sting causing plagues. The word *victory* answers to the Hebrew *destruction*. The word *where* implies that their past victorious destroying power and sting are now gone forever. The spirits in Hades being now freed by the resurrection, death's victory is no more. That will indeed be a happy day when the righteous are raised with bodies immortal to enter into heaven, there to die no more. No wonder Paul pictured the saints singing a song of triumph! "VICTORY IN JESUS!"

There is, therefore, a twofold yielding up in the resurrection at the last day—namely, one relating to the bodies in the grave and one relating to the spirits in Hades. Hades no more retains the souls of men after the resurrection than the graves do the bodies, but they each come from their respective temporary abodes and reunite. At this time Hades and the grave are superseded and abolished.

In harmony with the above passages of Scripture is the statement in Revelation 20:13–14: "And the sea gave up the dead that were in it; and death and Hades gave up the dead that were in them: and they were judged every man according to their works. And death and Hades were cast into the lake of fire." In the scene of the future—the last day—both death or the grave, the place of the bodies, and Hades, the place of disembodied souls, delivered up their dead. The sea and death have the bodies of all human beings; Hades has their spirits. As death and the sea gave up all the bodies, so Hades gave up all the spirits in order that they might be reunited to their resurrected bodies. Then death (or the grave) and Hades are both abolished. For after Christ comes again, neither the righteous in heaven nor the wicked in hell (Gehenna) will die any more in the sense of separation of body and spirit. Their souls and bodies will never again be separated, for the dead will be raised to die no more (Hebrews 9:27). Since the unseen world of disembodied spirits will be no more after the resurrection and the judgment, death and Hades cease to exist at the general resurrection. In this passage death and Hades are simply the personification of physical death; symbolically speaking, they are cast into the lake of fire. "The last enemy that shall be abolished is death" (1 Corinthians 15:26). How wonderful for the

---

1 James McKnight, D.D., *Apostolical Epistles,* Reprint Edition (Grand Rapids: Baker Book House, 1949), p. 207.

suffering and dying of this earth to know that death, the separation of the soul from the body, and Hades, the place and state of souls intervening death and the resurrection, shall one day be no more!

The Disembodied State

It follows, therefore, that since there is a period of time between one's death and the general resurrection and judgment at the last day, there is also a period during which the spirit is without a body. That disembodied period is what is called the intermediate state. All who believe in the resurrection of all mankind must admit that there is an intermediate state—that is, the time between death and the reuniting of the spirit once more with the resurrected body. Yet, there are those who deny that the Scriptures teach this, so note further truths concerning the intermediate state and its termination.

Old Testament Saints in Sheol

The Bible declares that the Old Testament worthies and those of the gospel dispensation will all be perfected together in heaven. "And these all, having had witness borne to them through their faith, received not the promise, God having provided some better thing concerning us, that apart from us they should not be made perfect" (Hebrews 11:39–40). This passage of Scripture affirms that all the righteous shall go up together, for one group of believers cannot attain to fullness without the other group. None of God's people in former ages are now made perfect (i.e., they are not in heaven); they will not be there until after the resurrection of saints on the last day. Hence, their present state (whatever it is and wherever it is) is an incomplete (or imperfect) one.

Christ Will Come for His Disciples

Christ promised His disciples a place He would prepare for them, and that when He returned from heaven He would receive them to it. "And if I go and prepare a place for you, I come again, and will receive you unto myself; that where I am, there ye may be also" (John 14:3). In this statement Jesus connects His returning with the Christian's entrance into the place He is now preparing, and not at the hour of death.

Christ's Parables Teach Rewards at the Judgment

In explaining the Parable of the Tares, Jesus said,

> The harvest is the end of the world; and the reapers are angels. As therefore the tares are gathered up and burned with fire; so shall it be in the end of the world. The Son of man shall send forth his angels, and they shall gather out of his kingdom all things that cause stumbling, and them that do iniquity, and

> shall cast them into the furnace of fire: there shall be the weeping and the gnashing of teeth. Then shall the righteous shine forth as the sun in the kingdom of their Father" (Matthew 13:39–43).

The harvest is at the end of the world, at which time there will be a separation of the righteous from the wicked. The wicked will be cast into the furnace of fire where there will be wailing and gnashing of teeth, and the children of the kingdom will shine like the sun.

Similar words are also in the Parable of the Net (Matthew 13:47–50). When the fishermen cast a net into the sea, it enclosed every kind of fish; when it was brought to shore, however, the fishermen divided the catch, keeping the good and disposing of the bad. "So shall it be in the end of the world," said Jesus. Here again the Lord declared that judgment is at the end of the world and will mean the end of this world order and the beginning of the eternal one. At that time God will introduce the righteous to the supreme joy of their eternal reward, and the wicked shall be severed from among the just.

Again this same truth is taught by Christ in the Parable of the Talents (Matthew 25:14–30). Not until the lord of those servants cometh does he say to the good and faithful, "Enter thou into the joy of thy Lord." Likewise, in the Parable of the Wise and Foolish Virgins, not until the bridegroom comes do the wise go into the marriage feast and the door is shut against the foolish (Matthew 25:1–13).

The Righteous Rewarded at the Last Day

Other passages speak only of the time when the righteous shall receive their reward. For instance, Jesus taught about acts of charity in these words:

> But when thou makest a feast, bid the poor, the maimed, thc lame, the blind: and thou shalt be blessed; because they have not wherewith to recompense thee: for thou shalt be recompensed in the resurrection of the just (Luke 14:13–14).

Concerning elders of the church doing their work of overseeing the flock in a faithful manner, Peter said, "And when the chief Shepherd shall be manifested, ye shall receive the crown of glory that fadeth not away" (1 Peter 5:4). The apostle also declared that the righteous are to be made glad with their reward "in the last time . . . at the revelation of Jesus Christ" (1 Peter 1:5–13; cf. 4:13).

The place where the righteous spirits go at death is not the same place to which they shall go after the second coming of Christ, the resurrection, and the final judgment. The day of judgment will be the day for the bestowal of each one's final reward.

Righteous and Wicked Separated at Judgment

The Lord's description of the judgment in Matthew 25:31–46 pictures Christ descending from heaven with His holy angels, and all nations summoned before Him. He then will proceed to separate the righteous from the unrighteous as a shepherd divides his sheep from the goats. To the righteous He will say, "Come," and to the wicked He will say, "Depart." "And these [the wicked] shall go away into [not back into] eternal punishment: but the righteous into [not back into] eternal life" (v. 46). The righteous souls at death do not go directly into heaven for their eternal reward. If so, they would be re-admitted after the resurrection of the body and the final judgment. If each individual were raised and judged, one by one, at death, there would be no need for a final resurrection and judgment. But a judgment makes it possible for all the dead to be raised together and the throne of judgment to be set for all mankind, at which time God will vindicate His moral government of the world.

Therefore, neither the saved inherit the kingdom nor do the condemned depart to their everlasting doom before the judgment day. At the same time the two groups enter on two opposite destinies. If all who die enter immediately into their respective eternal abodes, this would be before Hades is destroyed and the judgment, as well as before the righteous receive their immortal bodies. The Lord's statements, "Come, ye blessed of my Father, inherit the kingdom" and "Depart from me, ye cursed, into the eternal fire," cannot be true if all are judged immediately following death and before the resurrection. It is clear that an intermediate state is the plan that can be reconciled with the Scriptures on Hades and the general judgment.

Jesus Went to Hades

Jesus did not go to heaven the day He died; He went to Paradise (Luke 23:43). Christ ascended to heaven forty days after His resurrection (Acts 1:3–11; Mark 16:19). Neither the thief on the cross nor Christ went to heaven or to hell at death, but immediately to Hades. Peter on Pentecost said that Christ's soul was not left in Hades. Peter, referring to a prophecy of David, said, "For David saith concerning him [Christ] . . . Thou wilt not leave my soul unto Hades." And then later added: "Neither was he [Christ] left unto Hades" (cf. Acts 2:25–31).

John Saw Souls under the Altar

While on the isle of Patmos, John, in a vision, saw the souls of the martyred saints under the altar, where they were to rest yet for a little time (Revelation 6:9–11). In John's visions, after the judgment all the righteous were privileged to enter the new Jerusalem. If the redeemed were now in heaven in their complete glory, the souls that John saw would not have been pictured as underneath the altar, but as in heaven itself. Although these righteous dead were in a state of happiness (Revelation 14:13), this does not mean that the perfect, eternal heavenly age has yet begun.

Wicked Punished after Judgment

Other passages from God's Word teach that wicked men will not be fully punished until the Lord's second coming at the resurrection. Paul declared,

> at the revelation of the Lord Jesus from heaven with the angels of his power in flaming fire, rendering vengeance to them that know not God, and to them that obey not the gospel of our Lord Jesus Christ: who [i.e., some] shall suffer punishment, even eternal destruction from the face of the Lord and from the glory of his might, when he shall come to be glorified in his saints, and to be marvelled at in all them that believed . . . in that day (2 Thessalonians 1:7–10).

Paul affirmed God will recompense to one class affliction and to the other rest, which shall take place when the Lord Jesus shall be revealed from heaven with His mighty angels. At that time the one class "shall suffer punishment, even eternal destruction from the face of the Lord and from the glory of his might," and at the same time He shall "be glorified in his saints." Thus, this phase of eternal punishment begins with the rest and glory of the righteous. God "will render to every man according to his works." But when, Paul? "In the day when God shall judge the secrets of men . . . by Jesus Christ" (Romans 2:6–16).

The wicked are not now being punished in hell (Gehenna), but are being reserved in Tartarus to that day of judgment. Peter said:

> For if God spared not angels when they sinned, but cast them down to hell [*Tartarus,* Gr.] and committed them to pits of darkness, to be reserved unto judgment . . . The Lord knoweth how to deliver the godly out of temptation, and to keep the unrighteous under punishment unto the day of judgment (2 Peter 2:4–9).

The day of judgment is not at death, but after death, at the second coming of Christ. "Behold, the Lord came with ten thousands of his holy ones, to execute judgment upon all" (Jude 14–15). Hence, at the Lord's return, He will execute judgment upon all. Christ will send the wicked, both soul and body, to hell (Matthew 10:28; 25:46). But the wicked will not be cast into the furnace of fire to be punished with everlasting destruction until Christ comes again and judges the world.

Time between Death and Resurrection

So, according to the Scriptures, an intermediate state is between death and the resurrection. God's established order is that neither the righteous nor the wicked enter their final abode at death. The Bible teaches that all people go to Hades at death, and will remain there until the resurrection and judgment. The intermediate state is provisional, constituting neither the ultimate bliss of the saved nor the ultimate doom of the lost. Thus, the state and place of disembodied spirits between death and the resurrection is different from their final abode. Without a body, they can never be complete with reunion. To affirm, therefore, as some do, that at death the departing spirit goes immediately to heaven (if it be righteous) or to hell (if wicked) rules out an intermediate state of souls (Hades) between death and the judgment, and conflicts with many passages of Scripture. The Scriptures have answered these questions which are frequently asked: "Do the wicked at their death enter upon their full degree of punishment?" "Do the righteous at their death enter upon the full enjoyment of their reward?" "Do both the righteous and the wicked go to Hades at death? or just the wicked? or neither one?" All departing souls go to Hades to await the resurrection and final judgment.

Biblical Scholars Speak

Noted Biblical scholars have supported this interpretation of the Scriptures. Bloomfield commented: "The commencement, as well as the destruction of this intermediate state, are so clearly marked, as to render it almost impossible to mistake them."[1] A. G. Freed, a noted gospel preacher of a former generation and co-founder of Freed-Hardeman College, argued: "To preach that the righteous pass immediately into heaven at death, and the wicked into hell, is to render many plain scriptures meaningless."[2]

J. Patterson-Smyth expressed the same view:

> With educated people it should not be necessary to combat the foolish popular notion that at death men pass into their final destiny—heaven or hell—and then perhaps thousands of years afterwards come back to be judged as to that final destiny! To state such a belief should be enough to refute it. Those who hold it "do err not knowing the Scriptures": for the Scriptures have no such teaching.[3]

Consequently, as the Scriptures teach, and Bible scholars support, there is an intermediate state before the resurrection, when the spirits shall come from Hades and the bodies from the tomb at the end of time.

---

1 Samuel T. Bloomfield, *The Greek Testament with English Notes,* Vol. II (Philadelphia: Clark and Hesser, 1854), p. 603.

2 A. G. Freed, *Sermons, Chapel Talks, and Debates* (Nashville: Gospel Advocate Co., 1930), p. 159.

3 J. Patterson-Smyth, *The Gospel of the Hereafter* (New York: Fleming H. Revell Co., 1910), p. 33.

Questions for Discussion

1. Define Hades. How many times is the word found in the New Testament?
2. Who has the keys of Hades? When will He use them?
3. When will the Christian's victory over death be accomplished? How was it made possible?
4. What will happen to the spirits in Hades when the bodies are raised?
5. What is the duration of death and Hades? Explain 1 Corinthians 15:55.
6. What is meant by the intermediate state?
7. When will all men be raised and judged? Discuss some of the parables Jesus told about the judgment.
8. Are the righteous and the wicked judged and sent to their final destinies as soon as they die? Support your answer from the Bible.
9. How did Christ describe the judgment and the assigning of destinies in Matthew 25? When will the righteous enter heaven? When will the wicked go to hell?
10. Did Jesus go to heaven when He died on the cross? Explain Acts 2:27, 31.
11. Where are the righteous souls who have departed this life?
12. When will the final state of man come?

– 19 –

How Are the Righteous Dead with the Lord?

"But I am in a strait betwixt the two, having the desire to depart and be with Christ; for it is very far better"
Philippians 1:23

People often ask, "What is the purpose of the soul's waiting in Hades?" A man once remarked, "I believe the righteous go at death straight to their eternal reward. I do not believe the Lord keeps a man on 'cold storage' for centuries, awaiting the resurrection, before he lets him go to heaven."

Based upon the conclusions already drawn from God's Word, all departing souls do not go directly to their final destiny at death, for there is a state of existence which intervenes between death and the resurrection of the body and final judgment. This intermediate state for both the righteous and wicked spirits follows immediately after death.

Others erroneously affirm that today righteous souls go immediately to heaven at death, there being no Hades for them as for the wicked. They say divisions in Hades did exist prior to Christ's resurrection, but that Paradise in Hades for the righteous was abolished when Jesus arose from the dead. Here are some of their arguments:

- Character is formed in this life.
- The righteous dead are happy with the Lord.
- The righteous spirits left Hades at Christ's resurrection.
- The word *Paradise* refers to heaven.
- The righteous souls since A.D.70 now go directly to heaven.

We shall notice each of these objections in the light of Biblical teaching.

Character Formed in This Life

The objector says, "Character is formed in this life. Since destiny of all is fixed at death, then at that time the Christian goes to his final reward." True, character and works in this life determine one's destiny, and no change can be made after life has ended. But God will judge every man according to his works (2 Corinthians 5:10). What each individual receives is determined not only by what he did in this life, but also by the influences he has exerted, "for their works follow with them" (Revelation 14:13). Since the influence of a man's life will not be manifest until the very end of time, the final reward or punishment must be delayed until the ultimate results of every good and bad action can be surveyed as a whole and the fruit of the individual's doings are rightly estimated. The influence a man exerts outlives him and travels on, for good or for evil, to the end of time. In fact, the good or evil actually done in life may be very small compared with that which results from his influence after he is dead. The design of the judgment is the public declaration of God's righteous judgment, and the Lord has declared that all men will be present for this final judgment. The wicked will come for conviction, while the righteous will come for vindication. The Christian will be openly acknowledged in the day of judgment—just as he openly acknowledged Christ during his life (cf. Matthew 10:32–33; Luke 9:26; 1 John 4:15; Revelation 3:5).

Death, like an officer, arrests men; next they pass to the intermediate world of spirits—the righteous to Paradise to rest from their labors and await reward, the wicked to Tartarus to be held unto the day of judgment for final punishment. They are like prisoners awaiting trial. There is a day of reckoning at the end of time when justice will be meted out to all according to their works. The relation, therefore, between Tartarus and Gehenna is much like that of the county jail in which accused criminals are detained while waiting for their trial, and the state penitentiary to which they are assigned after the trial for their final earthly punishment. Unlike prisoners of the courts, the wicked will have an eternal punishment.

The Righteous Dead Happy with the Lord

When the righteous die they are absent from the body yet at home with the Lord (2 Corinthians 5:8). Scripture means by these expressions that the person departing goes into the care and keeping of the Lord, not that the spirit goes immediately to its *eternal* reward in heaven where Christ is. Paul did not expect at death to go immediately to his eternal reward, because he looked forward to the judgment day: "Henceforth there is laid up for me the crown of righteousness, which the Lord, the righteous judge, shall give to me at that day; and not to me only, but also to all them that have loved his appearing" (2 Timothy 4:8). According to Revelation 14:13, those who die in the Lord are, from that moment onward, in a state of blessedness. Death is for them emancipation from evil and their earthly labors, and the introduction into a condition of happiness. But Hades has not ceased for the righteous.

Although many believe that the righteous go to heaven immediately at death, they admit that during the time of the Old Testament the righteous spirits at death went to Sheol, or Hades, for Solomon in the Old Testament said that the spirit at death went back to God who gave it (Ecclesiastes 12:7). Likewise, David said, "If I make my bed in Sheol, behold thou art there" (Psalm 139:8). Again, he said, "Yea, though I walk through the valley of the shadow of death, I will fear no evil; for thou art with me" (Psalm 23:4). Thus, if the righteous dead went to God when Solomon and David wrote, and God was in Sheol, the righteous dead may now go to be with Christ and be in Sheol or Hades. The New Testament teaches that people do not go immediately to heaven when they die, nor does the Old Testament teach that before the cross of Christ the righteous went to their eternal award.

Again, according to Paul, the resurrection of the body is included in the Christian's complete redemption and glorification. He wrote that "the whole creation groaneth and travaileth in pain together until now . . . waiting for our adoption, to wit, the redemption of our body" (Romans 8:22–23). Paul spoke of the earthly, the intermediate, and the eternal stages of man in 2 Corinthians 5:1–8.

First: "We that are in this tabernacle do groan" (v. 4), that is, in a fleshly body, "the earthly house of our tabernacle" (v. 1), or man's earthly life.

Second: "Not for that we would be unclothed" (v. 4); there would be a time when the spirit would be out of the mortal body while in Hades awaiting the immortal body. In this state the spirit is "unclothed" and "naked."

Third: "We have a building from God, a house not made with hands, eternal, in the heavens" (v. 1) and are "longing to be clothed upon with our habitation which is from heaven" (v. 2), the eternal stage of the Christian's existence. So Paul makes it clear in 1 Corinthians 15 and 2 Corinthians 5:1–8 that the immortal body of the redeemed will be obtained at the resurrection at the end of time, and will be enjoyed only in heaven. The Scriptures never speak of any body save that which man now has (the earthly) and that which he will have at the resurrection (the eternal): the one natural, the other spiritual. So, even in Hades, while the spirit is unclothed, the spirit will not be separated from but present with Christ. Paul meant that the intermediate state is a less desirable alternative than the change to the resurrection-body without death. The intermediate state would not be undesirable, but nakedness of the soul is relatively undesirable as compared with the eternal blessedness in the immortal body. "But that we would be clothed upon" (v. 4), that is, receive the resurrection-body at the last day. This immortal body will be the "house not made with hands, eternal, in the heavens" (v. 1). But this permanent structure will be received when Christ comes again and not put on at the moment of death.

At death the spirit lays aside its earthly body, becoming a disembodied spirit until the eternal body is given. This state in the spirit's existence is the interim between death and the resurrection where the body is unclothed. In Hades the righteous are with Christ in a sense similar to the way He is on earth with His disciples (Matthew 28:20), and God was with the Old Testament saints (Psalm 23:4). Their fellowship is far richer than that ever experienced on this earth (Philippians 1:23). On earth the believer begins to know the meaning of being with Christ and enjoying His fellowship. Certainly, to be with the Lord after death means being with Jesus in a much closer and dearer relationship than can be experienced upon earth, for the Lord manifests Himself to the righteous souls waiting for the resurrection at the last day. For Christians death is a doorway that leads to greater happiness and more abundant living, where there are no cares and trials of this earth. Neither is there any more sickness, pain, or suffering. Death of the righteous is homecoming of the soul, the gathering into Paradise in Hades. Yet, the souls of the righteous dead have not arrived at their perfect and complete state of the glorified children of God, being still separated from their immortal bodies which are essential for fitness for heaven, the eternal abode. The original state of man was that of a spirit in a body. Death, which is the separation of the soul from the body, resulted from sin. Christ will redeem man's natural body from the grave at the resurrection when He comes again (1 Corinthians 15:42–47; Philippians 3:20–21). Hence, after the second advent of Christ the righteous shall be clothed with their glorified and immortal bodies and enter their eternal abode, heaven.

A Bible Scholar Speaks

For a number of years John T. Hinds, a Bible scholar and faithful gospel preacher, conducted the Question and Answer department of the *Gospel Advocate,* a religious magazine published for more than one hundred and fifty years in Nashville, Tennessee, advocating the principles of New Testament Christianity. In the April 2, 1931, issue of the paper, this teacher of God's Word answered two questions concerning this very point in this chapter. The questions and his answers follow:

A brother from Kentucky sends the following:

> According to my understanding, all who have died have gone to hell, and those who die will go there, to await the judgment; the righteous in a state of bliss, knowing that they will be in the resurrection unto salvation, and the unrighteous tormented by the thought that they will be in the resurrection unto damnation. The ones who pass the judgment will go to their reward and eternal life, but the others to the lake of fire. Is this right? As I understand it, Christ went to hell.

Paul said we would receive our reward at Christ's coming, and he seemed to include himself in that statement. Later he also speaks of departing and being with Christ. Do these statements contradict each other?

Brother Hinds responded:

The querist wanted to get "straightened out" on the subject of hell. This implies that he is mixed up on the question. He is not the only one who has been mixed up on this matter, which in the main can be charged to the King James translators. If this brother had carefully compared the Revised Version with the King James Version on those passages where the word *hell* occurs, most of his difficulty would have disappeared. The corrections made in the Revised Version in these passages are among the most important things accomplished in the making of the Revised text. Two entirely different Greek words are translated by the English word *hell* in the New Testament in the King James Version. One of them—*Gehenna*—means the final abode of the wicked, or what is generally understood by the word *hell*. This one is translated by the word *hell* in the Revised Version, because that is its meaning in the passages where it is used. The other—*Hades*—is simply spelled with English letters and appears in that form where it occurs in the Greek. In the passages where this word occurs in the Revised Version it does not mean hell. This at once eliminates a lot of trouble.

Hades literally means the "unseen," and applies to the state of spirits out of the body between death and the resurrection, and includes both bad and good spirits. There is a gulf or division between the two classes. (Luke 16:22–26.) Of course, the Spirit of Christ went to Hades, the unseen state, but not to hell. True, the King James Version virtually says so, but the Revised Version is correct and does not say so. With this explanation, the brother's idea is correct. All he says is true, except that Hades is the place instead of hell, the final abode of the wicked. That is where the wicked will go after the judgment.

There is no conflict between Paul's two statements. The final reward is after the judgment, which will take place at the Lord's coming. But when the righteous die, their spirits go to the place in the Hadean world prepared for the righteous; the place where Christ went and where Abraham was. Being with Christ means, at least, to be in that happy place that is prepared for the righteous, where we are conscious of His approval and rejoice in the glory that awaits us in the final state. We have no means of knowing where Hades is, or in what deep spiritual sense Christ, unappreciated by men in the flesh, is with the saved in that state.[1]

Did the Righteous Leave Hades at Christ's Resurrection?

Those who object to the intermediate state for the righteous falsely say, "At Christ's resurrection all the righteous souls were taken out of Paradise, and

1 John T. Hinds, "Gospel Advocate" (Nashville: Gospel Advocate Co., 1931), reprinted in the "Gospel Advocate," October 1, 1970, Vol. CXII, Number 40, p. 635.

at His ascension He carried them in triumph with Him to heaven; thus the intermediate state ended for the righteous with the resurrection of Christ." No passage of Scripture supports this idea. If the righteous had been removed from Hades to heaven, then Peter on Pentecost, ten days after Christ's ascension, made a mistake when He referred to David in his sermon and said, "For David ascended not into the heavens" (Acts 2:34). When Peter referred to David, David's body was still buried in the city of Jerusalem (1 Kings 2:10; Acts 2:29), and his body and spirit had not yet ascended into heaven. Although Christ had ascended into heaven, no man—not even David—had gone to heaven. Christ (His spirit) was not left in Hades; David and all other men were thus left. If David did not ascend to heaven, then other saints of his time did not. Therefore, the Holy Spirit through the apostle Peter taught that the intermediate state for the righteous did not end with the resurrection of Christ—David's soul was (and still is) in Hades.

Some use Hebrews 2:14–15 as proof that Christ released the righteous spirits from Hades when He arose; but this makes the statement of Scripture say too much. The writer of the epistle said that one object of the Incarnation was that Christ might through death "bring to naught [destroy, subdue] him that had the power of death, that is, the devil; and might deliver all them who through fear of death were all their lifetime subject to bondage." The deliverance mentioned in this passage is that which Christ accomplishes through the gospel. The bondage from which people are delivered is the fear of death and the consequences of it. The bondage is during their lifetime, and not after they have left this world by death. Christ died in order that He might win deliverance for men, nullify Satan's power, and free men from the terror of death. This He actually achieved by His death and resurrection. He emancipated men from that terrifying dread and gave hope even in death. Christ triumphed over Satan, death, and the grave (John 12:31; Colossians 2:15). The keys of death are now in His hands (Revelation 1:18). Christ's death and resurrection gave man deliverance from the enslaving fear of death. Man, looking forward to heaven's joys, can now be free from the fear of death, because Christ has "abolished death, and brought life and immortality to light through the gospel" (2 Timothy 1:10). Thank God! Death has been conquered by Christ, and ultimately all the dead shall be raised! "Precious in the sight of Jehovah is the death of his saints!" (Psalm 116:15). "Yea, though I walk through the valley of the shadow of death, I will fear no evil" (Psalm 23:4). Christ has not taken away death itself (for people still die), yet Christ has removed much of Satan's terrifying fear of death; He has extracted from it the unknown and its terrors.

Another passage used in support of this theory is Matthew 27:52–53: "And the tombs were opened; and many bodies of the saints that had fallen asleep were raised; and coming forth out of the tombs after his resurrection they entered into the holy city and appeared unto many." The tombs were opened when Jesus died on the cross, when the "earth did quake and the rocks were rent." The bodies of the saints came out of the graves "after his resurrection." The Bible does not say what happened to those bodies miraculously raised at the resurrection of Christ. To affirm that the raised bodies of the saints went to heaven when Jesus ascended is to advocate a personal opinion. The Bible does not say that the souls of the saints went to heaven.

Many of those who accept the above view that the raised bodies went with Christ to heaven find strength for their theory in Ephesians 4:8: "When he [Christ] ascended on high, he lead captivity captive, and gave gifts unto men." The verse says when the Lord ascended, not when He arose. The expression is figurative; it describes the ascension of the victorious Christ, the One who had conquered death and the grave. The gifts were manifestations, as on Pentecost when the Holy Spirit was given (Acts 2:1–4; 8:15–17; cf. Ephesians 4:11–13).

Some also theorize that the 144,000 that John saw in a vision (Revelation 14:1) were those Jesus had taken with Him to heaven when He ascended. This is wholly unscriptural. The purpose of this scene, like Revelation 7:4–9, is to encourage faithfulness by foretelling the final success true saints will have. The number sealed (144,000) is a symbolic number representing completeness of the redeemed of all ages. The idea is that when the final stroke is delivered, none of God's faithful shall suffer. The purpose of the book of Revelation was to give to the suffering saints an assurance of the final overthrow of all the evil forces which opposed them.

Does *Paradise* Refer to Heaven?

Another objection to the righteous now being in Hades is based upon Paul's statement of the third heaven and Paradise. "I know a man . . . caught up even to the third heaven. And I know such a man . . . how that he was caught up into Paradise" (2 Corinthians 12:2–4). Some say, "Paradise is now in heaven, and all righteous souls pass immediately into their eternal home at death; only the wicked now go to Hades to await the resurrection." In other words, they affirm, Paradise was transferred to heaven after Christ's resurrection.

In answer, *Paradise* is a Persian word and primarily means "a garden, a pleasure garden, or a park." Paradise signified during the time of the apostles a place of rest, pleasure, and delight. The word is used in the Scriptures in the following senses:

1. The Garden of Eden—a place of delight here on this earth (Genesis 2:8, 9, 10, 15, 16; 3:1–2, 8, 10, 23).
2. The place of rest for the righteous spirits after death (Luke 23:43), "Abraham's bosom" (Luke 16:22).

3. The eternal home of the redeemed, or heaven: "To him that overcometh, to him will I give to eat of the tree of life, which is in the Paradise of God" (Revelation 2:7). The picture of heaven is one of a Paradise in Revelation 22:1–5.

Hence, Paradise is appropriately applied to any place prepared for enjoyment, but more accurately, it signifies a condition rather than a place. The place where the condition exists must be learned from the context. For example, Dallas, Texas, is a city, but so are New York City and Tokyo. The word *city* does not mean in itself just which particular city. So, Paradise can be a proper description of the place of man's original home, a place where righteous spirits go at death to await the resurrection, or a place where the righteous go after the final judgment—heaven. Therefore, the three times the word Paradise occurs in the New Testament (i.e., Luke 23:43; 2 Corinthians 12:4; and Revelation 2:7) do not always refer to the same place. The context each time must determine its proper application.

In 2 Corinthians 12:4 Paul said one was caught up into Paradise and caught up even to the third heaven. Some ask, "Are Paradise and the third heaven the same place in this statement, or did Paul have two raptures?" Evidently, they mean the same. By the third heaven Paul surely meant the place where God dwells and manifests His glory. The Bible speaks of three heavens in this way:

1. The atmosphere above, or the aerial heaven where the birds fly (Genesis 1:7–8).
2. The place of the heavenly bodies, or the heaven where the stars are (Genesis 1:16–17; Psalm 19:1).
3. The dwelling place of God, or where the holy angels are and where the redeemed will dwell with God (Deuteronomy 26:15; Revelation 21:1–22:5).

Paradise, as used by Christ in His promise to the penitent thief ("Today shalt thou be with me in Paradise," Luke 23:43), did not embrace heaven. Jesus did not ascend to heaven in the interval between His death and His resurrection. He, in company with the robber, went to Paradise. Yet Christ was in Hades, according to Acts 2:27, 31. Therefore, Paradise, in Luke 23:43, is in Hades. And Paradise, in Hades, is not heaven. This Paradise—that is, the realm of Hades where righteous disembodied spirits await the resurrection of the body and consequent entrance into heaven—is the same as that designated by Christ as "Abraham's bosom" in the narrative of the rich man and Lazarus (Luke 16:22).

Near the end of the first century of the Christian era, the apostle John wrote, "No man hath beheld God at any time" (1 John 4:12). The hope of the

Christian is to see the Lord as He is (1 John 3:1–2). If now in heaven, it is inconceivable to think that the spirits of just men made perfect have not been privileged to see the Lord. Surely, then, the Christians who had died up to the time John wrote had not entered into heaven. The same would likewise be true of all saints who have died since then. Based upon the apostle's statement, one of two things is true: (1) one can occupy heaven and yet not see God, or (2) no one had entered into heaven when John wrote about seventy-five years after the resurrection and ascension of Christ. To affirm the first premise seems absurd; to affirm the second is to admit the correctness of Biblical teaching concerning the righteous remaining in Hades until the resurrection of the body at the end of time.

A statement that has given much study for serious Bible students is what Jesus said to Mary Magdalene on the day of His resurrection: "Touch me not; for I am not yet ascended unto the Father" (John 20:17). The idea seems to be, "Do not hold on to me, I am not immediately leaving the earth . . . but go unto my brethren, and say to them, I ascend unto my Father and your Father, and my God and your God." Definitely, Jesus did not go to the Father in heaven while His body was in the tomb; He went to Hades (Acts 2:27, 31).

Destruction of Jerusalem, A.D.70

As noted in the chapter on the second coming of Christ at the end of the world, Jesus did not come in person at the destruction of Jerusalem in A.D.70. There is no statement of Scripture that teaches that since that time all righteous souls now departing this life go directly to heaven. This is trying to make the destruction of Jerusalem mean too much.

Thus, we have answered some of the main arguments that are made in favor of righteous souls at death going directly to heaven. If they do, will God bring them out of heaven, take them to the judgment, and then send them back into heaven, where they have been since the time of their death?

Too, John wrote his Gospel of the life of Christ in the latter part of the first century—after the Lord had ascended into heaven. In chapter 3, verse 13, it is affirmed that Christ, alone, had ascended into heaven: "And no one hath ascended into heaven, but he that descended out of heaven, even the Son of man, who is in heaven."

Stages of Development

In God's plan of both the natural and the spiritual realms, there are stages of development. The world of botany has at least three stages of perfection—bud, blossom, and fruit. Each botanical process is a stage of perfection in its self.

Or take the example of the butterfly from the order of Lepidoptera which develops through three stages. Starting as eggs, they then go through the larva stage as hungry, grubby caterpillars to the pupa state (the chrysalis stage) when the insects hide in their cocoons, passing through a complete metamorphosis from caterpillars into the final stage as scaly-winged adult butterflies.

There are three stages of man's existence. The first state of human spirits is the earthly stage where the spirit is in union with a physical body. This fleshly state, where every accountable individual makes a choice between right and wrong, terminates at death, the body going to the grave, the immortal spirit to Hades. The second stage of man's existence is when human spirits are separated from their fleshly bodies in the intermediate state. This commences at death and terminates with the resurrection. In this period the souls of both the righteous and the wicked are in Hades, while their bodies are in the graves. The third is the final, eternal stage where the spirits dwell in their resurrected bodies forever. This state begins with the union of the spirit and the changed resurrected body and continues ever after, either in heaven or hell (Gehenna).

An Illustration Clarifies

Five circles in the diagram on the following page will clarify the teaching of this study on the words *Hades*, *Sheol*, *Paradise*, *Tartarus*, *Judgment*, *Heaven*, and *Gehenna* (hell).

Circle #1 represents the realm of this world where spirits dwell in a physical body. The righteous children of God in this life were saved from their past sins by obedience from the heart to the gospel (Romans 6:18–19), unlike innocent children who are safe. Still others in this world are lost in sin. The first state of human existence terminates in death, when the body goes to the grave and the immortal spirit to Hades. Death is the door of exit to the next world.

Circle #2 represents Sheol or Hades, the abode of all disembodied spirits. Here all souls are in a state of consciousness; the righteous are happy in Paradise, and the wicked are miserable in Tartarus. While in this intermediate state the human spirit is separated from its body. In Hades the gulf is fixed. This state commences at death and terminates with the resurrection. When the third state begins at the second coming of Christ, Hades will be destroyed.

Circle #3 represents the day of final judgment after the resurrection (Matthew 25:31–46; Romans 14:12; Revelation 20:11–15). At that time all mankind will give account of the deeds done in the body, whether good or bad; judgment will be pronounced, and the execution of judgment will begin (Matthew 7:21–23; Luke 12:47–48).

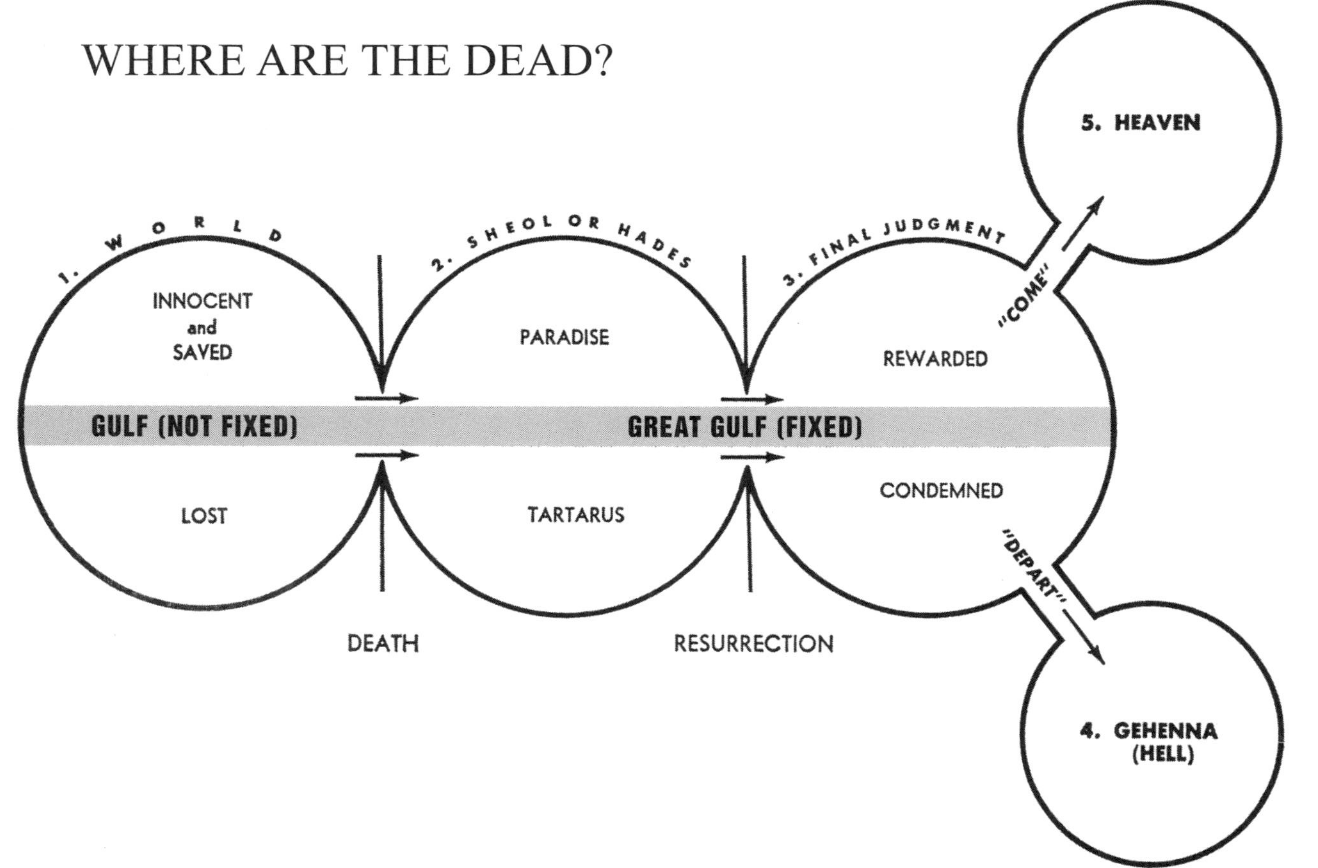
WHERE ARE THE DEAD?
1. WORLD
INNOCENT and SAVED
GULF (NOT FIXED)
LOST
DEATH
2. SHEOL OR HADES
PARADISE
GREAT GULF (FIXED)
TARTARUS
RESURRECTION
3. FINAL JUDGMENT
REWARDED
CONDEMNED
"COME"
"DEPART"
5. HEAVEN
4. GEHENNA (HELL)

Circle #4 represents heaven, the eternal home of the righteous where the redeemed shall be ushered after the judgment (Revelation 21:1–22:5; John 14:1–3). To the faithful on His right hand, the Lord will say, "Come, ye blessed of my Father, inherit the kingdom prepared for you from the foundation of the world" (Matthew 25:34). There the inhabitants will live in perfect peace and never grow old, for in God's presence there is fulness of joy and pleasures for evermore (Psalm 16:11).

Circle #5 represents Gehenna (hell), the eternal place of condemnation for all the wicked (Matthew 25:41, 46; 2 Thessalonians 1:9; Mark 9:45–48; 12:40; Revelation 21:8). At the judgment those on the left hand will hear the Lord say, "Depart from me, yet cursed, into the eternal fire which is prepared for the devil and his angels" (Matthew 25:41). "And these shall go away into eternal punishment" (v. 46).

Paradise (in Hades) for the righteous and Tartarus (in Hades) for the wicked denote places of rest and punishment after death and before the resurrection. Heaven and hell (Gehenna) are the final destinies that await all mankind after the resurrection; these two places are beyond the judgment, and for all who enter into either of the two places, their existence shall continue forever and ever. The Hadean realm (the intermediate state) is a condition out of the body wherein the spirit awaits the resurrected body.

Summary

Summarizing the study about disembodied spirits:

1. Man was created in the image of God and exists in three states: (a) body and spirit united in a physical body; (b) body and spirit separated, with the spirit in Hades and the body in the tomb; (c) resurrected body and spirit reunited and in the final eternal abode, heaven or hell. All souls, both good and bad, go to Hades at death. Although there are both joys and torments in Hades before the resurrection, ultimate pleasures and punishments must await the reunion of the spirit with the resurrected body and the final judgment. Whatever the state of the good and bad may be while in Hades, that state will certainly be exchanged for another of like nature at the resurrection.
2. The resting place of the soul after death is not the grave.
3. The abode of the spirit is Paradise for the righteous and Tartarus for the wicked.
4. The condition of the soul after death is not sleep or unconsciousness.
5. The Hadean realm is *not* a place of purgatory where change can be made by any soul or for any soul. In Hades the gulf is fixed.

6. The righteous in Hades have a "very far better" blessedness (a fellowship with Christ, and a hope of soon reaching the eternal home) than ever experienced on this earth.
7. Sinners in Tartarus are in misery while awaiting judgment of the great day, at which time they will be sentenced to Gehenna.

Hence, the final stage for man will be at the end of the age, after the general resurrection and judgment of all men, when all, with body and soul reunited, will be either in heaven or hell, the final abode. To be in heaven is to be in the eternal Paradise of God.

This teaching should help in the understanding of the condition of departed souls (spirits), especially concerning Hades. In Hades there is a place of comfort for the righteous (Abraham's bosom) and a place of torment for the wicked (Luke 16:22–31). After one's death he must wait until "the Son of man shall come in the glory of his Father with his angels; and then shall he render unto every man according to his deeds" (Matthew 16:27).

Jesus "is ordained of God to be the Judge of the living and the dead" (Acts 10:42; cf. Acts 17:31; John 5:22). We all will "be made manifest before the judgment-seat of Christ; that each one may receive the things done in the body, according to what he hath done, whether it be good or bad" (2 Corinthians 5:10).

After the day of judgment (Matthew 10:15; 11:22, 24; 12:36), the righteous will "be caught up in the clouds, to meet the Lord in the air: and so shall we ever be with the Lord" (1 Thessalonians 4:17), Paul said to Christians. After the day of judgment all the righteous will be with Christ forever in heaven. But the Bible does not teach that since the resurrection and ascension of Christ that the righteous no longer go to Hades, but directly to heaven. If a person objects to this teaching of God's inspired Word, it is well to ask him the question, "O man, who are thou that repliest against God?" (Romans 9:20).

Questions for Discussion

1. What do some teach concerning the righteous dead since Christ's resurrection?
2. Does one's influence continue after his death? For how long? What kind of influence?
3. What are the three stages of man's existence as given by Paul in 2 Corinthians 5:1–9?
4. When did Paul expect to receive his crown of life?
5. What is needed to make the believer complete in his redemption, according to Paul in Romans 8:23?
6. Can one be in Hades and still be with the Lord? Under the Old Testament, could one be in Sheol and still be with God?
7. Does the Bible say that all righteous souls left Hades when Christ arose? that all righteous souls since A.D.70 go to heaven?
8. Explain: "No one hath ascended into heaven" (John 3:13).
9. What does the word *Paradise* literally mean? How is it used in Scripture?
10. Name the three stages of man's existence as taught in the Bible, and give illustrations from nature of these stages.
11. Is the intermediate state as much needed to prepare man for the final state as this earthly life is to prepare him for the intermediate state?
12. Define *Hades*, *Sheol*, *Paradise*, *Tartarus*, and *Gehenna*, and show how each is used in the Bible.
13. Has any man been finally judged and sentenced to his eternal destiny?
14. When will the resurrection and final judgment occur?
15. Why have some called Paradise in Hades the ante-chamber of heaven?
16. Do not all passages of Scripture on this (and all other subjects) harmonize?
17. Did Peter on Pentecost say that David is now in heaven?
18. When will the redeemed enter into heaven? the wicked into hell?
19. How does one cross the gulf in this life?
20. Can one cross the gulf after he dies?

– 20 –

WHAT ABOUT THE MILLENNIUM?

". . . and they lived, and reigned with Christ a thousand years"
Revelation 20:4

This study has shown that Christ will return at some unknown point of time in the future. However, many affirm that Christ will rule a thousand years in His kingdom which is to be established on earth at His return. They ask, "When the millennium comes, will not the kingdom of Christ be established; will there not be some 'Golden Age' with Christ on earth before the final judgment at the end of time?"

The Theory Defined

The word *premillennialism* (*pre* "before," *mille* "a thousand," *annus* "a year," *ism* "a belief") is used to designate the supposed reign of Christ for a thousand years on this earth before the end of time. This theory affirms that Christ will return to this earth, establish His kingdom at Jerusalem, and reign over it for a thousand years. During this period universal peace and righteousncss will prevail on the earth with the devil being literally bound and unable to tempt people to sin. Following the period of one thousand years, Satan will be loosed for a little season. After Satan's brief release, the wicked will be judged. And that will be the end of time!

Most premillennialists speak of at least two distinct phases of Christ's second coming, all future: (1) a *first* second coming *for* the living and the dead saints, called by them "the rapture"; (2) a *second* second coming of Christ, seven years later, (after the marriage of the Lamb and the church) *with* the saints to this earth, called the revelation. At this time He will slay all the wicked, set up His kingdom, and begin His reign on earth. Hence, *premillennialism* is the doctrine that the second coming of Christ precedes the millennium, and the *millennium* means the thousand-year reign of Christ on this earth after His *second* second coming.

Those who hold this theory also have *three* bodily resurrections: (1) a resurrection of the righteous at the moment of the *first* second coming; (2) a resurrection of the tribulation saints at Christ's *second* second coming, seven years later (this is the second *first* resurrection); (3) a resurrection of the wicked dead for the final judgment after the millennial reign.

Many advocates of this theory go so far as to affirm that a person is not fundamental in his belief of Christ's second coming if he does not accept the premillennial doctrine; but for one to believe in the Biblical teaching on the second coming of Christ is one thing, and to hold to a theory about the millennial reign of Christ on earth is something altogether different. Premillennialists argue that one who denies their view of the millennial reign of Christ is not Scriptural in his teaching. (The word *millennium* is not in the Bible.)

The Proof-Text?

The advocates of premillennialism base their belief on the statements in Revelation 20:1–7. Note carefully what this passage says.

> And I saw an *angel* coming down out of heaven, having the *key* of the abyss and a great *chain* in his hand. And he laid hold on the dragon, the old *serpent*, which is the devil and Satan, and bound him for a *thousand years*, and cast him into the abyss, and shut it, and sealed it over him, that he should deceive the nations no more, until the *thousand years* should be finished: after this he must be loosed for a little time. And I saw *thrones*, and they sat upon them, and judgment was given unto them: and I saw the *souls* of them that had been *beheaded* for the testimony of Jesus, and for the word of God, and such as worshipped not the beast, neither his image, and received not the mark upon their forehead and upon their hand; *and they lived*, and *reigned* with Christ a *thousand years*. The rest of the dead lived not until the *thousand years* should be finished. This is the *first resurrection*. Blessed and holy is he that hath part in the *first resurrection*: over these the second death hath no power; but they shall be priests of God and of Christ, and shall *reign* with him a *thousand years*. And when the *thousand years* are finished, Satan shall be loosed out of his prison . . . (emp. added, PBC).

What Revelation 20 Does Not Teach

This passage of Scripture does not teach the premillennial theory concerning the Lord's second coming or His literal reign on earth for one thousand literal years. There are several things the passage in Revelation 20 does not mention, which are indeed essential elements in the premillennial theory:

1. *The Scripture does not mention the second coming of Christ*. John said, "I saw an angel coming down out of heaven" (v. 1). This is the first thing John saw. The second advent of Christ is not even remotely suggested in this verse. The second coming of Christ and the judgment are still be-

yond the little time (little season, KJV) that follows the thousand years. Premillennialists are usually bold to say, "The literal reign of Christ, with His saints, for a thousand years, on the earth, is plainly stated in the twentieth chapter of Revelation, for six times is the expression 'a thousand years' repeated."

2. *The Scripture does not mention a bodily resurrection.* The passage says, "I saw the *souls*" (v. 4), not bodies. The passage speaks of a reign of souls; the souls were in a disembodied state. No mention is made of a literal resurrection of bodies of the dead, a bodily resurrection.

3. *The Scripture does not mention a reign on earth.* The Scripture says, "I saw thrones, and they sat upon them . . . and they lived, and reigned with Christ a thousand years" (v. 4). John did not say that they lived and reigned with Christ on the earth a thousand years. The words "on the earth" are not even in the text. The passage does not say "on the earth after His coming" or "a thousand-year reign on the earth." Yet many have been made to believe that this is in the Scripture. It is a reign of certain souls with Christ, not the thousand-year reign of Christ on earth, that is mentioned. Those souls whom John saw in vision were reigning in some sense upon thrones, but it does not say "on the earth."

4. *The Scripture does not mention all the righteous.* The passage speaks of the "*souls* of them that had been *beheaded*" (v. 4). All the righteous as such are not mentioned; just the souls of the martyrs are in the picture. Hence, they [i.e., the souls of them that had been beheaded] lived, and reigned with Christ a thousand years. Is the beheading literal or figurative? If literal, as the "thousand years" parts of the passage is said to be, then one would have to be literally beheaded to get in the reign with Christ.

5. *The Scripture does not mention Christ on the earth.* There is no statement that Christ is on earth. In fact, there is no statement in the Scriptures which teaches that Christ will ever set foot on the earth again. At His coming the earth will be burned up (2 Peter 3:10), and all the righteous will meet the Lord in the air to be forever with Him (1 Thessalonians 4:17). Neither does the passage say, "Over the whole world." Nothing is said of Christ's temporal reign on earth. The throne of Christ, or the throne of David, is not mentioned in the passage. There is no passage of Scripture that speaks of Christ reigning over an earthly kingdom for any length of time, either before or after His second coming.

6. *The Scripture does not mention Jerusalem as the capital city, with Christ as King*. The passage does not mention a literal throne in any city, or the kingdom of Christ.
7. Finally, *the Scripture does not mention the length of Christ's reign*. The passage says, "They lived, and reigned *with Christ* a thousand years" (v. 4). But how long did Christ reign? The verse does not say. Note that the two verbs, *lived* and *reigned*, are both limited by the thousand years. The souls of the martyrs lived a thousand years and they reigned a thousand years. "They [both] lived, and reigned with Christ a thousand years." No mention is made of the duration of Christ's reign.

Now, since the passage of Revelation 20 does not mention any of these things that premillennialists say are in it, how can it teach all of them? Instead of reading out of the passage what it actually contains, they have the tendency to read into it what they think it ought to say. Hence, since a number of things necessary to the millennial theory of an earthly reign are missing from the chapter it must be in error (cf. Revelation 22:18).

Revelation a Book of Symbols

The entire book of Revelation abounds in symbols; the things were signified (sign-i-fied) unto John (Revelation 1:1). The visions and the truths they represent must be kept distinct. However, some seem to forget that Revelation is a book of signs and that the language is highly figurative. There are wild beasts in Revelation, but they are symbols; they symbolize a reality. Hence, the passage now under study cannot be given a literal meaning.

Moreover, those who make the one thousand years literal are not consistent, for they make the other parts of the prophecy symbolical. No premillennialist will interpret all of Revelation 20 with absolute literalness. (For example: key, chain, abyss, serpent, beheaded, etc.) They insist upon a literal interpretation only when it is useful to maintain their theory.

Written to Christians of the first century, the book of Revelation was given to encourage faithfulness to the Lord and to show the ultimate triumph of Christ over Satan; it was to comfort those who were being severely persecuted (Revelation 17:14; 12:11). Yet some students of God's Word today cannot understand that the things predicted in symbols were only pictures of them. Revelation 20 teaches that there will be a time when the influence of Satan will be greatly restrained, and a time when the church will enjoy great prosperity for a long period. But the figures cannot be interpreted literally because John's vision and what it meant were two different things. What the apostle saw were symbols of spiritual events. Besides, chapter 20 does not follow chronologically the nineteenth chapter (cf. 19:11–21 with 20:10); it presents another view leading up to the end of time with different symbols, stressing the overthrow of Satan. The chapter does not begin by saying, "And then, after this . . ." The chapter shows the ultimate victory over Satan and fulfills the key verse of the Bible, Genesis 3:15. He that "overcometh" is mentioned seventeen times in the book; the word "blessed" occurs seven times. The book of Revelation shows the ultimate triumph of the kingdom of God. The theme of the Bible is redemption.

Prophecy Literally Fulfilled?

To give to prophecy a literal interpretation is not correct. Take, for example, the prophecy concerning the coming and work of John the Baptist. Isaiah said:

> The voice of one that crieth, Prepare ye in the wilderness the way of Jehovah; make level in the desert a highway for our God. Every valley shall be exalted, and every mountain and hill shall be made low; and the uneven shall be made level, and the rough places a plain: and the glory of Jehovah shall be revealed, and all flesh shall see it together; for the mouth of Jehovah hath spoken it (Isaiah 40:3–5).

Was this prophecy fulfilled literally? No; but when John the Baptist was preaching in the wilderness of Judea, he identified himself as "the voice of one crying in the wilderness" (Matthew 3:1–4; Luke 3:3–6). Although John fulfilled Isaiah's prophecy, it was not in a literal sense. John was not a road builder. He did not pull down literal mountains and fill up literal valleys. These were all figurative expressions of his literal work of spiritual renovation. The Old Testament prophets, in order to teach spiritual truths, often used words and figures with which the people were familiar. And so did Christ and the apostles (cf. Matthew 5:13–14; Philippians 3:2). A prophecy can be clothed in figurative language and can be actually fulfilled without being literally fulfilled.

Figures of Speech

The Old Testament abounds in figures of speech. Even figurative expressions about the Lord cannot be understood in a literal way. For instance, "He shall cover thee with his feathers, and under his wings shalt thou trust" (Psalm 91:4 KJV). Surely God does not have literal wings and feathers!

Again, "The mountains and the hills shall break forth before you into singing, and all the trees of the field shall clap their hands" (Isaiah 55:12). Do literal trees clap literal hands? Do literal mountains literally sing?

To interpret these passages literally is to make them absurd and contradictory. The Holy Spirit never intended for them to be taken literally. Is Christ a literal vine? (John 15:1). Literal bread? (John 6:35).

The Safe Course

The safe and sane course is to interpret symbols in the light of plain statements of Scripture. Symbols from prophetic passages must be construed in harmony with plain truths which have been literally stated. If any theory based on any symbolic Scripture is in conflict with other plain verses of Scripture, it must be rejected as being false. If one's interpretation of any of these symbols in Revelation 20 contradicts the plain teaching of the Scriptures at another place, obviously his interpretation has gone astray, for there is no contradiction in Biblical teaching. The Word of God should always be interpreted by comparing Scripture with Scripture.

The Theory Contradicts the Bible

That the theory of premillennialism is inconsistent with the plain teaching of the Scriptures in several points is now to be observed.

Two Bodily Resurrections?

The theory makes two future bodily resurrections, separated by a thousand years. There will not be two distinct bodily resurrections, one of the righteous and one of the wicked, separated by an interval of time. The Scriptures affirm that *all* will be raised at the same time, the last day, when Christ comes again. Jesus distinctly said that all would come forth in the same hour, both they who have done good and they who have done evil:

> Marvel not at this: for the hour cometh, in which all that are in the tombs shall hear his voice, and shall come forth; they that have done good, unto the resurrection of life; and they that have done evil, unto the resurrection of judgment (John 5:28–29; cf. Daniel 12:2).

Paul also said: "For the trumpet shall sound, and the dead [i.e., all the dead] shall be raised incorruptible" (1 Corinthians 15:52).

Paul did say there is an order in the resurrection: Christ first, then they that are Christ's at His coming; then comes the end (1 Corinthians 15:23–24). But there is no mention made anywhere of a first and second resurrection with a space of one thousand years between them. Paul did not say: "But each in his own order: Christ the firstfruits; then the martyrs and all the righteous at His coming; then a thousand years afterward the rest of mankind; and then cometh the end." Nowhere in the Scriptures can one read of a resurrection of the bodies of believers followed after one thousand years by a resurrection of the bodies of unbelievers. There is only one future bodily resurrection of *all* the dead, both of the just and the unjust. Luke records Paul saying: "There shall be a resurrection [singular] both of the just and unjust" (Acts 24:15). Hence, no time interval is between the resurrection of the righteous and the wicked; the wicked as well as the righteous will be included in the one and only final resurrection.

Righteous Raised First?

The theory of premillennialism makes the righteous raised one thousand years before the last day, whereas the Scriptures teach that the righteous will be raised at "the last day." Speaking of the believers' resurrection, Christ said: "I will raise him up at the last day" (John 6:40; cf. vv. 39, 44, 54). No fewer than four times in one discourse did Jesus tell the people that He would raise the believer "at the last day." In addition, Jesus said that the wicked would be judged at the last day: "He that rejecteth me, and receiveth not my sayings, hath one that judgeth him: the word that I spake, the same shall judge him in the *last* day" (John 12:48). So the wicked also shall be raised and judged at the same time that the righteous will be raised, namely, at the last day. At the final judgment, the righteous and the wicked will all stand before the Judge to receive their individual sentences, for when Jesus comes again, then before Him shall be gathered all nations (Matthew 16:27; 25:31–46). All the dead, both good and bad, small and great, shall stand before God at the judgment (Revelation 20:12–15). All the wicked and the righteous will be raised and judged together, and both at the second coming of Christ at the end of time. Paul further said that Christ "shall judge the living [i.e., those living on earth at the time of His coming] and the dead [i.e., all the dead, who will then be raised], and by his appearing" (2 Timothy 4:1). Judgment will be when Christ comes, and not one thousand years after He comes. Both the righteous and the wicked will be raised and judged at the same time.

Thus, if any interpretation of any prophecy has the dead literally raised before the end of time, it contradicts the statements of God's Word. The righteous dead are all raised and the living saints are all changed at Christ's second coming. Likewise, the wicked are all raised and judged at the same time as the righteous are raised and judged—at the end of time. When the dead are raised and the living changed, then will all be gathered before the judgment seat of Christ. There the Judge will pronounce the irrevocable sentence and the righteous and the wicked will be separated, each departing to his eternal abode. The Lord will execute final judgment, a single event, upon all.

Since Scripture does not teach a period of time of one thousand year's duration between the resurrection of the righteous and that of the wicked, here again the theory of premillennialism is wrong. The wicked will be raised and judged at the same time that the righteous are raised and judged, which will be at the close of all human history. The Bible teaches a resurrection at the end of the age, both of the just and of the unjust, to be followed immediately with the judgment and eternity.

A Future Earthly Kingdom?

The premillennial view of the kingdom of Christ on earth is, in many respects, inconsistent with the Scriptures as to its establishment and nature. The theory makes the kingdom of Christ yet future. Perhaps more convincing than any other truth of the Scriptures, the theory of premillennialism is wrong because the Bible teaches that the kingdom of Christ has already been established, with Christ now reigning as King over His kingdom.

The church and the kingdom of Christ upon earth are one and the same institution. Jesus used the two terms, *church* and *kingdom,* to refer to the same organism. He said: "Upon this rock I will build my church . . . I will give unto thee the keys of the kingdom of heaven" (Matthew 16:18–19). Being the same, the time of the establishment of the church, therefore, is the time of the establishment of Christ's kingdom.

Some have said that the Lord intended to establish His kingdom when He came to earth the first time, but since the people rejected Him, God took Him back to heaven and established the church instead; and when Christ comes again, He will establish His kingdom. This idea makes the church an after-thought in God's plan. The Bible states, however, that the church was not an after-thought with God, but rather it was a part of His "eternal purpose" (Ephesians 3:11).

Too, the Scriptures teach that the kingdom of Christ is a spiritual one, Christ reigning and ruling in the hearts of His people. When on trial, Christ said to Pilate: "My kingdom is not of this world" (John 18:36). The theory of the millennium makes Christ king over a material kingdom. During Christ's personal ministry, the people did not grasp His teaching concerning the nature of the kingdom because they expected the Messiah to be a temporal prince; they wanted Him to break the yoke of the Roman government and restore the earthly kingdom of Israel (Matthew 22:20–28). At one time, some tried to take Jesus by force and make Him king (John 6:15), but Christ did not have in mind the establishment of an earthly kingdom. Throughout His personal ministry, Christ, time and again, spoke of the spiritual nature of His kingdom. He told Nicodemus that in order to enter the kingdom one had to be born again "of water and the Spirit"; that a spiritual kingdom demanded a rebirth of the spirit of man and not of the body (John 3:1–8). In spite of all that Christ had said, the people generally, including the apostles, even after His resurrection, continued to hold to the idea of an earthly ruler and kingdom (Luke 24:12; Acts 1:6). Following the coming of the Holy Spirit the apostles understood the spiritual nature of Christ's reign (John 16:13; Acts 1:8; 2:1–4).

Christ King Now, Kingdom Now

Is the kingdom of Christ *now* in existence? Is Christ *now* reigning as king? The Bible distinctly teaches that the kingdom was in existence in the days of the ministry of the apostles after the ascension of Christ, after the church was established (Acts 2:47), and Christians were citizens of it. Paul, a few years after Pentecost, about A.D.62, wrote a letter to those in Colossae who were in the kingdom. He told these Christians that they had been delivered out of the power of darkness, and translated into the kingdom of the Son of his love (Colossians 1:12–13). These believers were at that time in the kingdom. The apostle John, in writing the book of Revelation, said that he was a "brother and partaker with you in the tribulation and kingdom" (Revelation 1:9). These apostles preached the kingdom of God and Christ as a then present reality.

Moreover, this kingdom is still in existence, for the early saints were told that they were in a kingdom that could not be moved or shaken. The writer of Hebrews said: "Wherefore, receiving a kingdom that cannot be shaken . . . " (Hebrews 12:28). If it cannot be shaken, then it will stand forever, and it cannot end to let another begin (cf. Daniel 2:44). Thus, these passages of Scripture teach that the kingdom of Christ is now in existence and people by being born again are entering into it. If the kingdom has not been established, and Christ is not king, then the new birth is not a reality and no one is being born again.

Again, if the kingdom has not been established, then Christians cannot observe the Lord's Supper, which is only in the kingdom. Jesus said to His disciples, after instituting the Supper: "I appoint unto you a kingdom, even as my Father appointed unto me, that ye may eat and drink at my table in my kingdom" (Luke 22:29–30). However, the early Christians had the Lord's Supper. The members of the church at Corinth partook of the communion of the body and the blood of Christ, for Paul gave them instructions on the proper observance of it (1 Corinthians 11:18–34). Too, the disciples at Troas celebrated the Lord's Supper on the first day of the week, for Luke records: "And upon the first day of the week, when we were gathered together to break bread, Paul discoursed with them" (Acts 20:7). Then the kingdom must have been in existence in the days of these early disciples, or else they could not have observed the Lord's Supper.

It is false, therefore, to say that the kingdom of Christ has not been established and will not be until the Lord comes again. Christ is king now, the kingdom does exist now, and all Christians are in it. Christ is now reigning as king over His spiritual kingdom.

The Time Kingdom Established

The Bible teaches that the kingdom of Christ was established on Pentecost following the ascension of Christ. To prove from the Scriptures that the kingdom of Christ is now in existence is sufficient to disprove the theory of premillennialism regarding a future kingdom to be established on earth. Yet one can also learn from the Bible the exact day the kingdom was inaugurated.

- *The kingdom was to come with power*, that is, when the kingdom came, the power was to come. This would be during the lifetime of some of the disciples. Jesus said: "There are some here of them that stand by, who shall in no wise taste of death [die], till they see the kingdom of God come with power" (Mark 9:1).
- *The power was to come when the Holy Spirit came*. Jesus again said to His apostles after His resurrection: "But ye shall receive power, when the Holy Spirit is come upon you" (Acts 1:8).
- *The Holy Spirit came to the apostles on the day of Pentecost*. "And when the day of Pentecost was now come, they were all together in one place . . . And they were all filled with the Holy Spirit, and began to speak with other tongues, as the Spirit gave them utterance" (Acts 2:1–4).

This was in the city of Jerusalem, the place where Jesus told His disciples to wait for the Holy Spirit (Luke 24:47, 49). These passages establish that

- the kingdom was to come when the power came;
- the power was to come with the Holy Spirit;
- the kingdom was to come when the Holy Spirit came; therefore, the Spirit, power, and kingdom were all to come together, at the same time;
- the Holy Spirit came on the first Pentecost after Christ's resurrection and ascension;
- the kingdom came and was established on the first Pentecost after Christ's resurrection, in the city of Jerusalem.

This was the beginning of the reign of Christ and the Christian dispensation (Acts 11:15). Thus, the kingdom of Christ has been established for over nineteen hundred years. If the kingdom of Christ has not been established, then there are persons yet living on the earth who stood in the presence of Jesus when He said some would not die until the kingdom came with power (Mark 9:1). That would make them over nineteen hundred years old, twice the age of Methuselah when he died (Genesis 5:27).

The Prophets Foresaw Kingdom

Daniel saw in a vision the ascension and coronation of Christ:

> I saw in the night-visions, and, behold, there came with the clouds of heaven one like unto a son of man [i.e., Christ at His ascension, Acts 1:9], and he came even to the ancient of days [i.e., God the Father], and they brought him near before him. And there was given him dominion, and glory, and a king-

> dom, that all the peoples, nations, and languages should serve him: his dominion is an everlasting dominion, which shall not pass away, and his kingdom that which shall not be destroyed (Daniel 7:13–14).

Daniel's prophecy is clarified by Christ in the Parable of the Pounds: "A certain nobleman went into a far country, to receive for himself a kingdom, and to return" (Luke 19:12). In this parable Christ is the nobleman and heaven is the far country. Christ received the kingdom when He went to heaven—He will not receive it after He comes again.

In addition, the kingdom seen by the prophets is the kingdom of the Lord. For instance, Isaiah prophesied the beginning place and time of the kingdom. He referred to the Lord's kingdom as "the mountain of the Lord's house" and said it would have its beginning in Jerusalem: "For out of Zion shall go forth the law, and the word of Jehovah from Jerusalem" (Isaiah 2:3; cf. 1 Timothy 3:15; Luke 24:47). To this the prophets Micah and Zechariah assented (Micah 4:1; Zechariah 1:16). The kingdom was to begin in the "last days" (Isaiah 2:2). The Christian age or dispensation is the last days (Hebrews 1:1–2; Acts 2:17; Ephesians 3:21). People are now living in the last days of time. For this reason, the so-called millennium of Revelation 20 must be during the gospel dispensation.

Likewise, the prophet Daniel, in the interpretation of Nebuchadnezzar's dream, specified there would be four kingdoms—three kingdoms which would follow that of Babylon—and that in the days of the fourth kingdom, the God of heaven would set up His eternal kingdom (Daniel 2:36–45).

Daniel's Four World Empires

Note these four universal monarchies as they occurred in history:

1. The then then-present Babylonian (Chaldean) kingdom.
2. The kingdom of the Medes and Persians (they ruled together as one kingdom, called the Medo-Persian).
3. The kingdom of Greece (Macedonia).
4. The Roman kingdom.

It was in the days of the fourth kingdom—the Roman Empire—that God would establish the kingdom of Christ. Daniel also said that it would never be destroyed, that it would stand forever (Daniel 2:44). This was the kingdom the early Christians were in, according to Hebrews 12:28. The stone cut out of the mountain without hands that struck the image on its feet is no other than the kingdom of God (Christianity, Daniel 2:45). Now, since the old Roman Empire has long ceased to exist, it must be revived if Christ's kingdom has not been established.

Nevertheless, during the Roman Empire, the fourth kingdom, John the Baptist began his preaching by saying: "Repent ye; for the kingdom of heaven is at hand" (Matthew 3:2). Jesus, in His personal ministry, preached the same: "Now after John was delivered up, Jesus came into Galilee, preaching the gospel of God, and saying, The time is fulfilled, and the kingdom of God is at hand" (Mark 1:14–15). Likewise, did the Twelve and the Seventy (Matthew 10:7; Luke 10:9). John the Baptist, Christ, the Apostles, and the Seventy were telling the truth then—the kingdom was at hand. Paul, in prison at Rome, believed that his death was at hand (2 Timothy 4:6). Soon after this Paul died.

Likewise, in beautiful figures of speech the peaceful and prosperous reign of Christ was described by the Old Testament prophets (e.g. Isaiah 11:4, 6–9). These prophecies are all being fulfilled now in the gospel age as people turn from sin to live by the principles set forth by the Prince of Peace, King Jesus. It is so foolish for a person to think that all of those figurative prophetic descriptions of the Lord's reign must require a literal fulfillment. Paul, in Romans 15:12, quoted from Isaiah 11 and applied it to the Christian age in fulfillment. So, away goes the idea of the literal lion and lamb and a little child leading them in the so-called "millennium," with the reign of Christ on earth. Never is there from the pen of any inspired man in the New Testament a hint or suggestion to the effect that the reign of Christ, which God promised afore by His prophets, had been postponed to another (future) era. The kingdom of Christ has been established; all the Old Testament prophecies have been, and are now being fulfilled in the present Christian age. Jesus said to His disciples after His resurrection: "These are my words which I spake unto you, while I was yet with you, that all things must needs be fulfilled, which are written in the law of Moses, and the prophets, and the psalms, concerning me" (Luke 24:44).

Too, Amos said the tabernacle of David must be rebuilt, or else the Gentiles could not see God (Amos 9:11–12). This prophecy has been fulfilled in the conversion of the Gentiles to Christianity, as explained by the apostle Peter after the church was established (Acts 15:13–17). If not, then no Gentiles could be saved.

Likewise, the prophet Zechariah said that the Messiah would be a priest and king—both at the same time—on His throne: "Even he shall build the temple of Jehovah; and he shall bear the glory, and shall sit and rule upon his throne; and he shall be a priest upon his throne" (Zechariah 6:13). The book of Hebrews teaches that Christ is priest now (Hebrews 4:14; 8:1). Then Christ is king now, since He was to be priest and king on His throne at the same time, for He is priest now. Too, the Bible says that if Christ were on earth, He could not be a priest (Hebrews 8:4). This shows that Christ can never be a priest on earth, and disproves the theory of the millennial reign of Christ on earth. Christ's throne is in heaven. These prophecies are not yet future.

Pentecost, the Beginning

Up until the day of Pentecost (Acts 2), all statements about the kingdom pointed forward (e. g., Daniel 2:44; 7:13–14; Matthew 3:1–2; Mark 1:15; Matthew 10:7; Luke 10:9; 6:9–10; 16:18; Luke 22:18; 19:11; Mark 15:43; Acts 1:6, 8); but after that day all statements about the kingdom (or church) show that it had already been established and that Christ was king (e.g., Revelation 1:9; 2:1; 1 Timothy 3:15; Acts 13:1; 8:1; 11:22; 5:11; 2:47). That day was the beginning of the kingdom and of the reign of Christ. On Pentecost three thousand people were added to the kingdom, and souls continued to be added daily (Acts 2:47). This proves then that the kingdom was set up sometime between Christ's ascension into heaven and the close of events in Acts 2, the day of Pentecost, ten days later. The exact time, however, was the day of Pentecost and the place was Jerusalem. This fulfilled Old Testament prophecies. The "coronation ceremonies" have already occurred, nearly two thousand years ago. Peter stated regarding the Gentiles: "And as I began to speak, the Holy Spirit fell on them, even as on us at the beginning" (Acts 11:15).

"Thy Kingdom Come"

Too, during the personal ministry of Christ, before the kingdom was set up, Jesus taught His disciples to pray, "Thy kingdom come" (Matthew 6:10); but after Pentecost no inspired man ever told any one to pray for the kingdom to come. On Pentecost they received the kingdom. There is no need for one to pray this prayer now, for the kingdom has already come, and it exists today. It was future up until the day of Pentecost.

In reading the Bible one should always observe these rules: Who is the speaker in the verse? Who is addressed? Under what age or dispensation (Patriarchal, Jewish, or Christian) was the language spoken? This will help one in understanding what is read. So Christ told His apostles during His personal ministry—before the cross—to pray, "Thy kingdom come." But Christians are not told to pray this today—or even sing a song that teaches this!

The Church Age

Premillennialists talk much about the present "church age," the future "millennial age." They teach that the church must be done away before the kingdom of Christ can be established. Their view is without Scriptural foundation. The only kingdom yet future is the eternal phase of the kingdom of God which the redeemed shall enter when time is no more. Paul encouraged the Christians to "continue in the faith, and that through many tribulations we must enter into the kingdom of God" (Acts 14:22). And Peter exhorted saints to put into their lives virtue, knowledge, self-control, patience, godliness, brotherly kindness, and love. Then he said:

> Wherefore, brethren, give the more diligence to make your calling and election sure: for if ye do these things, ye shall never stumble: for thus shall be richly supplied unto you the entrance into the eternal kingdom of our Lord and Savior Jesus Christ (2 Peter 1:10–11).

At the resurrection and judgment the faithful will enter the everlasting kingdom, which is heaven (Matthew 25:34, 46).

Christ Now on David's Throne

The theory of premillennialism is wrong concerning the time Christ is to be on David's throne. The theory of the millennium is that during this time Christ will occupy David's throne in Jerusalem. From the many prophecies of the Old Testament it is clear that Christ in some sense was to be a king on David's throne (Psalm 2:6–8; Isaiah 9:6–7; Jeremiah 23:5–6) and while David slept with his fathers (2 Samuel 7:12). God promised His servant David that his throne would be established forever (2 Samuel 7:12–16), and this promise was later repeated (Psalm 89:3–4). The angel said to Mary that her Son would be given the throne of David (Luke 1:31–33). Hence, Peter, in his great sermon on Pentecost (the day of the establishment of the church), said that Christ had been raised up to sit on David's throne. He was speaking of Christ's resurrection in connection with David's prophecy when he said:

> Being therefore a prophet, and knowing that God had sworn with an oath to him, that of the fruit of his loins he [God] would set one upon his [David's] throne; he foreseeing this spake of the resurrection of the Christ, that neither was he [Christ] left unto Hades, nor did his flesh see corruption (Acts 2:30–31).

The inspired apostle Peter connected the fulfillment of the prophecy concerning Christ on David's throne with the resurrection and ascension of Christ, and not with His second coming in the future. All of the prophecies relating to David's throne have been fulfilled in the ascendancy of Christ to His throne in heaven. *Christ on David's throne is a present reality*. Christ is reigning now.

"The Lord's throne is in heaven" (Psalm 11:4 KJV). David's throne is now in heaven:

> Once have I sworn by my holiness that I will not lie unto David. His seed shall endure for ever, and his throne as the sun before me. It shall be established for ever as the moon, and as a faithful witness in heaven (Psalm 89:35–37 KJV).

Christ's resurrection and ascension fulfilled God's promise to David that his seed should sit upon his throne—sovereign power and dignity, a place occupied by one having authority. Christ now occupies that position of authority. The coronation ceremonies were held after Christ ascended back to the Father. Welcomed by the angels of glory at His ascension, the Father placed Him at His own right hand (a sign of power and dignity) and told Him to rule over His kingdom (Psalm 24:7–10; Hebrews 2:9; Philippians 2:9; Ephesians 1:20–22). Christ dispatched the Holy Spirit to the waiting apostles in Jerusalem on the day of Pentecost, and they began to preach repentance and remission of sins in His name (Luke 24:47; Acts 2:38). Guided by the Spirit, Peter used the keys of the kingdom on earth by announcing the Lord's terms of pardon to sinners. The terms of forgiveness were the same as the terms of induction into the kingdom.

So Christ began His reign as king on the day of Pentecost, and He is reigning now on David's throne or God's throne or His throne—they all mean the same. Christ's throne is in heaven (Acts 2:30–35; Zechariah 6:13; Hebrews 8:4). By "throne" is meant sovereign power and dignity.

All Authority Now

Christ has all authority now in heaven and in earth. Following His resurrection, He declared to His apostles: "All authority hath been given unto me in heaven and on earth" (Matthew 28:18). Christ, having all authority in religion, makes all laws of the kingdom. The King has such right. Christ is king now; He is now "Lord of lords, and King of kings" (1 Timothy 6:15; Revelation 17:14; 19:16). He is now exercising control over His kingdom.

The authority of King Jesus is expressed in the New Testament (cf. John 14:16; 16:13; 1 Corinthians 2:13; Galatians 1:11–12; 1 Thessalonians 2:13; 2 Timothy 3:16–17). Jesus Christ is the supreme authority in the Christian religion; He is king over His kingdom and head over His church. Citizens of the kingdom—those in His church—are to be subject to Christ (Colossians 1:18; Ephesians 1:22–23; 5:24). The authority is Christ, and the Scriptures are the tangible source of authority; they reveal the authority. The church has no power to alter New Testament instruction or to add laws to the Word of God. The legislative function of the church of the Lord Jesus Christ is a role reserved to Christ the King. The voice of Christ through the inspired Scriptures alone must rule the church.

Christ Not Reigning on Earth

Jeremiah prophesied concerning Coniah (Jeconiah): "Write this man childless, a man that shall not prosper in his days; *for no more shall a man of his seed prosper, sitting upon the throne of David, and ruling in Judah*" (Jeremiah 22:30). Although Christ is ruling on David's throne, He is not ruling in Judah, here on this earth. Furthermore, since He is not of the tribe of Levi; His priesthood cannot be based in Jerusalem (Hebrews 8:4).

All Requisites Now

As further proof that the kingdom now exists and that Christ is on David's throne is seen in the fact that all the requisites to the complete establishment and existence of Christ's kingdom are now present. The nature of the kingdom is seen in the six essentials that constitute it:

1. Christ is *king*.
2. His *territory* or spiritual domain extends over the whole earth.
3. His *throne* is a spiritual one and is in heaven.
4. The *subjects* of His kingdom are Christians.
5. The *law* that governs this kingdom is the New Testament (will) of Christ.
6. The *door* of entrance into this kingdom is the new (spiritual) birth, for the moment a person is born anew, or saved from his past sins, he is inducted into the kingdom of God on earth.

Phases of the Kingdom

The kingdom of Christ has existed in various phases or forms:

1. It existed in the mind of God, called the "eternal purpose" (Ephesians 3:10–11).
2. It existed in *promise* (Genesis 12:1–3; Galatians 3:8).
3. It existed in *prophecy* (Daniel 2:44; Zechariah 1:16, et al).
4. It existed in *preparation* (Matthew 3:1–5).
5. It began to exist in *perfection* (Acts 2).
6. It now exists in *perpetuity* by the Word (Luke 8:11; 1 Thessalonians 2:13).
7. It will exit in heaven in eternity (2 Peter 1:11), in the eternal Paradise of God. The kingdom of God on earth today is "the reign of heaven."

Old Judaism Revived

The premillennial theory is nothing less than a revival of the old Jewish idea of the Messiah's kingdom, that it is to be an earthly kingdom with Christ as an earthly king. It is foolish for people to refer to the Lord's second coming as the commencement of the millennium—a golden age with the kingdom of Christ on this earth. This false idea has been advocated in almost every century since the beginning of Christianity. The Jews expected the Messiah to establish a glorious earthly kingdom at Jerusalem, and present-day premillennialists are expecting the same thing to happen when Jesus comes again. The Jews could not conceive of a spiritual kingdom. They failed to see that the language of the prophets was figurative and symbolical. Since Jesus did not fulfill the prophecies according to their carnal misinterpretations of them, they rejected Him.

When the Kingdom Ends

The theory of premillennialism is contrary to the teaching of the Bible that the kingdom of Christ will end when He comes. The Bible not only teaches that the kingdom has been established and that Christ is now on David's throne and is now king, but also definitely states that Christ will cease His intercessory reign when He comes again. "For he [Christ] must reign [i.e., continue to reign], till he hath put all his enemies under his feet. The last enemy that shall be abolished is death" (1 Corinthians 15:25–26). Death will not be destroyed until Christ comes again, for then the dead will all be raised. "Then cometh the end, when he [Christ] shall deliver up the kingdom to God, even the Father [this is after the resurrection]; when he [Christ] shall have abolished all rule and all authority and power" (v. 24).

So Christ is not coming to *begin* His reign; He is reigning now and shall continue His personal mediatorial reign until all enemies have been abolished, and the last enemy to be destroyed is death. The second coming of Christ will mark the end—not the beginning—of the reign of Christ, at which time He will cease His reign and give back the kingdom to God the Father (v. 28). When Jesus comes the second time, then the church will enter into her everlasting state of glory. Christ is not going to set up a material kingdom on this earth and reign over the whole world when He comes again. The premillennial theory is inconsistent with the total teaching of the Scriptures. There is no passage of Scripture that speaks of Christ's reigning over an earthly kingdom for any length of time, either before or after His coming. The Bible teaches that Christ was to reign over a spiritual kingdom and not over a temporal one; this spiritual reign of Christ began on the day of Pentecost; it is now in operation at the present time, and it will continue until Christ shall come again. Instead of teaching that the Lord will come to set up His kingdom and rule on the earth for a thousand years, the Bible clearly teaches that the kingdom was established on the first Pentecost after His resurrection and that Christ is now king and has been reigning in heaven since the day of Pentecost following His resurrection.

The "First Resurrection"

Is the first resurrection in Revelation 20 a literal, bodily resurrection, or is this expression also figurative as other expressions in the context? When the entire chapter is studied, along with the total teaching of the Holy Scriptures concerning the second coming of Christ, the end of the world, the judgment, and the Lord's kingdom, this part of the chapter becomes clear. (However, a word of caution is always in order today in interpreting symbols of prophecy.)

A Spiritual Resurrection

The theory of premillennialism is in error in saying that the "first resurrection" is literal, whereas it is spiritual with figurative language. John, in Revelation 20, describes the revival of the *spirits* (souls) of the martyrs as the *first resurrection*, and on such the second death has no power. The resurrection here spoken of is a resurrection of souls—not of the bodies of men. They were not the souls of all the saints, but of "them that had been beheaded for the testimony of Jesus," the souls of the martyrs that lived. The martyrs were not under the altar crying for vengeance as they were in chapter 6. They were on thrones, reigning with Christ. This spiritual resurrection differs from the bodily resurrection at the end of time, when the thousand years are finished. It is not an actual resurrection from the grave. The dragon, the devil, was restrained by the Word of God (Matthew 4:1–11; cf. Matthew 12:29; Hebrews 2:14). The dragon, the chain, and the abyss are figures of speech. If the thousand years and the first resurrection are literal, then the other things in the chapter must be taken literally. In John's vision there is no literal resurrection of the literal bodies of the saints and no literal reign on this literal earth for a literal one thousand years.

Order of Events

Here is the order of events as pictured in Revelation 20:

1. The binding of Satan and the one thousand years' reign.
2. Satan's little season.
3. The second coming of Christ (called by some Bible students "the *parousia*").
4. The resurrection of all the dead.
5. The final judgment.

This order should not be reversed; however, this is exactly what is done when it is said that Christ is going to come before the millennium. Christ's personal coming will be at the end of time. Then, the heavens and the earth in their present form will end, with the resurrection and judgment, immediately following the first resurrection (vv. 11–15). Christ's return, the resurrection, and the judgment are linked in one perspective by the Scriptures. Therefore, it should be clear that the first resurrection is not a resurrection of the bodies of men, but a resurrection of the souls of the martyrs. The first resurrection must be understood as a figurative resurrection. In this way it harmonizes with all the passages of Scripture which speak of a simultaneous resurrection of all the dead. No basis is found in the symbolism for a literal reign of a literal one thousand years of saints with Christ on earth either before or after His second coming. John did not say that the bodies of the martyrs were to be raised from the dead, but the souls.

Rupturing the Rapture

Premillennialists believe Paul's language in 1 Thessalonians 4:16 teaches two future bodily resurrections:

> But we would not have you ignorant, brethren, concerning them that fall asleep [die]; that ye sorrow not, even as the rest, who have no hope. For if [since] we believe that Jesus died and rose again, even so them also that are fallen asleep

> in Jesus [Christians] will God bring with him [i.e., He will bring their spirits out of Paradise in Hades with Him when He comes, in order that these may be quickly united with their respective resurrected bodies]. For this we say unto you by the word of the Lord, that we that are alive, that are left until the coming of the Lord, shall in no wise precede them that are fallen asleep. For the Lord himself shall descend from heaven, with a shout, with the voice of the archangel, and with the trump of God: and the dead in Christ shall rise first; then we that are alive, that are left, shall together with them be caught up in the clouds, to meet the Lord in the air: and so shall we ever be with the Lord. Wherefore comfort one another with these words (1 Thessalonians 4:13–18).

Paul said that those who are alive and shall survive at the coming of the Lord, will by no means preceed (i.e., by entering into heavenly bliss) those who are already dead. Christ will bring the spirits of all believers who have died out of Hades with Him when He comes to raise their dead bodies. Yet the saints who are alive at His second coming, and who will also be caught up to welcome Him, cannot ascend until the bodies of the saints sleeping in the dust of the earth are raised to go with them. The righteous who are living at the time of Christ's return will have no advantage over those saints. The apostle stated that the "dead in Christ shall rise first." This does not mean two resurrections, one for those who are in Christ and the other for those who are not in Him, separated by a thousand years. When Jesus comes again, not only unbelievers but also believers will still be living on earth. Those who are dead in Christ will be raised with spiritual bodies and those who are still alive will be immediately changed into a spiritual state. Then all the saints will together ascend to meet the Lord in the air. This comparison is between the saints who are dead when Christ comes and those who are alive—two classes of believers—and not between the righteous and the wicked. Paul was not speaking of the resurrection of the wicked in this passage. Whether the wicked dead will be raised then, or at a later time, is not here stated. Paul was speaking of only believers, both dead and living, and not the wicked. (The fact that all the dead will be raised at the same time, at the last day, and their souls will be united with their proper bodies, is elsewhere stated in God's Word [cf. John 5:28–29; Acts 24:15].) The passage shows the order for the righteous when the Lord comes: the resurrection of righteous dead first; then the change of the living righteous second, immediately following the resurrection of the dead saints; then all together (both the raised and the living saints) will be caught up to meet the Lord in the air and live with Him forever—not seven years, and then come back to the earth and live for a thousand years. Those who are alive and remain until Christ's coming shall not precede or go before those who have died.

As for those still living, they shall not die as the others have, but their bodies will be changed from corruptible to incorruptible. However, the dead in

Christ shall rise before those then living shall be changed. Thus, those who are still living and whose bodies have not been dissolved by death shall have no advantage over their brethren who have died and whose bodies have gone back to dust. The living saints shall not go up to meet the Lord in the air while the saints of other ages are still under the dominion of death. "The dead in Christ shall rise first"—i.e., before the living saints ascend. In fact, those still alive will have to wait momentarily until the dead are raised.

This harmonizes with Paul's language in 1 Corinthians 15:22–24:

> For as in Adam all die, so also in Christ shall all be made alive. But each in his own order: Christ the firstfruits; then they that are Christ's, at his coming. Then cometh the end, when he shall deliver up the kingdom to God, even the Father; when he shall have abolished all rule and all authority and power.

Paul does not make the slightest reference here to the resurrection of the wicked. The whole chapter concerns the resurrection of believers. Christ certainly rose from the dead; so all His people shall rise; but each in his order; first, Christ, then they who are Christ's; then comes the end—the end of all things, the end of history. Again, Paul said: "We all shall not sleep [i.e., die], but we shall all [both dead and living] be changed [in body], in a moment, in the twinkling of an eye, at the last trump" (vv. 51–52). Also, in 1 Thessalonians 4:16 Paul said nothing about the judgment which will follow the resurrection of all mankind, but he did in other passages (cf. Romans 14:10, 12; 2 Corinthians 5:10).

So, something must happen to all bodies of the saints; a change must take place, either by dying and then being raised, or by being changed without experiencing death. (Christians cannot enter heaven in flesh-and-blood bodies.) But the premillennial idea of a rapture is nowhere taught in the Scriptures. The dead in Christ are placed in contrast with the living in Christ. In 1 Thessalonians 4:16–17, Paul discussed only Christians; the dead Christians and the living Christians. There is no contrast, therefore, between those in Christ (the believers) and those not in Christ (the unbelievers). Paul drew a contrast between the dead in Christ and those still-living in Christ at the Lord's return. These are the two groups. The passage should be read with the emphasis placed as follows: "The dead in Christ shall rise first; then we that are alive, that are left, shall together with them be caught up in the clouds, to meet the Lord in the air." The passage says nothing about a silent or secret rapture.

The word *rapture* is not found in any respectable English translation of the Bible. Neither is the idea of imminent rapture a fact of Biblical teaching. Several years ago Hal Lindsey's book *The Late, Great Planet Earth* taught this false doctrine of a rapture. Also in the early 1900s, W. E. Blackstone's book *Jesus Is Coming* taught the idea of a rapture. Too, the popular song "Jesus Is Coming Soon" was written to teach the "soon coming" of Christ. Christ will come again, but no one knows when.

Only One Second Coming

Christ Himself will come again only once. Nowhere does the Bible say that there will be more than one glorious return. He will come *with* His saints (the spirits from Hades) and also *for* His saints (those living on earth) at one and the same time.

Premillennialists are in error, therefore, when they split the second coming of Christ into *two* phases in order to make room for a great tribulation between the *first* phase of His second coming and the *second* phase of His second coming. The Bible does not teach that there will be a seven-year period of unparalleled tribulation preceding the end of this age.

The "Great Tribulation"

Daniel's prophecy and Christ's statement about a great tribulation were fulfilled in the siege of Jerusalem under Titus, A.D.70 (cf. Daniel 9:26; Matthew 23:37–38; 24:21). The great tribulation of prophecy is past. This "great tribulation" idea, with the tribulation saints being raised at the *second* second coming of Christ (called the "revelation" of Jesus), is just another unscriptural part of the over-all unscriptural doctrine of the theory of premillennialism.

The personal coming of Christ is placed by all inspired writers as the last event before the final judgment day; it is after the "one thousand years" period, and also after the overthrow of Satan in his last conflict, not before. The evident purpose of Revelation 20:1–10 is to present a brief review of Satan's overthrow from the time his power was restrained until he is banished in the lake of fire forever. The "little time" divides the thousand years from the final judgment.

Examples of Spiritual Resurrections

The Bible speaks of a spiritual resurrection. Elijah lived again. In the last chapter of the Old Testament is this prophecy: "Behold, I will send you Elijah the prophet before the great and terrible day of Jehovah come" (Malachi 4:5). The Jews properly understood the "day" to refer to the time of the Messiah, but they understood the prophecy literally and expected the same Old Testament prophet, Elijah, to reappear bodily as the harbinger of Christ. Yet the prophecy meant nothing of the kind, but simply that one having the spirit and power of Elijah should arise (Luke 1:17). Jesus Himself affirmed that this prophecy was fulfilled in the life and work of John the Baptist: "And if ye are willing to receive it, this is Elijah that is to come" (Matthew 11:14; cf. Matthew 17:10–12). The resurrection and reappearance of Elijah meant nothing more than simply that a man having his spirit and power should arise. In metaphorical language a man may be called by the name of another because of their resemblance to each other; so John the Baptist was called Elijah the prophet because he was like him.

The dry bones lived again. Again, take the prophecy of Ezekiel in which he predicted the return of fleshly Israel from literal Babylon under the symbol of a resurrection of a might army in the valley of dry bones (Ezekiel 37:1–14). Jehovah said to the prophet:

> Son of man, these bones are the whole house of Israel . . . Therefore prophesy, and say unto them, Thus saith the Lord Jehovah: Behold, I will open your graves, and cause you to come up out of your graves, O my people; and I will bring you into the land of Israel (vv. 11–12).

This was fulfilled, but not literally, when the Jews returned from Babylonian captivity to their homeland under the leadership of Zerubbabel and Ezra (Ezra 2:1–2; 7:6–7). So, there can be a resurrection when there is not a literal resurrection of literal bodies from literal graves. This is the same kind of resurrection as the first resurrection in the twentieth chapter of Revelation. The resemblance of John's prophecy to Ezekiel's prophecy is very striking. One was delivered to fleshly Israel, the other to spiritual Israel.

Sinners may come to life and be resurrected. Jesus made reference to a figurative or spiritual resurrection in the following language: "Verily, verily, I say unto you, The hour cometh, and now is, when the dead shall hear the voice of the Son of God; and they that hear shall live" (John 5:25). Thus, those dead in sin hear the voice of Christ, and those who harken to it live spiritually.

Later in the chapter (vv. 28–29), Jesus spoke of the resurrection of the body from the literal tomb. So in this chapter Jesus mentions *two* resurrections. The resurrection of verse 25 is something that is taking place every day in this present gospel dispensation. The moment a person is saved or born again this resurrection takes place, but it is not an actual resurrection from the tomb.

Still again, Paul spoke of those who had been quickened or made alive from death or sin in this manner: "And you did he make alive, when you were dead through your trespasses and sins" (Ephesians 2:1). In this instance Paul was speaking of their spiritual awakening or conversion. In obeying the gospel, the penitent believer is buried with Christ in baptism and is raised up to walk in newness of life (Romans 6:4). So, surely no one can deny that inspired men used the figure of people rising from the dead when their literal resurrection was not intended.

Furthermore, Christians—those who have been resurrected—are said to be priests of God and of Christ today. Peter said to Christians: "But ye are an elect race, a royal priesthood" (1 Peter 2:9; v. 5; cf. Revelation 1:6). Faithful Christians have no fear of being eternally lost, that is, experiencing the second death. The apostles are now on thrones, judging the twelve tribes of Israel [i.e., spiritual Israel] (Matthew 19:28); and Christians "reign in life through the one, even Jesus Christ" (Romans 5:17). This is not speculation.

Martyrs Live Again

The same principle can be applied to the passage in Revelation 20:5. The scene looks forward to a bright and glorious era for the church, in which the souls of the martyrs live again for a thousand years. The martyred saints live in the persons of others, as Elijah lived again in the person of John the Baptist and as the Jewish nation came out of their graves when they returned from their captivity in Babylon. Hence, in the figurative language of the apostle John in this passage, the lives of the primitive Christians shine forth in the lives of their faithful successors. The same persons are not to come back to earth, but their cause is to be judged and their blood avenged. In Revelation 6, the souls cried for vengeance; in chapter 20, they received it. They live again in the lives of the saints who, like themselves, hold the faith of the Lord and would die before becoming traitors to it. The spirits of the martyrs live again in the hearts of those who take up the fight to maintain pure New Testament Christianity—a resurrection of zeal, courage, and devotion, which shall precede the bodily resurrection. The triumph of the martyrs, the "first resurrection," and the chaining of Satan for a thousand years overthrew Satan's power in the persons who copied the lives of the martyrs. Hence, the first resurrection is spiritual and is before the resurrection of the literal dead.

Summary

From church history it would seem that faithful Christians are now in the millennium, which will end at an unknown time; Christians today are in the first resurrection. Satan is bound by the influence of God's Word. People are free to obey Christ if they so desire. Satan today is limited in his power to persecute and conduct a world-wide effort to erase Christianity from the earth (cf. Matthew 12:29). But he does persecute to some extent today.

There is no passage in the Bible that teaches Christ will come to this earth to begin a millennium with resurrected righteous saints—at any time. Going to be with the Lord might well be called a rapture (the word is not in the Bible), but it will not be one of seven year's duration, but ever with the Lord. There is no time between the resurrection of the righteous at the last day and the resurrection and judgment of the wicked at the last day for a millennium. Both the punishment of the wicked and the reward of the righteous will be given "at the revelation of the Lord Jesus from heaven" (2 Thessalonians 1:7). There is no intimation in all the Scriptures of a literal kingdom being established and a literal reign of a literal thousand years on earth being inaugurated. Furthermore, in all the passages referring to the Lord's second coming, the event is always singular—*coming*, not *comings*. There is just one future personal coming of Christ (Hebrews 9:28).

At the end of time Satan, who caused all the trouble to the faithful children of God, will be cast into hell (Gehenna) (Revelation 20:10). Satan's little time (vv. 7–9) is followed by Christ's return unto judgment (vv. 10–15), and the one and only literal resurrection, which includes all mankind. So if Christ comes before the "millennium," all the dead, both righteous and wicked, will be raised then, and there can be none left to be raised at the end of the millennium. On the contrary, the Scriptures teach that death and Hades will not be destroyed until the second coming of Christ and the end of the world (v. 14). The last enemy to be destroyed is death (1 Corinthians 15:26).

The premillennial theory is false because:

1. Christ is now reigning as king over His kingdom, and the kingdom of Christ is not an earthly, literal kingdom (John 18:36).
2. Since Christ's kingdom has already been established, it is not, therefore, future (Mark 9:1; Acts 1:8; 2:47); the second coming of Christ will mark the end of His reign instead of the beginning (1 Corinthians 15:24–28).
3. No Scripture reveals that Christ will ever set foot upon this earth again (2 Peter 3:10).
4. At His coming, Christ is no nearer to the earth than the clouds where the saints shall be caught up to meet the Lord in the air and ever be with the Lord (1 Thessalonians 4:17).
5. Christians are now in the millennium and in the first resurrection. The conclusion drawn harmonizes with every other truth of the Word of God.

Therefore, the reign of souls for a thousand years is through those on earth who imitate the faith of the early Christian martyrs. In this way the spirits of the early martyrs live again. Whenever Christ's followers are willing to lay all on the altar—even life itself—in service to their Lord, there is the spirits of the martyrs living in Christians today. Hence, in a vision, John said that the principles of true Christianity would again have prominence for a long, indefinite period of time—a thousand years—as if the martyrs were living again on the earth. However, the entire world will not be brought under the influence of Christianity during this period. Nevertheless, there is no intimation in any statement of Scripture of a literal earthly kingdom being established and a literal earthly reign of a literal thousand years being inaugurated at Christ's second coming. Nothing can be more opposed to the teaching of the Bible than that the kingdom of Christ is yet future and is not to be inaugurated until His second coming. Premillennialism is not a mere harmless belief!

The Book of Revelation

The plan of the book of Revelation seems to be as follows:

1. Introduction—chapter 1 (the prologue)

2. Letters to the seven churches of Asia—chapters 2–3
3. Preparatory vision (view in heaven)—chapters 4–5
4. The church and external foes—6:1–11:18
   a. round one—chapters 6–7
   b. round two—8:1–11:18
5. The church and internal foes—11:19–20:15
   a. round three—chapters 12–19
   b. round four—chapter 20
6. The final home of the righteous—21:1–22:5
7. Conclusion—22:6–21

David's Throne, Solomon's Throne, God's Throne, Christ's Throne

In the Old Testament David's throne, Solomon's throne, and God's throne were one and the same. This thought is clearly stated in Scripture: "Then Solomon sat on the throne of Jehovah as king instead of David his father, and prospered; and all Israel obeyed him" (1 Chronicles 29:23; cf. 1 Kings 2:12). Christ was promised David's throne; David's throne is now in heaven; Christ was raised up to sit on David's throne; Christ is now on David's throne, His throne, God's throne. "He that overcometh, I will give to him to sit down with me in my throne, as I also overcame, and sat down with my Father in his throne" (Revelation 3:21). Christ, "when he had made purification of sins, sat down on the right hand of the Majesty on high" (Hebrews 1:3). David, the king, ruling over God's Old Testament people on his throne, was a type of Christ, the King, ruling over God's New Testament people, on His throne.

"The Rapture"

The premillennial idea of the rapture does not mean just the lifting up of the saints to meet Christ in the air at the end of the world, but the secret catching away of the church, the resurrected and living saints, who will rise from the earth to meet the Lord in the air, who has secretly appeared just before the beginning of a great tribulation period on earth. This tribulation is to last seven years, at the beginning of which the Jews shall have returned to their homeland in unbelief, and at which time they have either rebuilt their temple or are in the process of rebuilding it. In unbelief of Christ, they will enter into a seven-year agreement with the antichrist.

After three and one-half years the true nature of the antichrist will be revealed. The kings of the earth then gather together to battle against Jehovah and Christ. When this occurs the Lord and His saints descend from heaven to deliver the faithful and to destroy the enemy. Jesus will break the power of the antichrist and bring the tribulation period to a close.

The martyrs during the tribulation period are then raised to reign over the earth with Jesus and their fellow saints in the millennial kingdom which is to be set up when Jesus returns to earth. The tribes of Israel are to be restored to their land.

That Jesus is to return in the air secretly and the church is to be caught away secretly to join Him and stay for seven years is nowhere taught in the Bible. There will be nothing secret about Christ's coming for His saints (1 Thessalonians 4:16; 2 Peter 3:8–13), except precisely when it will occur (2 Peter 3:10). When Jesus comes again it will be the end of the world and the beginning of eternity. However, according to the theory of premillennialism the first resurrection will take place at the rapture, when Christ comes for His saints: that is, all saints who have died (both during the Old Testament and New Testament periods) and all saints then living. This is the first part of the first resurrection. The resurrection of the tribulation saints seven years later will be the second part of the first resurrection.

This is false! In Revelation 20 we have the resurrection of a cause. The souls of the beheaded and the martyred were like Antipas (Revelation 2:13). They died as martyrs. Satan will be released for a brief period of apostasy. Then comes the final judgment (Revelation 20:11–15). But once one dies, his status before the Lord cannot be changed.

Questions for Discussion

1. What does the word *millennium* mean? Where is it found in the Bible?
2. What is commonly meant by the theory of premillennialism concerning Christ's second coming? What passage is used in support of the theory?
3. Name seven things, essential to the theory, not mentioned in the passage.
4. How should prophetic statements always be interpreted?
5. Why should not figures of speech be given a literal meaning?
6. How does the theory of premillennialism contradict the statements of the Bible on the following subjects: (1) the resurrection of all the dead, (2) the time the righteous will be raised, and (3) the establishment of Christ's kingdom?
7. What is the nature of Christ's kingdom on earth?
8. Give passages that show the kingdom of Christ was in existence in the days of the early Christians? What does that early existence prove?
9. What statements of Scripture prove the exact time and place for the beginning of the Lord's kingdom?
10. Are any of the apostles living on earth now?
11. Can Christians today pray "Thy kingdom come"? If so, how?
12. Where is the Lord's table? Who should partake of the Lord's Supper?
13. Is Christ king now? When did He begin His reign? Is He on David's throne? When will He cease His reign?
14. To whom is the church subject? What is the church?
15. What are the essentials of a kingdom? Do all of these exist now in Christ's kingdom? What is the eternal phase of the kingdom of God? (See 2 Peter 1:10–11; Acts 14:22; 2 Timothy 4:1.)
16. Is the spiritual kingdom (church) of Christ, which is now in existence, the kingdom the Old Testament prophets said would come? How do you know?
17. Name the four universal empires of Daniel 2.
18. When was the kingdom of God set up according to Daniel's prophecy?
19. Will there be another universal (world) empire?
20. Will there be another age after this present (Christian) age?
21. When will Christ cease His reign?
22. When will all the dead be raised? When will the righteous be raised? When will the wicked be raised?
23. During the personal ministry of Christ, what was the Jewish conception of the nature of the Messiah's kingdom? Discuss the premillennial theory of the Lord's kingdom as a revival of this old Jewish concept.
24. Does the Bible actually teach that the "thousand years" will be a period of absolute and universal peace of joy and righteousness?

25. Is Christ now on David's throne? Give proof.
26. Is the "one thousand years" literal or symbolic?
27. What divides the "one thousand years" from the judgment?
28. How do the apostles now rule? Christians?
29. Will Christ ever set foot on the earth again? How do you know?
30. When was the first gospel sermon in its fullness preached to man. By whom? What were the results? What empire (government) was then in effect?
31. What influence destroyed the last great empire of history?
32. Does the Lord rule over man's heart by moral suasion or by physical force?
33. Are members of the church also citizens of the kingdom? Do the church and the kingdom have the same head? the same conditions of entry? the same laws governing its citizens? What conclusions can we draw from these facts?
34. What did John see in the vision of Revelation 20?
35. What did John say was the first resurrection? Is this resurrection before or after the second coming of Christ? Is it a literal (bodily) resurrection? When did Job say man would rise again?
36. Should all the figures of this chapter—and the entire book of Revelation—be given literal meanings? Is it consistent to give some of them literal interpretations and not the others?
37. Give the exact order of events from the entire chapter of Revelation 20.
38. How can Satan, a spirit-being, be bound? What is the chain that binds him?
39. Does 1 Thessalonians 4:16 teach two future bodily resurrections? In what sense will the dead in Christ rise first?
40. How many "second" comings of Christ are mentioned in the Bible? How many phases of His second coming do some teach today?
41. When was the "great tribulation" of prophecy fulfilled?
42. In what sense could the spirits (souls) of the martyrs live again? How did Elijah live again? How did the dry bones in the valley come from their graves and live again?
43. Could the revival of true Christianity on the earth after the Dark Ages and for a long period of time be the fulfillment of the prophecy of Revelation 20 of the souls of the early martyrs living again? Why?
44. In what sense will there be a resurrection at the close of the "millennium" and before the end of time? How long will this period last? How long will Satan regain his power after the thousand years?
45. In the context of Revelation 20, what is meant by this statement: "After this he must be loosed for a little time"?

46. What kind of resurrection will be at the close of the little season?
47. Who are those called "the rest of the dead," and in what sense will they live again? Is this resurrection spiritual or literal?
48. From the study of this chapter, has the first resurrection occurred? Who are priests today?
49. Are Christians now in the millennium?
50. Will any one reign with the Lord one thousand years on this earth after He comes?
51. What are several reasons for saying that the premillennial theory is wrong as to (1) symbolic language, (2) two future bodily resurrections, (3) two phases of Christ's second coming, and (4) inconsistency in the use of symbolical language?
52. What is the main theme of Revelation 20? Is it the overthrow of Satan, or the reign of one thousand years?
53. Is the word *beheaded* to be understood literally?
54. Is the first resurrection an actual resurrection from the grave?
55. How many bodily resurrections will there be? What do premillennialists mean by "the rapture"? Is the word *rapture* in the Bible? Does the Bible teach their idea of the rapture?
56. In regard to the binding of Satan, does the Bible say by whom? Why? How? To what degree? When?
57. From 1 Thessalonians 4:16, in what sense are the dead in Christ raised first?
58. Define the word *prevent* as here used in the King James Version.

– 21 –

What about the Battle of Armageddon?

". . . to gather them to the battle of that great day of God Almighty . . . And he gathered them together into a place called in the Hebrew tongue Armageddon"
Revelation 16:14–16 KJV

Premillennialists talk much about the battle of Armageddon, which they say will take place just before the second phase of the second coming of Christ and will be raging when He comes, but He will put it to an end and then set up His universal material kingdom. Their description of this battle has great emotional appeal. Today every crisis that arises and every little skirmish in the Middle East is interpreted by them as the harbinger of the battle of Armageddon.

Sensational Preaching

The modern prophets of gloom and doom are making much money on the subject by the spread of their books and by their radio and television programs. Preachers of international fame talk glibly of a Golden Age upon earth when wars will end, sin will be no more, and vice and violence will vanish from the earth after the battle of Armageddon in the millennium. The anti-Christian propaganda of premillennialism is captivating and is capturing the minds of millions today all over the world who know very little about the Bible.

It is said that about seventy percent of all so-called Christendom today believes in premillennialism. People ask, "What is the battle of Armageddon?" "Will Russia, China, and other nations of the earth, be engaged in a great carnal warfare in the Valley of Meggido at the end of the seven-year period after the rapture?"

Satan's Little Season

From the language of Revelation 20, studied in the previous chapter, there is a resurrection at the close of the one thousand years. This is implied in the words: "The rest of the dead lived not until the thousand years should be finished" (Revelation 20:5). Then, did they live again when the thousand years were finished?

The resurrection that closes the thousand years is of the same nature as the one that begins it. This resurrection is also figurative and means that after the period of time in which the spirits of the martyrs live again and Satan is bound, the souls of the wicked will live again in the same way. Then, at that time, Satan will be loosed from his chains and wickedness shall again be revived and prevail on the earth. The loosing of Satan is no other than the revival of sin and paganism in the closing days of this world's history. Christ implied that the closing days of this dispensation will be a time of great wickedness, as in the days of Noah, before the flood, when He said:

> And as were the days of Noah, so shall be the coming of the Son of man. For as in those days which were before the flood they were eating and drinking, marrying and giving in marriage, until the day that Noah entered into the ark, and they knew not until the flood came, and took them all away; so shall be the coming of the Son of man (Matthew 24:37–39; cf. Luke 17:26–30).

Not only did the flood come suddenly upon the people who had rejected Noah's warning, but the world was very wicked at the time. Christ once asked, "Nevertheless, when the Son of man cometh, shall he find faith on the earth?" (Luke 18:8; cf. Matthew 24:44).

The clear implication of these passages is that paganism, once overthrown, shall be revived. As evidence of this world-wide decadence, people will relegate the Bible to the background and not follow its teaching. This period of time, however, shall be a temporary outbreak of evil; it will only be for "a little time" (Revelation 20:3). This will be an indication of Christ's coming in some sense, but no one knows the times.

Furthermore, this will be Satan's last struggle against the church, for after this his power will forever be at an end. Hence, the idea that the entire world will at length be converted to Christ just prior to His second coming is false. But John did say that before the second coming of Christ and the end of time there is to be a time of great and long prosperity (the thousand years), and this to be followed by a little time of decay and suffering, and then Satan is destroyed.

Armageddon

Satan's last struggle to destroy the true church is described in the book of Revelation as the battle of Armageddon (KJV) or Har-magedon (ASV).

> And I saw coming out of the mouth of the dragon, and out of the mouth of the beast, and out of the mouth of the false prophet, three unclean spirits, as it were frogs: for they are spirits of demons, working signs; which go forth unto the kings of the whole world, to gather them together unto the war of the great day of God, the Almighty . . . And they gathered them together into the place which is called in Hebrew Har-magedon [Ar-megedon]. (Revelation 16:13–16).

> And I saw the beast, and the kings of the earth, and their armies, gathered together to make war against him that sat upon the horse, and against his army. And the beast was taken, and with him the false prophet that wrought the signs in his sight, wherewith he deceived them that had received the mark of the beast and them that worshipped his image: they two were cast alive into the lake of fire that burneth with brimstone (Revelation 19:19–20).

> And when the thousand years are finished, Satan shall be loosed out of his prison, and shall come forth to deceive the nations which are in the four corners of the earth, Gog and Ma-gog, to gather them together to the war: the number of whom is as the sand of the sea. And they went up over the breadth of the earth, and compassed the camp of the saints about, and the beloved city: and fire came down out of heaven, and devoured them. And the devil that deceived them was cast into the lake of fire and brimstone, where are also the beast and the false prophet; and they shall be tormented day and night for ever and ever (Revelation 20:7–10).

Is It Literal?

Since there are so many symbols and figures of speech in the book of Revelation, the foregoing statements of Scripture raise the question: Is the war a literal, carnal battle? Or is this also symbolical? When is the last war? This surely is symbolic language and only indicates that in the final struggle the forces of good will prevail.

Why the Name

The word *Armageddon* comes from the tell (mound) of Megiddo which is far above the plain of Esdraelon in northern Palestine, in the fertile valley between Galilee and Samaria. The valley of Megiddon (Zechariah 12:11) is about twenty miles wide and forty-five miles long. It was on the caravan route from Egypt to Damascus. This valley is one of the most historic areas in Palestine, the scene of many famous battles. Here God's ancient people won two great victories: Barak over the Canaanites who were led by Sisera (Judges 4:5–24), and Gideon over the Midianites (Judges 7). Here, too, in this valley occurred the tragic death of King Josiah, when he went out to meet Egypt's ruler, Pharaoh-necoh (2 Kings 23:29–30; 2 Chronicles 35:22).

The battle of Armageddon will not be a literal battle in the literal valley of Megiddon in Palestine. Surely the idea is that of a moral and spiritual battle. A conflict rages today between good and bad, truth and error, right and wrong,

Christ and His church and the devil and his followers. This will be the last mighty struggle between good and evil, and will end with the final destruction of all the enemies of God, at the judgment. Christ will win! It would be ridiculous to think of that battle as a carnal conflict. It would be literally impossible for all the people of earth to assemble in this small valley for a carnal battle.

An Authority Speaks

In speaking of the mound of Megiddo, G. Ernest Wright says:

> For three thousand years this man-made hill was one of the most strategic spots in Palestine . . . So frequently was this spot a battleground that the word Armageddon (from the Hebrew har Megiddo, Mount Megiddo) has come to mean any cataclysmic conflict . . . By the time the 13-acre mound was abandoned about 400 B.C. so many violent and decisive battles had been fought on the plain below that Megiddo gave its name to Armageddon, the final battle between the power of God and the hosts of evil foretold in the book of Revelation.[1]

Hence, the apocalyptic language of the book of Revelation regarding the battle of Armageddon refers symbolically to the triumph of the church over the forces of evil. The spiritual battle is going on now. The language must not be taken literally. Since Har-magedon referred to a famous battlefield where decisive victories were lost and won, it figuratively was used by the Holy Spirit to describe the last decisive victory over the power of evil. Being such a noted place of Jewish wars, it became to the Jewish mind, like Marathon and Waterloo to other peoples of earth, emblematic of any decisive battlefield. Hence, it was appropriately used to represent Satan's final defeat. Evil on earth will be ended by the Lord at His coming. In symbol it is shown that in the final conflict between sin and righteousness, error and truth, the end will vindicate Christ and His teaching. In that day of final judgment it will then be evident that it pays to be on the winning side.

Spiritual Warfare

The church is locked in a life-and-death struggle in this world. Christians are at war with Satan. It is a spiritual warfare.

> For though we walk in the flesh, we do not war according to the flesh (for the weapons of our warfare are not of the flesh, but mighty before God to the casting down of strongholds), casting down imaginations, and every high thing that is exalted against the knowledge of God (2 Corinthians 10:3–5).

---

1 G. Ernest Wright, "Bringing Old Testament Times to Life" (*National Geographic Magazine,* Dec. 1957), pp. 852, 858.

Christians are encouraged to "fight the good fight of the faith" (1 Timothy 6:12), and to "suffer hardship . . . as a good soldier of Christ Jesus" (2 Timothy 2:3). Jesus said to His disciples during His personal ministry: "Think not that I came to send peace on the earth: I came not to send peace, but a sword" (Matthew 10:34).

Victory Assured

However, as has already been noted in a previous chapter, victory for the Lord's church is assured from the book of Revelation. "These shall war against the Lamb, and the Lamb shall overcome them, for he is Lord of lords, and King of kings; and they also shall overcome that are with him, called and chosen and faithful" (Revelation 17:14). How will the faithful overcome? "And they overcame him because of the blood of the Lamb, and because of the word of their testimony; and they loved not their life even unto death" (Revelation 12:11). Regardless of the number, whether few or many, those on the Lord's side will be on the winning side in the day of final judgment. This will be the outcome of the battle of Armageddon.

Although the second coming of Christ and the end of the world is always imminent in one sense, but "of that day and hour knoweth no one, not the angels of heaven, neither the Son, but the Father only" (Matthew 24:36). It is impossible, therefore, for any man to know from prophecy the day of the Lord's return.

The final effort to overthrow good will be followed by the one literal bodily resurrection of all mankind, when death and Hades shall give up their dead at the end of time. According to the Holy Scriptures, at the close of the millennial period evil will again exert its utmost power in a final conflict with righteousness. This will be a spiritual struggle, and like the figurative "thousand year reign of saints with Christ," that struggle will be prior to the Lord's second advent. Nevertheless, the overthrow of Satan and all of his agencies is guaranteed. In this Christians can rejoice.

The seat of the church after the millennium, after the battle of Armageddon and after the second coming of Christ is not to be on the earth, but in a new heaven and a new earth. (This will be our study in a later chapter.)

So the battle of Armageddon in the Apocalypse could well be used by the Holy Spirit as a symbol for the spiritual warfare in which the saints of God are engaged. The real warfare is that which Paul speaks of in Ephesians 6:10–18. As to Gog and Magog (Revelation 20:8), John had reference to the nations in the four corners of the earth—east, west, north, and south—the entire earth, not just Russia and China. Since in Biblical times some of the bloodiest and most decisive battles were fought in the valley of Megiddo, the battle of Armageddon is best understood as an apocalyptic symbol of warfare, much like in modern times when anyone suffers a crushing defeat he is said to have met his Waterloo.

So finally the Lord's faithful ones will be victorious, and they will rejoice. This is certain. Then John tells us what at the last will happen: "And the devil that deceived them was cast into the lake of fire and brimstone, where are also the beast and the false prophet; and they shall be tormented day and night for ever and ever" (Revelation 20:10).

Then John writes of the final judgment day:

> And I saw a great white throne, and him that sat upon it, from whose face the earth and the heaven fled away: and there was found no place for them. And I saw the dead, the great and the small, standing before the throne; and books were opened: and another book was opened, which is the book of life: and the dead were judged out of the things which were written in the books, according to their works. And the sea gave up the dead that were in it; and death and Hades gave up the dead that were in them: and they were judged every man according to their works. And death and Hades were cast into the lake of fire. This is the second death, even the lake of fire. And if any was not found written in the book of life, he was cast into the lake of fire (Revelation 20:11–15).

Following this John then writes of the beautiful eternal home of the soul, heaven (Revelation 21; 22:1–5). How wonderful it will be for all the redeemed to live in that city whose builder and maker is God! Then following this description, John brings the book of Revelation to a close with a few remarks (Revelation 22:6–21).

Questions for Discussion

1. Is the battle of Armageddon to be a spiritual or literal battle?
2. What finally will happen to Satan and his allies?
3. After the final judgment what will happen to "death and Hades"?
4. Will there be any more death—separation of spirit from body—after the resurrection and judgment?
5. Is the judgment of Revelation 20:11–12 for only the wicked, or for all?
6. Does the Bible emphasize that the events of wickedness and lawlessness which led to the flood in Noah's day will also be characteristic of the world just preceding Christ's second coming? Discuss your answer in light of Genesis 6:5–7 and Matthew 24:37–44.
7. Would the expression, "He met his Waterloo," be similar to the "battle of Armageddon" as found in the Bible? How and why did this expression originate?

– 22 –

WHAT ABOUT THE JEWS?

". . . and so all Israel shall be saved"
Roman 11:26

Premillennialists usually advocate the return of the Jews to Palestine and their conversion to Christianity just prior to the Lord's coming and the end of time. Some ask: "Will all the Jews be returned to Palestine and converted to Christ before the final judgment?" There are two different ideas within this question: (1) a future restoration of the Jews to Palestine and (2) their conversion to Christianity.

The Jews Have Returned to Palestine

God promised to Abraham's seed the land of Canaan for a possession. After Abraham arrived in Canaan, the Lord said to him: "Unto thy seed will I give this land" (Genesis 12:7; cf. 13:15; 15:18; 26:3; Numbers 34:12; Deuteronomy 34:4; Acts 7:5); and the Lord kept His promise to Abraham's descendents concerning the land. After leading the people into Canaan and getting the tribes settled, Joshua, just prior to his death, said to the people of Israel: "So Jehovah gave unto Israel all the land which he sware to give unto their fathers; and they possessed it, and dwelt therein . . . There failed not ought of any good thing which Jehovah had spoken unto the house of Israel; all came to pass" (Joshua 21:43, 45; cf. 23:14; 1 Kings 4:21, 24; Nehemiah 9:7–8). So, Israel once received the land of Canaan as Jehovah promised them.

However, with the passing of the centuries Israel sinned, and ten of the twelve tribes became captives of Assyria; later the two remaining tribes were taken to Babylon as captives. The promise to remain in the land was plainly conditional (Deuteronomy 4:25–27; 28:58–66; Joshua 23:15–16). They had to obey God; but the Israelites sinned and were removed from the land (2 Kings 17:1–23; 24:1–20; 25:1–21). Yet, God promised that they would return.

There are many predictions in the Old Testament which speak of a return of the Jews to their homeland, re-establishing a nation (Jeremiah 29:1–14;

30:1–3; Ezekiel 36:24, 33; 37:15–22). Jeremiah prophesied on the eve of the Babylonian captivity and Ezekiel gave his prophecies while the Jews were in Babylon, but all of these predictions of a return of the Jews were fulfilled when they returned from their Assyrian and Babylonian captivities (Ezra 1:1–4). This took place many years before Christ's personal ministry. There are now no unfulfilled prophecies for the Jews of any future temporal blessings in Palestine, or any other country. Instead of teaching that the Jewish nation would soon be restored, Jeremiah said that the nation "cannot be made whole again" (Jeremiah 19:11). The above-mentioned promises, which premillennialists offer as supporting a present-day Jewish restoration, were given either before or during the time of Israel's captivity in Babylon. The promises refer either to that captivity and restoration, or to the gospel era (the time of the Lord's spiritual kingdom on earth), which is neither earthly nor political. The Scriptures never speak of a future earthly kingdom or a return to Palestine for the Jews with Christ as King and Palestine as a whole for their possession. The Bible does not teach a future return of the Jews to their original homeland, as some modern-day "prophets" teach. Those who misconstrue Old Testament prophecies by applying them to a far-distant future after this gospel age are unaware of the return of the Jews from Babylonian exile. The prophecies did predict a restoration, and that restoration later came to pass. Just as the Jews rejected Christ because He failed to conduct Himself and kingdom business as they had anticipated, premillennialists now are mistaken as they look forward to the fulfillment of their expectations of the establishment of an earthly kingdom, the return of the Jews to their homeland, and their conversion to Christ.

"Zionism"

The recent Zionist movement—the return of the Jews to Palestine to repopulate their country—has brought many people to Palestine, and several modern cities have been built. This, however, for a number of reasons, is not the restoration of Israel, as mentioned in the Scriptures. Even if all the Jews were taken to Palestine to live, the little country (about nine thousand square miles, about one-fourth the size of the state of Indiana) could not hold all of them. Only a small fraction of the more than sixteen million Jews in the world today could live in that small area. Too, many Jews do not want to go to Palestine to live, because the Holy Land is now a very poor country. America is the "Promised Land" to a great many Jews today. They are content to live there. The establishment of the state of Israel on May 14, 1948, was not the fulfillment of any Biblical prophecy, and it did not include all of Palestine.

Although it must be granted that there has been a degree of success to the political movement of Zionism, this is far from proof that God is miraculously restoring the Jews to Palestine while they abide still in unbelief and rebellion against Christ. Their presence in the country now means nothing insofar as national restoration is concerned. The Jews have no divine right to Palestine today, but this is a part of the premillennial theory, and they are determined to make Palestine a Jewish state. The wars in the Middle East (June, 1967, and following) have given rise to a flurry of speculations concerning Biblical prophecy—the return of the Jews, the rapture, the battle of Armageddon, and the millennium. Modern-day sensational preachers on radio and television are making false claims about all of this being the fulfillment of Old Testament prophecies about the Jews and the end of the world.

The Real Point of Issue

After all, the real question of this issue is not, "Will the Jews regain Palestine from the Gentiles?" The Lord does not care who owns the land today, whether the Jews live in Jerusalem or in Dallas, Texas, is not of concern in God's plan for Israel now. The real point has to do with the theory that Jerusalem is to be rebuilt during a millennium and then be occupied by the Jews, all converted to Christ, with the Lord on earth on a literal throne, reigning over the whole world in universal peace from the city for a thousand literal years, with the resurrected saints reigning with Him. The theory is one, however, that cannot be proved by any correct interpretation of the Holy Scriptures.

Spiritual Restoration Is Now

Premillennialists misunderstand Acts 3:21: "Whom the heaven must receive until the times of restoration of all things, whereof God spake by the mouth of his holy prophets that have been from of old." Peter here was speaking of Christ shortly after Pentecost, after Christ had returned to heaven and the church had been established. He affirmed that the heaven must receive (i.e., retain) Him until all things were restored.

The "restoration"—whatever it contemplates—must be accomplished while Christ is in heaven. This idea was contrary to the ideas of the Jewish people, just as it is to the ideas of premillennialists now. On the other hand, there is to be no restitution to absolute sinlessness as in the Garden of Eden. The restoration of Acts 3:21 is spiritual in nature and has been going on since Peter preached the sermon on Pentecost (Acts 2), and will continue to the end of time. Since it is a moral and spiritual restoration unto God, it is accomplished by the power of the gospel (Romans 1:16). Some of the "all things" had been fulfilled and were then being fulfilled at the very time Peter said the words of Acts 3:21. Christ was then in heaven, and heaven is to receive or retain Him until the end, until all that the prophets have spoken—although not until all that some have speculated—have been fulfilled. He "shall appear a second time, apart from sin [i.e., a sin offering] to them that wait for him, unto salvation" (Hebrews

9:28). This also agrees with the statement in Hebrews 10:12–13, which says that Christ is now in heaven "on the right hand of God; henceforth expecting [i.e., waiting] till his enemies be made the footstool of his feet" (cf. Psalm 110:1). His second coming marks the end of that period.

The "Regeneration" Is Now

"And Jesus said unto them, Verily I say unto you, that ye who have followed me, in the regeneration when the Son of man shall sit on the throne of his glory, ye also shall sit upon twelve thrones, judging the twelve tribes of Israel" (Matthew 19:28). The regeneration is during the Christian dispensation.

If the millennium is a part of the restoration, then it must come and go before Jesus leaves heaven. Heaven must receive (or retain) Him until all is accomplished; He must reign till He hath put all enemies under His feet, and the last enemy that shall be destroyed is death. This is clearly stated by Paul:

> For since by man came death, by man came also the resurrection of the dead. For as in Adam all die, so also in Christ shall all be made alive. But each in his own order: Christ the firstfruits; then they that are Christ's, at his coming. Then cometh the end, when he shall deliver up the kingdom to God, even the Father; when he shall have abolished all rule and all authority and power. For he must reign, till he hath put all his enemies under his feet. The last enemy that shall be abolished is death (1 Corinthians 15:21–26).

Premillennialists would have Christ return to make the restoration predicted, but the regeneration with the apostles on thrones is now in progress (Matthew 19:28). This is the time when men are being regenerated (born anew) (John 3:3, 5; Titus 3:4–7). Christ will never set foot on earth again. At His coming the earth will be burned up (2 Peter 3:10), the righteous and the wicked raised (John 5:28–29), and all will be judged and assigned their eternal destiny (Matthew 25:31–46).

Furthermore, Peter's statement in Acts 3:19 teaches that the enjoyment of "times of refreshing" from God's presence is inseparably connected with man's obedience to God. Christ's return to God gives the Christian these spiritual blessings. The future hope of the Christian is not some place in Palestine or in some universal, political kingdom of this world. According to Peter in his first epistle to the saints, the child of God can look forward to "an inheritance incorruptible, and undefiled, and that fadeth not away, reserved in heaven for you" (1 Peter 1:4). "In heaven" is not the same as "in Palestine." The Christian is in hope of eternal life (Titus 1:2).

Many Jews Have Been Converted to Christ

Since the beginning of the Lord's church on the day of Pentecost (Acts 2), the word has been preached to the Jews, and many of them have obeyed the gospel and become Christians. The apostle Paul was an Israelite (Philippians 3:4–7; Romans 11:1), and he earnestly desired the salvation of his own Jewish brethren of the flesh (Romans 9:1–5; 10:1–3).

God loves the whole world (John 3:16) and sent Christ to die for all mankind (Hebrews 2:9). His blessings of salvation are for all nations, for every creature (Matthew 28:19; Mark 16:15), but all will not be saved (Matthew 7:13–14; 25:46). So the Jews may obtain salvation in Christ Jesus (2 Timothy 2:10).

> For the scripture saith, Whosoever believeth on him shall not be put to shame. For there is no distinction between Jew and Greek: for the same Lord is Lord of all, and is rich unto all that call upon him: for, Whosoever shall call upon the name of the Lord shall be saved (Romans 10:11–13).

The Lord does not want anyone to be lost (2 Peter 3:9).

Although Jews may be converted to Christ today, the Bible announces no special plan of salvation for the Jews in this present gospel age. God no longer deals with them as a chosen people, but as individuals to whom salvation is offered by faith in Christ. The Lord is not now preventing the Jews from being converted to Christianity in order to punish them for the murder of Christ.

True Israelites Today

Contrary to the belief of many, God's children in this Christian Age are not fleshly Israelites, but spiritual Israelites, regardless of race or color—that is, Christians. The children of God today are all those—Jew and Gentile—who have been born anew of water and the Spirit (John 3:3, 5; 1 Peter 1:23). God's Word teaches that man's sins are forgiven by the grace of God through faith (Ephesians 2:8) or by one's obedience to the gospel (Romans 6:16–18); that all spiritual blessings are in Christ (Ephesians 1:3); that salvation is in Christ (2 Timothy 2:10), in His name and in no one else (Acts 4:12); that Christ's way is the only way to the Father (John 14:6); and that all men must believe in Christ or be lost (John 8:24, 21). The apostles, inspired by the Holy Spirit (John 16:13), proclaimed the terms of reconciliation, and urged all men to be reconciled to God (2 Corinthians 5:17–21). Both Jew and Gentile are reconciled to God in Christ, in the church (Ephesians 2:12–16); 1:22, 23). The saved are added by the Lord to the church (Acts 2:38, 41, 47; Mark 16:16). Acts 2:38 is a parallel to Acts 3:19. All who thus obeyed the Lord in the first century were saved, made Christians, and added to God's spiritual family, the church. The same is true today; the Lord has no other plan.

Paul made clear who the true Israelites today are when he said: "For he is not a Jew who is one outwardly . . . but he is a Jew who is one inwardly" (Romans 2:28–29). Again,

> For ye are all sons of God, through faith, in Christ Jesus. For as many of you as were baptized into Christ hath put on Christ. There can be neither Jew nor Greek, there can be neither bond nor free, there can be no male and female; for ye all are one man in Christ Jesus. And if ye are Christ's, then are ye Abraham's seed, heirs according to promise (Galatians 3:26–29).

In this present Christian dispensation national distinction plays no part in a person's acceptance by the Lord, but faith and obedience. According to the New Testament, it is taught in simple, unmistakable language that believers in Christ are the seed of Abraham. They are the true Israel of God, spiritual Jews in this sense. The fleshly Jews are no longer God's chosen people, rather Christians are the true offspring of Abraham. Today the Lord's people are not limited by geography, race, or culture; Jew and Gentile alike—that is, men of all nations—can find common ground in God's family, His universal kingdom or church.

Paul, in writing to the Philippians, identified the house of Israel today when he said: "For we are the circumcision [i.e., Israel of God], who worship by the Spirit of God, and glory in Christ Jesus, and have no confidence in the flesh" (Philippians 3:3). Again, to the Romans: "For they are not all Israel, that are of Israel: neither, because they are Abraham's seed, are they all children" (Romans 9:6–7). Christians are now the only true Israel of God that there is. "Know therefore that they that are of faith, the same are the sons of Abraham" (Galatians 3:7). So, not all of the fleshly Jews are of the true spiritual Israel of God today; spiritual Israel does not embrace all Israelites of the flesh. However, God did not cast off the Jews because they were Jews, for He saved those who accepted Christ; but they cut themselves off from God because of their unbelief (Romans 11:1–6, 20–23). Although many of the Jews obeyed the gospel and became Christians, it was but a remnant that obeyed in comparison with the entire nation. The true spiritual nation today is composed of both Jews and Gentiles who have been born again. They are the true seed of Abraham and heirs.

Are the Jews—who deny Christ—a holy nation today? Are they the chosen people of God? The Jews who deny Christ as their Messiah are not a holy nation. They are not now the chosen people. The unbelieving Jew is no Israelite in any Scriptural sense. Now God's Israel consists of all believers in Christ. The true Israel of God today is the whole body of God's redeemed people—composed of the election (the remnant of converted natural Jews) and believers among the Gentiles. Christians are now a holy nation, a royal priesthood (1 Peter 2:9; Revelation 1:5–6). These only are the true spiritual seed (children) of Abraham, who inherit the promises of God.

"All Israel" Saved

Paul's statement, "and so all Israel shall be saved" (Romans 11:26), is often referred to as proof that all the Jews will finally be converted to Christianity prior to the end of time; that this is one prophecy yet to be fulfilled. Is it? The context (Romans 9, 10, and 11) shows that Paul is here describing the how (manner) the Jews would be saved—that is, by accepting Christ as the Deliverer. The word *so* in the passage is an adverb, and means in this manner, or in the way described. It answers the question, "How?" The passage says nothing at all in answer to the question, "When?" Paul did not say, "and then all Israel shall be saved," as if God planned to deal first with the Gentiles, and then after all the Gentiles have been converted, all Israel shall be saved, commencing with the Jews once more. (This would be true if the premillennial theory were true.) Paul said, "And so [in this manner or in this way and not in any other way] all Israel shall be saved," just as Paul and some of the other Israelites had been saved. The only way Israel can be saved is to accept Christ individually through a living, obedient faith. God no longer deals with the Jews as a nation. God does not extend any favors to the Jews (fleshly Israel) today, except those which He offers to the whole world, and on exactly the same terms.

Translations, Errors Taught

Often some of the new translations of the Bible or versions—more correctly, "perversions"—contain renderings that teach premillennialism. For example, The Living Bible Paraphrased has Romans 11:26 read: "And then all Israel will be saved." It changes the word *so* to *then*. This is certainly error. Likewise, The Scofield Reference Bible says: "Israel is yet to be saved nationally" (p. 1206). Even *Zerr's Commentary on the Bible* on this passage falls into the same trap by saying that this is one prophecy yet to be fulfilled before the Lord's return and the end of time.

Both the King James (Authorized) Version (1611) and the American Standard Version (1901) render this verse accurately: "so all Israel shall be saved." The word *so* in the passage, meaning in the manner described, answers the question as to how Israel is to be saved. They all will be saved "so"—and in no other way; and they must be saved before the day of gospel salvation comes to an end. In other words, Paul simply said that all the Israelites can be saved just like a few of them have already been saved.

Today any and all of the physical Israelites can come into the spiritual family of God and be saved at any time that they obey the gospel. Jews and Gentiles are saved in the same way, that is, by grace through faith (Ephesians 2:8; cf. Acts 10:34–35; 15:7–11).

Two Olive Trees

Paul showed how God can save Israel by the illustration of the wild and good olive trees (Romans 11:19–23). He said: "God is able to graft them in again"; and He will do so, "if they continue not in their unbelief." The gospel of Christ "is the power of God unto salvation to every one that believeth; to the Jew first, and also to the Greek" (Romans 1:16). Thus, the unbelieving Jews can be saved; but Scripture makes their salvation hinge entirely on their faith, the same as of other men. The word *if* in verse 23 is the same *if* that conditions the salvation of any Gentile. The salvation of the Jews is conditional just the same as that of other nationalities. God will not, through an arbitrary display of irresistible power, convert the Jews against their will. Salvation is offered to all classes and races of men on the same terms. No one can be saved without obeying the gospel; there is no other way of salvation for anyone. The Jews were cut off because of their unbelief in Christ; they rejected Him and He rejected them. The unbelieving Jews, because of unbelief, were taken from the tree of Israel (God's favor) and the believing Gentiles were grafted in. The remnant of the Jews who were saved were not chosen by the Lord after an arbitrary manner, but were all who truly believed in Christ. So now, it all depends upon their individual acceptance or rejection of Jesus Christ. The Jews may be saved today as many of them were in the first century. They can get back in covenant relationship with God, but if a Jew refuses to accept Christ, he has no hope. They are like every other man who fails to obey the Lord (Hebrews 5:9). Since God is no respecter of persons (Acts 10:34–35; cf. 15:8–9), Jews have no special place in God's plan today. Nothing now remains for the natural Israel, but promises do exist for the spiritual Israel. The gospel is the power of God for salvation to all, both Jews and Gentiles (Romans 1:16).

No Special Favors

Indeed, God will restore Israel to His favor anytime, "if they continue not in their unbelief" (Romans 11:23). The receiving of the Jews back to the favor of God must be through Christ (Ephesians 1:3; 2 Timothy 2:10) and by means of the gospel, God's only power to save (Romans 1:16).

The Bible does not teach that there will be conversions of any race when the Lord comes again on the clouds of heaven. At His coming, all opportunity for repentance will have passed. This is not to say, however, that God has forgotten the Jews (He still desires their salvation); but Scripture does not predict any national conversion of them when the Lord returns. If the Jews will believe on Christ and accept Him, individually, they will be grafted in again, the same as the Gentiles. "For there is no distinction between Jew and Greek: for the same Lord is Lord of all, and is rich unto all that call upon him" (Romans 10:12).

The "Antichrist"

Premillennialists are also very bold in affirming that near the end of time a certain world ruler will arise as the antichrist. The Bible does not teach this. By comparing 1 John 2:18; 4:3; and 2 John 7, one can observe that the antichrist is not any one specific person. At the time the apostle wrote, near the end of the first century, the antichrist was already present. "Little children, it is the last hour; and as ye heard that antichrist cometh, even now have there arisen many antichrists; whereby we know that it is the last hour" (1 John 2:18). The antichrist was one who stands in opposition to Christ. The man of sin whom Paul describes (2 Thessalonians 2:3–12) is identical with the antichrist to whom John refers. However, John does not use the term in the sense of a proper name; he speaks not of the antichrist, but of antichrists.

"Jacob's Trouble"

Premillennialists are claiming that Israel is returning to Palestine in unbelief, and that their rejection of Christ will lead the nation to make a pact with the "antichrist," who will disannul the agreement and then launch an attack against the Jews. The persecution will fulfill the time of Jacob's trouble as mentioned in Jeremiah 30:7: "Alas! for that day is great, so that none is like it: it is even the time of Jacob's trouble; but he shall be saved out of it." The return of Christ will mean the salvation of Israel and their deliverance, and then will begin the millennium with Christ ruling on David's throne in Jerusalem. From this verse they try to find proof of a return of the nation of Israel and a Scriptural basis for Zionism. But, as already observed, the captivity mentioned by Jeremiah is the Babylonian captivity, which lasted for seventy years (Jeremiah 25:11). The time of trouble of which Jeremiah speaks in Jeremiah 30:7 refers to this captivity. There is no justification in expecting any future fulfillment of the prophecy. The promise of a return does not have to do in any way with the Jews being in Palestine today. Jeremiah 30:10 was fulfilled when the remnant returned from captivity. It is false doctrine to teach that the Jews have a divine right to Palestine today.

"The Fulness of the Gentiles"

Clearly, in the Christian Age, although God has provided salvation for the Jews, He has also provided blessings for the Gentiles. Yet there are two other passages of Scripture which are often improperly applied to support the idea of Jews being saved after the Gentiles, namely, Romans 11:25 and Luke 21:24. Paul said "that a hardness in part hath befallen Israel, until the fulness of the Gentiles be come in" (Romans 11:25). But Paul did not say what would happen to the Jews after "the fulness of the Gentiles." Christ, after having foretold the destruction of Jerusalem and the dispersing of the Jews, said: "Jerusalem shall be trodden down of the Gentiles, until the fulness of the times of the Gentiles be fulfilled" (Luke 21:24). But He, too, did not say what would happen to Jerusalem after this. With that His prediction ended. He did not specify either how long that would be or what would occur to the city after that. The "times of the Gentiles" must have begun from the destruction of the city in A.D.70, for from that event to the present time, God's work has been mainly among the Gentiles. It would be false to try to make Christ say that when the times of the Gentiles are ended, near the close of the gospel age, then the Jews will be reconstructed as a nation and will repossess their ancient country, and all (or nearly all) will be converted to Christianity. It is more in harmony with total Scripture and history to say "the fulness of the Gentiles" and "the times of the Gentiles" referred to the time when the Gentile Christians gained their full freedom in Christianity by complete victory over Jewish objections and persecutions—until no Jewish prejudices effectively hindered admission of the Gentiles into the church of God. When this happened, soon after the destruction of Jerusalem, this was the fulness of the Gentiles, or the times of the Gentiles. The Gentiles then had fulness of opportunity and freedom to grow.

The times of the Gentiles then is the dispensation of the Gentiles, or the entire Christian dispensation. During this era, Gentiles have access to all God's spiritual blessings in Christ Jesus, along with the Jews. The times of the Gentiles will cease when the Christian Age ends, at the Lord's return. The hardness, or "blindness in part" (KJV), was a hardening that came to some of the Jews as punishment for sin. There were those who rejected Christ and the preaching of the apostles. The Lord's wrath fell on them in A.D.70, when their temple, city, and nation were destroyed. Although many of the Jews are still unconverted to Christianity, this is due to their individual prejudice and hardness of heart, not to a certain direct curse placed on them by the Lord. They can become the children of God by accepting Jesus as the Messiah.

The "Last Days"—The Gospel Age

Another error in this connection which should be noted has to do with the idea of the last days of time. Scripture teaches that man is now living in the last age of the world, an age which shall close to usher in eternity, and has been since Pentecost. Peter, guided by the Holy Spirit, quoted the prophet Joel on the day of Pentecost: "And it shall be in the last days . . ." (Acts 2:17), and he applied it to this Christian dispensation as the last days. Likewise, the writer of the book of Hebrews called this New Testament age "the last days" (Hebrews 1:1–2). Peter, in his first epistle, called this present gospel age "the end of the times" (1 Peter 1:20), and the apostle John called it "the last hour" (1 John 2:18). There cannot be another earthly age after this one. There is to be no millennial age with literal thrones on earth following the Christian age. The gospel dispensation is the last age. Nothing but eternity remains after the Christian era.

Christ's second coming will be at the end of the world, when time shall have run its course, in the last day of this last age of time. The destruction of the world, the resurrection of both righteous and wicked, and the judgment will occur at the end of time, at the Lord's second coming. After speaking of the second coming of Christ and the resurrection, Paul said: "Then cometh the end" (1 Corinthians 15:24). This renders a literal thousand year reign of Christ on earth an impossibility. Christ began His reign on Pentecost; He will continue this reign until the end, when He comes again, at which time He will give up the kingdom to God (1 Corinthians 15:24–26). The Lord's return, the resurrection of all the dead, and the final judgment are all connected in Scripture as occurring at the same time, and will mark the end of all opportunity of salvation, for both Jew and Gentile. At the second coming of Christ and the end of the world, the resurrection will be followed by the transformation of the living (1 Corinthians 15:51–52); and at the judgment, all will pass to their eternal destiny. How near man is to that day no one knows. But definitely, Christ will remain in heaven until "the end"—not until the beginning of an earthly reign.

Summary

The Bible is silent as to the establishment of a future earthly kingdom, the rapture, saints resurrected in body and living and reigning on earth, the return of the Jews to the land of Palestine, and the conversion of the Jewish people to Christianity. The whole millennial program is utterly void of Scripture.

When the New Testament speaks of physical Israel it never speaks of her restoration to the land of Palestine, or of her exaltation over the nations of the earth. It does speak of Israelites coming into Christ through faith (Romans 11:20–24; Galatians 3:26–28).

When God called Abraham to leave his country He made to him three promises: (1) his descendants would make a great nation; (2) a land in which this nation would live; and (3) in him all the families of the earth would be blessed (Genesis 12:1–3; cf. 18:17–18; 22:15–18; 26:2–4; 28:13–14). The third promise is the one which was the most important. The promised seed was Christ (Genesis 22:18; Galatians 3:8, 16–29). If one is in Christ (a Christian) he is one of Abraham's blessed seed (a child of Abraham), and an heir to the promise. Conversion of Jews to Christianity by the gospel has nothing to do with a restoration to the land of Palestine and the establishment of a worldwide political government wherein Jews will have the ascendancy. That which God set out to do through Abraham and through Israel, He has fulfilled, and is fulfilling now through Christ and the church.

Whatever future blessing awaits the Jew must await him in Christ, and only if he accepts Christ on the terms of the gospel. Whenever any people turn to the Lord they shall be saved, but if they continue in their unbelief they shall be lost forever.

Scholars Speak

We close this chapter by giving two quotations from Bible scholars. The first is from Albert Barnes in his comments on Acts 3:21.

> The passage means that the heavens must receive the Lord Jesus until all things spoken by the prophets in relation to his work, his reign, the spread of the gospel, the triumph of religion, etc., shall have been fulfilled.[1]

Commenting on Romans 11:25–27, the eminent Bible scholar R. L. Whiteside said:

> Paul does not reveal to us what the coming in of the fulness of the Gentiles is. What Paul does not say, some commentators and other writers fill in with their own assumptions . . . But the preposition "until" does not tell what will follow the event or events mentioned in the phrase it introduces, or governs . . . "And Samuel came no more to see Saul until the day of his death" (1 Samuel 15:35).
>
> That implies nothing as to what Samuel did after the death of Saul… As the Gentile population grew in the church, hardness among the Jews increased until the church became almost, if not entirely, Gentile in membership—until the fullness of the Gentiles came in; then the hardness among the Jews apparently became complete . . . *So* is an adverb of manner; it is here a translation of a Greek word, which means, "in this way (manner), so, under these circumstances." Paul had shown how Gentiles had been grafted into God's favor, and how the Jews, the broken-off branches, might also be grafted in again . . . all would be saved as others had been saved—salvation was open to all on the same terms. The Deliverer is Christ Jesus . . . And so, in this manner, or in this way, shall all Israel be saved.[2]

---

1 Albert Barnes, *Commentary on the New Testament, Acts* (Grand Rapids: Baker Book House, 1949), p. 70.

2 R. L. Whiteside, *Paul's Letter to the Saints at Rome* (Clifton, TX: Mrs. C. R. Nichol, 1945), pp. 240–241.

Questions for Discussion

1. Did God promise the land of Canaan to the descendents of Abraham? Did He keep His promise?
2. When did the seed of Abraham possess the land? Were they later removed from that land, and if so, why?
3. What do the prophecies of Jeremiah and Ezekiel say about the Jews returning to their homeland? Did they return?
4. Are there any Old Testament prophecies of a return of the Jews to Palestine which have not been fulfilled?
5. What is the meaning of the modern movement of Zionism? Do all Jews want to return to Palestine? Are any Biblical prophecies being fulfilled in this movement?
6. According to Acts 3:21, how long will Christ remain in heaven?
7. Does God desire the conversion of the Jews? How can they be saved?
8. How does anyone—Jew or Gentile—become a child of God in this Christian age?
9. Who are the true Israel of God today?
10. What is the meaning of "and so all Israel shall be saved"?
11. What are some of the errors taught in some of the modern "versions" of the Bible?
12. What does Paul's illustration of the two olive trees teach?
13. Why are so many Jews not Christians today? Will they be eternally lost if they fail to believe in Christ?
14. Who (what) is the "antichrist"? Has he come?
15. When will the "fulness of the Gentiles" be completed?
16. What age will follow the present gospel age? What are the "last days"?
17. Does the Bible teach that the entire Jewish nation will one day be converted to Christ? Defend your answer.
18. What were the three promises God made to Abraham? Which one was the most important? Why?
19. Discuss Romans 11:36: "In this way all Israel will be saved" (McCord's Translation).

– 23 –

WILL HELL BE ETERNAL PUNISHMENT?

"And these shall go away into eternal punishment"
Matthew 25:46

There are only two ultimate destinies for mankind, heaven (a state of rewards), and hell (a state of punishment). Final retribution begins at the last day, and not at death, nor in death. The wicked will be sent to hell (*Gehenna*), both soul and body. Jesus said, "And be not afraid of them that kill the body, but are not able to kill the soul: but rather fear him who is able to destroy both soul and body in hell" (Matthew 10:28). This is the second death (Revelation 20:14). As has been learned in this study, the separation of the soul from the body is called death. (This is physical, ordinary death.) The ultimate and final separation of the soul from God, after the judgment, is called the second death. The New Testament refers to those in this present life who are separated from God by reason of sin as "dead through your [their] trespasses and sins" (cf. Ephesians 2:1, 5; 1 Timothy 5:6).

The Final Issue of Evil

Thus, the full and final sentence of retribution will take place at judgment, immediately after the resurrection (John 5:28–29). The doctrines of heaven and hell must stand or fall together. If one believes in good and its final reward of light, he must also, if consistent, believe in evil and its final harvest of darkness.

Great Suffering in Hell

The Bible represents the final doom of the wicked as a state of great suffering. John the Baptist said of Christ, "The chaff he will burn up with unquenchable fire" (Matthew 3:12). Jesus said the sentence to the wicked at judgment would be: "Depart from me, ye cursed, into the eternal fire which is prepared for the devil and his angels" (Matthew 25:41).

Jesus made it certain that there is a hell, a real place of unending anguish. He first mentioned eternal punishment in the Sermon on the Mount. There He affirmed: "Whosoever shall say, Thou fool, shall be in danger of the hell of fire" (Matthew 5:22; cf. vv. 29–30; 7:19). He also described it in terms of exclusion, and producing sorrow: "But the sons of the kingdom shall be cast forth into the outer darkness: there shall be weeping and gnashing of teeth" (Matthew 8:12). In one parable He informed:

> As therefore the tares are gathered up and burned with fire; so shall it be in the end of the world. The Son of man shall send forth his angels, and they shall gather out of his kingdom all things that cause stumbling, and them that do iniquity, and shall cast them into the furnace of fire: there shall be the weeping and the gnashing of teeth (Matthew 13:40–42).

Again, "The angels shall come forth, and sever the wicked from among the righteous, and shall cast them into the furnace of fire: there shall be the weeping and the gnashing of teeth" (Matthew 13:49–50).

Consider this:

> And if thy hand cause thee to stumble, cut it off: it is good for thee to enter into life maimed, rather than having thy two hands to go into hell, into the unquenchable fire . . . where their worm dieth not, and the fire is not quenched (Mark 9:43–48).

Thus, eternal punishment for the wicked is a prominent doctrine of Jesus Christ Himself. He is the one with whom all opponents of this tenet are in conflict. Jesus, in His account of the final judgment, said the wicked "shall go away into eternal punishment" (Matthew 25:46). Any man who asserts that the wicked will not be punished slanders the Word of God—he preaches the doctrine of Satan! Christ could not have warned men, frequently and earnestly, against "the fire that never shall be quenched," were there no future peril to correspond fully to it. Jesus described hell as a place of endless suffering and woe, where there is eternal punishment for the wicked (cf. Matthew 22:13; 23:15, 33; 25:30). Christ did not teach that all men will finally be holy and happy.

Suffering after Death

Misery for the wicked begins immediately after death, as taught by Christ in the narrative of the rich man and Lazarus (Luke 16:19–31); but the punishment of the wicked indicated by the word *hell* (Gehenna) follows man's final sentence at the judgment. Hell is the place of torment, the lake of fire, where "the smoke of their torment goeth up for ever and ever" (Revelation 14:11). All the incorrigibly wicked and the devil, too, will be in this fire.

> And the devil that deceived them was cast into the lake of fire and brimstone, where are also the beast and the false prophet; and they shall be tormented day

> and night for ever and ever . . . And if any was not found written in the book of life, he was cast into the lake of fire (Revelation 20:10–15).

If there is not a lake of fire, how can all these be cast into it?

Eternal *(aionios)*

According to Christ, the punishment of the wicked will last as long as the happiness of the blest. The same word measures the duration of both. Hell is eternal punishment, as proved by the fact that the word *eternal* (everlasting) is from the Greek word *aionios,* an adjective which means unending, age-lasting. *Aionios* is the word used for the everlasting (eternal) happiness of the righteous in Matthew 25:46: "And these shall go away into eternal punishment: but the righteous into eternal life" (*zoen ten aionios*). Exactly the same word—*aionios,* eternal—is used by our Lord to describe the happiness of the saved and the punishment of the wicked. This teaches the endlessness of punishment of the wicked even as it describes the endless blessed life of the godly. It denotes the duration of the enjoyment in heaven and the misery in hell (cf. Mark 3:29; Revelation 19:3).

Aionios depicts the unending joys of the righteous in another statement made by Jesus: "But he shall receive a hundredfold now in this time . . . and in the world to come eternal life" (Mark 10:30). Again, "For God so loved the world, that he gave his only begotten Son, that whosoever believeth on him should not perish, but have eternal life" (John 3:16). It is the word used by the rich young ruler when he asked, "Teacher, what good thing shall I do, that I may have eternal life?" (Matthew 19:16). If *aionios* describes endless joy, it likewise describes endless punishment. The pains of the wicked in hell will be as enduring as the joys of the righteous in heaven, since the same phraseology denotes the duration of both.

Others Speak

Likewise, Paul declared: "Who [i.e., the wicked] shall suffer punishment, even eternal destruction from the face of the Lord and from the glory of his might" (2 Thessalonians 1:9). Daniel foretold: "And many of them that sleep in the dust of the earth shall awake, some to everlasting life, and some to shame and everlasting contempt" (Daniel 12:2).

In addition, both Jude and Peter referred to future punishment of transgressors. Jude in his epistle spoke of "the punishment of eternal fire," and the wicked as "wandering stars, for whom the blackness of darkness hath been reserved for ever" (Jude 7, 13). Peter said the wicked are those "for whom the blackness of darkness hath been reserved" (2 Peter 2:17). Hence, the punishment of the wicked is called "eternal," "forever"; it is spoken of as co-existent and co-eternal with the blessedness of the righteous.

Three words in the New Testament are used to express the never-ending torment of the wicked. These are *eternal, everlasting,* and *forever.* In fact, the same words that measure punishment of the lost, as observed, are used to describe the eternal or unending existence of God—"The eternal God" (Romans 16:26), "the King eternal" (1 Timothy 1:17), and "Thy throne, O God, is forever and ever" (Hebrews 1:8).

In whatever image future punishment is set forth, suffering is invariably connected with it. Eternal punishment is described as a place of darkness, a furnace of fire, a lake of fire, a banishment from the feast, a place of weeping, wailing, and gnashing of teeth, of torment forever and ever. It is impossible for one to comprehend all the horrors associated with eternal punishment.

Hell (*Gehenna*)

The Bible teaches that there is an undesirable place of pain and no relief called hell. As observed earlier in the study, *hell* is from the Greek word *Gehenna,* found twelve times in the New Testament (Matthew 5:22, 29, 30; 10:28; 18:9; 23:15, 33; Mark 9:43, 45, 47; Luke 12:5; James 3:6). It denotes the final abode of the wicked, the hell of fire. In both the King James and the American Standard versions *Gehenna* is always translated hell. (The word *Sheol* in the Old Testament, sometimes translated hell in the King James Version, does not refer to the place of eternal punishment. The same is true of Hades in the New Testament. Sheol in the Old Testament and Hades in the New, refer to the realm of disembodied spirits.) With the exception of the one time James used *Gehenna* (James 3:6), Jesus is the only one in the New Testament who used it.

"Valley of Hinnom"

Gehenna at first literally referred to a valley southeast of Jerusalem where refuse was burned continuously, sometimes called the valley of Hinnom (2 Chronicles 28:3; 33:6; Jeremiah 7:31; 19:1–5; 2 Kings 23:10–14). Symbolically, Gehenna stands for the eternal punishment of the damned. Surely Jesus did not mean that all the wicked would dwell forever in that little valley; He meant continual suffering, so fitly represented by the perpetual burning in the literal valley. That valley of Hinnom, where the refuse of Jerusalem and the corpses of criminals were burned, was literally a famous garbage dump. It contained both dry and wet material—the dry, added to daily, burned incessantly; the wet, consisting of discarded meat, rags, etc., seethed with indescribable worms. The moral character of God demands hell; and Jesus said the morally filthy and corrupt will go into this garbage dump, there "their worm dieth not, and the fire is not quenched."

The word *worm* here must surely be understood figuratively to represent the consciousness of the sinner in torment for his sins, by memory of evil deeds committed, which prey upon him like a worm. Remorse is the worm and anguish is the fire. In this figurative language Jesus simply said that hell is a place where remorse of conscience will never end and anguish of soul will never cease. Hence, Christ illustrated spiritual things by material things. The literal valley of Hinnom, a most loathsome and terrible place, was chosen to picture the endless misery in the final, everlasting abode of the damned. So Jesus used popular language to describe the valley and warn men of the terrible consequences of sin. The word *Gehenna,* regardless of its origin, as used by Christ, had no other meaning than the place of future punishment; it designated the eternal state of things after the second coming of Christ and the judgment.

In view of these facts, then, hell will not be literal fire, brimstone, and worms. Christ used figurative language. Else, how could He speak of literal fire and literal darkness? That would be contradictory. However, it will be something best represented by these, and perhaps far worse that these. So, although fire is symbolic of a real, serious spiritual thing, one must believe in the fact of punishment for sin. The word *fire* represents the intensity of suffering. The suffering will be no less than it would be were it actually a lake of fire and brimstone. The language then stands for a terrible reality, a torment of severity and Divine vengeance for the reprobate, that no description can equal. The fire spoken of in Scripture concerning the eternal torment of the damned, then, is not literal fire, nor the worm a literal worm. The finally impenitent will have no material bodies to be acted upon by elemental fire; but mental faculties will be retained. The fire depicts the internal and spiritual suffering which results from the soul's sense of wrong and from the accusations of conscience. The suffering in hell will be no less than it would be, however, were it actually a lake of fire. Surely no human language can describe the horrors that will be in hell!

Therefore, if people would think of heaven and hell less carnally, and regard these eternal states as the perfection of either an earthly life of holiness or one of sin, there would be less difficulty in understanding future rewards and punishments.

The Inhabitants of Hell

Hell was not originally intended for man, but "prepared for the devil and his angels" (Matthew 25:41), yet the occupants of hell will be the wicked of all ages. When man chooses to violate divine law, he must suffer the consequences (Ezekiel 18:20). No one can escape the final results of his misdeeds. "For ye know of a surety, that no fornicator, nor unclean person, nor covetous man, who is an idolater, hath any inheritance in the kingdom of Christ and God" (Ephesians 5:5; cf. 1 Corinthians 6:9–10). The companionship of woe is still further indicated: "But the fearful, and unbelieving, and abominable, and murderers, and fornicators, and sorcerers, and idolaters, and all liars, their part shall be in the lake that burneth with fire and brimstone; which is the second death" (Revelation 21:8). Those who became Christians but left the Lord never to return, as well as those who heard the gospel and never obeyed, will be lost in hell with the devil and his angels and all the wicked.

A Loving God

There are those who assert that a merciful and loving God, as described in the Bible, will not punish His creatures in torment forever. So, the Universalists claim that all men, good and evil, will finally be saved in heaven, that all men will finally become reconciled to God, holy, and therefore happy. They affirm that God desires the salvation of all mankind, and that His love is great for the whole world.

God does love the whole world (John 3:16). "God is love" (1 John 4:8), and He is also just (Genesis 18:25). Man must respond to God's love in order to be saved. Christ is "unto all them that obey him the author of eternal salvation" (Hebrews 5:9; cf. Matthew 7:21; Revelation 22:14). Man has the power by his own choice to reject salvation and die in his sins (John 5:40; 8:21, 24). God's wishes for people are not always accomplished, for man is a free moral agent and can refuse obedience to Jehovah. Since the Bible teaches that eternal salvation is conditional, the doctrine of Universalism has no foundation in Scripture. Sin against God is a serious matter. There is no contradiction between the love of God and the wrath of God—they must be in harmony (cf. Romans 11:22). All men are responsible to God for their conduct. If God allows eternal torment upon the wicked, His enemies, man cannot say that such is not right. The God who determines the reward of virtue ordains the punishment of evil. Sin has its reward: "For the wages of sin is death" (Romans 6:23). So, it is a "righteous thing with God to recompense affliction to them that afflict" the saints of God (2 Thessalonians 1:6). God's justice requires that sin must be punished with everlasting punishment. God's love prompts Him to warn of the direful consequences of disobedience. The Lord permits suffering in this life and in hell, and this is consistent with His nature.

One Reaps as He Sows

Men reap hell for themselves by their own wickedness. Hence, the life of sin, continued without repentance, means damnation of the soul; and God's love will not prevent it. When man flatly refuses to obey God, the Lord cannot do otherwise than let him reap the consequences of his own sinful sowing.

> Be not deceived; God is not mocked: for whatsoever a man soweth, that shall he also reap. For he that soweth unto his own flesh shall of the flesh reap

> corruption; but he that soweth unto the Spirit shall of the Spirit reap eternal life (Galatians 6:7–8).

"God is no respecter of persons" (Acts 10:34). Thus, if some are eternally lost, it will be the doom they have deliberately chosen in spite of God's warnings and entreaties to save them from it.

The Scriptures teach that eternal life and eternal death are conditional. For instance, "He that believeth on the Son hath eternal life; but he that obeyeth not the Son shall not see life, but the wrath of God abideth on him" (John 3:36). In eternity, surroundings must correspond to character. Hell is not only a place but also a condition. Many have a dislike, even loathing and hate, for the worship of God and fellowship with His children here in this world. Man's destiny in eternity will result from his character made in this life. He will go to hell of his own accord, and because he has a character suitable for that place. It is said of Judas that he went "to his own place" (Acts 1:25). So will each person.

Still as of old
Man by himself is priced.
For thirty pieces Judas sold
Himself, not Christ.

The wicked will not be forced by Jehovah into a sphere unsuited to them in eternity. A soul in love with sin can find no restful place in a holy heaven. For this reason, men will get in eternity exactly what they have made themselves fit, while living here on earth (Revelation 14:13). The quality of character will be the same after death as it was before. So the final condition of the impure and wicked is outside the heavenly city, where the holy are admitted. "Without are the dogs, and the sorcerers, and the fornicators, and the murderers, and the idolaters, and every one that loveth and maketh a lie" (Revelation 22:15).

Sin Must Be Punished

Sin is the transgression of God's law: "Sin is lawlessness" (1 John 3:4). Every law has its penalty, else it is no law. Sir William Blackstone, an expert on law, said: "Where there is no law there can be no wrong or violation." Man's freedom demands hell; law demands a penalty. Since sin must be punished, hell must exist. For example, in every free society the citizens realize that if the penalty is not going to be carried out, the law might as well be abolished. Those who break the law are punished for their crimes. God, therefore, cannot be deceived; He cannot be mocked, and man left to his own course must reap as he has sown. The penalty for sin must be carried out.

The Bible contains God's laws for man and the penalty for their violation. God cannot be just and say to the impenitent murderer or hardened traitor:

"Enter thou into the joys of heaven, even in your sins." For God to place the wicked in heaven would be to destroy a sense of reward and make obedience to His will useless. Paul declared: "For the wrath of God is revealed from heaven against all ungodliness and unrighteousness of men" (Romans 1:18). Moses, prior to his death, pleaded with his people in these words: "I have set before thee life and death, the blessing and the curse: therefore choose life" (Deuteronomy 30:19). These are still two ways opened before each individual, as Jesus taught in the Sermon on the Mount (Matthew 7:13–14), and as Joshua said to the children of Israel (Joshua 24:15). John Oxenham expressed it beautifully in these words:

> To every man there openeth
> A highway, and a low,
> And every man decideth
> Which way his soul shall go.

There are some who think that the Lord will keep His promise to the righteous but will not punish the wicked. However, Paul said: "If we are faithless, he abideth faithful; for he cannot deny himself" (2 Timothy 2:13). Regardless of what men may think, God will be faithful to do all that He has said He will do. One can believe what God has promised to the wicked the same as one can depend upon His promises to the obedient. If He fails to punish those whom He said He would punish, one has no assurance that He will bless those whom He has said He would bless. But God's Word can be depended upon; He will do what He said—to both the wicked as well as to the righteous. Finite man is incompetent to judge the penalty which sin deserves. So long as moral creatures are opposed to God and reject the offered mercy of the Savior, they deserve punishment.

Payday Someday

Every transgressor of God's law has been warned of a final payday. All of God's accounts are not settled in October, like the farmers. Jesus will one day come with His angels to judge and avenge:

> Behold, the Lord came with ten thousands of his holy ones, to execute judgment upon all, and to convict all the ungodly of all their works of ungodliness which they have ungodly wrought, and of all the hard things which ungodly sinners have spoken against him (Jude 14–15).

He will come and render "vengeance to them that know not God, and to them that obey not the gospel of our Lord Jesus: who shall suffer punishment, even eternal destruction from the face of the Lord and from the glory of his might" (2 Thessalonians 1:7–9).

However, the Bible teaches that God was longsuffering in the days of Noah while the ark was being prepared (1 Peter 3:20). God is still longsuffering in giving men time to repent before He destroys the world by fire (2 Peter 3:9–10). Payday will come someday.

The Fear of Hell

The Lord intended the fear of hell to keep people from plunging into sin (Romans 2:4–5). The emphasis on the future, everlasting punishment of the wicked brings home to man the woe and fear of hell. Although not the only or highest motive for morality and obedience to God, this teaching has helped to restrain evil and provoke submission to the Lord. Some today need to smell the sulphurous flames of hell to be shocked into a realization of the heinousness of sin and the reality of its punishment. God would have "all men to be saved, and come to the knowledge of the truth" (1 Timothy 2:4). The Lord is "longsuffering to you-ward, not willing that any should perish, but that all should come to repentance" (2 Peter 3:9). However, if one is determined to go to hell, God will not stop him; He will only plead with him through the Scriptures to repent and live. If any man will meet the Lord's terms of salvation, offered by His mercy and proclaimed in the gospel, he can escape the eternal fires of torment.

Degrees of Punishment?

Will all lost souls suffer equally in torment? This question of whether there will be degrees of punishment in hell has been discussed pro and con over the years. This is not an idle question. Notice now some statements of Scripture which teach that there will be different degrees of punishment in the final state.

1. Each person will be rewarded according to his works. The misery of the future world is always represented in the Scriptures in the way of direct result and consequence of this life; the one is necessary to the other. This life and the future life are connected like cause and effect—like sowing and reaping (cf. Romans 2:5–11; 2 Corinthians 5:10; Galatians 6:7–8; 2 Timothy 4:14). God "will render to every man according to his works" (Romans 2:6). Man at death is unclothed of the mortal, and in the resurrection he is clothed with the immortal body; but he will still be the same being—retaining the consciousness of all that he participated in while here on this earth.

> The tissue of the life to be
> We weave with colors all our own,
> And in the field of destiny
> We reap as we have sown.
> —John Greenleaf Whittier

The wicked are going to be judged "according to their works" (Matthew 16:27; Revelation 20:12). The Lord will give to every man "according as his work shall be" (Revelation 22:12). Just as sinners on earth are not equal in character, neither will they be in hell.

2. Jesus talked about greater condemnation. In His last public discourse in the temple, Jesus denounced the scribes and Pharisees for pretense in making long prayers, and added: "They that devour widows' houses, and for a pretense make long prayers; these shall receive greater condemnation" (Mark 12:40; Luke 20:47).

The word *greater* is comparative. Greater condemnation means severer punishment. There is a difference in not knowing God's law and in knowing the law and not obeying it (cf. Acts 17:30). This distinction of sins was also in the Mosaic law; there were some sins called sins of ignorance and some called sins of presumption (Numbers 15:27–36). Degrees of punishment, due to greater or lesser opportunities to know the truth, were also suggested by Christ in His analogy of the two servants:

> And that servant, who knew his lord's will, and made not ready, nor did according to his will, shall be beaten with many stripes; but he that knew not, and did things worthy of stripes, shall be beaten with few stripes (Luke 12:47–48).

Again, Jesus, in speaking of the opportunities of those who heard Him preach and of those who had lived in ancient times, said: "It shall be more tolerable for the land of Sodom and Gomorrah in the day of judgment, than for that city [that refuses to listen to His messengers]" (Matthew 10:15). Still further:

> Then began he to upbraid the cities wherein most of his mighty works were done, because they repented not. Woe unto thee, Chorazin! woe unto thee, Bethsaida! for if the mighty works had been done in Tyre and Sidon which were done in you, they would have repented long ago in sackcloth and ashes. But I say unto you, it shall be more tolerable for Tyre and Sidon in the day of judgment, than for you. And thou, Capernaum, shalt thou be exalted unto heaven? thou shalt go down unto Hades: for if the mighty works had been done in Sodom which were done in thee, it would have remained unto this day. But I say unto you that it shall be more tolerable for the land of Sodom in the day of judgment, than for thee (Matthew 11:20–24).

The phrase *more tolerable* means "more easily borne." The truth taught here is that highly favored people will be punished accordingly if they abuse their privileges. Hence, there must be degrees or grades of woe in hell, depending upon the life lived and the opportunities neglected.

Christ said to Pilate, while on trial: "He that delivered me unto thee hath greater sin" (John 19:11). There will be a difference among those who will stand condemned at the judgment. It shall be more tolerable for some than for others. In eternity, each man will be punished exactly as his conduct on earth merits by the all-wise, merciful, and just Judge. Hence, the Scriptures indicate that diverse degrees of severity of punishment will be proportioned to the aggravation of guilt. But to think one can live a wicked life all of his physical existence and never repent, and the most that he would have to fear would be physical annihilation is a false comfort.

How Long Eternity?

Eternity, like God Himself, cannot be fully measured nor comprehended by man. Time from creation to the end of the world is but a fragment of eternity, a break between eternity past and eternity future. Soon—God only knows when—time will be no more, and only eternity will remain.

Every living person today is very near eternity. How sad for anyone to be lost forever!

Questions for Discussion

1. What are the options men have in choosing a final destiny?
2. What, according to Scripture, is the final destiny of the wicked?
3. How is the suffering in hell described in Scripture?
4. Why do some want to think that the Bible is not speaking the truth in regard to hell?
5. What does the Greek word *aionios* mean? Define eternal punishment.
6. What does *Gehenna* mean as used in the New Testament? How did the word originate? Why did Christ use it?
7. Who will be the inhabitants of hell?
8. Is the love of God for man inconsistent with eternal punishment?
9. Is hell a place? a condition? or both?
10. Must every law have its penalty? What is the law of sowing and reaping?
11. Would the wicked enjoy heaven if they should go there?
12. How does each man decide where he will dwell in eternity?
13. Why is it a righteous thing with God for the wicked to suffer forever?
14. Does God desire that any person go to hell? What is the doctrine of Universalism?
15. How should the fear of hell affect man's life on earth?
16. Does the Bible teach that there will be different degrees of suffering in hell? If so, on what basis?
17. On what basis will all be rewarded or punished? Can two people be in the same place and yet not be equally affected?
18. Will death work a change in the sinner's character?
19. Why cannot man fully comprehend eternity? In what sense are all who now live near eternity?

– 24 –

WILL THE WICKED BE ANNIHILATED?

". . . and the day that cometh shall burn them up"
Malachi 4:1

Hell does not mean instantaneous annihilation or absolute extinction of the impenitent wicked. Annihilationists believe those in Christ will be saved and become immortal, but the wicked will cease to be (be annihilated) both in body and spirit at the resurrection and judgment. According to them, this is the meaning of the second death (Revelation 2:11; 20:6, 14; 21:8). To them, there will be no endless misery of the wicked; but this is not the meaning of the "eternal punishment" of the Bible.

When Jesus comes again, He will raise the dead, both the just and the unjust. At this time all mankind will be summoned before His judgment-seat, the righteous will inherit eternal life, the wicked shall go away into everlasting punishment (Matthew 25:31–46; 2 Thessalonians 1:7–9; 2 Peter 2:17; Jude 13).

Theory of Annihilationism False

The theory of annihilation (although comforting to the wicked) must be rejected as false, for a number of reasons.

Death Not Non-Existence

First, annihilationists are wrong in their definition of the second death. They define death as mere non-existence, and the second death as a second non-existence, a total extinction of being.

As observed already in this study, there is no ground in the Bible for the utter destruction of personality or for conditional immortality. Certainly, if a person ceases to exist at the judgment, he would cease suffering in eternity. But the Scriptures do not teach that death is mere non-existence. *Death* means separation, physical or spiritual. The decree, "For in the day that thou eatest thereof thou shalt surely die" (Genesis 2:17), did not mean that Adam and Eve would die sooner or later—the bodies at the end of life on earth and the souls at the judgment. The death threatened was spiritual, a loss of God's favor; and it fell upon the transgressors that day, as God said. But Adam did not become extinct on that day (cf. Genesis 5:5).

Similarly, in the Scriptures *life* and *eternal life* mean more than mere existence. The terms *life* and *death* are used metaphorically in the Bible to indicate conditions of existence. Eternal life is an eternal existence in a right relationship with God; eternal death is an eternal existence without the blessings of eternal life. Thus, eternal life is not a synonym for immortality; it is a "gift of God" to those who already have a conscious, eternal existence; it does not mean endless existence, and it can never be possessed by the wicked. "For the wages of sin is death; but the free gift of God is eternal life in Christ Jesus our Lord" (Romans 6:23).

As eternal life is assured the faithful, so the opposite, eternal death, is the inevitable, continuing destiny of the disobedient. Remember that death means separation, and the theory of annihilation vanishes. Whether figuratively or literally used, this aspect of the word is always dominant. Literal death involves separation of the soul and body; figuratively, death involves the separation of the individual from God, and the second death means eternal separation from the fullness of joy which those in possession of eternal life experience in heaven. In the New Testament eternal life never suggests mere existence, but always relates to the joy associated with God and all the redeemed. So the opposite, eternal death, never denotes mere non-existence; but it refers always to separation from God and the loss of heaven, and all that it means. Jesus said that in the day of judgment He will say to some, "Depart from me, ye that work iniquity" (Matthew 7:23). So, separation from Christ will be part of the eternal punishment. As eternal life is synonymous with unending happiness, so eternal death denotes ceaseless misery. Concerning the wicked, it is written: "And the devil that deceived them was cast into the lake of fire and brimstone, where are also the beast and false prophet; and they shall be tormented day and night for ever and ever" (Revelation 20:10). Again, "And the smoke of their torment goeth up for ever and ever; and they have no rest day and night" (Revelation 14:11). This is the lake into which Satan shall be cast with all of God's foes. If one substitutes the materialist's meaning of the words *life* and *death* in the Scriptures, the reading does not make good sense and is contradictory.

Man's exit from this world in physical death is not extinction. He leaves either in a saved or a lost condition. The penalty prescribed for those dying in sin is the second death, but this refers to a certain condition of everlasting existence, a circumstance of being, never non-existence. The second death, therefore, is a symbolical way of speaking of eternal punishment; it does not mean eternal non-existence.

Since only the body dies in a literal sense, death of the soul in hell can be affirmed only in a moral and figurative sense. In this sense, the second death is existence in the lake of fire and brimstone forever and ever: "And death and Hades were cast into the lake of fire. This [i.e., existing in the lake of fire] is the second death, even the lake of fire" (Revelation 20:14). However, God says to the Christian, "He that overcometh shall not be hurt of the second death" (Revelation 2:11). There is no intimation, therefore, in any passage of Scripture that anyone ceases to exist in the lake of fire and brimstone. Rather, existing in the lake forever is the second death: they were "cast alive into the lake of fire that burneth with brimstone" (Revelation 19:20). This is the sinner's final, eternal separation from God, who

> will render to every man according to his works: to them that by patience in well-doing seek for glory and honor and incorruption, [He will render] eternal life: but unto them that are factious, and obey not the truth, but obey unrighteousness, shall be wrath and indignation, tribulation and anguish, [and this will be] upon every soul of man that worketh evil, of the Jew first, and also of the Greek; but glory and honor and peace to every man that worketh good, to the Jew first, and also to the Greek: for there is no respect of persons with God (Romans 2:6–11).

In this passage, the culmination of eternal life is glory, honor, and incorruption; while eternal death is indignation, wrath, tribulation, and anguish. God will not forever pour out wrath and indignation upon an extinct object. Tribulation and anguish cannot be felt by a non-entity. Eternal death is the doom of the wicked, and the adjuncts of that death are said by Paul to be "wrath and indignation, tribulation and anguish."

"Inherit the Kingdom"

The expression, "inherit the kingdom," found often in the New Testament, is a parallel to receiving eternal life. For instance, at the final judgment, the righteous will inherit the kingdom (Matthew 25:34), or go "into eternal life" (v. 46), a place of joy and happiness. Similarly, the second death meted out to sinners will be the lake of fire and brimstone. This is not extinction, but continuous and endless suffering.

"Eternal Punishment"

The second reason why the annihilationist is wrong is in his misinterpretation of the meaning of *punishment*. The idea of punishment suggests suffering while there is a living being to feel it. Punishment implies conscious existence; it is the penalty for wrong doing, and it can be inflicted only where there is capacity for feeling pain, either mental or physical. To speak of punishing a house or rock is nonsense. Pain and suffering implies a conscious subject; and if the person does not exist, he cannot be punished. The individual, therefore, must exist in a conscious state to be punished. So everlasting punishment must be endless conscious suffering. An annihilated person would experience no suffering beyond the moment of extinction, for if there is no eternal person there can be no eternal punishment. Annihilationists cannot avoid the obvious Scriptural meaning of *aionios, eternal,* or *everlasting,* which describes both the joys of the righteous and the torments of the wicked. No one argues that the blessedness of the righteous will cease after a term of years, because the Bible declares it is eternal. In addition, Christ taught that the punishment of the wicked is eternal. If the sufferings of the lost are not unending, the Scriptures are in error.

Annihilationists say that the eternal or punishing part is the sinner's non-existence, because it is a punishment of which the effect continues forever. They are in error, for obviously the word eternal does not mean final, but everlasting. The person exists as long as the punishment continues, and that is forever. Since the punishment, according to the Scriptures, is eternal, there can be no eternal punishment in the absence of eternal conscious existence. Since the punishment is to last forever, the one tormented in hell must consciously suffer forever. In view of this fact, it becomes evident that souls in hell will have unending conscious misery, remorse, and despair. Materialists are wrong in their definition of eternal punishment, since consciousness is an essential element of torment . . . and the punishment is everlasting.

Both Heaven and Hell Eternal

Both places—hell and heaven—are alike described as permanent states or conditions. Enjoying eternal life or suffering eternal death demands conscious existence. Suppose the wicked should cease to exist, what would become of the place into which they were sent? The place of punishment and the punishment cannot continue when those who have entered into it have ceased to exist. The eternal life does not end in extinction of being, but the Lord affirmed that the misery of the wicked will be as durable as the joys of the righteous. Jesus said of the people who will be sentenced at the judgment: "And these [the wicked] shall go away into eternal punishment: but the righteous into eternal life" (Matthew 25:46).

Degrees of Punishment

Third, the annihilationists are wrong, for there are degrees of punishment. If annihilation of the sinner at the judgment were the penalty for sin, then the punishment of all will be precisely alike. However, Scripture never uses the expression of *annihilation* as the fate for the sinner to escape. There is not a warning or admonition in all the Bible to provoke faith in Christ by the threat of annihilation. If the second death were annihilation, then every description of that death should indicate freedom from all suffering by termination of all existence. There could be no weeping and wailing and gnashing of teeth from those who have been annihilated. If annihilation were the punishment, then the wicked have very little to fear after the judgment.

Annihilated Twice?

Fourth, according to annihilationists there is no difference between the state of the sinner at physical death and after the resurrection. If spirits are blotted out of existence at death, reproduced at the resurrection of the body, then sent back into non-existence, they suffer exactly the same penalty before as after the resurrection. The theory involves the difficulty of making the wicked become nothing twice, for they are brought from non-existence, then go back into and remain in non-existence forever. It seems foolish to annihilate wicked men once, then bring them back into existence at the judgment for a second annihilation.

Too, if death means becoming non-existent, and punishment is simply annihilation, then martyrs who suffered death by fire or sword experienced the same suffering as that which awaits the wicked at the judgment.

Righteous Punished?

Fifth, annihilationists falsely consign the righteous to the same non-existence from death to the resurrection, as will be the lot of the wicked after the last day. The theory demands that the souls of the righteous become extinct with the death of the body, and this is all that the souls of the wicked are said to suffer after the final judgment.

Encourages Unrighteous Living

The sixth reason the system of annihilation is erroneous is that if it were true, then bad men would have the additional encouragement of a doctrine that closes their responsibility. The results would surely be that sinners would lead corrupt lives, knowing that later they would cease to be. Evil men have always liked this doctrine.

The ancient Epicureans believed in no future life. Their maxim was, "Let us eat and drink, for tomorrow we die" (1 Corinthians 15:32). If such be the moral influence of the doctrine of no resurrection and future life, the same would be the effect of the doctrine of a resurrection only to be annihilated.

With reference to Judas, Christ implied that the terrible doom awaiting him was so bad it would have been better if he had never been born than to encounter it (Matthew 26:24). However, if Judas is to be annihilated at the judgment, this would simply restore things as they were before he was born; but according to Christ's statement, his fate will be much worse than annihilation or non-existence.

In harmony with this thought, the writer of the book of Hebrews warned of a much sorer [graver] punishment than physical death for those who would tread under foot the Son of God and count His blood an unholy thing and do despite to the Holy Spirit (Hebrews 10:28–29). Yet if death of the body is extinction of being, and this is the exact penalty for the wicked after they are raised and judged, then there is no sorer punishment than physical death. However, since Jesus said God was able to "destroy both soul and body in hell" (Matthew 10:28), final punishment is obviously much worse than physical death. Christ also taught a fate worse than physical death, even if that death be most horrible, when He said if one should cause "one of these little ones that believe on me to stumble, it is profitable for him that a great millstone should be hanged about his neck, and that he should be sunk in the depth of the sea" (Matthew 18:6). Physical death, then, is not worthy of comparison with the doom after death. But according to the Bible, for the wicked there will be a more terrible death—the second death, the damnation of the soul and body in hell *(Gehenna)*—everlasting punishment.

Wicked Burned Up

Seventh, the annihilationists are in error when they speak of the wicked being burned up as meaning put out of existence. Annihilationists think of God's vengeance as a literal wood fire, and the soul as combustible material. Man is a spirit, and God's wrath does not decompose a spirit in order to punish it. A law of the universe says literal burning annihilates nothing, but merely changes its elemental form and it continues to exist.

The passage of Scripture most used by annihilationists to argue for the burning up of the wicked is from Malachi:

> For, behold, the day cometh, it burneth as a furnace; and all the proud, and all that work wickedness, shall be stubble; and the day that cometh shall burn them up, saith Jehovah of hosts, that it shall leave them neither root nor branch . . . And ye shall tread down the wicked; for they shall be ashes under the soles of your feet in that day that I make, saith Jehovah of hosts (Malachi 4:1–3).

This is a prophecy concerning the first coming of Christ. The burning up could have related to the destruction of Jerusalem in A.D.70 and to those who had rejected Christ's personal ministry. The Romans trod down the wicked people, the wicked place, set fire to the temple, and trod the ashes thereof under their feet. The righteous, following instructions, escaped this destruction; but unbelievers were slaughtered in great numbers, and their city, Jerusalem, was laid waste. All of this was described in symbolic language by the prophet Malachi. There was no extinction of immortal spirits.

The last two verses of the chapter read:

> Behold, I will send you Elijah the prophet before the great and dreadful day of Jehovah come. And he shall turn the heart of the fathers to the children, and the heart of the children to their fathers; lest I come and smite the earth with a curse (Malachi 4:5–6).

This Elijah who was to come was none other than John the Baptist. Gabriel said of him before his birth:

> And he shall go before his face [i.e., the Messiah, Christ] in the spirit and power of Elijah, to turn the hearts of the fathers to the children, and the disobedient to walk in the wisdom of the just; to make ready for the Lord a people prepared for him (Luke 1:17).

Moreover, Jesus said of John: "This is Elijah, that is to come" (Matthew 11:14; cf. Mark 9:11–13). John the Baptist was Elijah, and he was sent "before the coming of the great and dreadful day of the Lord." Christ visited His chosen people with sore judgments. He made Mount Zion a perpetual desolation. Christ "burned up" the proud Jews who did wickedly when he spoke terror by condemning their lives and false teaching, which was finally culminated in the destruction of Jerusalem and the Jewish nation by the Romans.

It is evident, therefore, that this burning up of the wicked, an idea upon which annihilationists depend so much, falls short of annihilation of anything, and has absolutely no reference whatever to the final destruction of the wicked. Figures of speech were used to describe both the coming and work of John the Baptist and the Messiah.

Other Figures of Speech

Finally, annihilationists incorrectly use other Biblical terms, as *hewn down, devoured, consumed, destroyed, perish, cut off, damned,* and *lost* to support their theory. None of these words denote annihilation. The sheep, for example, in the Lord's parable, was lost, but had not ceased to exist (Luke 15:3–7). Jesus came to save the lost, but those He came to redeem had not ceased to exist; they were away from God in their sins (Luke 19:10). *Destruction* and *annihilation* are two different words. Destruction occurs when something has been laid waste or seriously injured (cf. Exodus 10:7). For instance, a city is laid waste or destroyed by a tornado, but this does not mean the people and town were annihilated. *Destroy* never means to annihilate (cf. Job 19:10; Hosea 4:6; Romans 14:15; Hebrews 2:14).

If *perish* means to go out of existence, then both the wicked and the righteous shall be annihilated: "The righteous perisheth, and no man layeth it to heart" (Isaiah 57:1; cf. Micah 7:2). The wicked shall perish—be condemned and sent away into eternal punishment. Their existence, like the world which perished by the flood (2 Peter 3:6), shall continue to exist forever. Moses warned Israel that if she sinned she would utterly perish from off the land (Deuteronomy 4:26), but by that he did not mean the people would suffer annihilation. On the contrary, they were to be scattered among the nations about them. Although ruin and destruction would be theirs, they would continue to exist among the heathen.

In John 3:16, the fate of those who do not believe in Christ is described as perishing, the alternate to possessing eternal life. The word *consume* does not mean annihilation (cf. Ezekiel 13:14). Surely David did not think the jealous King Saul would annihilate him when he said: "I shall now perish [be consumed KJV] one day by the hand of Saul" (1 Samuel 27:1; cf. Psalm 6:7; 31:10). In admonishing Christians to dwell together in brotherly love, the apostle Paul said: "But if ye bite and devour one another, take heed that ye be not consumed one of another" (Galatians 5:15). He did not mean that Christians by quarreling would annihilate each other. So *perish* means the same as *lost* (cf. 1 Samuel 9:3, 20), ruined, dispersed, laid waste, destroyed, or consumed.

Eternal Punishment after Judgment

Punishment of the wicked is not annihilation but positive and conscious suffering which shall never end (Matthew 13:42, 50; 18:8; 22:13; Mark 9:43–48). When Jesus separates the wicked from the righteous at the day of final judgment, "these [the wicked] shall go away into eternal punishment: but the righteous into eternal life" (Matthew 25:46). Future everlasting punishment for the wicked is taught by the prophet Daniel: "And many of them that sleep in the dust of the earth shall awake, some to everlasting life, and some to shame and everlasting contempt" (Daniel 12:2).

Nevertheless, in the theory of annihilationism there is no pain, no suffering, no shame or everlasting contempt; the wicked simply die again—cease to be (exist) the second time. Sin and everlasting punishment are light affairs in such a system. Regardless of what a person would like to believe, the Scriptures describe for the wicked a condition of separation hereafter from Christ and the holy. The wicked will be excluded from the joys of heaven, and have companionship with only the wicked in their woes.

Way of Escape Provided

Although hell exists, there is no necessity for anyone's going there. God offers pardon to all, and is not willing that any should perish (2 Peter 3:9).

Through the mercy of God, in Christ sins and transgressions which have been committed can be forgiven (Ephesians 2:8–9; Acts 2:38; Mark 16:15–16); but all who die in willful disobedience to the gospel of Christ shall suffer endless punishment (2 Thessalonians 1:7–9). God cannot save a man against that person's will. God will not do for man what he can do for himself. The Lord has made it possible for all men to be saved, but salvation also depends upon man's willingness to be saved. The universal invitation of the Lord is: "He that will, let him take the water of life freely" (Revelation 22:17); no one is excluded. So, if a person is lost eternally, that does not mean that God ordained it thus to be. It will be because that person failed to place himself within the scope of God's redemption, by yielding to His will.

God has done everything possible to prevent man from suffering forever in torment. He takes no pleasure in the plight of those who reject His mercy. "As I live, saith the Lord Jehovah, I have no pleasure in the death of the wicked; but that the wicked turn from his way and live: turn ye, turn ye from your evil ways; for why will ye die?" (Ezekiel 33:11).

In the last two chapters the three "r's" of hell have been noted: (1) The *reality* of hell; (2) the *residents* of hell; and (3) the *redemption* God has provided through Christ to escape hell.

Questions for Discussion

1. What is the theory of annihilation concerning eternal punishment?
2. What is the Biblical definition of death? the "second death"?
3. How do annihilationists err in their definition of death?
4. Who is the only competent witness as to the punishment of the wicked?
5. What is the Biblical meaning of "eternal life"?
6. Does punishment of a person necessarily imply conscious existence?
7. What is the meaning of "eternal (everlasting) punishment"? Does the word *eternal* describe the conscious existence of the person who endures the punishment?
8. Does the Bible ever speak of a person's being annihilated?
9. Can there be degrees of punishment in annihilation?
10. If death means annihilation, how can a person be annihilated twice? How could the righteous be annihilated?
11. How does the theory of annihilation encourage sinful living?
12. What can God do with both soul and body?
13. How and when was Malachi's prophecy (3:1–2; 4:1) fulfilled?
14. Define *lost, damned, perish,* and *consumed,* as used in the Scriptures? Do the words mean annihilation?
15. How may one escape the punishment of everlasting torment?
16. Does God desire that anyone be eternally lost in hell?
17. What has the infinite mercy of God provided for every man through Jesus Christ? If any person is lost, whose fault will it be?
18. Discuss (1) the reality of hell; (2) the residents of hell; (3) the redemption God has provided to escape hell. Review each one of these points.
19. What is the last word in the Old Testament?
20. Matthew Henry in his commentary on Malachi, among other things, said regarding verse 4:11, "Now this was fulfilled (1) when Christ, in his doctrine, spoke terror and condemnation to the proud Pharisees and the other Jews that did wickedly . . . (2) when Jerusalem was destroyed by the Romans . . ." (Vol. IV, p. 1502). What do you think of this explanation?

–25–

Will Any Infants Be Lost?

". . . for to such belongeth the kingdom of heaven"
Matthew 19:14

In recent years, medical science has resulted in improvement of health and lengthened life-span for man in the Western world. Now, a larger percentage of mankind attains the age of maturity. Nevertheless, people ask, "What happens to the souls of those who die in infancy; will they be saved in heaven or lost in hell?"

Not Born in Sin

The theory of original sin is that children are born with the taint of Adam's sin through inheritance; and because of this depravity, all infants should be baptized. Infants are not born with sin. God's Old Testament prophet Ezekiel made this very clear:

> The soul that sinneth, it shall die. The son shall not bear the iniquity of the father, neither shall the father bear the iniquity of the son: the righteousness of the righteous shall be upon him, and the wickedness of the wicked shall be upon him (Ezekiel 18:20).

The apostle John said that sin is an act: "Sin is lawlessness" (1 John 3:4). It is man's own individual sins that separate him from God: "Your iniquities have separated between you and your God, and your sins have hid his face from you, so that he will not hear" (Isaiah 59:2). "And you did he make alive, when ye were dead through your trespasses and sins" (Ephesians 2:1).

Although men inherit the consequences of Adam's sin—physical death—they do not inherit sin. Thus, because of Adam's sin, all are born with a nature subject to death; and because of Christ, all will be raised from the dead. For Paul wrote, "For as in Adam all die [i.e., physically], so also in Christ shall all be made alive [i.e., at the resurrection]" (1 Corinthians 15:22).

All men suffer physical death as a result of Adam's sin, but they do not suffer the responsibility or guilt of it. The Scriptures affirm that death passed unto all men, not sin. The act of Adam brought universal death; the act of Christ will bring universal resurrection—to all alike. The Bible does not teach hereditary total depravity—that man is wholly bad by nature, and that guilt of inherited sin is upon every person born into the world. The Scriptures teach that infants are pure and innocent. Jesus said, "For of such is the kingdom of heaven" (Matthew 19:14 KJV). Infants are not born in sin; they do not inherit sin, Adam's or anyone's. They are sinless.

Infant Baptism?

The view that unbaptized babies will be lost but baptized ones will not be is based upon the false notion that babies are born in sin. Baptism, in order to be valid, must, according to Sacred Writ, be preceded by teaching, hearing, faith, repentance, and confession of faith in Christ as the Son of God. Christ authorized His apostles to baptize: "Go ye therefore, and make disciples of all the nations, baptizing them into the name of the Father and of the Son and of the Holy Spirit" (Matthew 28:19). Since Christ commanded that teaching must precede baptism, infants are excluded from obedience to this command because they cannot grasp spiritual concepts.

Mark records the Lord's Great Commission thus: "Go ye into all the world, and preach the gospel to the whole creation. He that believeth and is baptized shall be saved; but he that disbelieveth shall be condemned" (Mark 16:15–16). So faith also precedes Scriptural baptism, but infants are incapable of believing. In Samaria, after the church was established, it was said that "when they believed Philip preaching . . . they were baptized, both men and women" (Acts 8:12). No infants were baptized here, for first they heard and believed. Concerning those at Corinth who were baptized, the Bible says, "Many of the Corinthians hearing believed, and were baptized" (Acts 18:8). No infants were baptized, because only those who heard and believed were baptized in the first century church.

On the day of Pentecost when believers asked what to do, the apostle Peter, guided by the Holy Spirit, commanded, "Repent ye, and be baptized every one of you in the name of Jesus Christ unto the remission of your sins" (Acts 2:38). Thus, the Bible teaches that baptism for (unto) the remission of sins is to a believing penitent. Infants cannot repent, for they have not sinned.

The Ethiopian treasurer confessed his belief that Jesus is the Christ the Son of God, and was then baptized and went on his way rejoicing.

> Then Philip opened his mouth, and began at the same scripture, and preached unto him Jesus. And as they went on their way, they came unto a certain water: and the eunuch said, See, here is water; what doth hinder me to be baptized? And Philip said, If thou believest with all thine heart, thou mayest. And he answered and said, I believe that Jesus Christ is the Son of God. And

> he commanded the chariot to stand still: and they went down both into the water, both Philip and the eunuch; and he baptized him. And when they were come up out of the water, the Spirit of the Lord caught away Philip, that the eunuch saw him no more: and he went on his way rejoicing (Acts 8:35–39 KJV).

The confession is important: "For with the heart man believeth unto righteousness; and with the mouth confession is made unto salvation" (Romans 10:10).

Infants cannot confess Christ. Infants cannot be taught the gospel; they cannot believe in Christ; they cannot repent; they cannot with their mouths confess Christ as Lord. The Bible gives neither command for, nor example of, infant baptism. Infants, therefore, are excluded from baptism.

To prove infant baptism, the accounts of household baptisms are often cited—Lydia and the jailer and their households (Acts 16:15, 32–33). It is merely assumed that these households included infants. The Bible does not say that there were infants in them. The statements of Jesus, recorded in Matthew 19:14 and Mark 10:15, about little children invited to the Master, likewise do not mention baptism.

Infants Not Lost

Furthermore, only the lost need to be saved, and only those who need to be saved need to be baptized. Infants and little children have neither inherited nor committed any sin that will bar them from heaven. Little children are innocent—they are safe. They are not in a lost condition and do not need to be baptized. For infant baptism to be necessary, it must first be proved by the Scriptures that infants are guilty of sin and lost because they are sinners.

Sprinkling Is Not Baptism

Besides, sprinkling water on a little child, as most usually do today in the act called baptism, is not Bible baptism in any sense of the word for at least two reasons: (1) the act is unscriptural, for baptism is a burial and resurrection (immersion) (Romans 6:4; Colossians 2:12; Acts 8:38–39), and (2) baptism is for (unto) the remission of sins only to a penitent believer (Acts 2:36–38; 22:16). Thus, a christening service, in which the word *baptism* is used, fails to meet Bible requirements of baptism. Two things are wrong then with the practice of baptizing infants. The first is that the act done is not really baptism (immersion), and the second is that it is performed on one who has no need of baptism.

The approval of the practice by men does not make it right (cf. Matthew 15:9). Christ has all authority (Matthew 28:19). The church has no right to legislate; the church is to obey the King, and the Lord nowhere authorizes infant baptism. If infants should be baptized for the forgiveness of sins, without any teaching, faith, repentance, or confession of faith, then that would be water salvation, for water, and water alone, dominates the ceremony. The Bible does not teach baptismal regeneration. On the contrary, it teaches that baptism—coupled with faith, repentance, and confession—is a condition of remission of sins, yet not a meritorious cause. People are cleansed by the blood of Christ and through the grace of God (1 John 1:7; 2:2; Ephesians 2:8; Titus 3:4–5) when they comply with the terms of pardon (1 Peter 3:20–21).

When Accountable?

The Bible does not set the age of one's accountability. This depends upon home training, mental ability, and other things. With proper spiritual guidance and correct Biblical teaching, children come to reach the age in life when they themselves desire to accept Christ in genuine faith and put Him on in baptism. Definitely, the Scriptures teach that one's obedience to the gospel must be "from the heart" (Romans 6:17; cf. John 6:45). So, until children reach the age of sensibility or accountability and sin against God, they need not be baptized.

Parents have the responsibility of bringing up their children "in the nurture and admonition of the Lord" (Ephesians 6:4 KJV); but they should not subject them to a religious rite unauthorized by the Lord, which might later keep them from obeying the Savior in Scriptural baptism. Those "baptized" in infancy should realize they were not then responsible and should want to be baptized Scripturally later. Now, as accountable persons, they must render obedience to God through baptism unto the remission of their sins, thereby becoming the children of God (cf. 1 Peter 1:22).

Infants Not Excluded from Heaven

Thus, the conclusion must be that the Bible nowhere excludes infants, baptized or unbaptized, whether born to believing or unbelieving parents, from the eternal joys of heaven. Where there is no accountability, there is no responsibility. (This principle would also apply to the mentally incompetent.) Parents, therefore, need not worry about the destiny of their precious children who pass away before they reach the age of accountability. They are safe in the arms of Jesus. For an infant to pass from this life into the next in purity and innocence is sweetness unsurpassed.

David's Faith

When King David lost his child by death he made this familiar statement: "I shall go to him, but he will not return to me" (2 Samuel 12:23). Fathers and mothers can now say the same when giving up a baby in death. When parents contemplate the spiritual and physical dangers with which the world is environed, they often are grateful because their little ones were freed from such things.

Fathers and mothers had rather their children die in infancy than later to grow up and go down to a hopeless grave (cf. Mark 14:21).

Words of Comfort

There are other words of Scripture that give bereaved parents comfort. "And we know that to them that love God all things work together for good, even to them that are called according to his purpose" (Romans 8:28). The Lord sympathizes with those who have lost loved ones. Jesus wept at the tomb of Lazarus (John 11:35). Parents who are not Christians may be drawn closer to heaven when their child dies. In one sense, "a little child shall lead them" (Isaiah 11:6). The Good Shepherd "will gather the lambs in his arm, and carry them in his bosom" (Isaiah 40:11).

A poet has said:

Oh, not in cruelty, not in wrath,
The reaper came that day;
'Twas an angel visited the green earth,
And took the flowers away.

Parents should be moved by the memory of a departed little one to do the Lord's will, so they too may go to heaven. If parents fail to obey Christ, then their child will be in heaven, but they themselves shall not be there. As parents, their prayer should be, as another poet has written:

Lord God, the Spirit! Purify
My thoughts, bind fast my life to Thee;
So shall I meet my babes on high,
Though they may not return to me.

The compassion of Christ for those who mourn over the loss of their children is great. Once while on earth, Jesus met a funeral procession going out of the city of Nain. A widow was going to bury her only son. The sight of this weeping mother went straight to the Lord's heart. Immediately, the compassion He felt for her expressed itself in the soothing, loving words, "Weep not." He then delivered her son to her alive, removing the cause of her tears (Luke 7:11–15). Jesus Christ continues to have loving compassion on all those who now weep. What a friend we have in Jesus!

What Time Is It?

Parents, being older and accountable, should prepare for death, if they are not already Christians, and be as ready as little children when the time comes to die.

It is not of any great importance how or when one dies. Eternity will be just as long for each individual, regardless of the time spent on earth. Each person should resolve to live for Christ and trust Him to decide when to call him from this world.

With many people life is about gone. They need to be thinking of their own soul's salvation. Someone has taken the average of seventy years for a normal life span and likened it to the dial of a clock. Suppose 6:00 A.M. is birth, and 12:00 midnight is age seventy, what time is it for you?

If you are 15, it is 8:51 A.M.
If you are 20, it is 11:08 A.M.
If you are 25, it is 12:25 P.M.
If you are 30, it is 1:25 P.M.
If you are 35, it is 2:59 P.M.
If you are 40, it is 4:16 P.M.
If you are 45, it is 5:33 P.M.
If you are 50, it is 6:50 P.M.
If you are 55, it is 8:07 P.M.
If you are 60, it is 9:24 P.M.
If you are 65, it is 10:41 P.M.
If you are 70, it is almost midnight!

Since life is like "a vapor that appeareth for a little time, and then vanisheth away" (James 4:14), salvation through Christ becomes the most urgent message of the hour. Dying to sin in order that one might not die in sin now represents one's most serious need. It is not surprising, then, that Jesus urged His disciples to seek first the kingdom of God and His righteousness (Matthew 6:33). One of the beauties of Christianity is the fact that it offers the best that is here, plus the promise of an eternal glorious hereafter in heaven.

Let no one, therefore, look at the above chart and conclude he has many years left to obey God. The Lord can advance the hands to midnight at any moment. Thousands are taken from this life without ever seeing midnight—or even 3 P.M. Thinking there is plenty of time to obey the Lord will cause many souls to be lost eternally.

Remember Jesus said: "Except ye turn, and become as little children, ye shall in no wise enter into the kingdom of heaven" (Matthew 18:3). The dear, precious little ones who leave this world before they know sin are simply transplanted from earth to heaven to grow, to bloom, to flourish in the beautiful garden of God forever. Two Christian parents put on their departed infant's tombstone: "Budded on earth to bloom in heaven."

"Limbus Infantum"

Some imagine a separate place in hell for unbaptized children, called the *Limbus Infantum*. The term means the place and state pertaining to the departed souls of unbaptized infants. The term is not found in the Sacred Oracles. Those who practice infant baptism, however, logically imply that the unbaptized who die in infancy will be lost. The practice of baptizing infants grew out of the false notion that infants are born totally depraved. If infants are born in sin, people reasoned, then since baptism is for the remission of sins, babies should be baptized as quickly as possible. But the death in 1 Corinthians 15:21–22 is physical death, and the resurrection spoken of is the resurrection of the body. Adam introduced sin and death into the world, but there is a difference between the consequences of an act and the guilt of that act (cf. Romans 5:12–21). All are not born sinners just because Adam sinned.

Questions for Discussion

1. What question is often asked concerning infants who die?
2. Define *Limbus Infantum*. Is this term found in the Scriptures?
3. Are infants born in sin or without sin? What is the doctrine of total hereditary depravity?
4. Do infants inherit sin? If so, whose sin? Is it Adam's sin?
5. Whose sin separates a person from God?
6. What did Ezekiel say the son would not inherit from his father?
7. What is the Biblical definition of sin? Is it an act?
8. Of whom was Jesus speaking when He said, "Of such is the kingdom of heaven"?
9. What are the prerequisites of Scriptural baptism?
10. Does the Bible teach "baptismal regeneration" or "water salvation"?
11. Does the mention of household baptisms in the book of Acts necessarily imply that infants were baptized?
12. How does infant baptism fail to fulfill the requirements of Scriptural baptism? Is the religious practice of infant baptism wrong?
13. Is there an example of, or instruction for, an infant receiving baptism for any purpose in all the Bible?
14. What theory concerning sin caused the origin of infant baptism?
15. What is the condition of all infants who die?
16. Does the Bible state the physical age when a person reaches accountability?
17. What are parents instructed to do concerning their children?
18. If one had a ritual called baptism in his infancy, what should he, as a responsible person, now do?
19. Who, according to Scripture, will be lost eternally and who saved?
20. What should be one's most urgent concern?
21. Which religious bodies (denominations) practice "infant baptism"?

– 26 –

What Is Heaven Like?

"And I saw a new heaven and a new earth"
Revelation 21:1

Heaven, the eternal abode of the Redeemer and the redeemed, is described at the close of God's revelation in man's sublime, yet limited, language. In the Scriptures the language establishes the fact of eternal life.

Heaven Is a Place

God has not given any definite information on the physical location of heaven. Heaven is somewhere in the region of God's creation, the place where His throne is (cf. Deuteronomy 26:15; John 6:38, 62; 13:1; 16:27–28; 20:17; Ecclesiastes 5:2). A song says that heaven is "above the bright blue."

The fact of heaven is certain, and saints of all ages have believed in and looked forward to the abode of the blessed as their eternal home after this life. For example, Abraham, while sojourning in the land of Canaan, expected future happiness after death. He looked to the permanent abode of the righteous, "the city which hath the foundations, whose builder and maker is God" (Hebrews 11:10). This great man, together with the heirs of promise with him, desired "a better country, that is, a heavenly: wherefore God is not ashamed of them, to be called their God; for he hath prepared for them a city" (Hebrews 11:16). Every Christian may likewise believe he has in heaven "a better possession and an abiding one" (Hebrews 10:34). "For we have not here an abiding city, but we seek after the city which is to come" (Hebrews 13:14).

Heaven is a place, not a myth. When Jesus was about to leave His disciples and return to His Father, He said: "I go to prepare a place for you" (John 14:2). In heaven the redeemed of all ages and of every nation will one day be gathered together to live with the Lord and His holy angels. Here in their eternal home, the Father's house, the children of God will enjoy the most blessed fellowship. Jesus is already there, and His promise to His disciples is: "Where

I am, there ye may be also" (John 14:3). Hence, heaven is a real place and the inhabitants are real people in glorified resurrected and changed bodies.

Heaven Is a Condition

Instead of thinking of heaven altogether as a place to go, one should think of it as something he has to be. He must not think that everybody would enjoy heaven if he only got there, for heaven is also a state, a condition of heart. Heaven presupposes union with God with one thing certain: there will be no heaven for those whose heaven does not begin first within their souls. Jesus said: "Blessed are the pure in heart: for they shall see God" (Matthew 5:8).

Again, John, in speaking of heaven, wrote: "And there shall in no wise enter into it anything unclean, or he that maketh an abomination and a lie: but only they that are written in the Lamb's book of life" (Revelation 21:27). Hence, the inhabitants of heaven are those who are righteous. The unrighteous and unholy shall not inherit heaven (Revelation 20:15). Men must prepare for heaven while they are living on earth by letting heaven get into them here before they can get into heaven there. Heaven is a prepared place and condition for a prepared people. Heaven is only for those who prove their love to the Lord by developing a Christ-like character. People must develop heaven within them while they are here in order that they may enjoy heaven after a while. Therefore, eternal destiny depends upon character; only the pure in heart will enjoy God's fellowship in heaven.

Not All in Heaven

Some, because of sin, are not going to enter into heaven, for the Bible says:

> Or know ye not that the unrighteous shall not inherit the kingdom of God? Be not deceived: neither fornicators, nor idolaters, nor adulterers, nor effeminate, nor abusers of themselves with men, nor thieves, nor covetous, nor drunkards, nor revilers, nor extortioners, shall inherit the kingdom of God (1 Corinthians 6:9–10).

Of course, all will say that they want to enjoy heaven after they die, but they do not want to be heavenly minded while on earth. The society of heaven will be the holy men and women of all ages and of all nations, those who have been redeemed, and the innocent ones. The writer of the book of Hebrews admonished Christians in these words: "Follow peace with all men, and holiness, without which no man shall see the Lord" (Hebrews 12:14 KJV). Holiness is the essence of God-likeness. Peter said heaven will be a place "wherein dwelleth righteousness (2 Peter 3:13). Again, John tells us in the book of Revelation who will not go to heaven: "But for the fearful, and unbelieving, and abominable, and murderers, and fornicators, and sorcerers, and idolaters, and all liars, their part shall be in the lake that burneth with fire and brimstone;

which is the second death" (Revelation 21:8). "Without are the dogs, and the sorcerers, and the fornicators, and the murderers, and the idolaters, and every one that loveth and maketh a lie" (Revelation 22:15). To the Jew, the dog was the emblem of all that was wild, unclean, and offensive. How blissful must be that society from which the unholy and vile are forever excluded, and in which the holy and the good of all ages are gathered!

Who Will Be in Heaven

God, Christ, the Holy Spirit, the holy angels, the redeemed, and infants will be in heaven. Abraham, Isaac, and Jacob, and others like them who lived in the Patriarchal age, which lasted from Adam to Moses, will be in heaven. Moses and the prophets and the obedient ones who lived during the Jewish age will be there. Finally, Paul, Peter, John, and all the righteous who lived during the Christian age will be there. Jesus at the judgment will send all the righteous into eternal life (Matthew 25:34, 46).

Types of Heaven

Heaven is sometimes described in type as "Eden," "Canaan," and "Jerusalem." Because each of these originally was important to man, God has used them to picture the place and the beauties of heaven. They are figures of speech.

Eden was a type of heaven. This lovely earthly Paradise of delight, man's first home (Genesis 2:8–10), dimly shadows the beautiful heavenly Paradise where the tree of life will reappear. "To him that overcometh, to him will I give to eat of the tree of life, which is in the Paradise of God" (Revelation 2:7). The Lord's promise to the Christian is that to inherit heaven will be Paradise regained. The book of Genesis tells of a Paradise that was lost; the book of Revelation pictures a Paradise restored (Revelation 22:1–2). As already learned, the bliss of the righteous in Hades is also Paradise (Luke 23:43). The word *paradise* means a place of pleasure.

Canaan was a type of heaven. This earthly Canaan was a place of inheritance and a home for the people of God. This land, flowing with milk and honey, prefigured the heavenly Canaan or the eternal inheritance for God's children. Compared with that land of this earth, heaven is "a better country" (Hebrews 11:16). Peter spoke of Christians as having been begotten again to "an inheritance incorruptible, and undefiled, and that fadeth not away, reserved in heaven" (1 Peter 1:4).

Jerusalem presented a type of heaven. After Israel settled in Canaan, Jerusalem became the chief place in the land and here God was worshipped. The Lord, through the apostle John on the isle of Patmos, presented heaven as a glorious and holy city. This is the grand finale.

In Revelation 1:11 Jesus instructed John to write what he saw in visions. Here is one of John's detailed accounts.

> And I saw a new heaven and a new earth: for the first heaven and the first earth are passed away; and the sea is no more. And I saw the holy city, new Jerusalem, coming down out of heaven from God, made ready as a bride adorned for her husband. And I heard a great voice out of the throne saying, Behold, the tabernacle of God is with men, and he will dwell with them, and they shall be his peoples, and God himself shall be with them, and be their God. And he shall wipe away every tear from their eyes; and death shall be no more, neither shall there be mourning, nor crying, nor pain, any more: the first things are passed away . . . And he carried me away in the Spirit to a mountain great and high, and showed me the holy city Jerusalem, coming down out of heaven from God, having the glory of God: her light was like unto a stone most precious, as it were a jasper stone, clear as crystal: having a wall great and high; having twelve gates, and at the gates twelve angels; and names written thereon, which are the names of the twelve tribes of the children of Israel: . . . and the wall of the city had twelve foundations, and on them twelve names of the twelve apostles of the Lamb . . . And the city lieth four-square, and the length thereof is as great as the breadth: and he measured the city with the reed, twelve thousand furlongs: the length and the breadth and the height thereof are equal. And he measured the wall thereof, a hundred and forty and four cubits, according to the measure of a man, that is, of an angel. And the building of the wall thereof was jasper: and the city was pure gold, like unto clear glass. The foundations of the wall of the city were adorned with all manner of precious stones . . . And the twelve gates were twelve pearls: each one of the several gates were of one pearl: and the street of the city was pure gold, as it were transparent glass. And I saw no temple therein: for the Lord God the Almighty, and the Lamb, are the temple thereof. And the city hath no need of the sun, neither of the moon, to shine upon it; for the glory of God did lighten it, and the lamp thereof is the Lamb. And the nations shall walk amidst the light thereof: and the kings of the earth bring their glory into it. And the gates thereof shall in no wise be shut by day (for there shall be no night there): and they shall bring the glory and the honor of the nations into it . . . And he showed me a river of water, bright as crystal, proceeding out of the throne of God and of the Lamb, in the midst of the street thereof. And on this side of the river and on that the tree of life, bearing twelve manner of fruits, yielding its fruit every month: and the leaves of the tree were for the healing of the nations. And there shall be no curse any more: and the throne of God and of the Lamb shall be therein: and his servants shall serve him; and they shall see his face; and his name shall be on their foreheads. And there shall be night no more; and they need no light of lamp, neither light of sun; for the Lord God shall give them light: and they shall reign for ever and ever (Revelation 21:1– 22:5).

How Beautiful Heaven Must Be!

Herein is recorded a glorious picture of the final and complete joys of the saved in a place and condition men call heaven. In the imagery of the happy abode of the saved—the church in her new and perfect state—there is a blending of the city of Jerusalem as the symbol and the Garden of Eden as the type. Revelation 21:1–7 shows the fellowship with God; 21:9–26, shows the protection of God; and 22:1–5, tells of the provisions from God.

The Verses Outlined

An outline of this description is as follows (Revelation 21):

1. A vision of a new heaven and a new earth, the first heaven and earth having passed away at the second coming of Christ and the judgment (v. 1).
2. A vision of the holy city, with a general statement of what will be the condition of the saved in heaven (vv. 2–4).
3. God's command to John to make a record of these things, for the truth and certainty of the blessed state are ratified by the word and promise of God (v. 5).
4. A general description of those who will dwell in the wonderful city of God and those who will not (vv. 6–8).
5. A more detailed description of the New Jerusalem, both in the exterior and the interior parts of it—its appearance (vv. 11, 18, 21), walls (vv. 12, 18), gates (vv. 12–13, 21), foundations (vv. 14, 18–20), size (vv. 15–17), light (vv. 23–24), temple (v. 22), access (v. 25), and inhabitants (v. 27).
6. The eternal home is set forth as a city in a garden; here is Paradise regained, with the river and tree of life, free from the evils of the first Eden (vv. 1–3).
7. Here in this sinless summerland with the blessed Lord the righteous shall reign forever and ever; the life of heaven will be eternal (vv. 4–5).

New Heaven, New Earth

The expression, "a new heaven and a new earth," does not mean that heaven will be here on this earth after it has been purified with fire. The earth will be burned up (2 Peter 3:10). The expression means that the eternal home of the soul will be new to the saved, a new order; referring rather to the place and happiness which the saints are to enjoy in heaven after the resurrection in the final state. The Father's house is already being built (John 14:2), and the inheritance is already prepared and is now reserved in heaven for the righteous (1 Peter 1:4). The new heaven will be new in quality or kind.

Why in Symbols?

God did not intend for man to take all of the expressions about heaven in a literal sense, such as a street of gold, walls of jasper, foundations of precious stones, and gates of pearl. All these descriptions are figurative; the beauty of heaven and the happiness of the redeemed are described in imagery. Let no one make heaven materialistic. The Bible gives a material description of something that is spiritual—not material. Yet heaven is real, and what these symbols represent are real and actual, though one may poorly comprehend what the Lord has said about heaven due to his limited faculties. Heaven will be equal in beauty, majesty, and glory to God's description—and more so. God could not fully describe heaven to man due to man's inability to fully comprehend. For example, how can one now describe the beauties and delights of the tropical region to one who has never known anything but ice and snow? How can one fully explain calculus to a three-year-old child? So it is not a question of God's ability so much as that of human capacity. This, then, is the situation confronting one when he reads the Scriptures on heaven or any phase of the life beyond the grave. God had to use figures and words of this life with which the people were familiar in order to teach spiritual truths about the other world. It was, therefore, under beautiful imagery that God presented heaven to John on the Isle of Patmos. The language is a description of a heavenly thing in earthly terms. The words describe conditions that will obtain in the eternal state for the righteous; they are the symbols of its glory, its beauty, and its purity. The description John saw in the vision and what it represents are different things. The vision is surely but a dim representation of what heaven really is. All unseen states must be presented through the medium of what is seen and understood. What God has said about heaven is a figurative description of the place; man can only comprehend it to a certain degree.

An Illustration

The story is told of a little child born blind. After several years of blindness, doctors were permitted to perform a delicate operation which would probably enable the child to see. After surgery, and the removal of bandages, the teenager was taken to a window. God's big, wonderful, and beautiful world was beheld for the first time. As faces of loved ones and friends and the scenes of nature appeared, the shout rang out: "Oh, Mother! How wonderful! Why didn't you tell me how beautiful everything really is?" To this the mother, in tears, replied, "Darling, I tried to, but I couldn't." Then the mother explained how it was impossible to describe fully unto one born blind the beauties of this wonderful world.

So it shall be with all the redeemed when they reach heaven. That country is so great and so wonderful a place that man should be willing to sacrifice everything in this world for it. Heaven is worth more to a man than the whole world and everything in it (Matthew 16:26). Christians want to go to heaven. This is their all-consuming passion.

Eternal Life in Heaven

The righteous will have eternal life in heaven, and eternal glory (Matthew 25:46; 1 Peter 5:10). This will be much more than mere eternal existence. This will be real life, life in union and fellowship with God forever, life in the fullest possible sense of the word. The Bible teaches that obedience to God brings blessings "a hundredfold now in this time . . . and in the world to come eternal life" (Mark 10:30; cf. Matthew 19:16; John 3:16; 4:36; 6:68; 10:27–28; 12:25; 17:2–3; Romans 2:7; 1 Timothy 6:12; Titus 1:2; Romans 8:24–25; 1 John 2:25).

The tree of life and the river of the water of life are in heaven, indicating the pure joy of the holy life flowing from God. Abundant life is for all throughout the whole city with a perpetual abundance of spiritual blessings, happiness, and immortality. The Bible teaches that heaven will be a life of abounding joy and happiness. In fact, heaven will be the summit of felicity. There will be no disappointments in heaven, for in that eternal world of delight there will be nothing to cloud the Christian's happiness or to break in upon his rest. There will be perfect peace. All know that perfect happiness cannot be found on earth.

The world can never give
The bliss for which we sigh.

The Walls of the City

The great walls of the city represent security and protection. Separated from the wicked, no enemy can ever touch the saved again. The twelve gates represent entrance with free admission to all the redeemed from every tribe and land; they are guarded by angels to keep all others out.

The foundations of the city are twelve (from the apostles of Christ—their teaching), and of the most precious stones. The city John saw was not only foursquare, but also a perfect cube: the length, width, and height were equal—twelve thousand furlongs (about fifteen hundred miles) in every direction. This symbol must surely indicate the ample provision that God has made for all His obedient children in the eternal home.

Worship in Heaven

There will be worship in heaven. No special place for a temple is in the city, for the whole city will be a place to meet and worship God, and the worship will be celebrated forever. The saved will join in singing, with tongues immortal, and bow before the throne of God and offer thanksgiving and praise to the Lord. The worship of God on earth is but preliminary to the worship of the Lamb in heaven. John described the singing in heaven in these words: "And I heard a voice from heaven, as the voice of many waters, and as the voice of a great thunder: and the voice which I heard was as the voice of harpers harping with their harps" (Revelation 14:2). The singing was like that of mighty waters and thunders. Yet this heavenly music had sweetness "as harpers harping with their harps." Nothing has ever been heard comparable to this music which one shall hear when he shall reach that land that is fairer than day.

Serve in Heaven

Again, the Bible says: "His servants shall serve him." Although heaven is a place of rest from the toils of this life (Job 3:17; Hebrews 4:9), it will not be a place of inactivity. Work shall be there, but no one shall grow tired or weary with his serving as here on earth. Only God knows the work of redeemed souls in heaven, but in this earthly life fidelity prepares them for greater things in the other world.

Mysteries Made Clear

In the heavenly state there will be an unraveling of the mysteries of this earthly life. In the history of men there have been providential dealings which were mysterious to them; but there all shall know why the good were afflicted and the wicked man prospered. Here on earth sources of knowledge are limited, but there man will be able to see more clearly. The redeemed shall then see that the Lord was doing what was proper, holy, and just. When all His judgments have been made manifest, things will appear entirely in a different light. (See Romans 8:28; 2 Corinthians 4:17.)

There is much truth in these words:

Not now but in the coming years,
It may be in a better land,
We'll read the meaning of our tears,
And there, sometime, we'll understand.
—Maxwell N. Cornelius

Degrees in Heaven?

In a sense, there are different degrees of happiness in heaven, just as there are different degrees of honor and happiness of the saints here on earth in the church. All Christians do not enjoy equally the worship and service of the Lord here below. That there are degrees of happiness in heaven may be inferred from God's goodness and justice. Those who suffer much and endure hardness as good soldiers of Christ should receive a corresponding reward by being highly glorified with Him. True, the saint who has been less useful will be happy; but his happiness, although to him eternal and full, will not be as intense. This difference of happiness among the righteous will spring from the different capacities of their souls, and not from things external. For example, "A" and "B" may go to a musical performance together, and each one enjoy it to the fullest of their capacities; but "A" may have a greater power to really appropriate such a program to his enjoyment than "B" has. In like manner, in heaven, sources of happiness may be full and inexhaustible, but the extent to which any saint enjoys them will depend upon his receptive faculty.

Thus, heaven will be alike to all, and yet on account of their various capacities, all will not be alike in heaven. The Bible is alike to all Christians, and yet all are not equally blessed by its truths. Those who are more advanced spiritually and are strong find in the Book strong meat, while those less advanced and are babes in Christ find milk (Hebrews 5:12–14), and yet it is the same Word of God to all. So heaven will be to all everything that God promised, and yet these will be enjoyed in various degrees. Hence, inasmuch as the saints are far from being equal in grace and happiness in the kingdom of God in this life, so the different degrees of service rendered on earth will determine the different degrees of glory in heaven. Do you think we will enjoy heaven as much as will the apostle Paul?

God No Respecter of Persons

There is no respect of persons with God (Romans 2:11). If, then, those who are the least of all saints should be exalted to the same degree of honor and happiness as those who have been greatest, it would seem as if God were partial, and a respecter of persons; but He has said that He is a respecter of works and of character, and that He will reward every man "according to what he hath done, whether it be good or bad" (2 Corinthians 5:10; cf. Revelation 20:12). Every passage of Scripture which declares that God will render to all according to their works indicates different degrees of reward in heaven. Thus, if the saints are rewarded in heaven according to their works on earth, as the Bible says, then there must still continue to be the same difference in glory as there is on earth. Those greatest here will be greatest there, and those least here will be the least there. One must believe that there are higher degrees of glory for those that have done and suffered most.

To use an old illustration: vessels of different sizes may all be full, and yet some will contain much more than others. A little pail can be as full of water as is a big tub, but the tub will hold much more than the pail. Rewards, therefore, in heaven will be equal, in the sense that each saved person will be filled with good; but rewards will vary, in the sense that the capacity of one will be greater than that of another.

Although there will be degrees of blessedness and honor for the righteous, proportioned to the capacity and fidelity of each redeemed soul, each will receive as great a measure of reward as he can contain. There can be degrees of happiness proportioned to the capacity of each soul. Each redeemed child of God will receive as great a measure of reward as he deserves and is prepared for.

John, while on Patmos, saw the redeemed host and was asked:

> These that are arrayed in white robes, who are they, and whence came they? And I said unto him, My Lord, thou knowest. And he said to me, These are they that came out of the great tribulation, and they washed their robes, and made them white in the blood of the Lamb. Therefore are they before the throne of God; and they serve him day and night in his temple: and he that sitteth on the throne shall spread his tabernacle over them. They shall hunger no more, neither thirst any more; neither shall the sun strike upon them, nor any heat: for the Lamb that is in the midst of the throne shall be their shepherd, and shall guide them unto fountains of waters of life: and God shall wipe away every tear from their eyes (Revelation 7:13–17).

Face to Face with Christ

Perhaps the crowning glory of heaven will be to see the blessed Savior face to face. The longing of the pilgrim below is to see the King in His beauty, and to become an inhabitant of the land that is afar off (Isaiah 33:17). The prospect cheers him in his pilgrimage, lightens every burden borne, and sweetens every sorrow that comes. The redeemed shall see the King some day. "They shall see his face." They shall be in the presence of their dear Lord and Savior. The beloved apostle John declared to Christians: "We shall be like him; for we shall see him even as he is" (1 John 3:2). In heaven the divine presence will be a glorious reality. In the description of heaven that John gave, he said: "Behold, the tabernacle of God is with men, and he shall dwell with them." The redeemed will be like Him and will be with Him.

Saints of old have looked forward to this blessed event, and God's children now look forward to seeing the Lord Jesus Christ, who loved them and died for them. How many times have children been away from home, happily staying with friends. Yet when the time to go home draws near, they become eager to see familiar faces! They can hardly wait to reach home. Although the journey be long, how wonderful to finally reach home and to see dear friends and loved ones! David looked forward to seeing the Lord one day: "As for me, I shall behold thy face in righteousness; I shall be satisfied, when I awake, with beholding thy form" (Psalm 17:15). Christ, in His prayer to the Father concerning His disciples, said: "Father, I desire that they also whom thou hast given me be with me where I am, that they may behold my glory, which thou hast given me" (John 17:24). Christ's loving presence will make heaven a magnificent home for the child of God. Christians often sing:

Just to be near the dear Lord I adore
Will through the ages be glory for me.

Again:

Face to face with Christ my Savior,
Face to face—what will it be,
When with rapture I behold Him,
Jesus Christ who died for me?
—Mrs. Frank A. Breck

Surely one's eyes have never seen anything that is equal to the beauty that shall burst upon his enraptured vision when he enters the eternal home of the soul, there to meet the dear Lord and many loved ones and friends who have gone on in death. It is not the place so much as the company that will make heaven so beautiful. This is heaven—to be forever with the Lord, and all the saved (1 Thessalonians 4:17).

The Way to Heaven

Finally, the way to heaven is made clear in Scripture. Jesus said: "I am the way, and the truth, and the life: no one cometh unto the Father, but by me" (John 14:6). It is through faith in Christ—an obedient, living, active faith in the Son of God that one finally reaches the everlasting abode of the righteous. Jesus again said: "Not every one that saith unto me, Lord, Lord, shall enter into the kingdom of heaven; but he that doeth the will of my Father who is in heaven" (Matthew 7:21). The last beatitude of the Bible says: "Blessed are they that do his commandments, that they may have right to the tree of life, and enter in through the gates into the city" (Revelation 22:14 KJV). Indeed, "the path of the righteous is as the dawning light, that shineth more and more unto the perfect day" (Proverbs 4:18). For "man goeth to his everlasting home" (Ecclesiastes 12:5). "We Are Going down the Valley One By One" is a song often sung. But the way to reach heaven, when this earthly life is completed, is to follow the teaching of the Bible. Jesus says, "Come unto me, all ye that labor and are heavy laden, and I will give you rest" (Matthew 11:28). "And the Spirit and the bride say, Come" (Revelation 22:17). To all those in sin God offers forgiveness. He does not want anyone to be lost (2 Peter 3:9). And to the Christian, the Lord through John wrote, "Be thou faithful unto death, and I will give thee a crown of life" (Revelation 2:10).

Conclusion

Man receives eternal life as a free gift of God (Romans 6:23), and not upon his own meritorious works. Yet the Father offers salvation through Christ upon condition of obedience to the gospel; but such obedience does not purchase salvation. Salvation has been provided for all as a free gift from God; it is up to man to comply with the conditions set forth in the gospel in order to obtain that free gift. Jesus Christ is "the author of eternal salvation unto all them that obey him" (Hebrews 5:9 KJV; cf. 1 Peter 1:22).

So the words *eternal* and *everlasting* are from the same Greek word *aionios* in the New Testament. If one is in Christ and living faithfully the Christian life, he has the promise of eternal life. But sometimes the promise is in the present tense; for example, in 1 John 5:11: "And the witness is this, that God gave unto us eternal life, and this life is in the Son." Yet in 1 John 2:25, he wrote: "And this is the promise which he promised us, even life eternal." Paul declared that he was "in hope of eternal life" (Titus 1:2). Hope is made up of desire and expectation; one does not hope for that which he already has (Romans 8:24–25). Heaven, or eternal life, is not now in this life a present possession; it is a promise to the faithful child of God. He has it in prospect, in promise, but not in realization. This reward will be given to the faithful children of God at the consummation of all things at the final judgment. Then the righteous will go away "into eternal life" (Matthew 25:46; cf. Mark 10:29–30).

We read of a place that's called heaven,
It's made for the pure and the free;
These truths in God's Word He has given,
How beautiful heaven must be,

How beautiful heaven must be,
Sweet home of the happy and free;
Fair haven of rest for the weary,
How beautiful heaven must be.
—Mrs. A. S. Bridgewater

Earth holds no treasures but perish with using,
However precious they be;
Yet there's a country to which I am going:
Heaven holds all to me.

Heaven holds all to me,
Brighter its glory will be
Joy without measure will be my treasure:
Heaven holds all to me.
—Tillit S. Teddlie

"Wherefore, my beloved brethren, be ye steadfast, unmoveable, always abounding in the work of the Lord, forasmuch as ye know that your labor is not in vain in the Lord" (1 Corinthians 15:58). How great to hear one day these words: "Enter thou into the joy of thy Lord" (Matthew 25:21). This is the glorious hope that every faithful child of God possesses (Titus 1:2; 3:7).

Questions for Discussion

1. Why do most people like to read about heaven?
2. Is heaven a place, a state, or both?
3. Upon what does our eternal destiny depend?
4. Why will all people not go to heaven?
5. How was Eden a type of heaven? the land of Canaan? Jerusalem?
6. Where is God's description of heaven found in the Scriptures? What are some of the things said about it?
7. Should all the expressions about heaven be taken literally? Explain your answer.
8. Why did God use figures of speech, or comparisons, in describing heaven?
9. Is it possible for man to fully grasp the meaning of all of these terms about heaven?
10. Who will be the inhabitants of heaven? Will there be room enough for all?
11. What do the walls of the city represent?
12. Will there be worship and work in heaven? Why will there be no temple in heaven?
13. What kind of bodies will the righteous have in heaven?
14. Why will the saved then be able to understand the mysteries of this life?
15. What is said about the joys of heaven?
16. Whose face shall the redeemed behold?
17. Name some things that will not be in heaven. Who will not be there?
18. Does the Bible teach degrees of happiness in heaven? Upon what basis?
19. How can all get the same reward in heaven and yet be different?
20. How may one reach heaven?
21. When is the time for one to make preparations for going to heaven? (Luke 13:23–24; Matthew 7:13–14).

– 27 –

What about Future Recognition?

"I shall go to him, but he will not return to me"
2 Samuel 12:23

Finally, "Will the redeemed know each other in heaven?" Few questions asked about heaven are of more concern to Christians than the one that pertains to future recognition. Dear ones of this earth—linked to individuals by the most tender ties—have died and gone into the beyond. Their bodies have been tenderly laid to rest in the tomb to sleep till the great awakening at the resurrection. Many believe that at the last day the redeemed shall see and know their own whom they have known and loved here, while others, just as sincere, doubt it. Although the Bible does not speak directly on the subject, many passages of Scripture seem to imply that they will.

Arguments for Recognition

The following arguments are usually offered in favor of the idea that the saved shall know their friends and loved ones in heaven.

First, the heart yearns for future recognition. Such belief has been generally received by Christians in all ages and among all classes. Not only have all nations and all tribes believed in God and future life—the immortality of the soul—but likewise in the mutual recognition of each other in that life in the glory world. These deep universal beliefs and desires of the human heart are thought by many to be prophetic of their fulfillment. Man wants a happy reunion before the throne of the Lamb. His loved ones are still linked to him by the ties of memory and affection. Love is eternal; one loves the dead even as the living. One wants to see them again, just like he wants to live again; he believes that this human feeling can find its consummation only in a recognized personal reunion in heaven. God must have planted in the human breast this desire, just as He did the desire to live again, and that it will be fulfilled in personal recognition. Hence, man believes he will meet his loved ones again in unmolested realms of happiness in the resurrection morning, and that it seems foreign to his deepest ideas of future happiness for heaven to be otherwise. He believes that God would hardly have put this yearning in the hearts of His people if it were never to be gratified.

In the next place, men will continue as separate personalities through eternity. Memory and personal identity, which are the essential elements for future recognition, will be retained in the future life. In the judgment day each person stands there in his own distinctive character, having a full and thorough recollection of this life (Matthew 25:34–46). One must retain his personal identity to say he failed to visit the sick, feed the hungry, and such like. The state after the resurrection, therefore, is one in which there is preserved the individuality of each person and a memory of his past life, even though one will be in a different body. In Hades, the rich man was told, "Son, remember . . ." (Luke 16:25).

In addition, the phrase *future life* implies remembrance of this earth life. Man is to know himself as himself at the judgment and in eternity, and also possess the power to make himself known as himself. Even the idea of rewards in the future life for deeds done in this life implies the memory of such deeds as the person's. The memory of the present life is clearly implied in the song the redeemed will sing in heaven:

> Thou art worthy to take the book, and to open the seals thereof: for thou wast slain, and hast redeemed us to God by thy blood out of every kindred, and tongue, and people, and nation; and hast made us unto our God kings and priests (Revelation 5:9–10 KJV).

Each one in the company remembers being a sinner saved by the blood of the Lamb. Even the souls John saw under the altar retained their memory:

> And when he opened the fifth seal, I saw underneath the altar the souls of them that had been slain for the word of God, and for the testimony which they held: and they cried with a great voice, saying, How long, O Master, the holy and true, dost thou not judge and avenge our blood on them that dwell on the earth? (Revelation 6:9–10).

They knew they had been slain upon the earth and that some day their martyrdom would be avenged.

Since sameness of person and fidelity of memory are necessarily the conditions of future recognition, and souls cannot lose their memories (their affections and their individualities), it seems logical to say there will be reunion and recognition of the saints in glory. No soul in heaven will ever lose, at any time, the distinct individuality of his consciousness or his past experiences. His personality shall persist, and the knowledge acquired in this life will be retained in its fullness in the life beyond.

Third, the Bible indicates future recognition by taking the doctrine for granted. If, for instance, those sleeping in the night were awakened the next morning, they would awake the same persons, recognizable and recognizing, as when they lay down to sleep. If a traveler, for example, visited in a country and saw many church buildings, he would reasonably infer that the people of that land were religious. So it is, many Christians believe, with the doctrine of future recognition.

Jesus taught the sociability of the heavenly state under the figure of a feast: "And I say unto you, that many shall come from the east and the west, and shall sit down with Abraham, and Isaac, and Jacob, in the kingdom of heaven" (Matthew 8:11). Man is a social being. The communion of the saints on earth is a rich blessing. Heaven will be the family of God of all ages in the Father's house (John 14:2). This statement, therefore, from Jesus implies that Abraham, Isaac, and Jacob will be known; and if they are known surely others also will be known. Although many people never knew Abraham, Isaac, and Jacob personally in this life, they shall know these Old Testament characters in heaven. If one is to know them individually there, then one shall know those there whom in this life he did know. The redeemed shall behold all the saved and enjoy their company. So the fellowship of the saints in heaven is another reason for one's believing in personal recognition.

Again, Jesus said to His disciples prior to His return to the Father: "And if I go and prepare a place for you, I come again, and will receive you unto myself; that where I am, there ye may be also" (John 14:3). Here is implied future recognition of Christ and mutual association together.

Later, Christ presented heaven to the apostle John as a city, implying community and fellowship (Revelation 21). In fact, every true idea of the eternal home for the redeemed stresses fellowship with God, Christ, the Holy Spirit, angels, and all the saved. The inhabitants of heaven will not find the place a solitary country, but everyone will feel at home. Assembled in one place and united in one society, the saved will have knowledge of each other's presence and will recognize those known in a former state. This will be one of the chief privileges of eternal blessedness.

Too, the Lord was recognized by His disciples after His resurrection when the body raised was identified by the apostles as "that same Jesus" (John 20:18–20, 26–28; Acts 2:32). Does this not imply that those who now know one, as the disciples were acquainted with Jesus before His death, shall in the future world be able to see in that one recognizable features? All the redeemed shall see and know in heaven the Lord Jesus Christ as the one who was slain for their sins (John 17:24; 1 John 3:2).

Furthermore, future recognition is intimated by John's experience on the isle of Patmos. There the apostle saw the resurrected and glorified body of Christ, and he saw "one like unto the Son of man" (Revelation 1:13 KJV). John knew the person looked like Jesus. The Lord possessed a glorified likeness of what He was on earth.

The transfiguration scene, in which Moses and Elijah re-appeared on earth and talked with Christ in the presence of Peter, James, and John, implies that Moses and Elijah recognized each other, that both recognized Christ, and that the three apostles recognized them as Moses and Elijah.

> And after six days Jesus taketh with him Peter, and James, and John his brother, and bringeth them up into a high mountain apart: and he was transfigured before them; and his face did shine as the sun, and his garments became white as the light. And behold, there appeared unto them Moses and Elijah talking with him. And Peter answered, and said unto Jesus, Lord, it is good for us to be here: if thou wilt, I will make here three tabernacles: one for thee, and one for Moses, and one for Elijah. While he was yet speaking, behold, a bright cloud overshadowed them: and behold, a voice out of the cloud, saying, This is my beloved Son, in whom I am well pleased; hear ye him (Matthew 17:1–5).

Certainly, Moses and Elijah knew or remembered themselves as Moses and Elijah; their memories reached back to the past and they knew they were the ones whose names they bore, though they had lived in different periods of the world, hundreds of years apart, and had not known each other on earth.

When his child was dead but the body unburied, David said: "I shall go to him, but he shall not return to me" (2 Samuel 12:23). This surely meant, "I shall soon rejoin him there." Is there not also implied the expectation of recognition? What comfort could David find in the thought that he would go to his child, if that child would never be known to him on the other side of death?

The Scriptures regard life as a pilgrimage on this earth and death as a going home (Hebrews 11:9–16). All shall soon die and be "gathered to his people," like it was said of many in the long ago (Genesis 25:8–9, 17), and finally all shall one day go to their eternal home. Although the separation after death will be brief, to the Christian a glorious and eternal reunion with those gone before awaits. This is clearly brought out in the writings of the apostle Paul when he said he would be made happy in heaven to know that those whom he had converted had remained faithful and would be among the saved "that I may have whereof to glory in the day of Christ, that I did not run in vain neither labor in vain" (Philippians 2:16); "Wherefore, my brethren beloved and longed for, my joy and my crown . . ." (Philippians 4:1); "For what is our hope, or joy, or crown of glorying? Are not even ye, before our Lord Jesus at his coming? For ye are our glory and our joy" (1 Thessalonians 2:19–20); "we are your glorying, even as ye also are ours, in the day of our Lord Jesus" (2 Corinthians 1:14); "knowing that he that raised up the Lord Jesus shall raise up us also with Jesus, and shall present us with you" (2 Corinthians 4:14). This language implies that the apostle thought that those saved through his ministry would be personally known to him in the heavenly state. Paul's converts, if faithful to God in this life, would be to him a crown of joy and rejoicing in the day of the Lord. The language certainly implies that they would know each other in the final day. Evidently Paul took pleasure in imagining himself meeting his friends and brethren in Christ whom he had known in different parts of the world. Obviously, Paul knew that memory would not be annihilated. He anticipated the delightful renewing of old associations, recounting of mutual trials, and of giving thanks to God. Thus, he exhorted his brethren to faithfulness.

Recognition in Hades

The idea of future conscious recognition and company in Hades (the unseen realm of disembodied spirits) is surely implied in the language of Jesus to the dying thief on the cross: "Today shalt thou be with me in Paradise" (Luke 23:43). If such is true in Paradise in Hades, then may it not also be true in heaven?

Moreover, future recognition is asserted as a fact in the Hadean world in the narrative that Christ gave of the rich man and Lazarus. In Hades the rich man recognized two persons: Lazarus, the poor beggar who was once "laid at his gate, full of sores," and Abraham, the father of the faithful. The rich man begged for mercy (Luke 16:22–23). Then, from this case of actual future recognition, it is suggested that the saved in heaven, too, shall be able to recognize each other. Spirits have the means of knowing each other because the dead know and are known, and they recognize and are recognized.

Also in this narrative, as previously learned in this study, death destroys neither personality nor memory. The rich man was conscious that he was himself and remembered he had five brothers still alive in the present world; his acts on earth were still remembered (vv. 25–27). Thus, the Scriptures teach that the impressions of this present life are faithfully preserved and are capable of being reproduced in the next life.

Arguments against Recognition

Although personal recognition beyond the grave is a Bible idea, some object to this along several lines of arguments. First, to affirm that men will continue as separate personalities, which involves the preservation of memory, presents a difficulty to some people. They ask, "How can memory continue when the brain is dissolved?" According to their assumption, memory is a product of the brain, but this cannot be true because memory remains while the brain tissue is constantly changing. It is better to say that memory is a function of the mind and is merely expressed through the brain in this life. The mind is immortal.

The second objection to the idea of future recognition is that one spirit cannot recognize another spirit in heaven when both are formless and featureless beings. The answer to this objection is that the redeemed will not be ghost-like wraiths, and it is only an assumption that spiritual beings will be formless and invisible. Certainly, the Bible says the resurrection-body will be a spiritual one; yet it will be a body. The saved will be real people in heaven, formal and visible. It is not a mere spirit that is possessed by the saints in glory, but "a spiritual body"—an incorruptible, glorious, powerful, immortal, spiritual body. (This has already been studied in the chapter on the resurrection. See 1 Corinthians 15:42–54.) Body and soul shall constitute glorified humanity in heaven.

The third objection is that the bodily changes which will be undergone in death and the resurrection make future recognition highly improbable if not impossible. The Scriptures intimate that the redeemed shall retain all those marks and characteristics of individuality by which they were here distinguished and known. Just like the seed that is sown, every seed gets its own body again, and is known as that particular kind. Bodily changes occur with people on earth, and yet one continues to recognize them and remember his past experiences with them. For example, the grown son recognizes his aged mother as the one who used to care for him so tenderly; he recalls that she nursed him on her lap in her bosom. Now those earthly forms are different because the mother is old and feeble, and the son strong and full grown. But they both know that they are the same persons and recognize each other as the same persons although the bodily forms have been changed. So, even in this life one's personality, whatever it is, is not dependent entirely upon his physical organism. Now, in heaven one will not have his physical body but a spiritual body, and with the same individuality, live on and on forever; and he shall be the same identical person as before. Hence, the objection does not seem to be a valid one. The ability to remember continues in the other world.

A fourth objection is often made that since Christ said, "For in the resurrection they neither marry, nor are given in marriage, but are as angels in heaven" (Matthew 22:30), this means personal recognition must cease with this life. This conclusion is false because the Savior asserted that the marriage relation will not be continued in another life. He did not say that the saints shall be unacquainted with each other. It is not the remembrance of this relationship that is to be obliterated, but simply the earthly relation itself that is not to be continued in heaven—only spiritual ties will abide there. The redeemed will be equally immortal as the angels. Jesus said, "For neither can they die any more" (Luke 20:36). Nevertheless, the saints will remember that they had such relationships to one another on earth. Since bodies undergo changes here, and people recognize each other and remember that these conditions once existed in a former state, then why couldn't they be recognized in heaven?

As recorded by Luke, Christ taught two facts about the resurrection state; namely, that neither marriage nor death will have a place with those raised from the dead.

> And Jesus said unto them, The sons of this world marry, and are given in marriage: but they that are accounted worthy to attain to that world, and the resurrection from the dead, neither marry, nor are given in marriage: for neither can they die any more: for they are equal unto the angels; and are sons of God, being sons of the resurrection (Luke 20:34–36).

Births will be unknown; none will die; all will be immortal. In teaching that this corruptible body will be replaced by an incorruptible one, Christ contradicted the false doctrine of the Sadducees who denied the resurrection. They said that if there were a resurrection, it would imply a complete resumption of all human relations in the body and in society. This was their mistake in reasoning. In reply to them, Jesus did not say there would be no resurrection, that the souls of men would remain forever without bodies, or that fellowship is not resumed in heaven. On the contrary, He asserted the fact of a resurrection as something presupposed by this life, and further taught that family relations, as known to people in this life, would not continue after the resurrection, since men would no longer be subject to death.

A fifth objection urged against future recognition is the idea that sorrow would be experienced from missing some friends and relatives who might not be in heaven. The answer to this objection is that God has promised that the redeemed in heaven will be perfectly happy and He can make it so, for He is infinite in power and mercy. There God "shall wipe away every tear from their eyes . . . neither shall there be mourning" (Revelation 21:4). Furthermore, the redeemed in heaven will then realize that God has done right with all mankind and submit to His decree. Even Aaron held his peace when his two sons, Nadab and Abihu, died in the wilderness at the tabernacle for offering "strange fire before Jehovah, which he had not commanded them" (cf. Leviticus 10:1–3). Aaron knew that sin had to be punished, even if it did include his own sons. In fact, even the damned in Gehenna (hell) will realize that perfect justice has been done to them. We must constantly remind ourselves that God is too good to be unkind and too wise to make mistakes. We must trust Him totally and fully to do what is right. As Abraham said: "Shall not the Judge of all the earth do right?" (Genesis 18:25).

Moreover, the sufferings of the impenitent will be distinctly known by the Lord and the angels (Revelation 14:10); but God, Christ, the Holy Spirit, and the angels will still be happy in heaven while knowing that some are damned forever. Who has loved souls more than the Savior? He died on the cross for all men. However, even the damned, suffering now in torment (Tartarus), do not mar His joy in His glorified state. If the just punishment of the wicked and the unfaithful children of God (2 Peter 2:20–22) does not pain Christ and the angels, it will not be to those redeemed among men. Also, Jesus taught there are ties higher than fleshly kindred; there are spiritual affections as well as natural affections (Matthew 12:46–50).

If one has relatives who will be lost in hell, they certainly will not want any of their loved ones there; they never want to see them again. Surely no one wants to be lost because a relative will be lost. The rich man in torment did not want any of his brothers to come to that place of suffering (Luke 16:27–28).

Therefore, God in some way will see that the redeemed are happy in heaven. He, in His infinite power, may cause the saved to finally forget those from whom they are separated as they become absorbed with the joys and beauties of that eternal home. To say the least, man cannot make human feelings the standard of God's actions or measure the Infinite by the finite.

A gospel preacher, F. W. Smith, once ably expressed the idea of future recognition in these words: "While there is no direct teaching on the subject in the Bible, there are numbers of passages that are to me absolutely meaningless without that idea." This author agrees with these words.

A Source of Consolation

The doctrine of future recognition should be a source of consolation for the righteous. Christians have the glorious prospect of a meeting with their departed friends and loved ones in a better world to come. They have the blessed hope in knowing that they shall meet one another again and live forever in heaven with the Lord. "Wherefore comfort one another with these words" (1 Thessalonians 4:18).

Man's knowledge of heaven and the future life is, of course, necessarily limited while he is on earth. He has only hints of the pleasures that await beyond the grave. The apostle John expressed this thought in these words: "Beloved, now are we the children of God, and it is not yet made manifest what we shall be. We know that, if he shall be manifested, we shall be like him; for we shall see him even as he is" (1 John 3:2; cf. Deuteronomy 29:29). However, with the sublime teaching of the Scriptures on life in the hereafter, all can now have a clearer understanding of the nature of man and what awaits him beyond the grave. The grave hides the dear objects of one's affection from his sight, but he knows that the separation is only for a time. They are not lost, but gone before. They are not extinct; they live. He shall see them again and, if a Christian, dwell with them forever. The separation will be brief and the reunion glorious because they shall meet to part no more. This hope should be a source of great comfort to one in his hours of bereavement. One need not forget his dear loved ones, for a time will be when he shall see them again. Hence, the separation that comes to relatives and friends at death will be only until the Lord comes again and the resurrection; there will be a reunion in heaven one day for all the righteous. Therefore, one's prayer should be:

Up to that world of light,
Take us, dear Savior:
May we all there unite,
Happy, forever.

Nevertheless, let the truth be deeply impressed upon each heart, that if one would see his loved ones and friends in heaven, his first duty is to become a Christian, and then live faithfully the Christian life. No others shall enter through the gates into that blissful city. "Blessed are they that wash their robes, that they may have the right to come to the tree of life, and may enter in by the gates into the city" (Revelation 22:14).

Oh, how sweet it will be, in that beautiful land,
So free from all sorrow and pain,
With songs on our lips, and with joy in our hearts,
To meet one another again.

As the days come and go, the faithful child of God can say:

One sweetly solemn thought
Comes to me o'er and o'er:
Today I'm nearer to my home
Than e'er I've been before.

May all those who now miss the touch of the vanished hand and the sound of the quieted voice still find comfort in God's Holy Word until they reach the eternal home of the soul.

Epilogue

Heaven, the wonderful city of God, is described in the most beautiful imagery. Only through the eye of faith can the beauties of heaven be envisioned. It is a state of eternal joy and happiness, a land without sickness, pain, death, or sad farewells.

There the saints of all ages in harmony meet,
Their Savior and brethren transported to greet,
While the anthems of rapture unceasingly roll,
And the smile of the Lord is the feast of the soul.

As John Newton said in his great hymn "Amazing Grace":

> When we've been there ten thousand years,
> Bright shining as the sun,
> We've no less days to sing God's praise
> Than when we first begun.

How wonderful it will be to live in that eternal city whose builder and maker is God!

This is my faith, the faith which has helped me, and the faith which in the hour of sorrow I bring for the comfort of those who mourn. "Comfort ye, comfort ye my people, saith your God" (Isaiah 40:1).

Closing Appeal

When the end of time comes and the parting of the nations of men, will it be found that your name is recorded in the Lamb's book of life? Will you be among the righteous to inherit the land that is fairer than day? My prayer is that we may enter into that beautiful home of the soul, the land "Beyond the Sunset," and dwell forever with all the redeemed in the eternal Paradise of God. There is life after death.

And now,

> The Lord bless thee, and keep thee:
> The Lord make his face to shine upon thee,
> And be gracious unto thee:
> The Lord lift up his countenance upon thee,
> And give thee peace.
>
> —Numbers 6:24–36 KJV

Death can be the gateway to life more abundant, or it can be the gateway to eternal separation from God and from all who love Him—an eternity of conscious joy, or an eternity of conscious torment. Which will it be?

May the Lord bless all of us in walking in the light of His Word, through grace to glory, that we may be with God forever; and not only with God who created us, but with our loved ones, not lost but gone before, with the sweet little ones who shall be gathered there, and with all the redeemed of every age and country and clime.

So Christians do not view death in the same way as those who are not Christians. They look, with Paul, to be reunited with their loved ones and friends and in heaven to enjoy the beautiful home of the soul forever and ever (1 Thessalonians 4:13–18). There God shall wipe away every tear from their eyes; and death shall be no more (Revelation 21:4). God has promised it and He will do it. What a glorious thing Christians have to look forward to! They will be reunited with those they love who have gone on before them!

Questions for Discussion

1. Does the Bible give an answer to the question of future recognition?
2. Does the Bible intimate there will be recognition in the hereafter?
3. What are the two essentials for future recognition? Does the Bible teach that they will exist in the future life?
4. Did God create man a social being? Will the desire for association continue in the eternal state?
5. Does the transfiguration of Christ imply recognition?
6. Does David's statement about going to his son imply faith in recognition?
7. Does the apostle John's recognizing Christ on Patmos imply recognition?
8. Why could Paul look forward to rejoicing at the judgment over his converts?
9. Does the Bible teach recognition in Hades?
10. What are some of the objections usually offered regarding future recognition? Are they valid objections?
11. What do you think is true of the redeemed in heaven being all together?

These chapters that have been studied affirm that after the resurrection the souls, dislodged at death, shall be united with their raised and immortal bodies, never again to be separated from them.

Since God breathed into man something of Himself, man is endowed with capacity to exist forever. Neither the spirits of the wicked nor of the righteous cease to exist at death. Is it any wonder then that the great mass of men have in all ages and in all nations believed in the continued existence of the soul after death? The immortality of man is a doctrine firmly established in God's eternal word.

– 28 –

POEMS[1]

When I Must Leave You

When I must leave you
    for a little while,
Please go on bravely
    with a gallant smile;
And for my sake and in my name,
    Live on and do all things the same.

Spend not your life
    in empty days,
But fill each waking hour
    in useful ways;
Reach out your hand
    in comfort and in cheer,
And I in turn will comfort you
    and hold you near.

My Beautiful Mother Has Gone Away

A part of my heart is in Paradise today;
    My beautiful mother has gone away.
I wasn't ready for her to leave;
    But God called her home and I grieve.

1 Over the many years of preaching and conducting funeral services, the author has often used these poems.

The angels took her by the hand,
    And guided her to a bright new land;
A land completely free of pain;
    A land of sunshine and never rain.

As she walked the golden stairs,
    She left behind earth's troubles and cares;
Waiting to welcome her at heaven's door,
    Were all the dear loved ones who have gone before.

Mother wouldn't understand our cry;
    She was born again—she didn't just die.
Her life didn't really end;
    It is only now to begin.

Death is another bend in the road
    On the way to a heavenly abode.
But someday in a far away land,
    I will see my mother once again.

God gave her to us for a little while
    To give us love, to make us smile;
My mother lived a wonderful life;
    Beloved mother, and beloved wife.

She wanted to live, not just exist;
    Oh how much she will be missed.
She wiped away so many tears;
    She shared my pain through the years.

But this pain she cannot help share;
    I must bear it alone with God's care;
God help those who are left who sorrow;
    Help us to live through each tomorrow.

Our hearts feel as if they will break;
    Help us God, oh help us for our sake;
The emptiness engulfs my heart today;
    My dear beautiful, wonderful mother has gone away.

—Selected

Looking for the Sunrise

I'm not looking for the sunset
    as the swift years come and go;
I'm looking for the sunrise
    and the golden morning glow.

Where the light of heaven's glory
    will break forth upon my sight
In the land that knows no sunset
    nor the darkness of night.

I'm not going *down* the pathway
    toward the setting of the sun
Where the shadows ever deepen
    when the day at last is done;

I am walking *up* the hillside
    where the sunshine lights the way
To the glory of the sunrise
    of God's never-ending day.

I'm not going *down* but *upward*
    and the path is never dim,
For the day grows even brighter
    as I journey on with Him.

So my eyes are on the hilltops
    waiting for the sun to rise,
Waiting for *his* invitation
    to that *home* beyond the skies.
        —Albert Simpson Reitz

"Earth hath no sorrow that Heaven cannot heal."
—Thomas Moore, English Author, 1478–1535

God Saw She Was Getting Tired

God saw she was getting tired
And a cure was not to be.
So He put His arms around her,
And whispered, "Come with Me."

With tearful eyes we watched her suffer,
And saw her fade away.
Although we loved her dearly,
We could not make her stay.

A golden heart stopped beating,
Hard working hands to rest.
God took her from this earth to prove . . .
He only takes the best.

God's Garden

God looked around His garden,
and He found an empty place.
He then looked down upon
this earth and saw your tired face.

He put His arms around you
and lifted you to rest.
God's garden must be beautiful,
He always takes the best.

He knew that you were suffering;
He knew you were in pain,
He knew you would never
get well on this earth again.

So He closed your weary eyelids
and whispered, "Peace be thine."
He then took you up to heaven
with hands gentle and so kind.

But you did not go alone,
for part of me went with you,
The day God called you home,
home in the beautiful garden of God.

I'm Free

Don't grieve for me, for now I'm free;
    I'm following the path God laid for me.
I took His hand when I heard Him call;
    I turned my back and left it all.

I could not stay another day
    To laugh, to love, to work or play.
Tasks left undone must stay that way;
    I found that place at close of day.

If my parting has left a void,
    Then fill it with remembered joy.
A friendship shared, a laugh, a kiss;
    Ah yes, these things I, too, will miss.

Be not burdened with times of sorrow;
    I wish you the sunshine of tomorrow.
My life's been full, I savored much;
    Good friends, good times, a loved one's touch.

Perhaps my time seemed all too brief;
    Don't lengthen it now with undue grief.
Lift up your hearts and share with me;
    God wanted me now, He set me free.

"I have fought the good fight, I have finished the course, I have kept the faith: Henceforth there is laid up for me the crown of righteousness, which the Lord, the righteous judge, shall give to me at that day" (Paul, the apostle).

"The best is yet to be."
    —Robert Browning, English Poet, 1812–1889

Each tick of the clock brings each one of us closer to death and to eternity.

Inside the Gate

Loved ones in glory are waiting for me,
    Just inside the gate;
Some golden morning their faces I'll see,
    Just inside the gate.

There will be shouting and singing up there,
    Glory forever with them we shall share,
When we shall enter our mansion so fair,
    Inside the gate.

Inside the home gate, where friends for me wait,
    With angels of light all robed in pure white;
'Twill be a glad day, a wonderful day, when we enter
    that home
Just inside, inside the beautiful gate.

—J.W. Vaughan

The Last Mile of the Way

If I walk in the pathway of duty,
    If I work till the close of the day,
I shall see the great King in His beauty
    When I've gone the last mile of the way.

If for Christ I proclaim the glad story,
    If I seek for His sheep gone astray,
I am sure He will show me His glory
    When I've gone the last mile of the way.

Here the dearest of ties we must sever,
    Tears of sorrow are seen every day;
But no sickness, no sighing forever
    When I've gone the last mile of the way.

Refrain:
When I've gone the last mile of the way,
    I will rest at the close of the day,
And I know there are joys that await me
    When I've gone the last mile of the way.

—Wm. Edie Marks

"So teach us to number our days,
that we may apply our hearts unto wisdom."
(Psalm 90:12 KJV)

The Eternal Goodness
(Selected verses)

Yet, in the maddening maze of things,
And tossed by storm and flood,
To one fixed stake my spirit clings:
I know that God is good.

And so, beside the Silent Sea
I wait with muffled oar;
No harm from Him can come to me
On ocean or on shore.

I know not where His islands lift
Their fronded palms in air;
I only know I cannot drift
Beyond His love and care.
—John Greenleaf Whittier

A Psalm of Life
(Selected verse)

Lives of great men all remind us
We can make our lives sublime,
And, departing, leave behind us
Footprints on the sands of time.
—Henry Wadsworth Longfellow

Never Grow Old

I have heard of a land on the far away strand,
'Tis a beautiful home of the soul;
Built by Jesus on high, where we never shall die,
'Tis a land where we never grow old.

In that beautiful home where we'll nevermore roam,
We shall be in the sweet by and by;
Happy praise to the King through eternity sing,
'Tis a land where we never shall die.

When our work here is done and the life-crown is won,
And our troubles and trials are o'er;
All our sorrows will end, and our voices will blend,
With the loved ones who've gone on before.

Refrain:
Never grow old, never grow old,
In a land where we'll never grow old;
Never grow old, never grow old;
In a land where we'll never grow old.

—James C. Moore

Life
(Selected verses)

Life, we have been long together
through pleasant and through cloudy weather;
'Tis hard to part when friends are dear,
perhaps will cost a sigh, a tear.

Then steal away, give little warning,
choose thine own time;
Say not "Good Night," but in some brighter clime
bid me "Good Morning."

—Anna L. Barbauld

You Tell Me I Am Getting Old

You tell me I am getting old:
I tell you that's not so!
The house I live in is worn out,
And that, of course, I know.
It's been in use a long, long while,
It's weathered many a gale;
I'm really not surprised you think
It's getting somewhat frail.

The color's changing on the roof;
The windows getting dim.
It's walls a bit transparent
And looking rather thin.
The foundation's not as steady
As once it used to be;
My house is getting shaky,
But my "house" isn't me!

My few short years can't make me old:
I feel I'm in my youth.
Eternity lies just ahead,
A life of joy and truth.
I'm going to live forever there;
Life will go on, it's grand!
You tell me I am getting old?
You just don't understand!

The dweller in my little "house"
Is young and bright and gay;
Just starting on a life to last
Throughout eternal day.
You only see the outside,
Which is all that most folks see;
You tell me I am getting old?
You've mixed my "house" with me!

—Dora Johnson

I Would Not Live Alway
(Selected verse)

Where the saints of all ages in harmony meet,
Their Savior and brethren transported to greet;
While the anthems of rapture unceasingly roll,
And the smile of the Lord is the feast of the soul.
—William Augustus Muhlenberg

If There Were No Christ

If there were no Christ,
And have never been,
To save the sinner from the throes of sin,
What a dreadful place
This would be.
But there is a Christ for you and me.

God Has Not Promised

God has not promised skies always blue,
Flower-strewn pathways all our lives through;
God has not promised sun without rain,
Peace without sorrow, joy without pain.

But God has promised strength as our day,
Rest for the labor, light for the way,
Grace for the trials, help from above,
Unfailing kindness, and undying love.

Life's race well run,
Life's work well done,
Life's crown well won,
Now comes rest.
—President Garfield's Epitaph

The Mansion of Heaven

This world, however beautiful,
  was never meant to be
The place that we would call our home
  for all eternity.
And though we would not choose to leave,
  a loving God knows best;
And in His time He lifts us
  to a place of rest.

For He has built a mansion
  where his children will abide
Free from pain and sorrow,
  forever at His side.
He said He'd never leave us
  to face our trials alone,
And though sometimes we fail Him,
  He never fails His own.

And though these ones we love so much
  have left our present sight
And passed into a better world
  of majesty and light,
Someday we'll be together
  in our Father's home above
Where we'll thank Him for His mercy
  and praise Him for His love.

You Told Me of Jesus

When the voice of the Master is calling,
  And the gates of the city unfold;
When the saints arise in His likeness,
  And are thronging the city of gold
How your heart shall rejoice in that morning,
  If *one* of the ransomed shall say:
"You guided my steps to heaven;
  You told me of Jesus, the way."

When We All Get to Heaven
(Selected verse)

When we all get to heaven,
    What a day of rejoicing that will be!
When we all see Jesus,
    We'll sing and shout the victory.
        —E. E. Hewitt

Thanatopsis
(Selected verse)

All that tread
The globe are but a handful to the tribes
That slumber in its bosom
        —William Cullen Bryant

Angel Child

Dear God, our little child left here
    To come and live with You.
Won't You take special care of him,
    As only You can do?

He is so little and alone,
    Your world so strange and new;
Won't You hold him in Your arms,
    As only You can do?

Dear God, please gently tuck him in,
    And smooth his little brow,
Hold his little hands in Yours,
    For he's an angel now.

God, grant us a faith that will endure,
    That will keep us brave and true,
And guide us to our angel child,
    As only You can do.

I Do Not Go Alone

If Death should beckon me with outstretched hand
    and whisper softly of an "Unknown Land,"
I shall not be afraid to go;
    for though the path I do not know
I take Death's hand without a fear,
    for He who safely brought me here
Will also take me safely back;
    and though in many things I lack,
He will not let me go alone
    into the valley, that "Unknown";
So I reach out and take Death's hands
    and journey on to the "Promised Land"!

—Helen Steiner Rice

I went home for Christmas;
    I hope you don't mind.
I wanted the day to be happy,
    and things worked out just fine.
You are still celebrating Christ,
    while I see Him face to face.
I'm having the best Christmas ever,
    in this blessed place.

—Author unknown

Like a ship that's left its mooring
    and sailed bravely out to sea,
So Someone Dear has sailed away
    in calm serenity:
But there's a promise of greater joy
    than earth could have in store,
For God has planned a richer life
    beyond the Unseen Shore.

—Author unknown

My Heavenly Home

There is a place up in heaven,
My Lord has gone to prepare.
Mansions resplendent in glory,
That saints of all ages shall share.

A Home of such beauty and splendor,
This world has naught to compare.
Its light is the face of my Savior,
Its warmth, the glow of His care.

And when I reach that fair haven,
After my labors are o'er;
There I will rest with my Savior,
Safe on that beautiful shore.
—Alta C. Carroll

Should You Go First

Should you go first, and I remain to walk the road alone;
I'll live in memory's garden, dear, with happy days we've known.
In spring I'll watch the roses red, when fade the lilac blue;
In fall when the brown leaves call, I'll catch a glimpse of you.

Should you go first, and I remain for battles to be fought;
Each thing you've touched along the way will be a hallowed spot.
I'll hear your voice, I'll see your smile, tho' blindly I may grope;
The memory of your helping hand will buoy me on with hope.

Should you go first, and I remain to finish out the scroll;
No length'ning shadows shall creep in to make this life seem droll.
We've known so much of happiness, we've had our cup of joy;
And memory is one gift of God that death cannot destroy.

Should you go first, and I remain, one thing I'd have you do:
Walk slowly down that long, lone path, for soon I'll follow you.
I want to know each step you take, that I may walk the same;
For some day, down that lonely road, you'll hear me call your name.
—Albert Kennedy "Rosey" Rowswell

Over the River, They Beckon Me

Over the river, they beckon to me,
    Loved ones who've crossed to the other side.
The gleam of their snowy robes I see,
    But their voices are drowned in the rushing tide.

There is one of ringlets of sunny gold,
    And eyes the reflection of heaven's blue;
She crossed in the twilight gray and cold,
    And the pale mist hid her from mortal view.

We saw not the angels that met her there,
    The gates of the city we could not see,
But over the river, over the river,
    My dear mother stands waiting and watching for me.

On her bosom she folded her dimpled hands,
    And entered the phantom bark.
We watched it glide from the silver sands,
    And all our sunshine grew strangely dark.

We know she's safe on the farther shore,
    Where all the ransomed angels be,
For over the river, over the river,
    My darling mother is waiting for me.

Over the river another stands,
    Anxiously watching, her outstretched hands
To me are beckoning her hair so white
    Gleams silver in the heavenly light.

Ah, those dear hands, how they labored for me,
    In labors of love, then I could not see;
But I see it now since she's crossed the tide,
    How her love would woo me to the Savior's side.

Yes, I will keep the promise I made her that night,
    I'll make the start, though a struggle it be,
For over the river, the mystic river,
    My dear mother is waiting and watching for me.

Sometime We'll Understand
(Selected verses)

Not now, but in the coming years,
It may be in a better land;
We'll read the meaning of our tears,
And there, sometime, we'll understand.

We'll catch the broken thread again,
And finish what we here began;
Heaven will the mysteries explain,
And then, ah then, we'll understand.

We'll know why clouds instead of sun
Were over many a cherished plan;
Why song has ceased when scarce begun,
'Tis there, sometime, we'll understand.

Then trust in God thro' all thy days;
Fear not, for He doth hold thy hand;
Tho' dark the way, still sing and praise,
Sometime, sometime, we'll understand.
—Maxwell Newton Cornelius

A Little Hand

Dear Lord, I do not ask
that Thou shouldn't give me
Some high work of Thine,
Some noble calling, or some wondrous task.
Give me a little hand to hold in mine;
Give me a little child to point the way
Over the strange, sweet path
that leads to Thee.
Give me a little voice to teach to pray;
Give me two shining eyes Thy face to see.
The only crown I ask, dear Lord, to wear
Is this: that I may teach my little child.
I do not ask that I may ever stand
Among the wise, the worthy, or the great;
I only ask that softly, hand in hand,
My child and I may enter at the gate.

Safely Home

I am home in heaven, dear ones;
    Oh so happy and so bright!
There is perfect joy and beauty,
    In this heavenly light.

All the pain and grief are over,
    Every restless tossing passed;
I am now at peace forever,
    Safely home in heaven at last.

Then you must not grieve so sorely,
    For I love you dearly still;
Try to look beyond earth's shadows,
    Pray to trust our Father's will.

There is work still waiting for you,
    So you must not idle stand;
Do your work while life remaineth,
    You shall rest in Jesus' land.

When that work is all complete,
    He will gently call you home;
Oh, the rapture of the meeting,
    Oh, the joy to see you come!

Heaven Holds All to Me
(Selected Verses)

Earth holds no treasures but perish with using,
However precious they be;
Yet there's a country to which I am going:
Heaven holds all to me.

Heaven holds all to me,
Brighter its glory will be;
Joy without measure will be my treasure:
Heaven holds all to me.

—Tillit S.Teddlie

I'll Lend You a Child

"I'll lend you for a little while a child of Mine," God said,
"For you to have her while she lives and mourn for when she's dead.

"It may be six or seven years or twenty-two or three;
But will you, till I call her back, take care of her for Me?

"She'll bring her charms to gladden you, and should her stay be brief,
You'll have her lovely memories as a solace for your grief.

"I cannot promise she will stay; since all from earth return,
But there are lessons taught down there I want this child to learn.

"I've looked the whole world over, in search for teachers true,
And from the throngs that crowd life's land, I have chosen you.

"Now will you give her all your love nor think the labor vain?
Nor hate Me when I come to take this lent child back again?"

I fancied that I heard them say: "Dear Lord, Thy will be done.
For all the joys Thy child will bring the risk of grief we'll run.

"We'll shelter her with tenderness, we'll love her while we may,
And for the happiness we've known, forever grateful stay.

"But should the angels call for her much sooner than we've planned,
We'll brave the bitter grief that comes and try to understand!"

—Edgar Guest

How Beautiful Heaven Must Be
(Selected Verses)

We read of a place that's called heaven,
It's made for the pure and the free;
These truths in God's Word He has given,
How beautiful heaven must be.

How beautiful heaven must be,
Sweet home of the happy and free;
Fair haven of rest for the weary,
How beautiful heaven must be.

—Mrs. A. S. Bridgewater

A Mother's Love

A Mother's love is something
that no one can explain,
It is made of deep devotion
and of sacrifice and pain,

It is endless and unselfish
and enduring come what may
For nothing can destroy it
or take that love away . . .

It is patient and forgiving
when all others are forsaking,
And it never fails or falters
even though the heart is breaking . . .

It believes beyond believing
when the world around condemns,
And it glows with all the beauty
of the rarest, brightest gems . . .

It is far beyond defining,
it defies all explanation,
And it still remains a secret
like the mysteries of creation . . .

A many splendored miracle
man cannot understand
And another wondrous evidence
of God's tender guiding hand.
—Helen Steiner Rice

Oh, may I join the choir invisible
Of those immortal dead who live again.
—The Choir Invisible, George Eliot

Psalm 23
KJV

The Lord is my shepherd; I shall not want.
He maketh me to lie down in green pastures;
He leadeth me beside the still waters.
He restoreth my soul:
He leadeth me in the paths of righteousness
for his name's sake.

Yea, though I walk through the valley
of the shadow of death,
I will fear no evil: for thou art with me;
Thy rod and thy staff they comfort me.

Thou preparest a table before me
in the presence of mine enemies:
Thou anointest my head with oil;
my cup runneth over.
Surely goodness and mercy
shall follow me all the days of my life:
And I will dwell in the house of the Lord for ever.

Beyond the Sunset

Beyond the sunset, O blissful morning,
When with our Savior heav'n is begun
Earth's toiling ended, O glorious dawning,
Beyond the sunset, when day is done.

Beyond the sunset, no clouds will gather,
No storms will threaten, no fears annoy;
O day of gladness, O day unending,
Beyond the sunset, eternal joy!

Beyond the sunset, a hand will guide me
To God, the Father, whom I adore;
His glorious presence, His words of welcome,
Will be my portion on that fair shore.

Beyond the sunset, O glad reunion,
With our dear loved ones who've gone before;
In that fair homeland we'll know no parting;
Beyond the sunset forever more!

—Virgil P. Brock